RADIANT

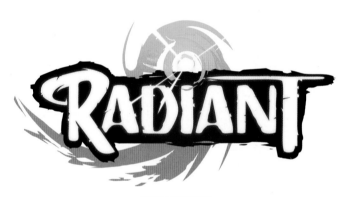

TONY VALENTE

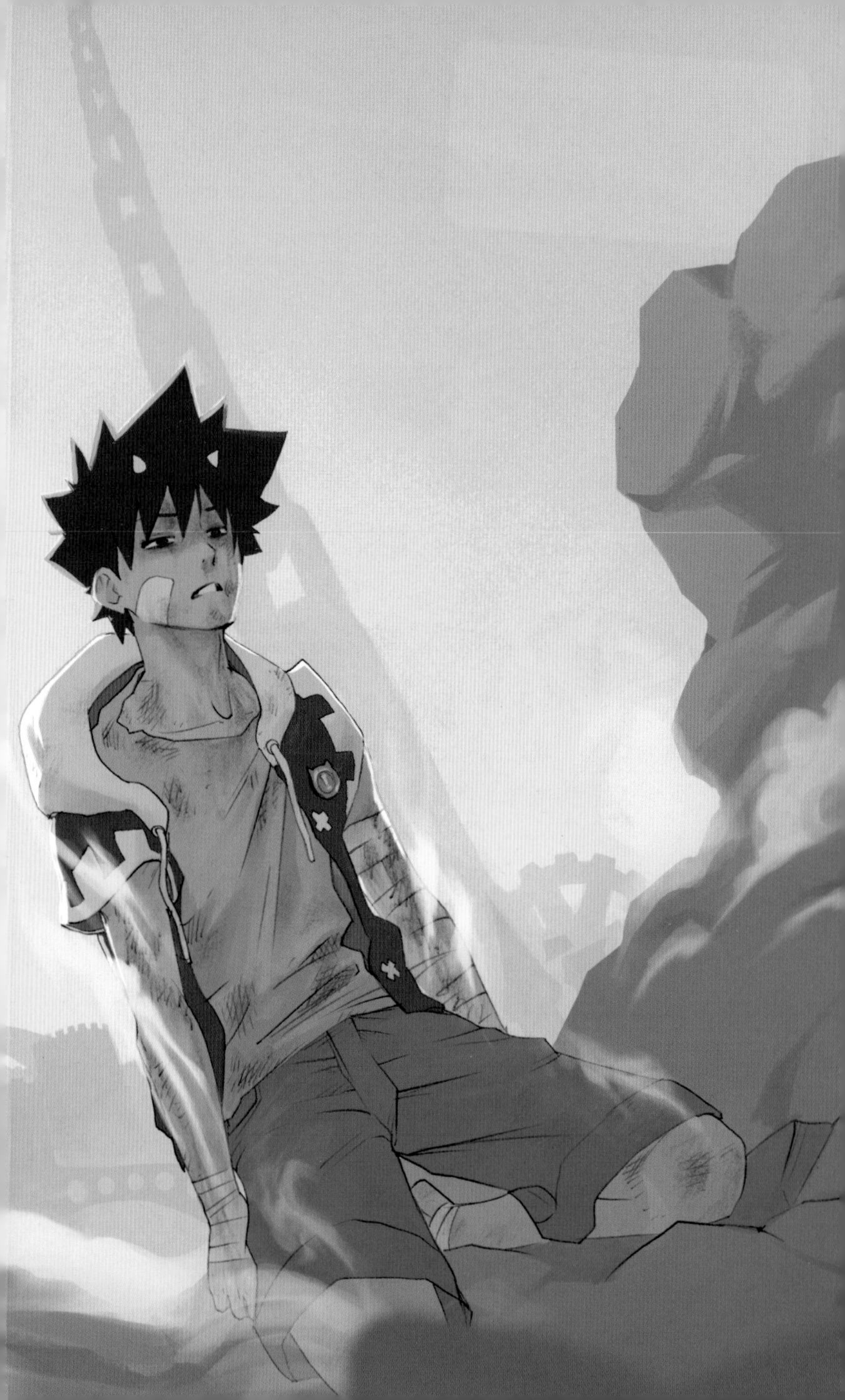

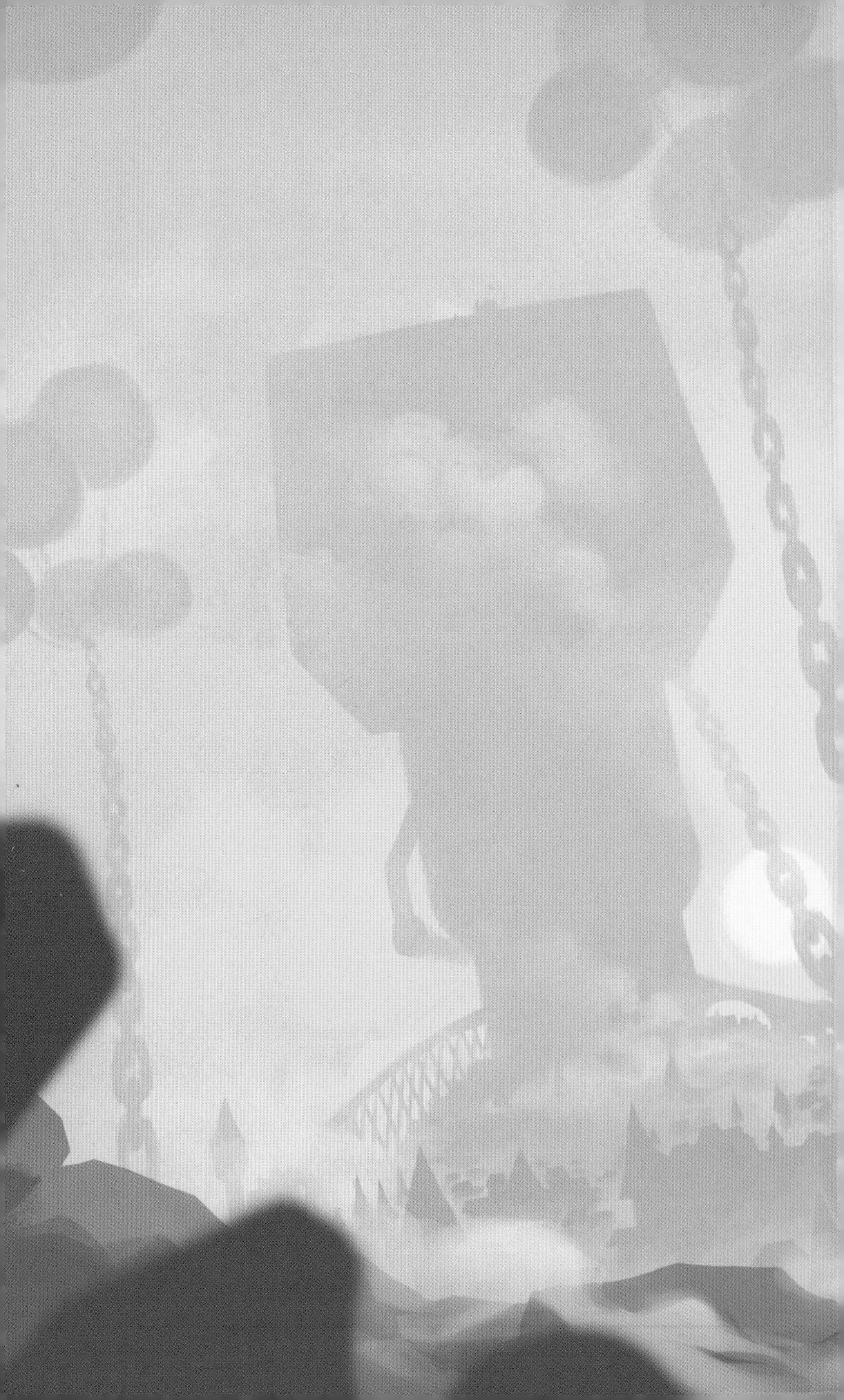

CONTENTS

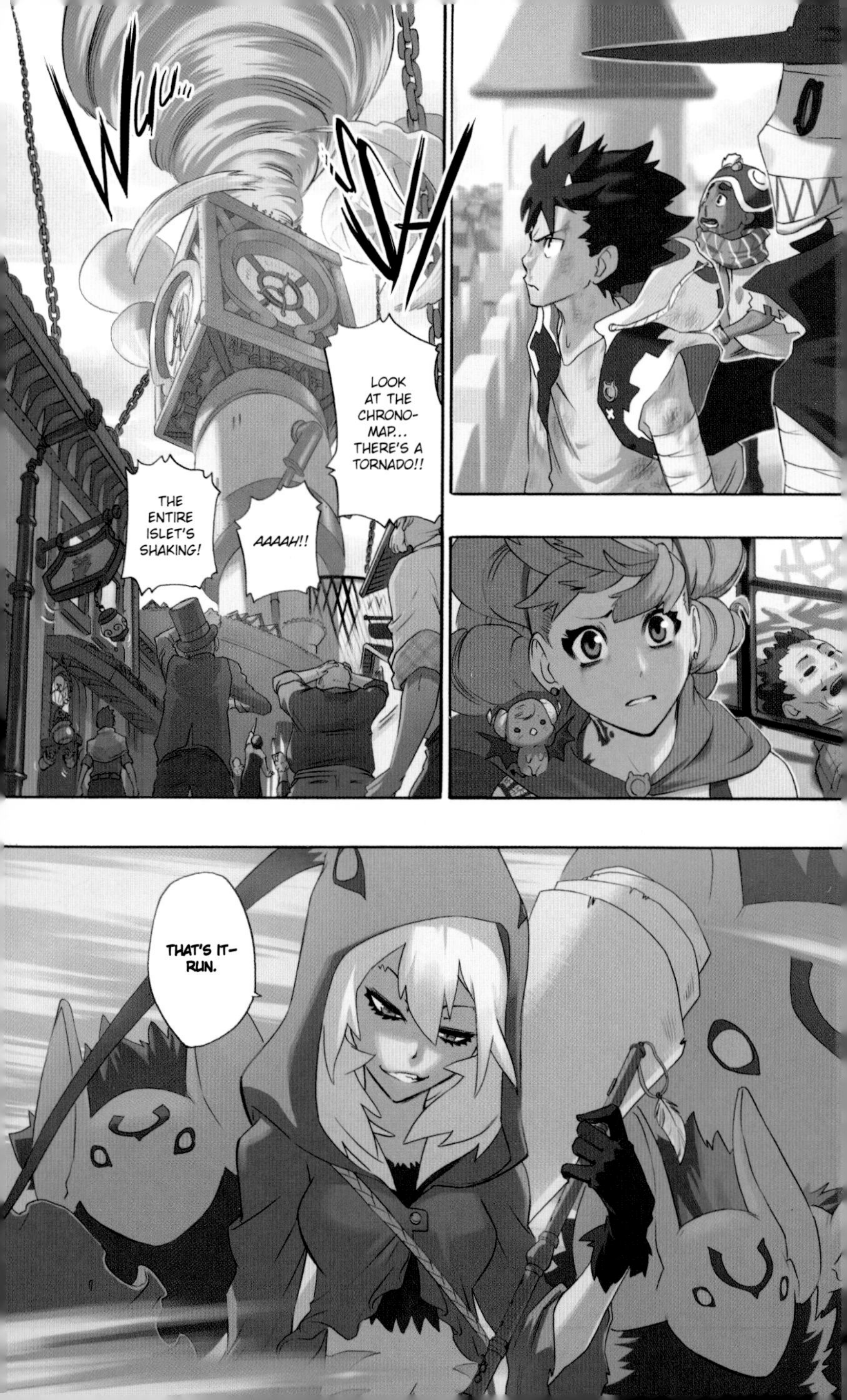
WUU...
SCH
LOOK AT THE CHRONO-MAP... THERE'S A TORNADO!!
THE ENTIRE ISLET'S SHAKING!
AAAAH!!
THAT'S IT- RUN.

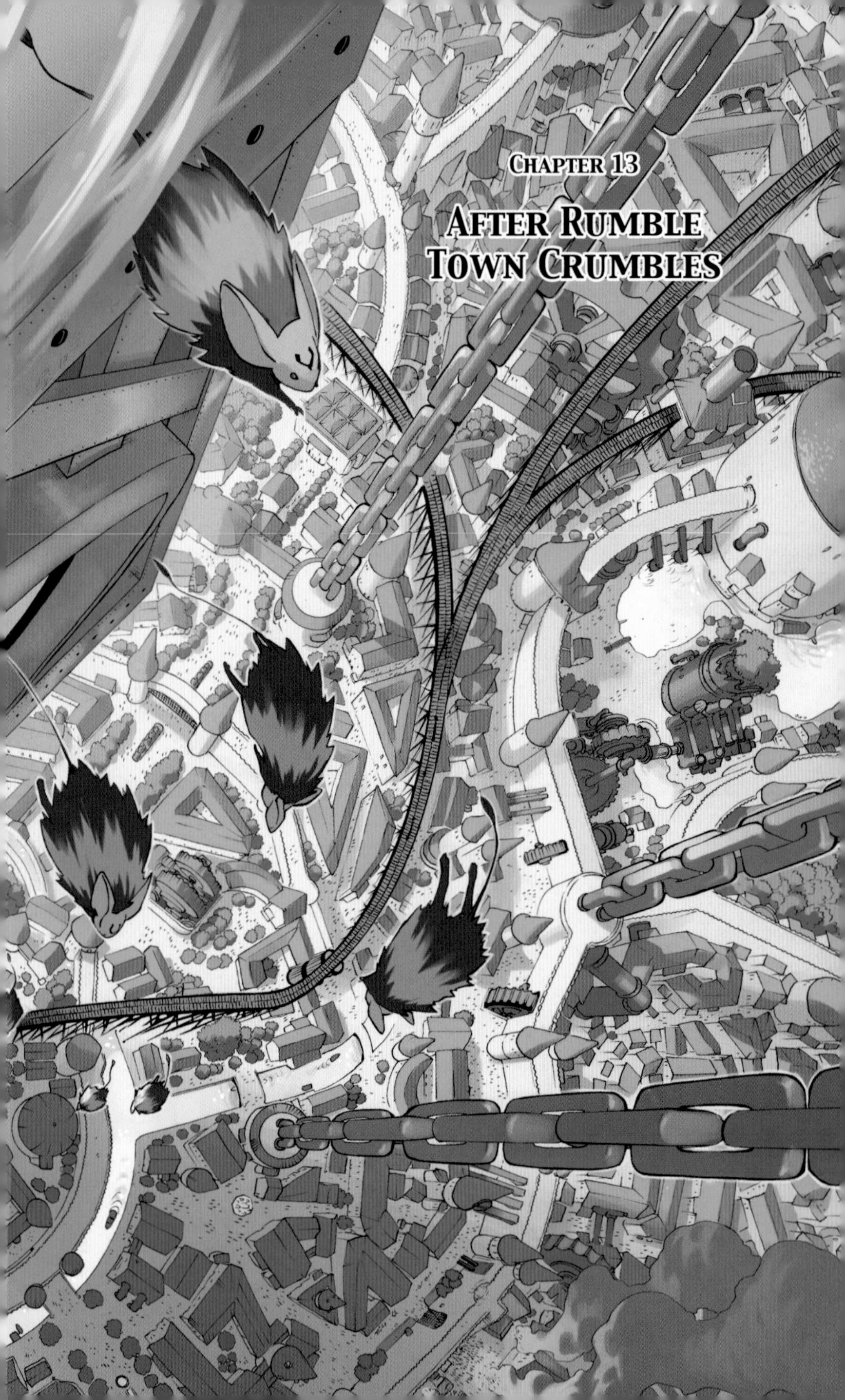
Chapter 13
After Rumble Town Crumbles

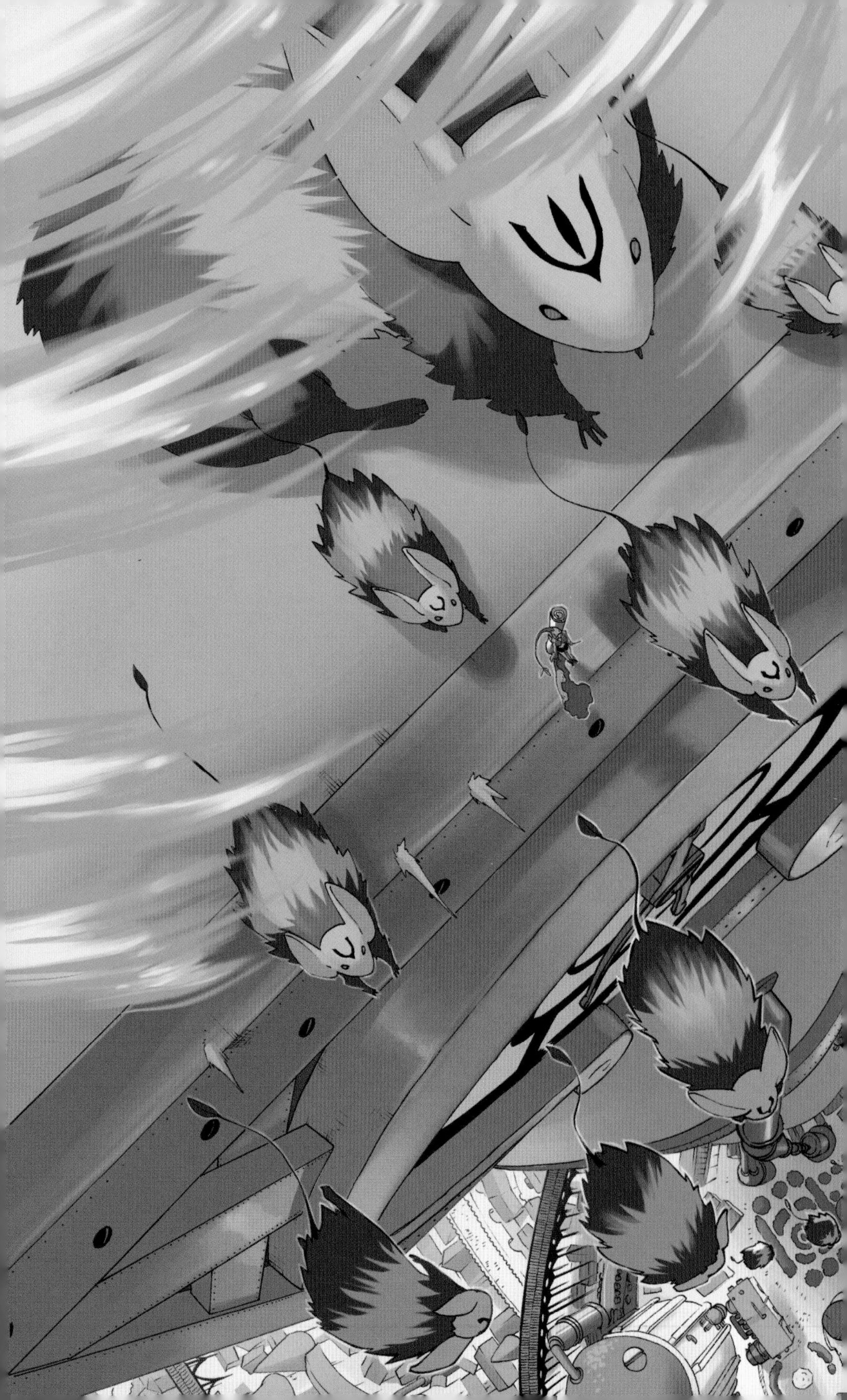

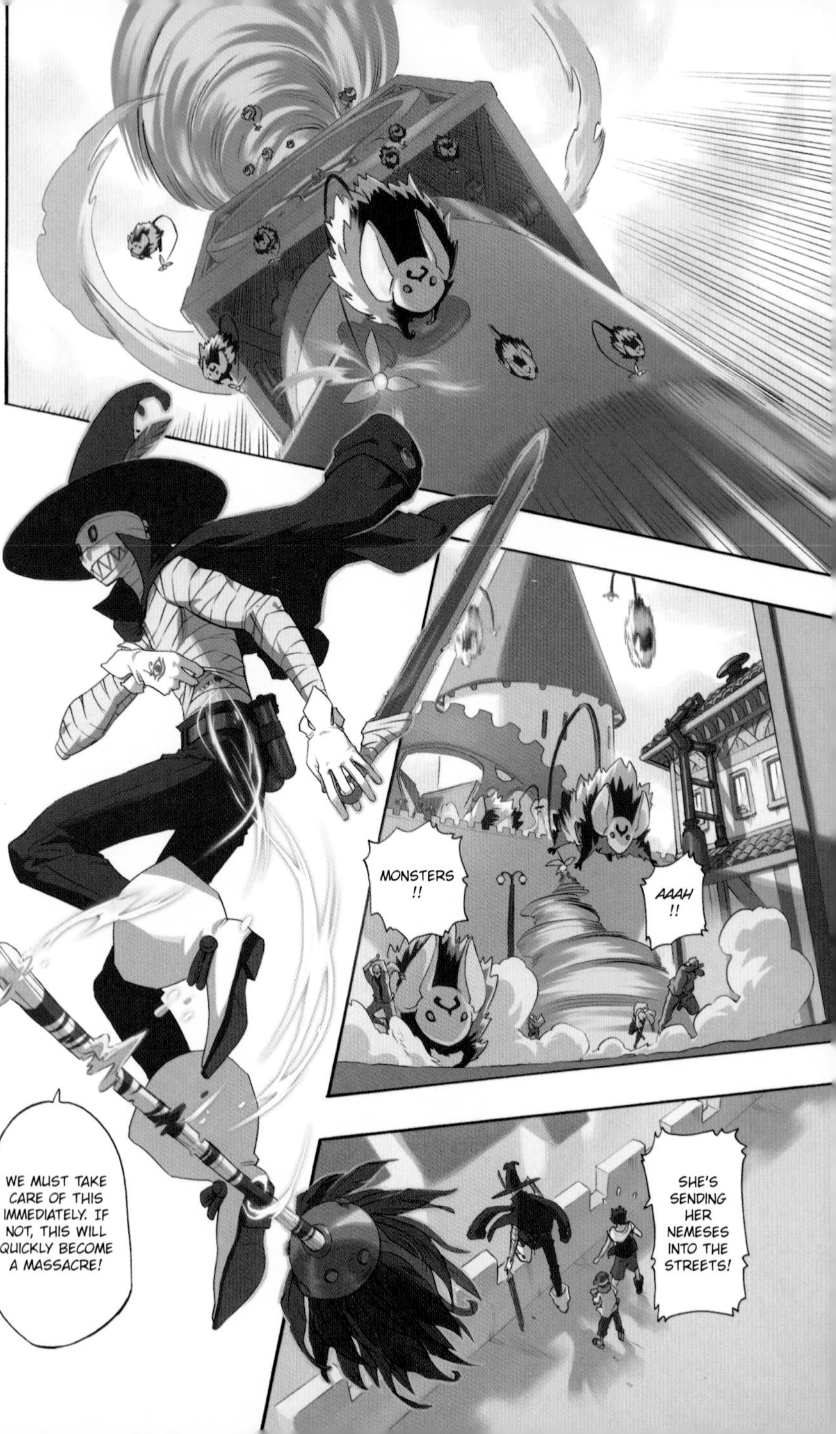

MONSTERS !!
AAAH !!
WE MUST TAKE CARE OF THIS IMMEDIATELY. IF NOT, THIS WILL QUICKLY BECOME A MASSACRE!
SHE'S SENDING HER NEMESES INTO THE STREETS!

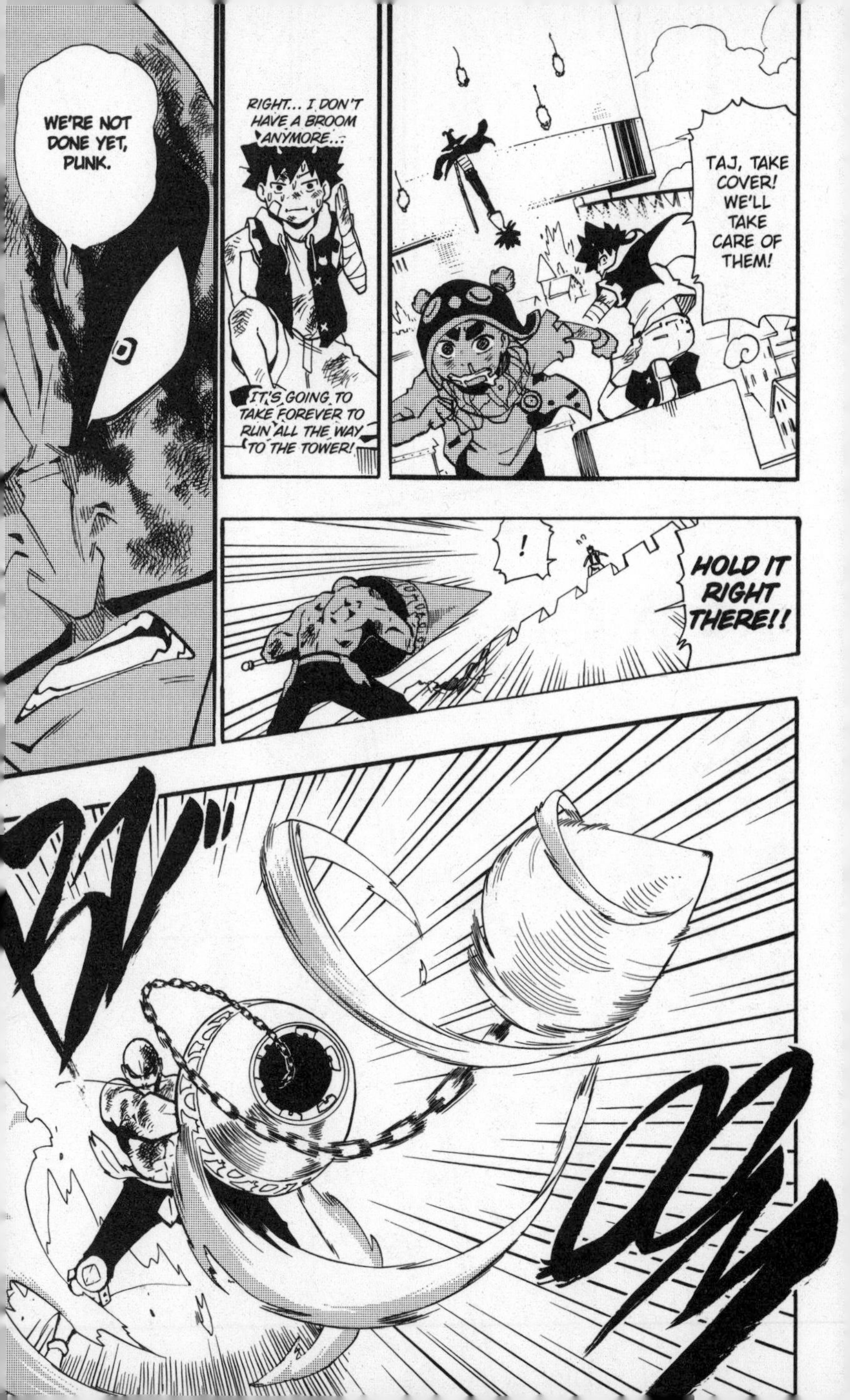
TAJ, TAKE COVER! WE'LL TAKE CARE OF THEM!
RIGHT... I DON'T HAVE A BROOM ANYMORE...
IT'S GOING TO TAKE FOREVER TO RUN ALL THE WAY TO THE TOWER!
WE'RE NOT DONE YET, PUNK.
!
HOLD IT RIGHT THERE!!

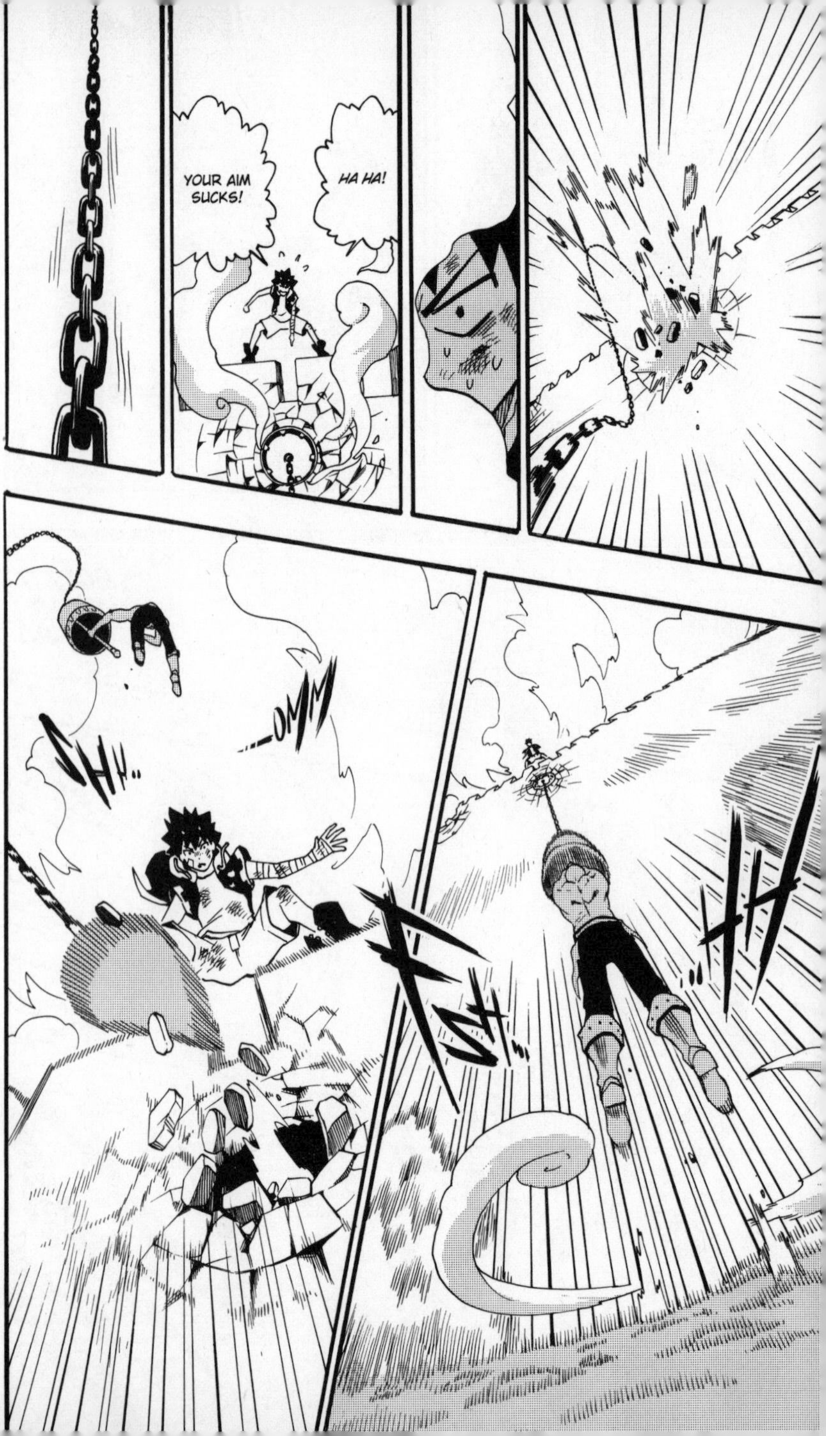
HA HA!
YOUR AIM SUCKS!

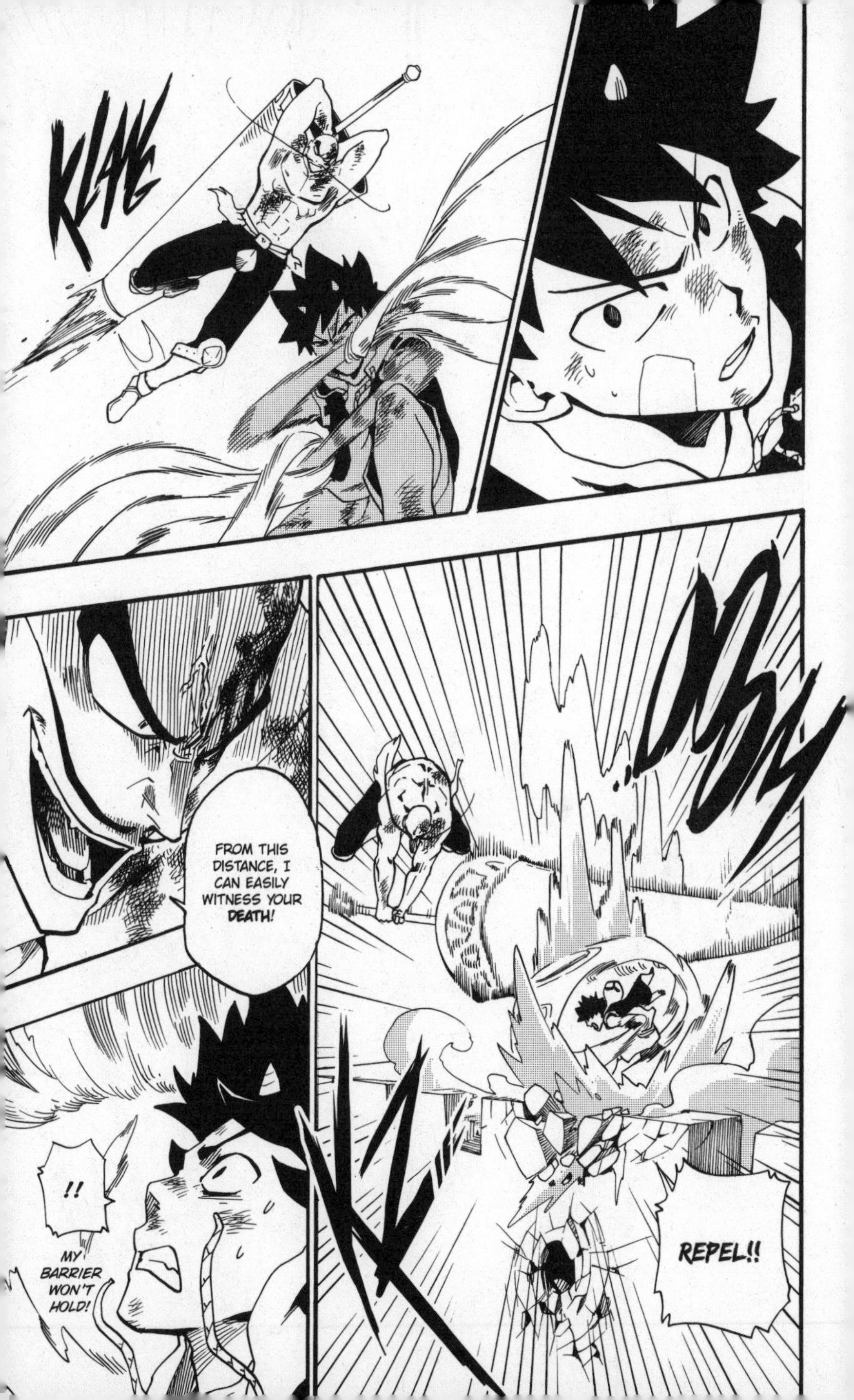
REPEL!!
FROM THIS DISTANCE, I CAN EASILY WITNESS YOUR DEATH!
!!
MY BARRIER WON'T HOLD!

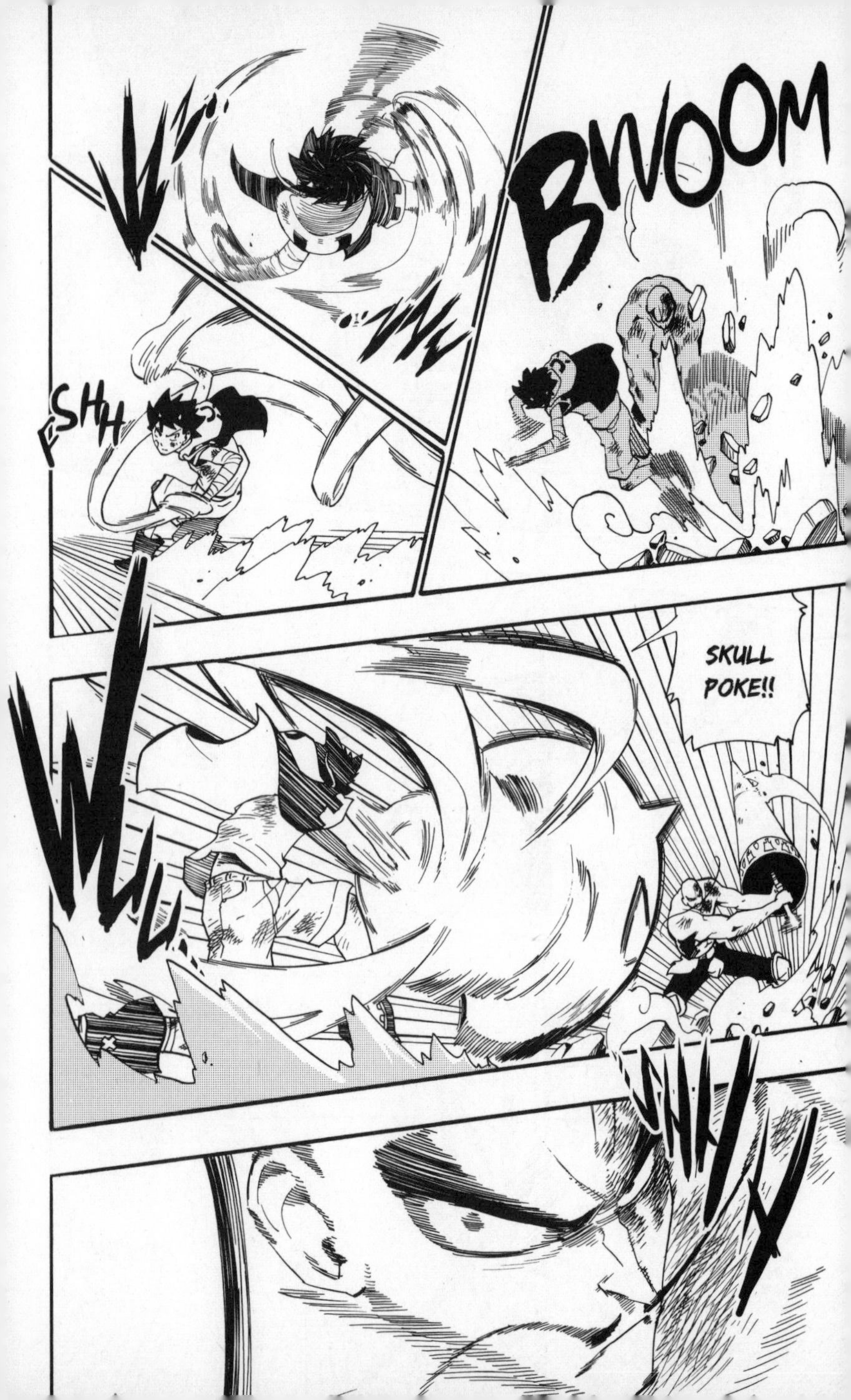
BWOOM
FSHH
SKULL POKE!!

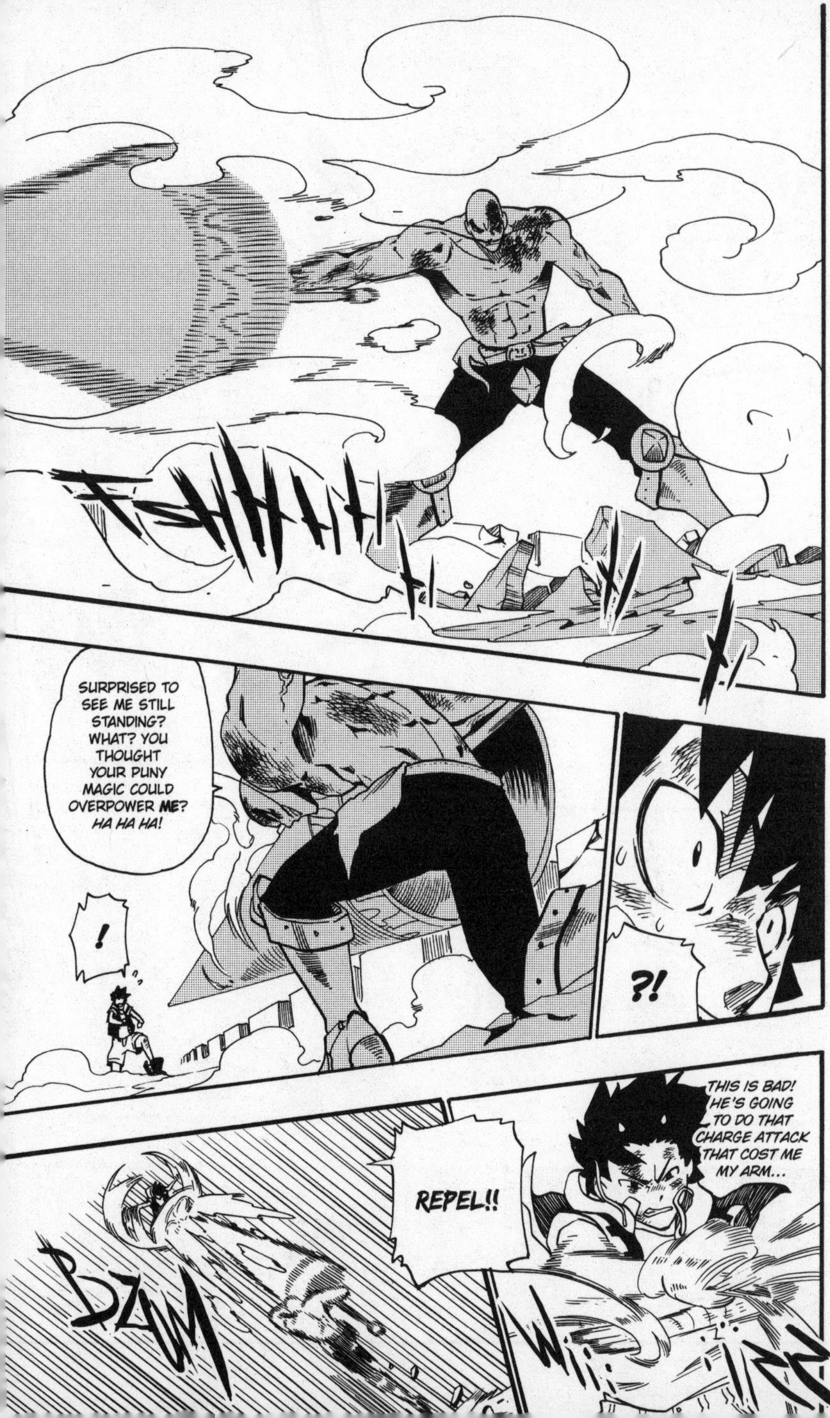
?!
SURPRISED TO SEE ME STILL STANDING? WHAT? YOU THOUGHT YOUR PUNY MAGIC COULD OVERPOWER ME? HA HA HA!
!
THIS IS BAD! HE'S GOING TO DO THAT CHARGE ATTACK THAT COST ME MY ARM...
REPEL!!
BZAM

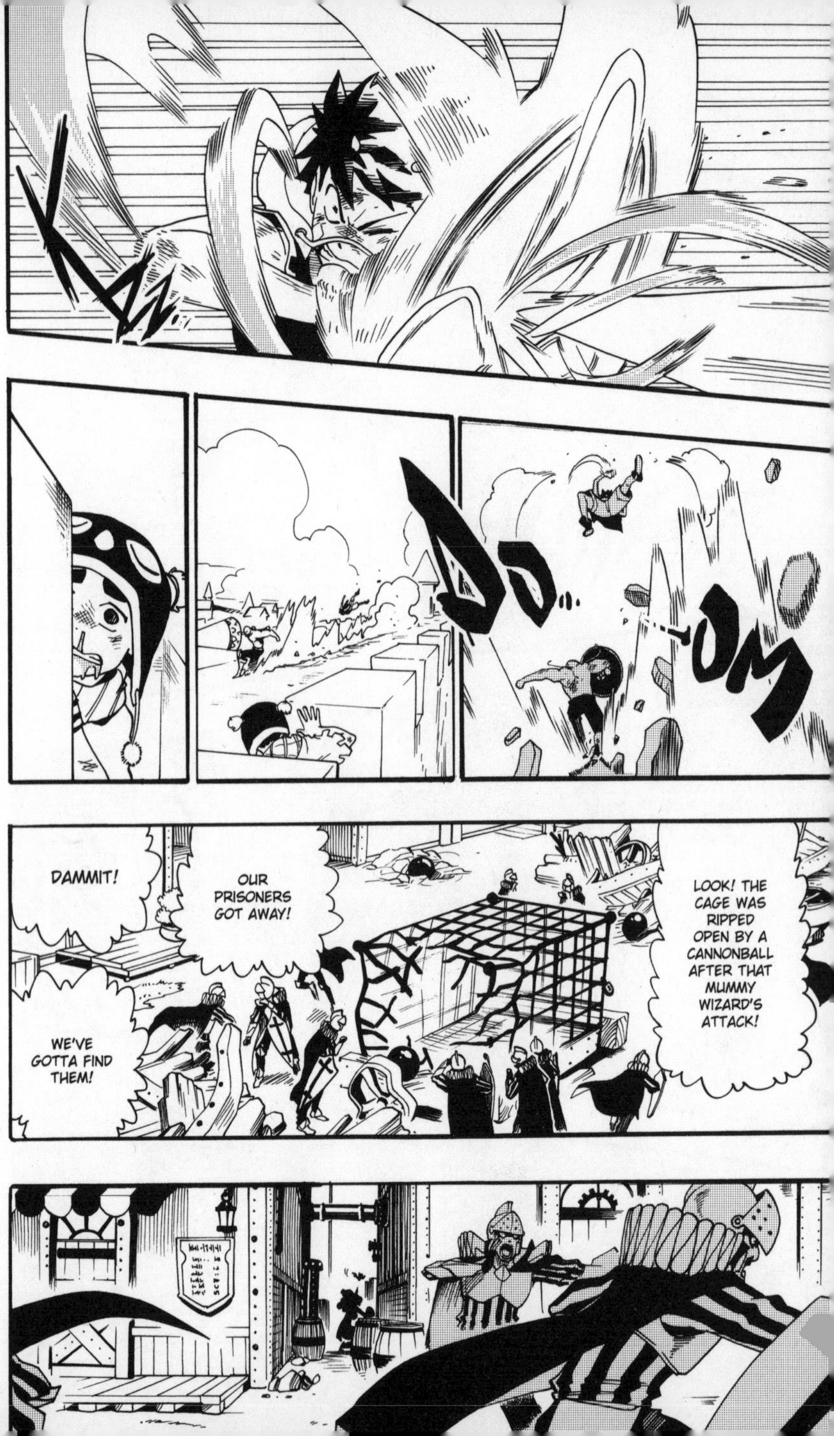
LOOK! THE CAGE WAS RIPPED OPEN BY A CANNONBALL AFTER THAT MUMMY WIZARD'S ATTACK!
OUR PRISONERS GOT AWAY!
DAMMIT!
WE'VE GOTTA FIND THEM!

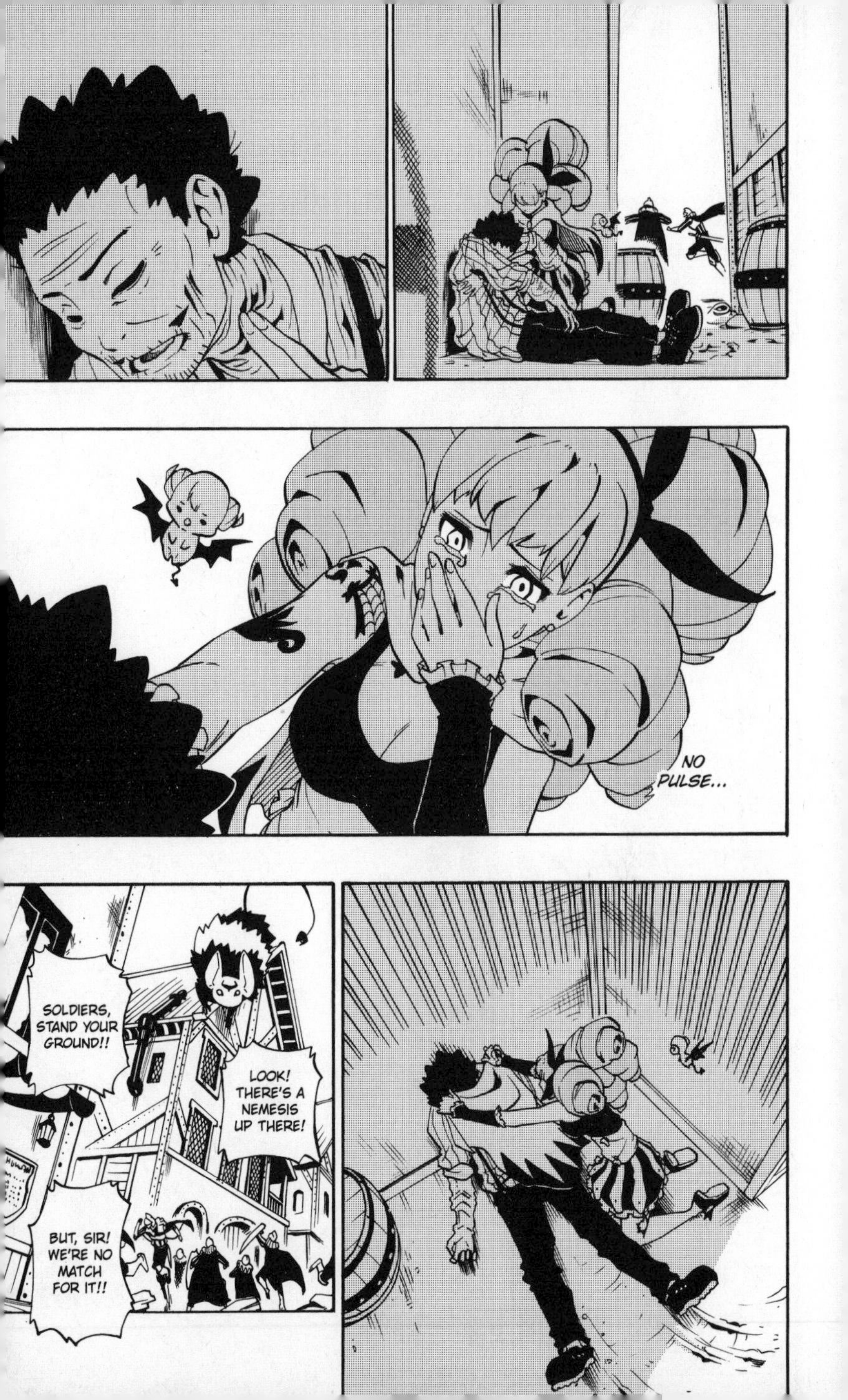
NO PULSE...
LOOK! THERE'S A NEMESIS UP THERE!
SOLDIERS, STAND YOUR GROUND!!
BUT, SIR! WE'RE NO MATCH FOR IT!!

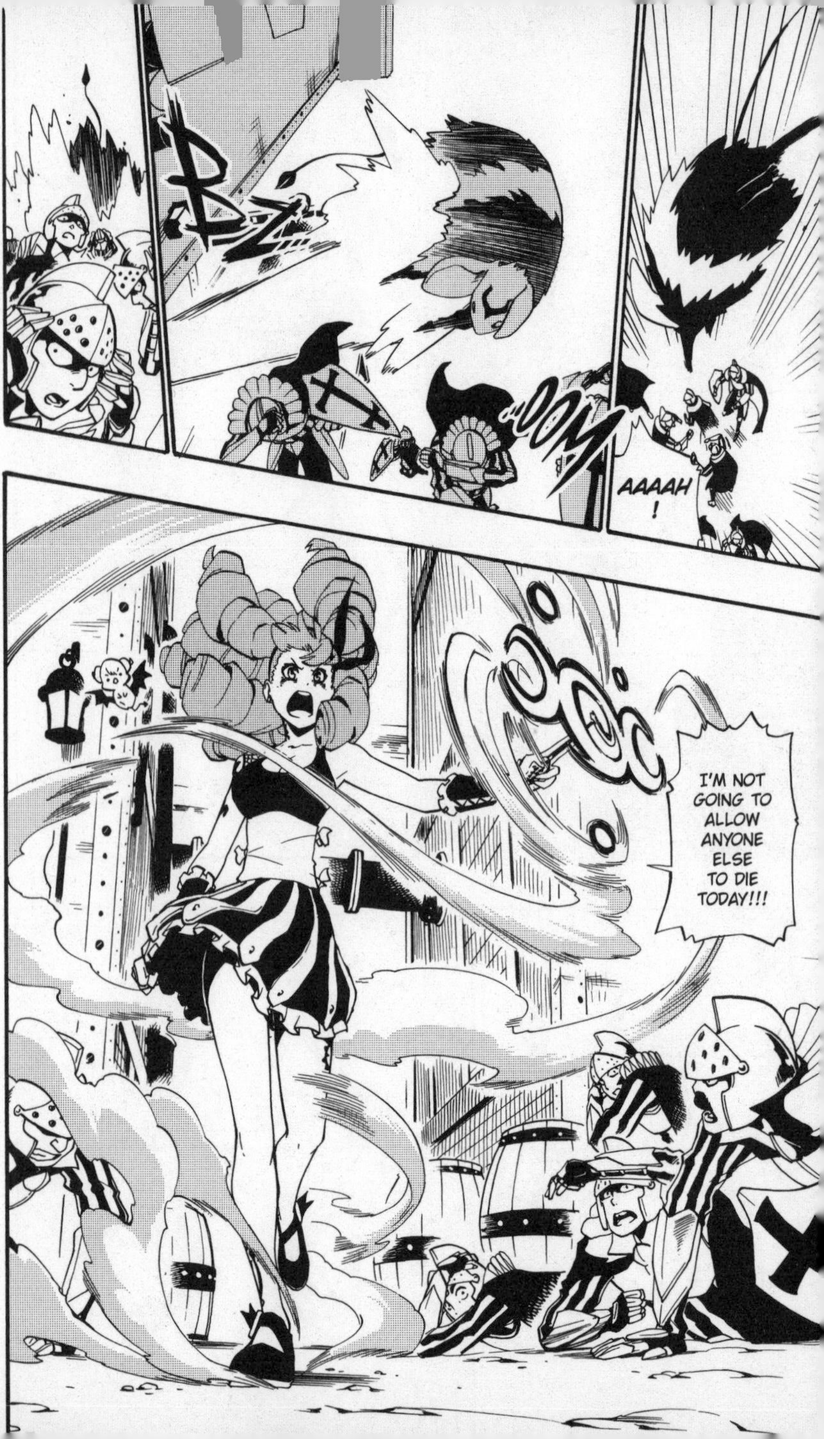
BZZ...
WOOM
AAAAH!
I'M NOT GOING TO ALLOW ANYONE ELSE TO DIE TODAY!!!

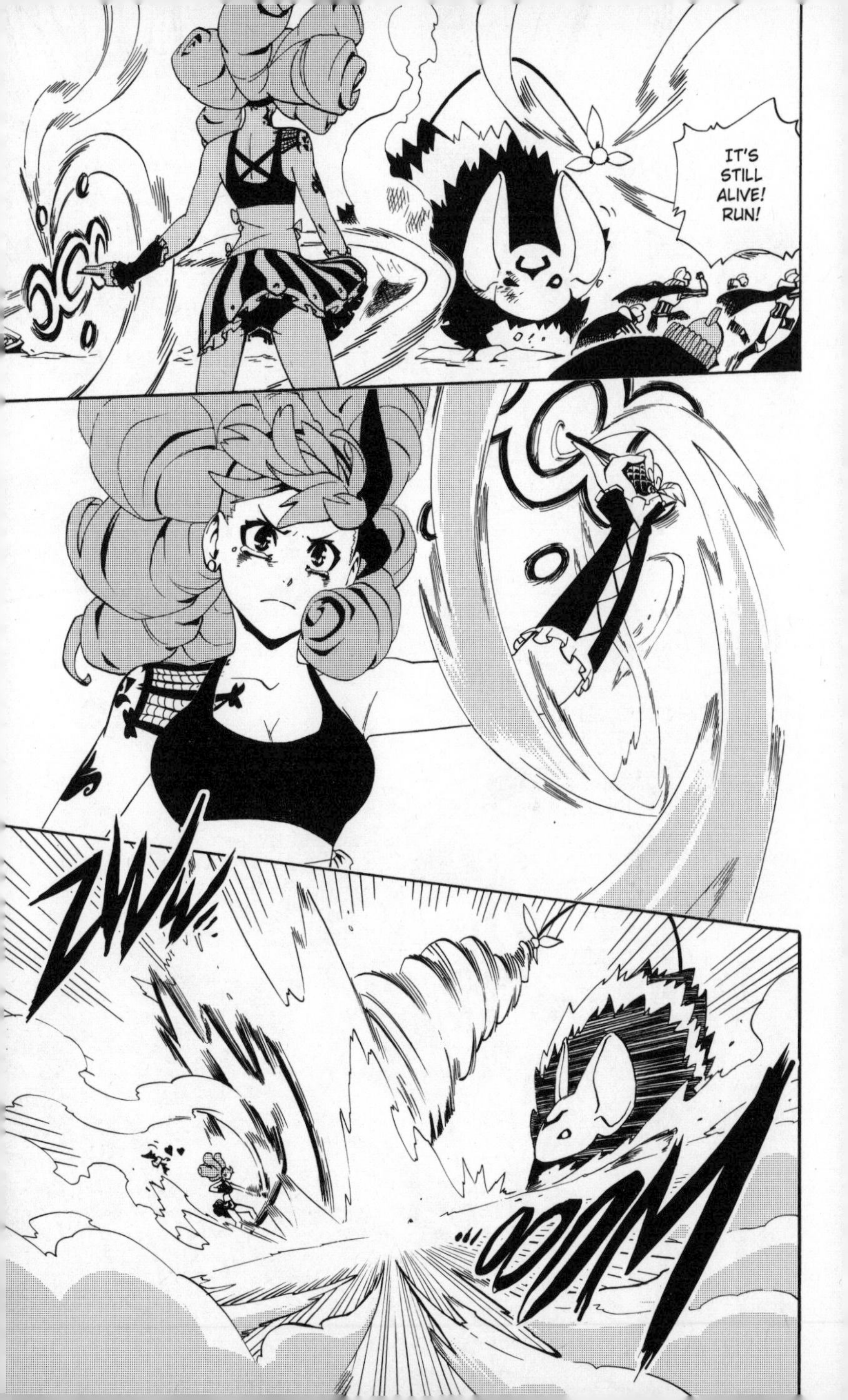

IT'S STILL ALIVE! RUN!
ZWW
WOOM

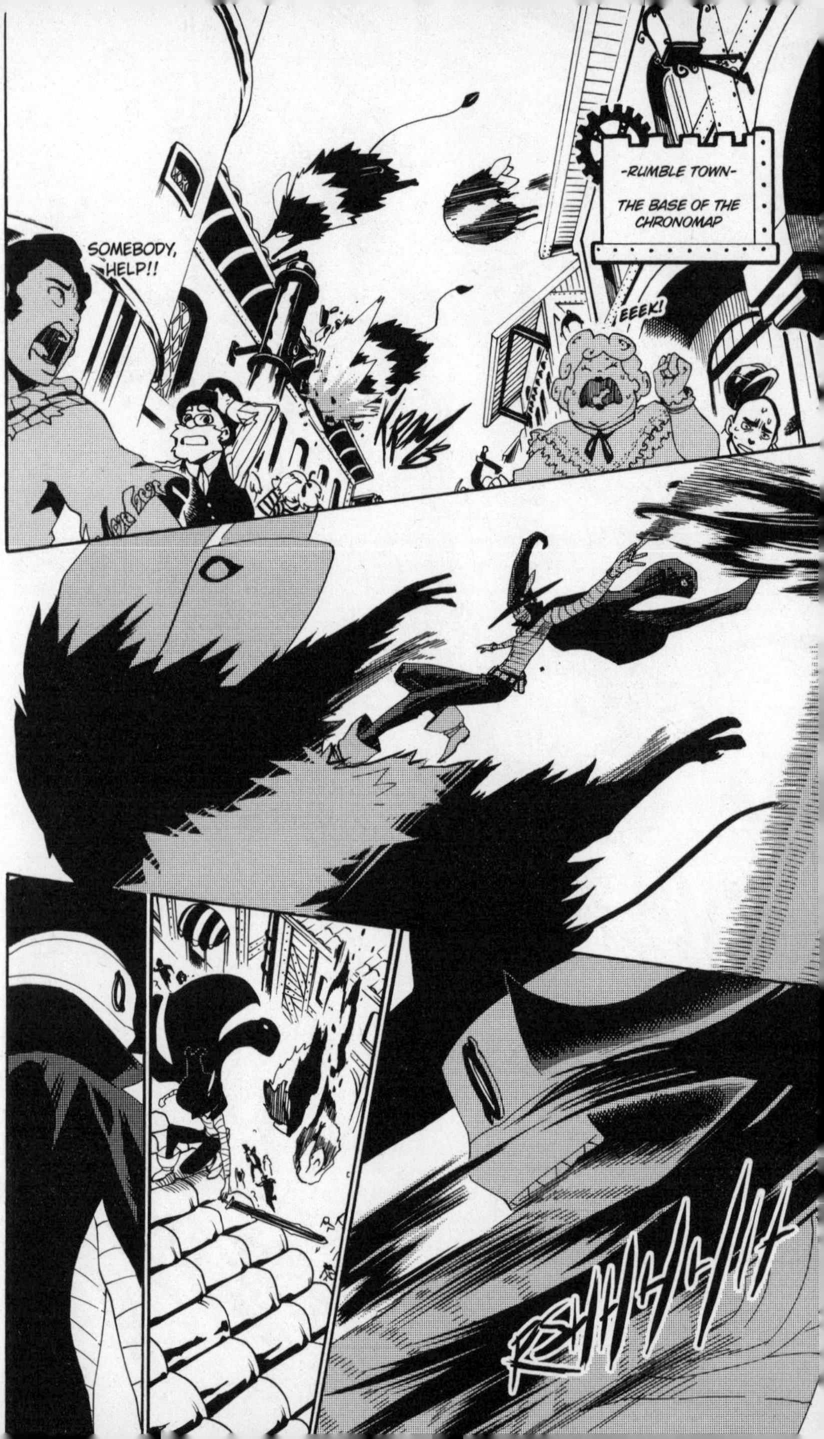
-RUMBLE TOWN-
THE BASE OF THE CHRONOMAP
EEEK!
SOMEBODY, HELP!!

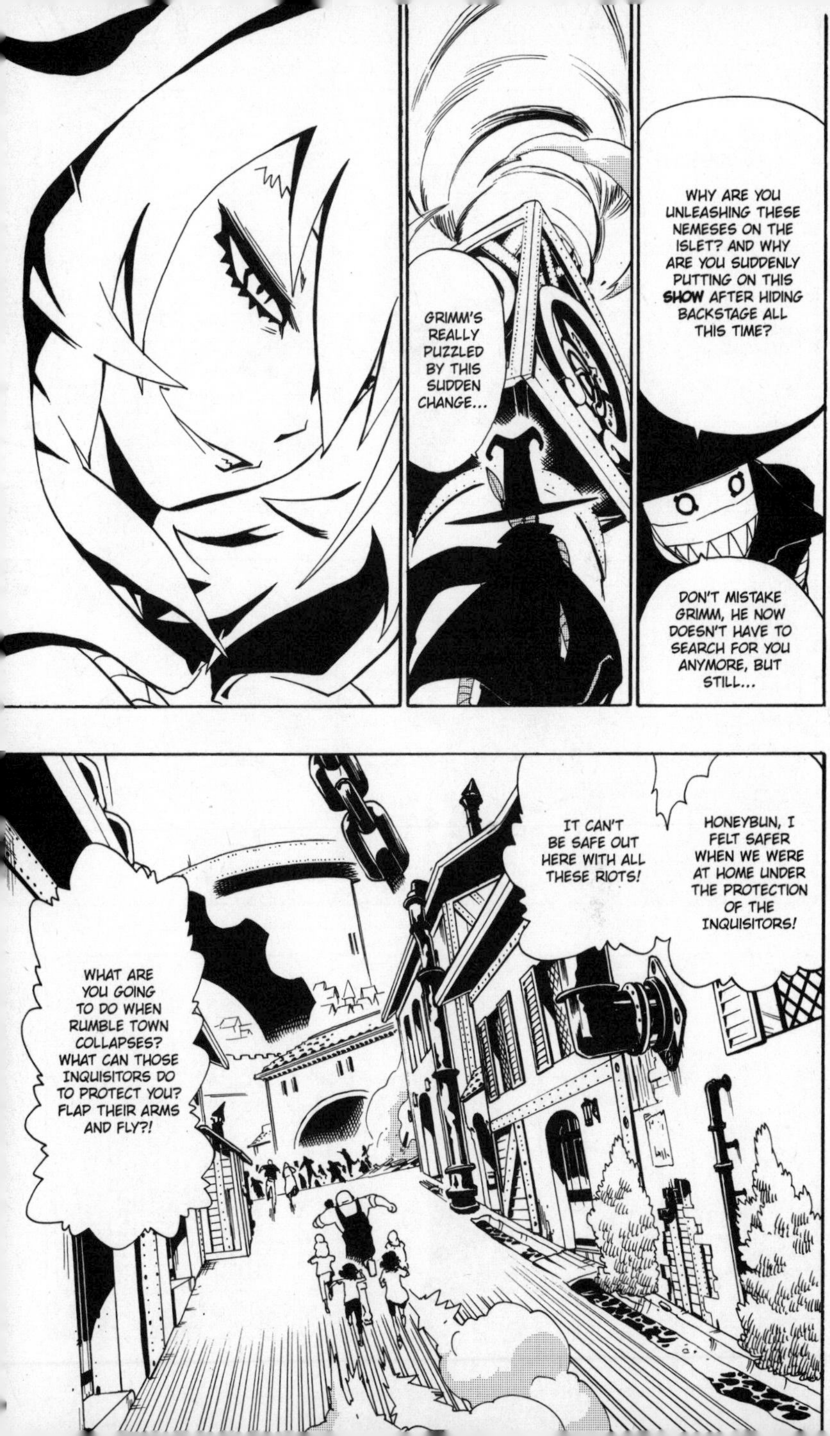
WHY ARE YOU UNLEASHING THESE NEMESES ON THE ISLET? AND WHY ARE YOU SUDDENLY PUTTING ON THIS **SHOW** AFTER HIDING BACKSTAGE ALL THIS TIME?
DON'T MISTAKE GRIMM, HE NOW DOESN'T HAVE TO SEARCH FOR YOU ANYMORE, BUT STILL...
GRIMM'S REALLY PUZZLED BY THIS SUDDEN CHANGE...
HONEYBUN, I FELT SAFER WHEN WE WERE AT HOME UNDER THE PROTECTION OF THE INQUISITORS!
IT CAN'T BE SAFE OUT HERE WITH ALL THESE RIOTS!
WHAT ARE YOU GOING TO DO WHEN RUMBLE TOWN COLLAPSES? WHAT CAN THOSE INQUISITORS DO TO PROTECT YOU? FLAP THEIR ARMS AND FLY?!

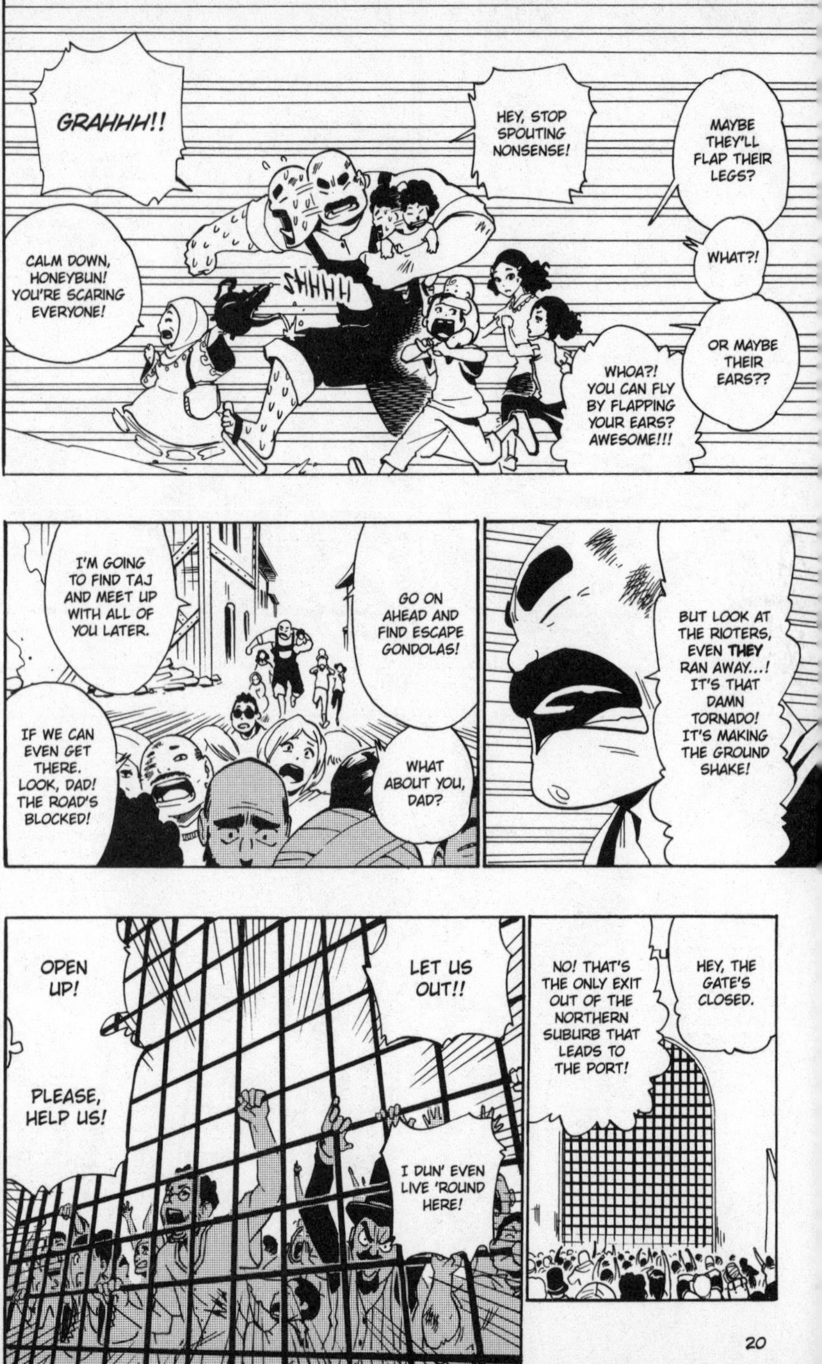
MAYBE THEY'LL FLAP THEIR LEGS?
HEY, STOP SPOUTING NONSENSE!
GRAHHHH!!
WHAT?!
OR MAYBE THEIR EARS??
WHOA?! YOU CAN FLY BY FLAPPING YOUR EARS? AWESOME!!!
SHHHH
CALM DOWN, HONEYBUN! YOU'RE SCARING EVERYONE!
BUT LOOK AT THE RIOTERS, EVEN THEY RAN AWAY...! IT'S THAT DAMN TORNADO! IT'S MAKING THE GROUND SHAKE!
GO ON AHEAD AND FIND ESCAPE GONDOLAS!
I'M GOING TO FIND TAJ AND MEET UP WITH ALL OF YOU LATER.
WHAT ABOUT YOU, DAD?
IF WE CAN EVEN GET THERE. LOOK, DAD! THE ROAD'S BLOCKED!
HEY, THE GATE'S CLOSED.
NO! THAT'S THE ONLY EXIT OUT OF THE NORTHERN SUBURB THAT LEADS TO THE PORT!
LET US OUT!!
OPEN UP!
I DUN' EVEN LIVE 'ROUND HERE!
PLEASE, HELP US!

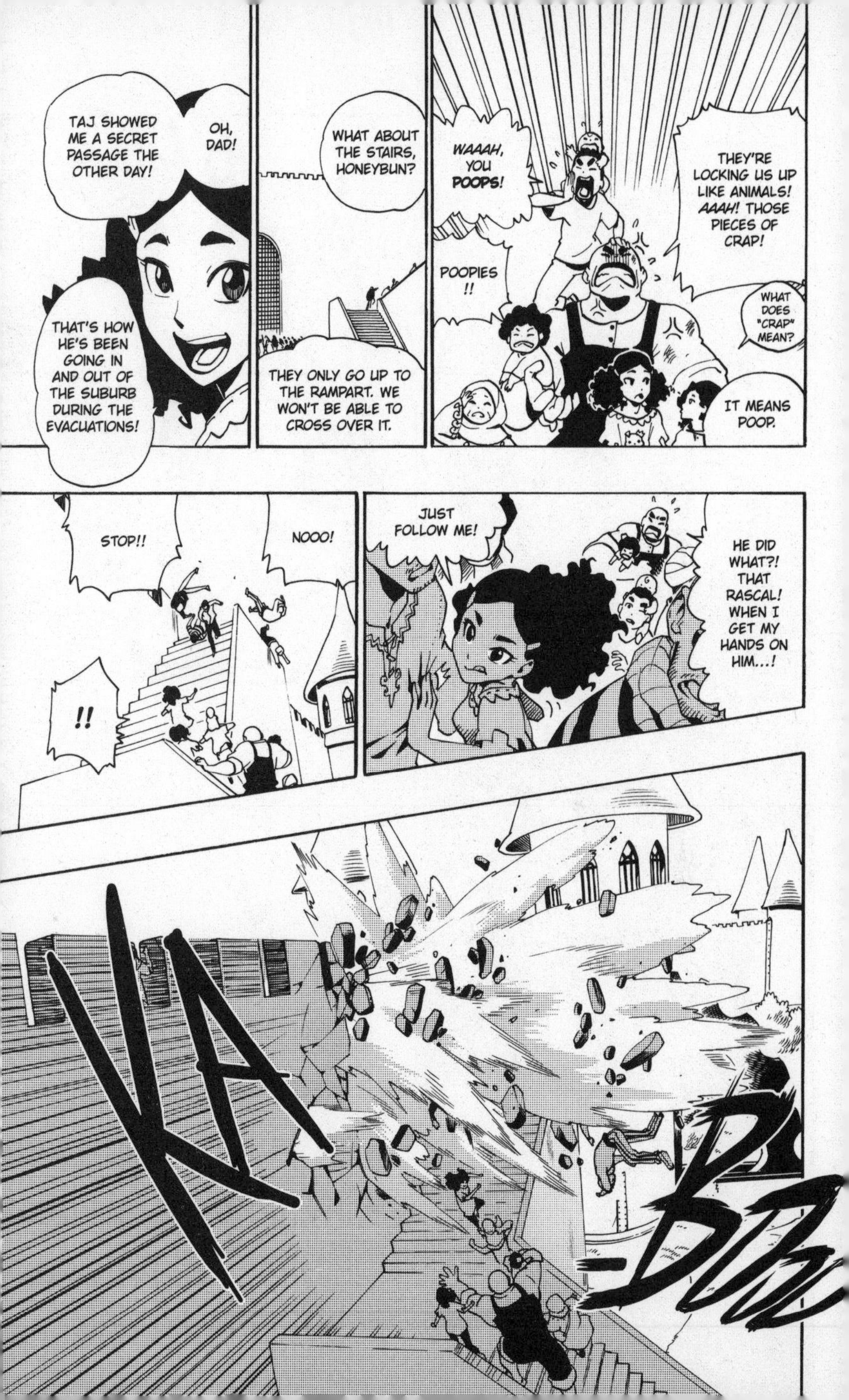

TAJ SHOWED ME A SECRET PASSAGE THE OTHER DAY!
OH, DAD!
THAT'S HOW HE'S BEEN GOING IN AND OUT OF THE SUBURB DURING THE EVACUATIONS!
WHAT ABOUT THE STAIRS, HONEYBUN?
THEY ONLY GO UP TO THE RAMPART. WE WON'T BE ABLE TO CROSS OVER IT.
WAAAH, YOU POOPS!
POOPIES !!
THEY'RE LOCKING US UP LIKE ANIMALS! AAAH! THOSE PIECES OF CRAP!
WHAT DOES "CRAP" MEAN?
IT MEANS POOP.
STOP!!
NOOO!
!!
JUST FOLLOW ME!
HE DID WHAT?! THAT RASCAL! WHEN I GET MY HANDS ON HIM...!
KA-BOOM

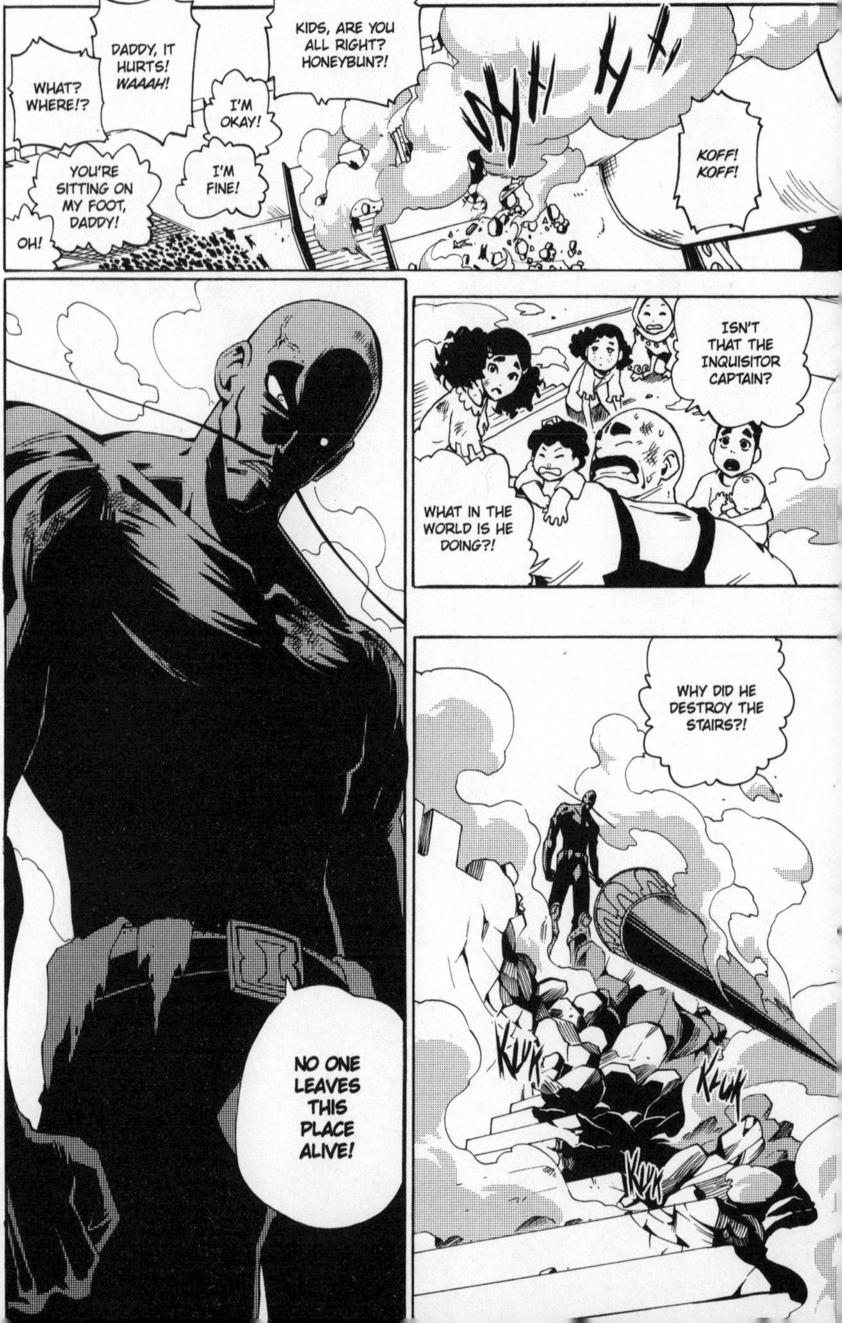
KOFF! KOFF!
KIDS, ARE YOU ALL RIGHT? HONEYBUN?!
I'M OKAY!
I'M FINE!
DADDY, IT HURTS! WAAAH!
WHAT? WHERE!?
YOU'RE SITTING ON MY FOOT, DADDY!
OH!
ISN'T THAT THE INQUISITOR CAPTAIN?
WHAT IN THE WORLD IS HE DOING?!
WHY DID HE DESTROY THE STAIRS?!
NO ONE LEAVES THIS PLACE ALIVE!

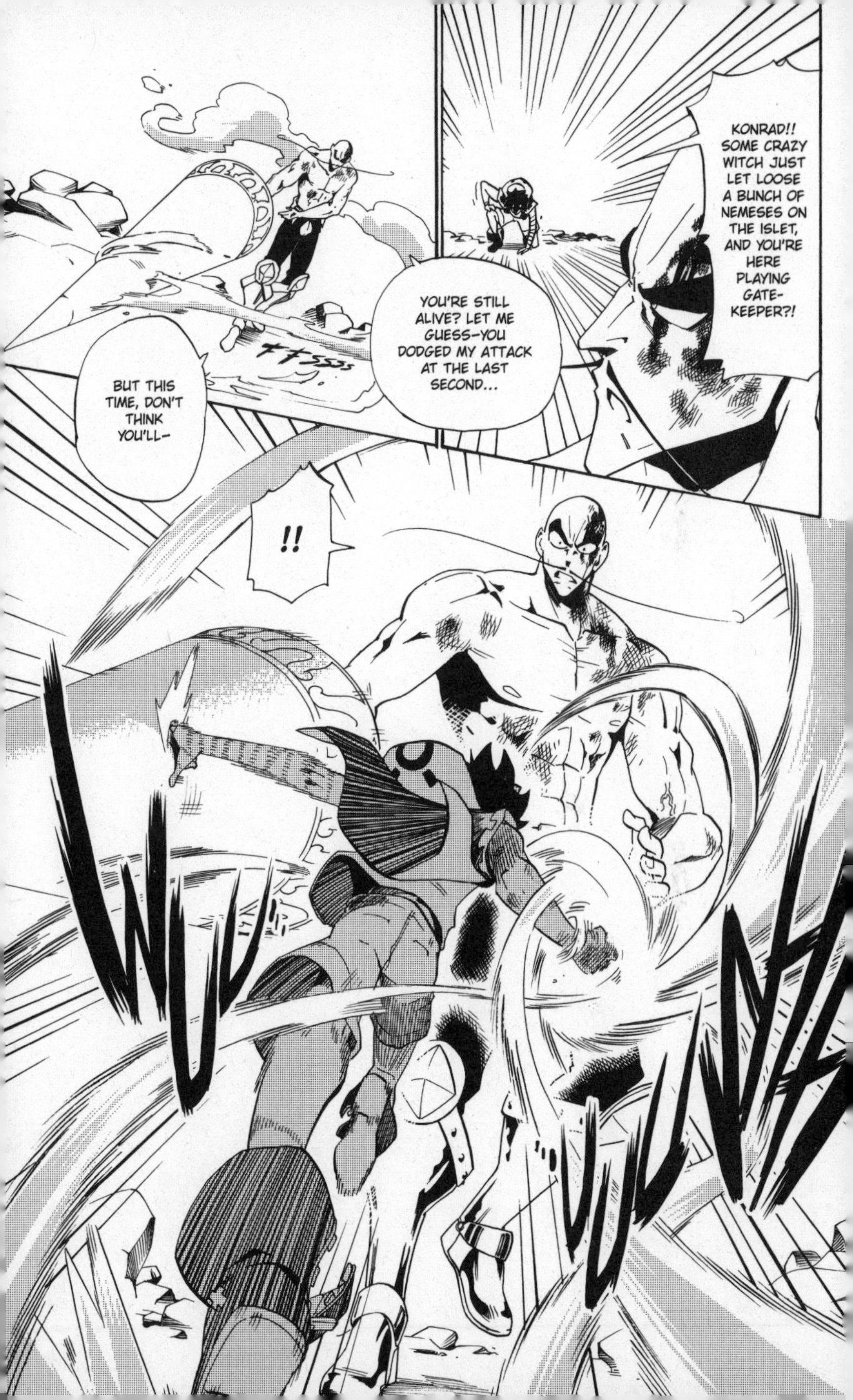
KONRAD!! SOME CRAZY WITCH JUST LET LOOSE A BUNCH OF NEMESES ON THE ISLET, AND YOU'RE HERE PLAYING GATE-KEEPER?!
YOU'RE STILL ALIVE? LET ME GUESS—YOU DODGED MY ATTACK AT THE LAST SECOND...
BUT THIS TIME, DON'T THINK YOU'LL—
!!

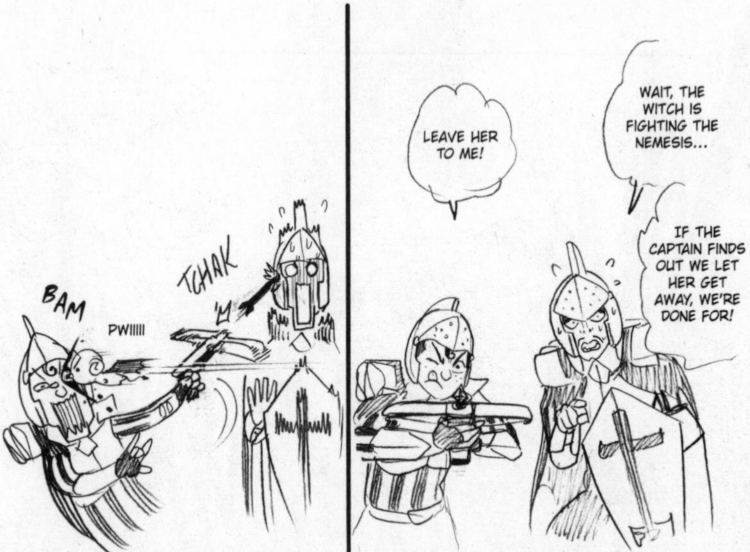
BAM
PWIIII
TCHAK
LEAVE HER TO ME!
WAIT, THE WITCH IS FIGHTING THE NEMESIS...
IF THE CAPTAIN FINDS OUT WE LET HER GET AWAY, WE'RE DONE FOR!

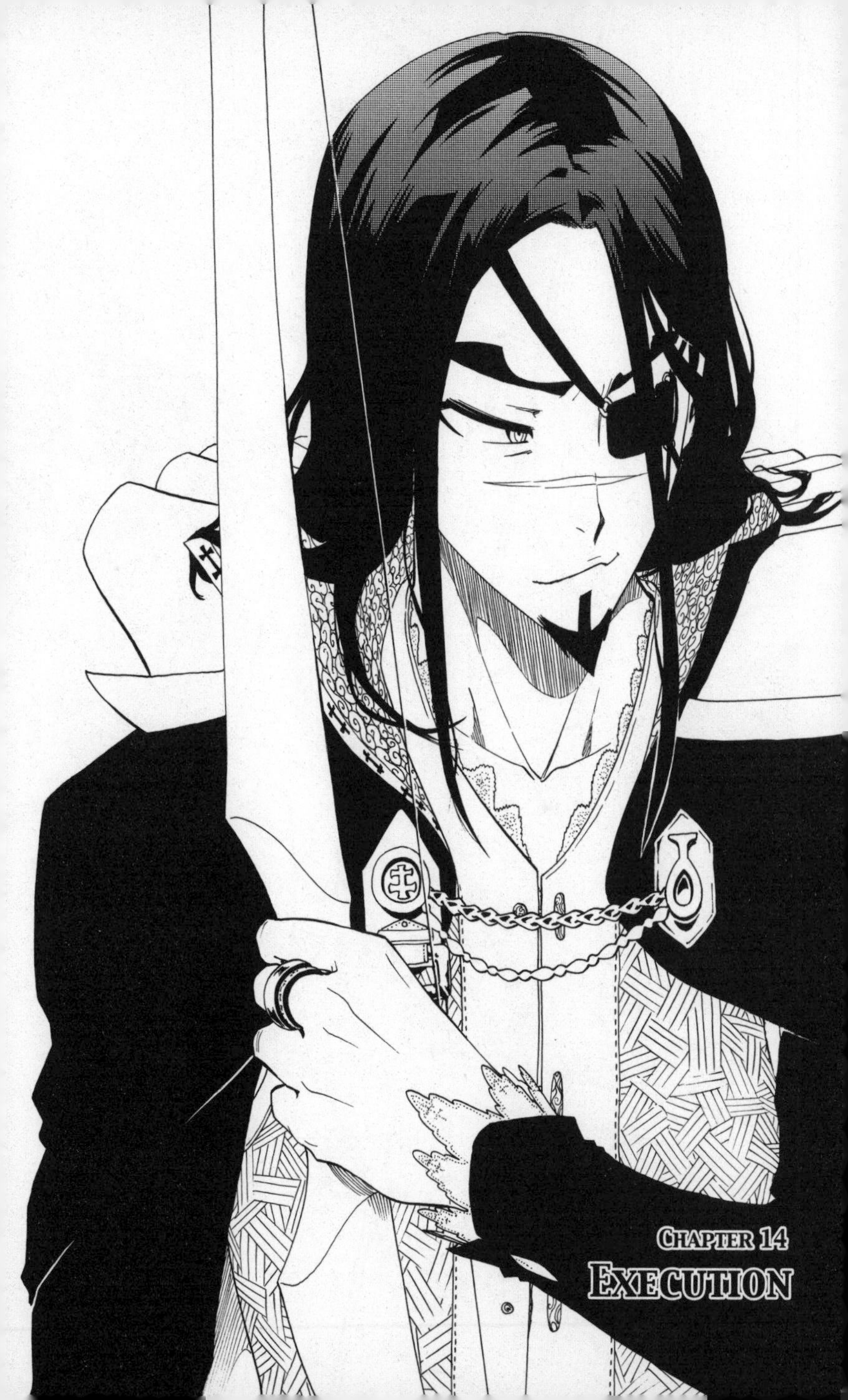
Chapter 14
Execution

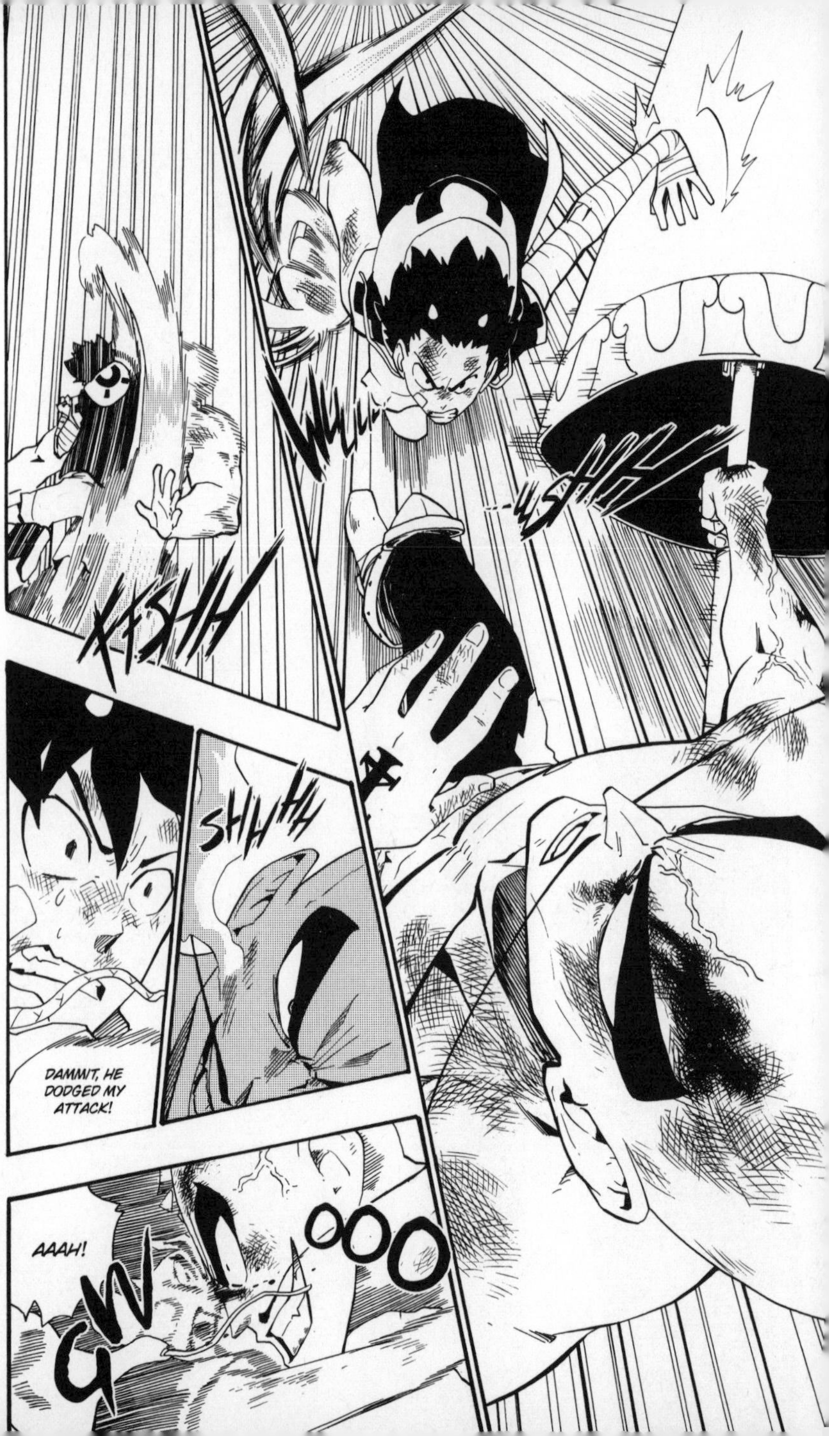

SHHH
KFSHH
SHHHH
DAMMIT, HE DODGED MY ATTACK!
AAAH!
GWOOO

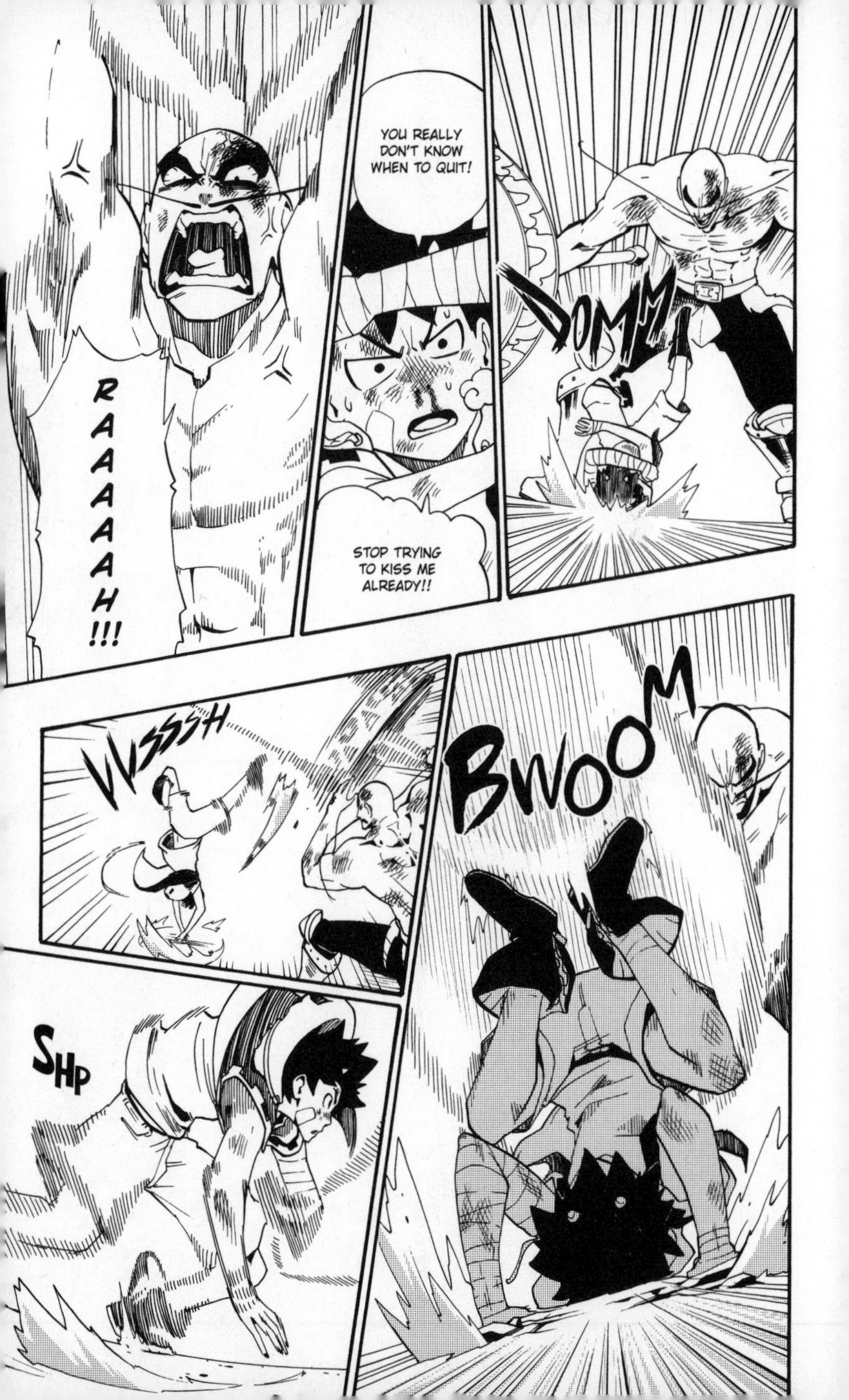

DOMM
YOU REALLY DON'T KNOW WHEN TO QUIT!
STOP TRYING TO KISS ME ALREADY!!
RAAAAAAH!!!
BWOOM
WSSSH
SHP

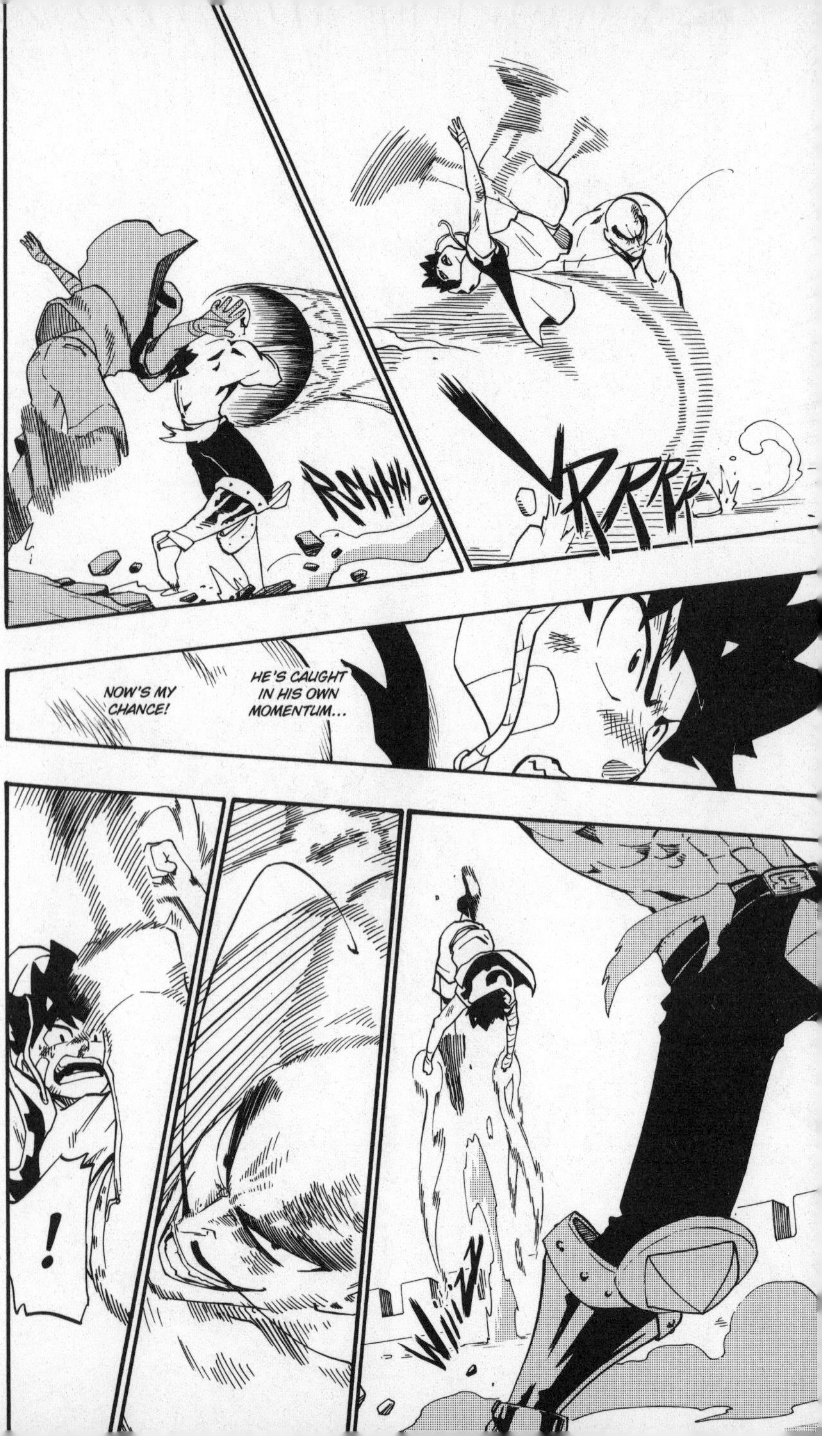
VRRRR
RSHHH
HE'S CAUGHT IN HIS OWN MOMENTUM...
NOW'S MY CHANCE!
!

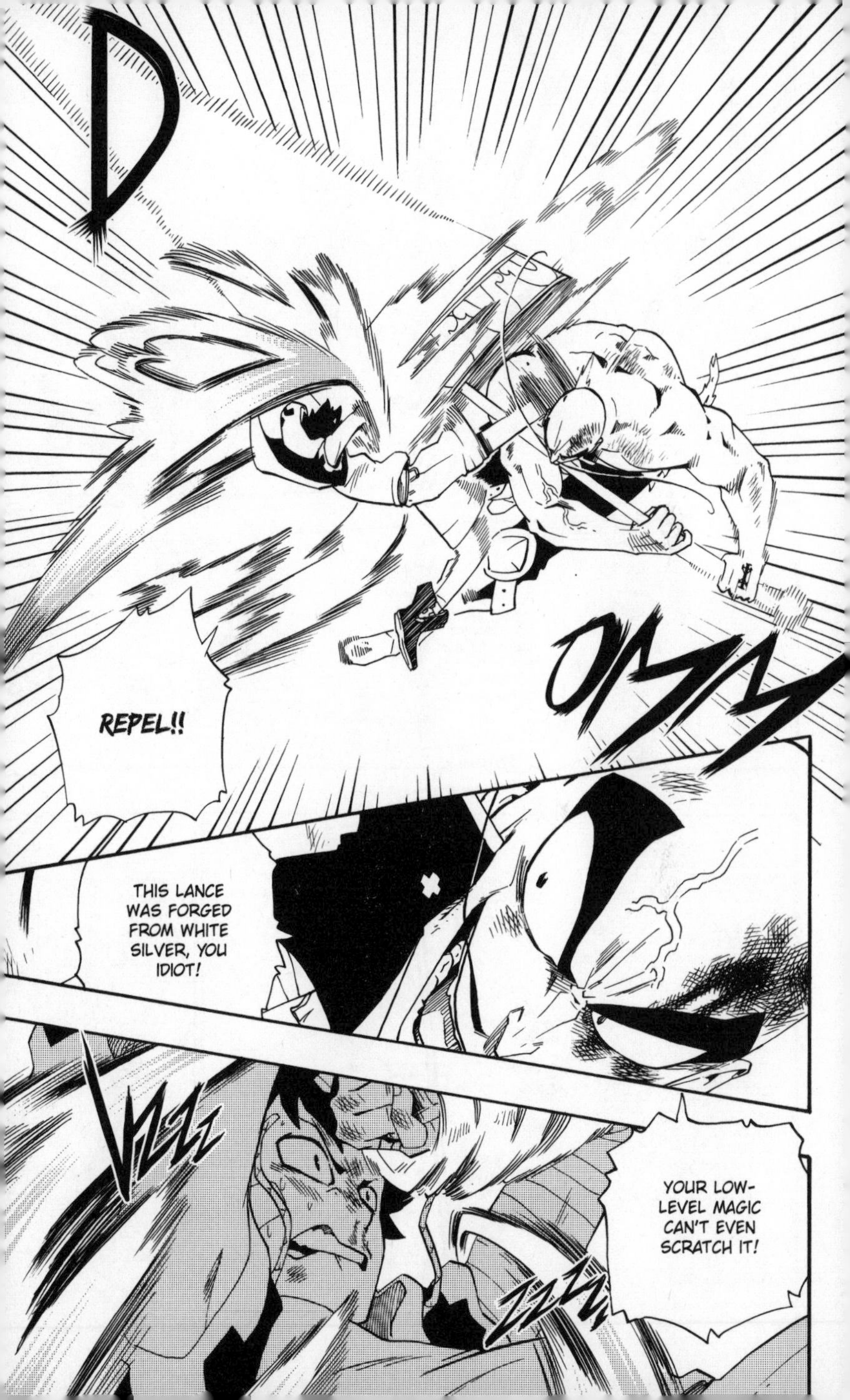
D
OMM
REPEL!!
THIS LANCE WAS FORGED FROM WHITE SILVER, YOU IDIOT!
YOUR LOW-LEVEL MAGIC CAN'T EVEN SCRATCH IT!

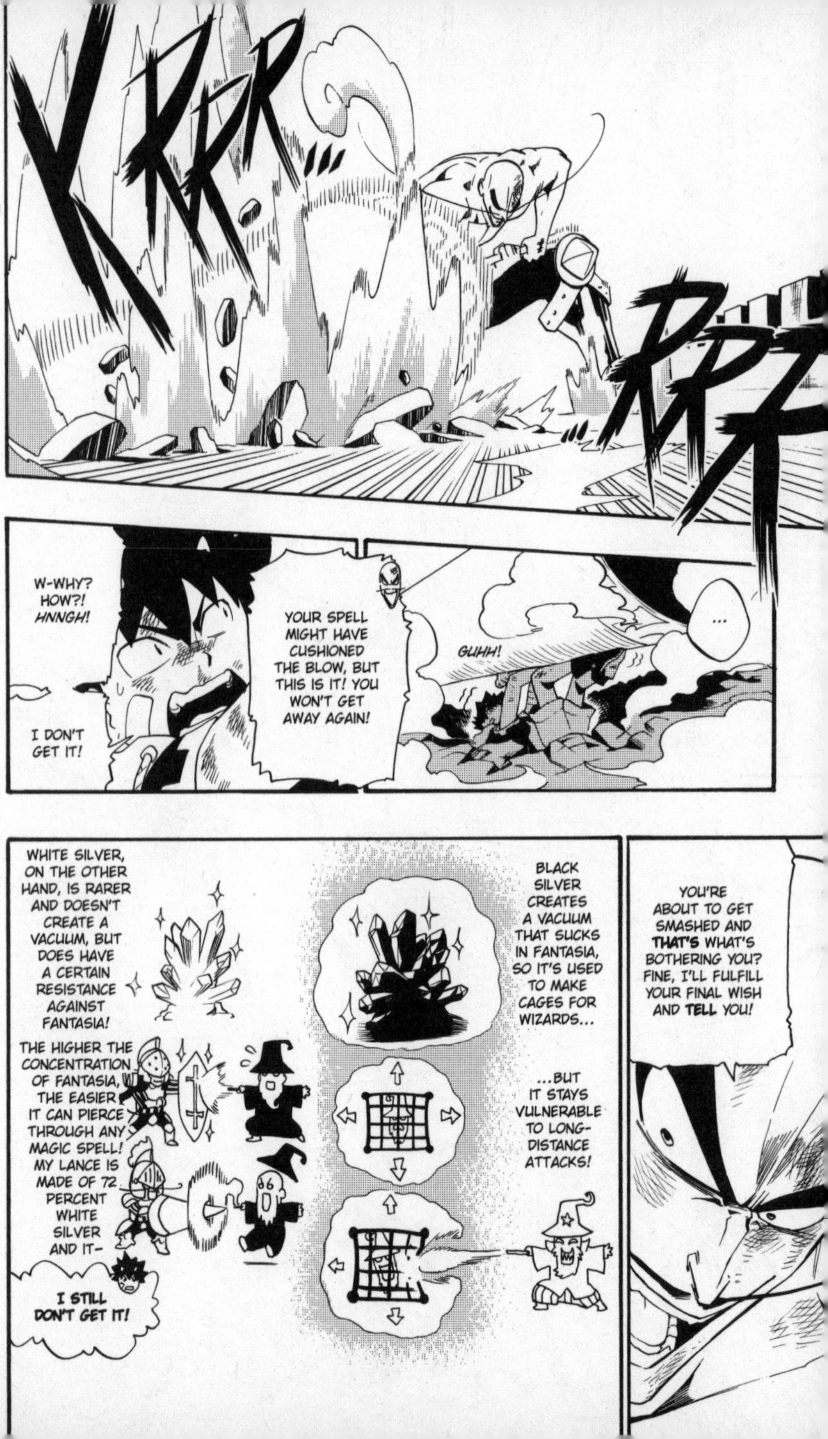

KRRR
RRR
...
GUHH!
YOUR SPELL MIGHT HAVE CUSHIONED THE BLOW, BUT THIS IS IT! YOU WON'T GET AWAY AGAIN!
W-WHY? HOW?! HNNGH!
I DON'T GET IT!
YOU'RE ABOUT TO GET SMASHED AND **THAT'S** WHAT'S BOTHERING YOU? FINE, I'LL FULFILL YOUR FINAL WISH AND **TELL** YOU!
BLACK SILVER CREATES A VACUUM THAT SUCKS IN FANTASIA, SO IT'S USED TO MAKE CAGES FOR WIZARDS...
...BUT IT STAYS VULNERABLE TO LONG-DISTANCE ATTACKS!
WHITE SILVER, ON THE OTHER HAND, IS RARER AND DOESN'T CREATE A VACUUM, BUT DOES HAVE A CERTAIN RESISTANCE AGAINST FANTASIA!
THE HIGHER THE CONCENTRATION OF FANTASIA, THE EASIER IT CAN PIERCE THROUGH ANY MAGIC SPELL! MY LANCE IS MADE OF 72 PERCENT WHITE SILVER AND IT-
I STILL DON'T GET IT!

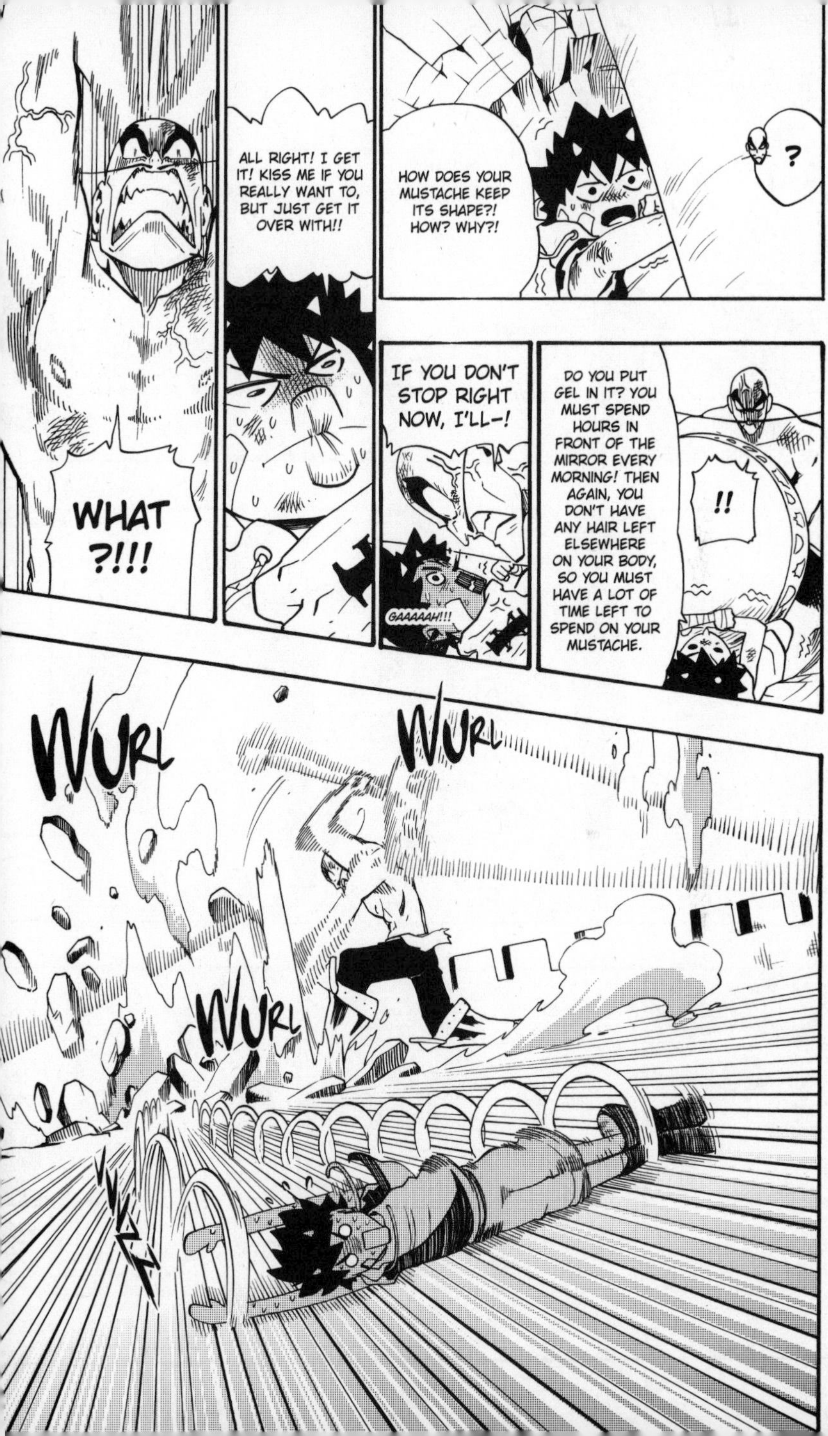
?
HOW DOES YOUR MUSTACHE KEEP ITS SHAPE?! HOW? WHY?!
DO YOU PUT GEL IN IT? YOU MUST SPEND HOURS IN FRONT OF THE MIRROR EVERY MORNING! THEN AGAIN, YOU DON'T HAVE ANY HAIR LEFT ELSEWHERE ON YOUR BODY, SO YOU MUST HAVE A LOT OF TIME LEFT TO SPEND ON YOUR MUSTACHE.
!!
IF YOU DON'T STOP RIGHT NOW, I'LL-!
GAAAAAH!!!
ALL RIGHT! I GET IT! KISS ME IF YOU REALLY WANT TO, BUT JUST GET IT OVER WITH!!
WHAT ?!!!
WURL
WURL
WURL

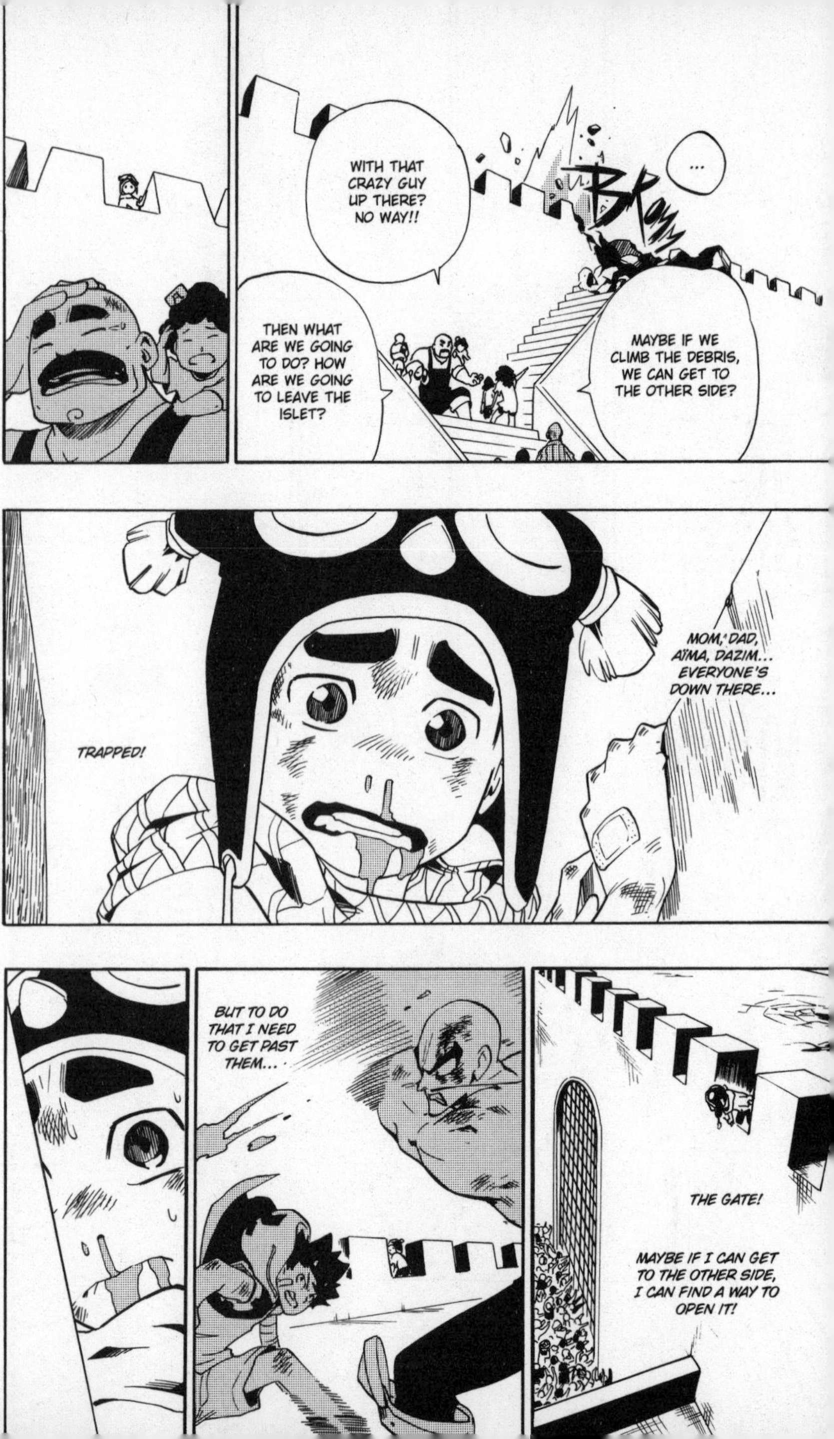
WITH THAT CRAZY GUY UP THERE? NO WAY!!
BROW
...
THEN WHAT ARE WE GOING TO DO? HOW ARE WE GOING TO LEAVE THE ISLET?
MAYBE IF WE CLIMB THE DEBRIS, WE CAN GET TO THE OTHER SIDE?
TRAPPED!
MOM, DAD, AÏMA, DAZIM... EVERYONE'S DOWN THERE...
BUT TO DO THAT I NEED TO GET PAST THEM...
THE GATE!
MAYBE IF I CAN GET TO THE OTHER SIDE, I CAN FIND A WAY TO OPEN IT!

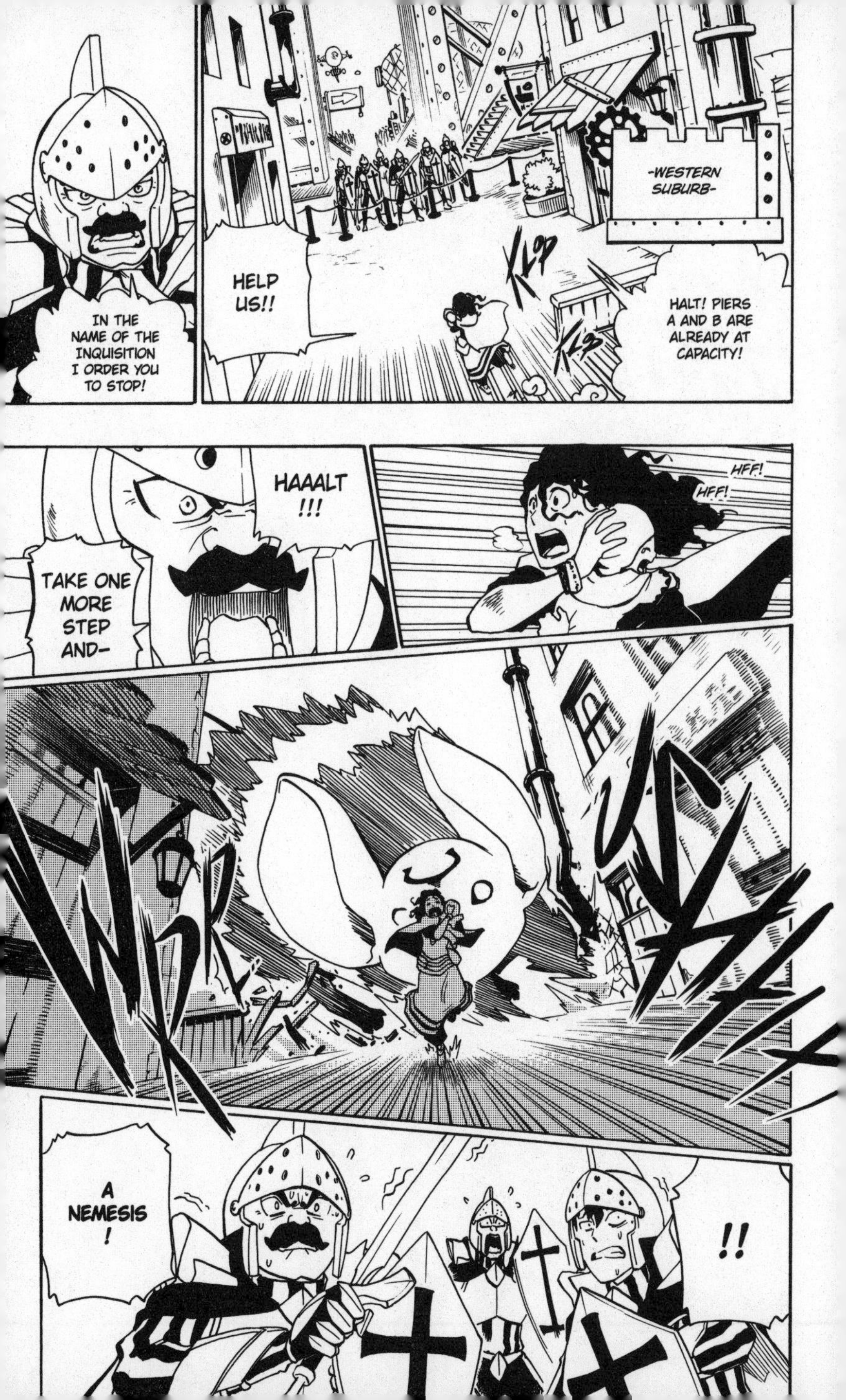

-WESTERN SUBURB-
HALT! PIERS A AND B ARE ALREADY AT CAPACITY!
KLOP
KLOP
HELP US!!
IN THE NAME OF THE INQUISITION I ORDER YOU TO STOP!
HFF! HFF!
HAAALT!!!
TAKE ONE MORE STEP AND–
!!
A NEMESIS!

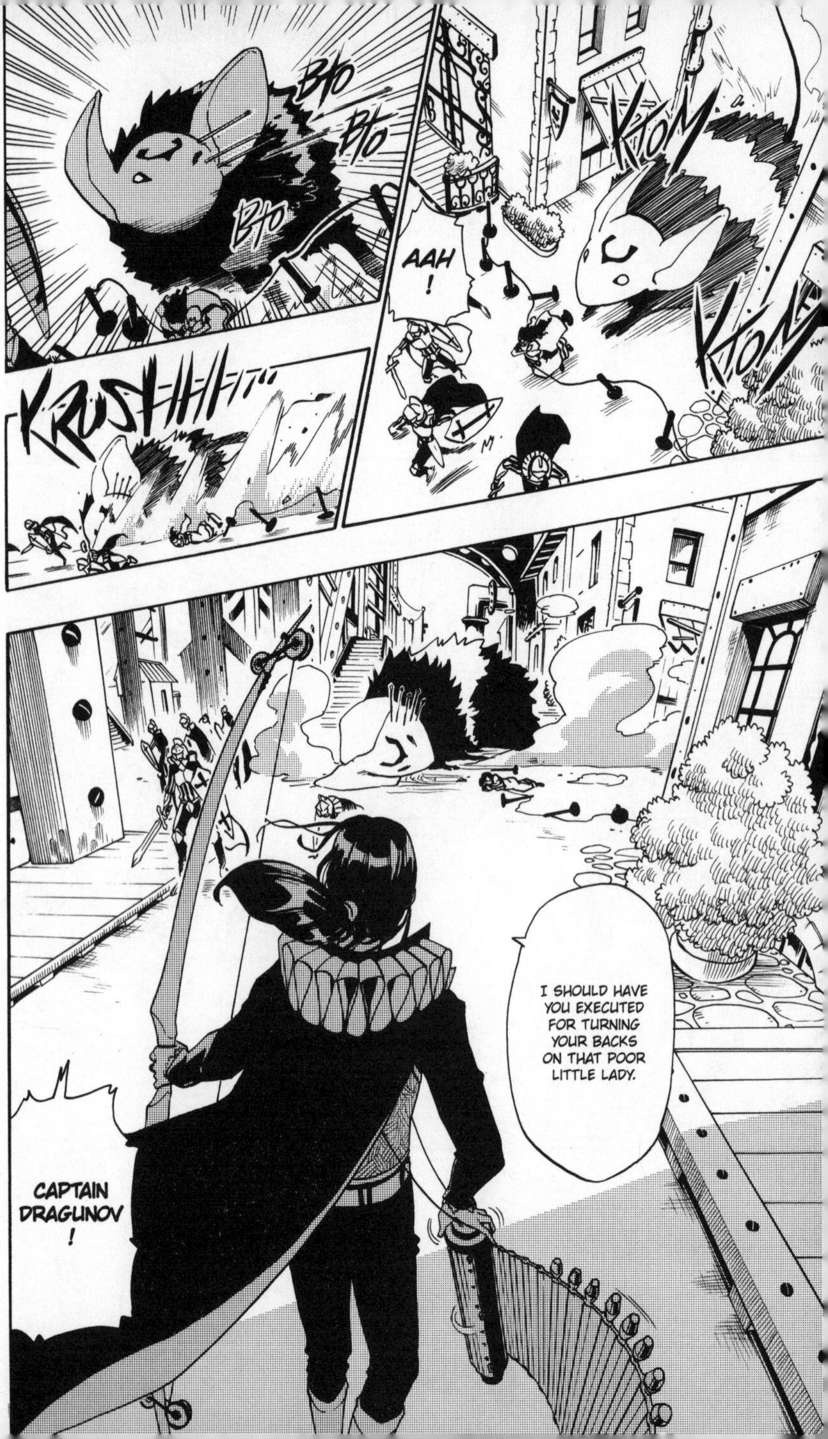
KTOM
KTOM
AAH!
BTO
BTO
BTO
KRUSHHH
I SHOULD HAVE YOU EXECUTED FOR TURNING YOUR BACKS ON THAT POOR LITTLE LADY.
CAPTAIN DRAGUNOV!

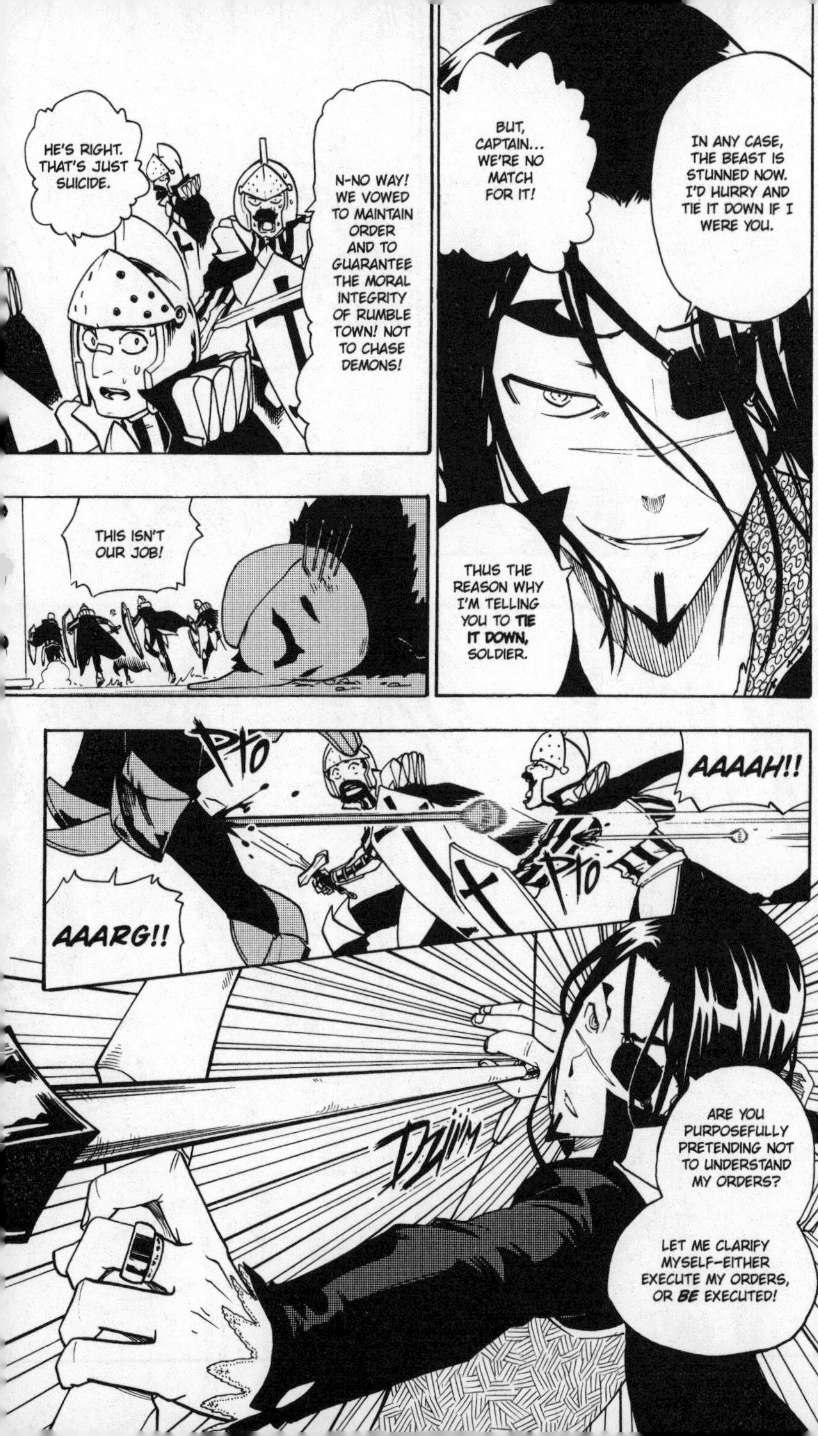
N-NO WAY! WE VOWED TO MAINTAIN ORDER AND TO GUARANTEE THE MORAL INTEGRITY OF RUMBLE TOWN! NOT TO CHASE DEMONS!
HE'S RIGHT. THAT'S JUST SUICIDE.
THIS ISN'T OUR JOB!
BUT, CAPTAIN... WE'RE NO MATCH FOR IT!
IN ANY CASE, THE BEAST IS STUNNED NOW. I'D HURRY AND TIE IT DOWN IF I WERE YOU.
THUS THE REASON WHY I'M TELLING YOU TO **TIE IT DOWN,** SOLDIER.
PTO
AAAAH!!
PTO
AAARG!!
DZIIIM
ARE YOU PURPOSEFULLY PRETENDING NOT TO UNDERSTAND MY ORDERS?
LET ME CLARIFY MYSELF—EITHER EXECUTE MY ORDERS, OR ***BE*** EXECUTED!

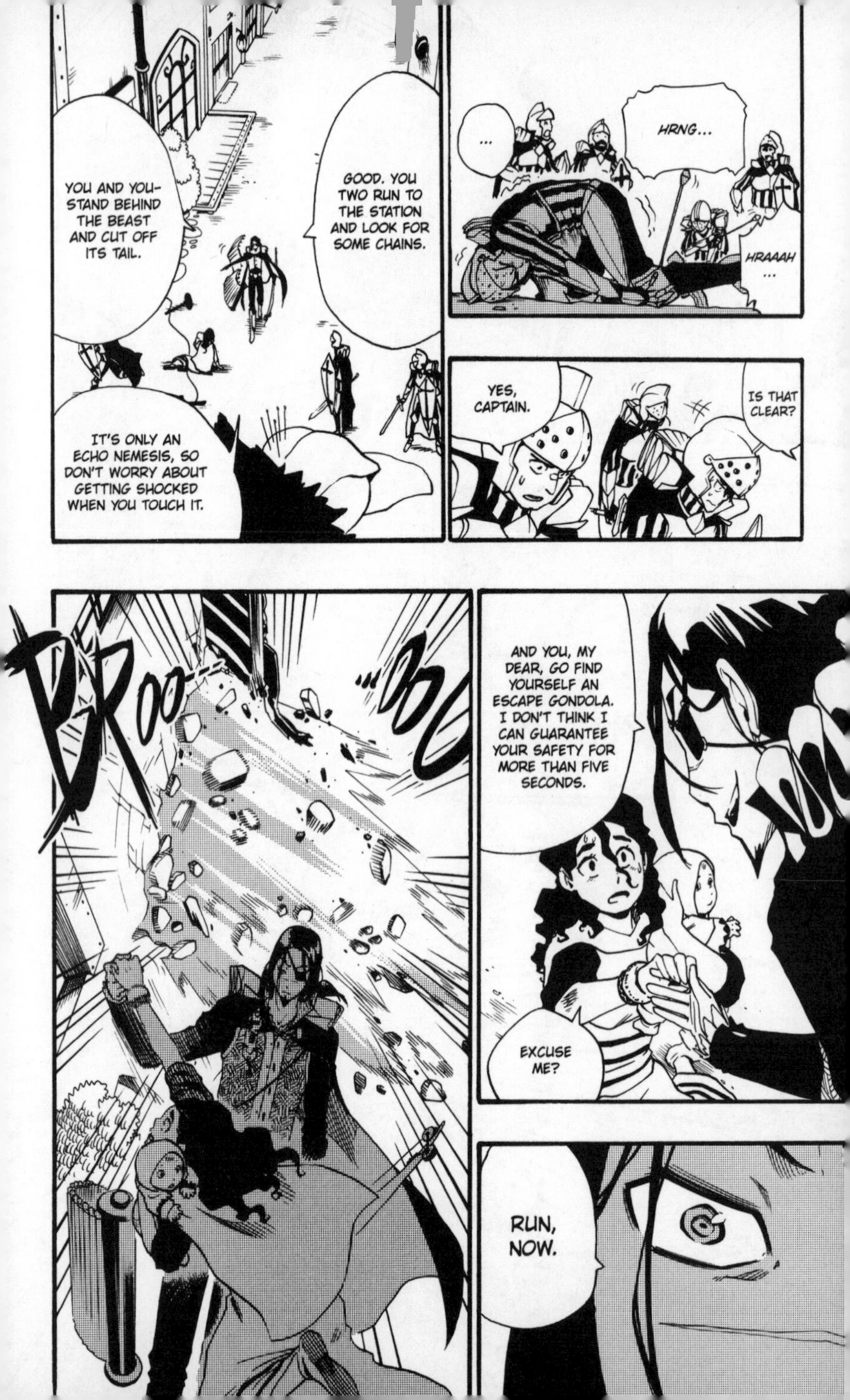
YOU AND YOU—STAND BEHIND THE BEAST AND CUT OFF ITS TAIL.
GOOD. YOU TWO RUN TO THE STATION AND LOOK FOR SOME CHAINS.
IT'S ONLY AN ECHO NEMESIS, SO DON'T WORRY ABOUT GETTING SHOCKED WHEN YOU TOUCH IT.
...
HRNG...
HRAAAH...
IS THAT CLEAR?
YES, CAPTAIN.
BROO...
AND YOU, MY DEAR, GO FIND YOURSELF AN ESCAPE GONDOLA. I DON'T THINK I CAN GUARANTEE YOUR SAFETY FOR MORE THAN FIVE SECONDS.
EXCUSE ME?
RUN, NOW.

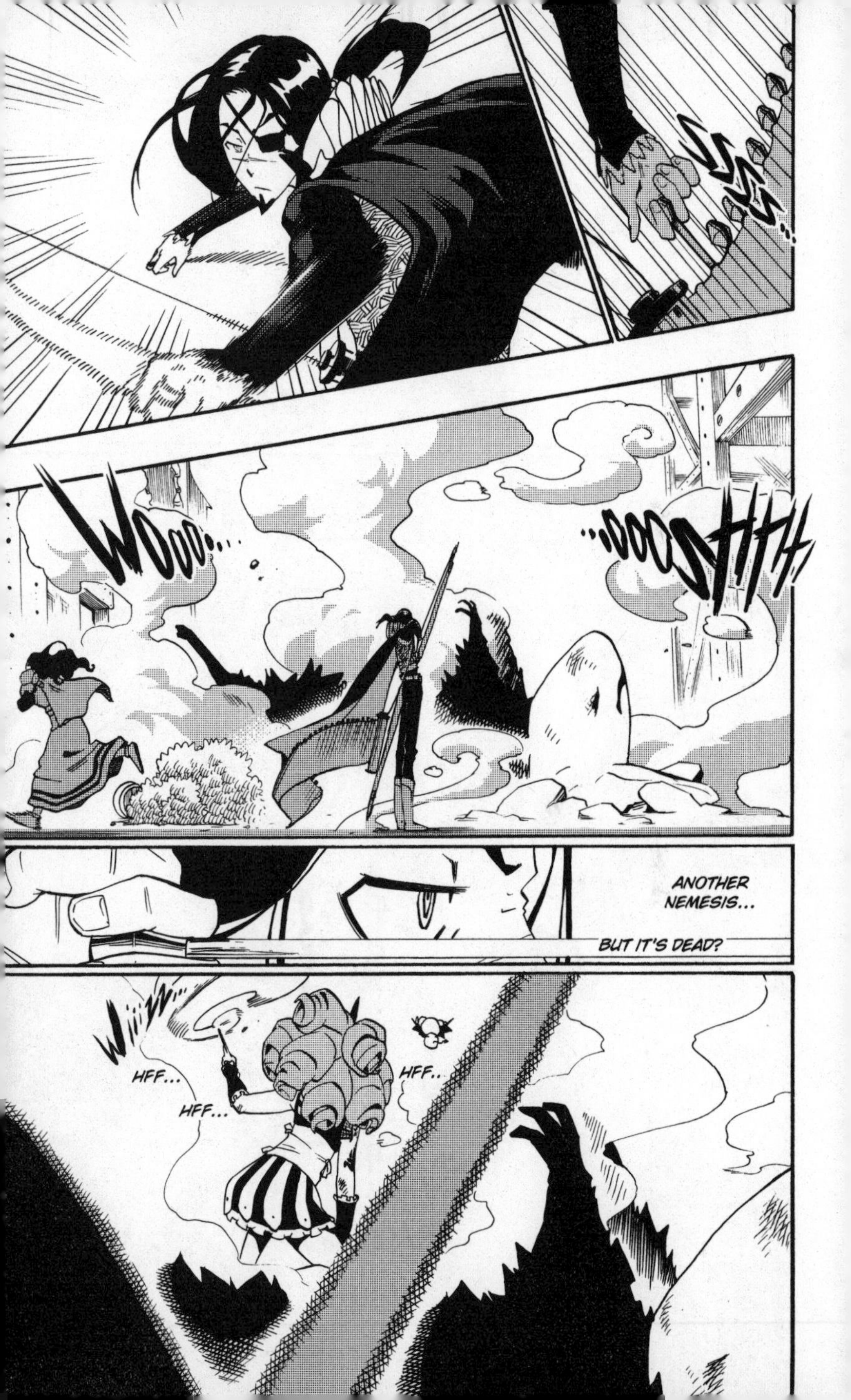
SSSS...
WOOO...
...OOSHHH!!
ANOTHER NEMESIS...
BUT IT'S DEAD?
WIIIN
HFF...
HFF...
HFF...

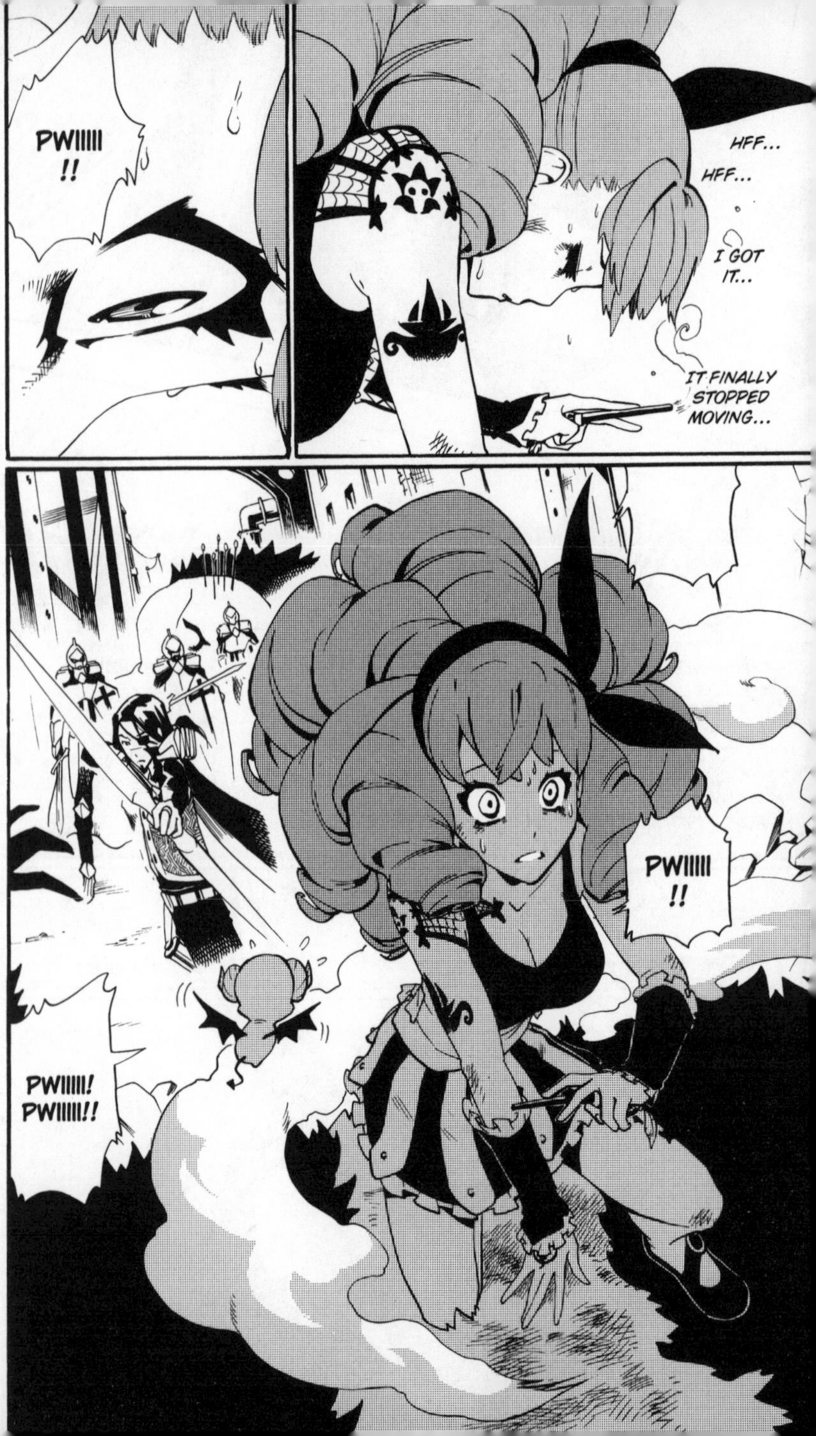
HFF...
HFF...
I GOT IT...
IT FINALLY STOPPED MOVING...
PWIIIII !!
PWIIIII !!
PWIIIII! PWIIIII!!

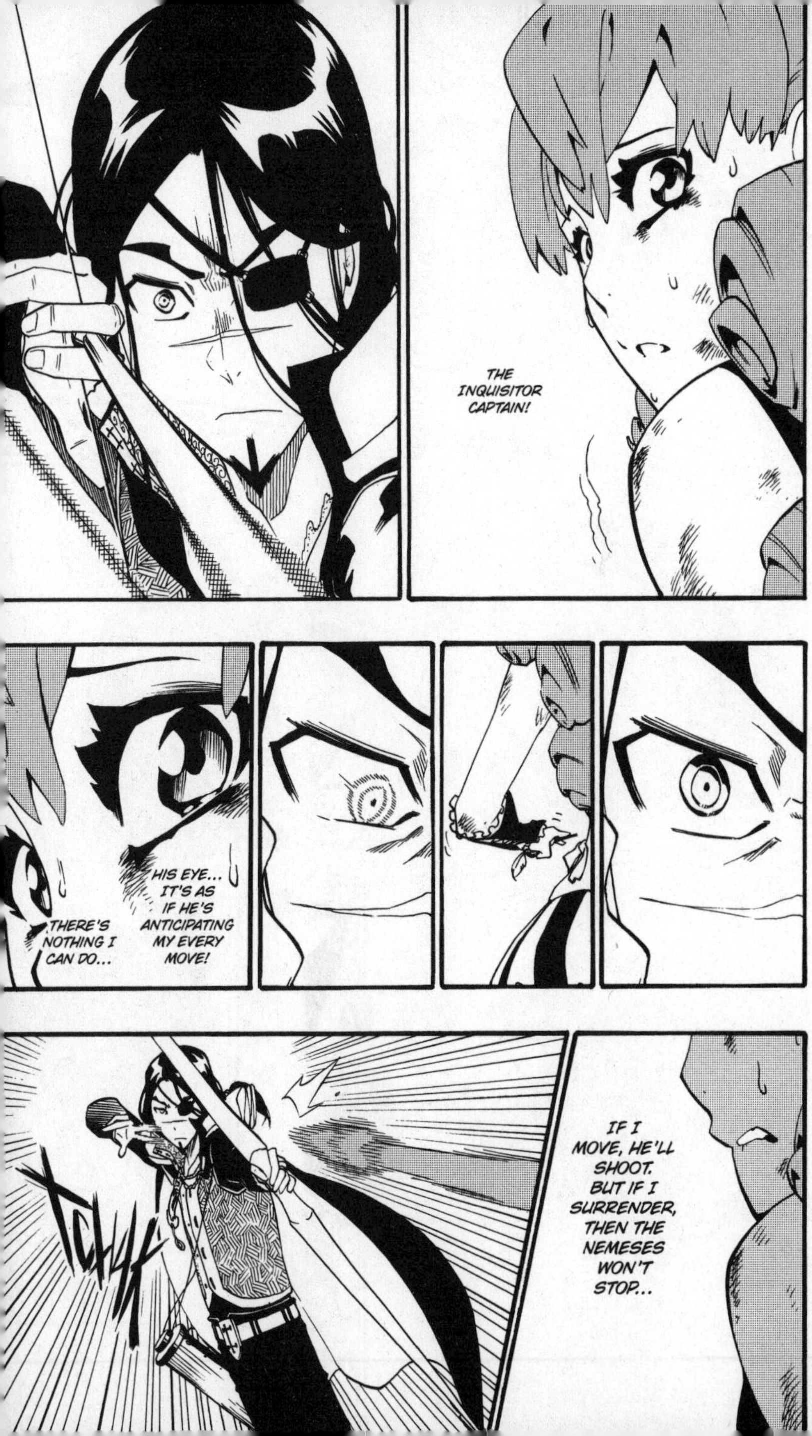
THE INQUISITOR CAPTAIN!
HIS EYE... IT'S AS IF HE'S ANTICIPATING MY EVERY MOVE!
THERE'S NOTHING I CAN DO...
IF I MOVE, HE'LL SHOOT. BUT IF I SURRENDER, THEN THE NEMESES WON'T STOP...
TCHUK

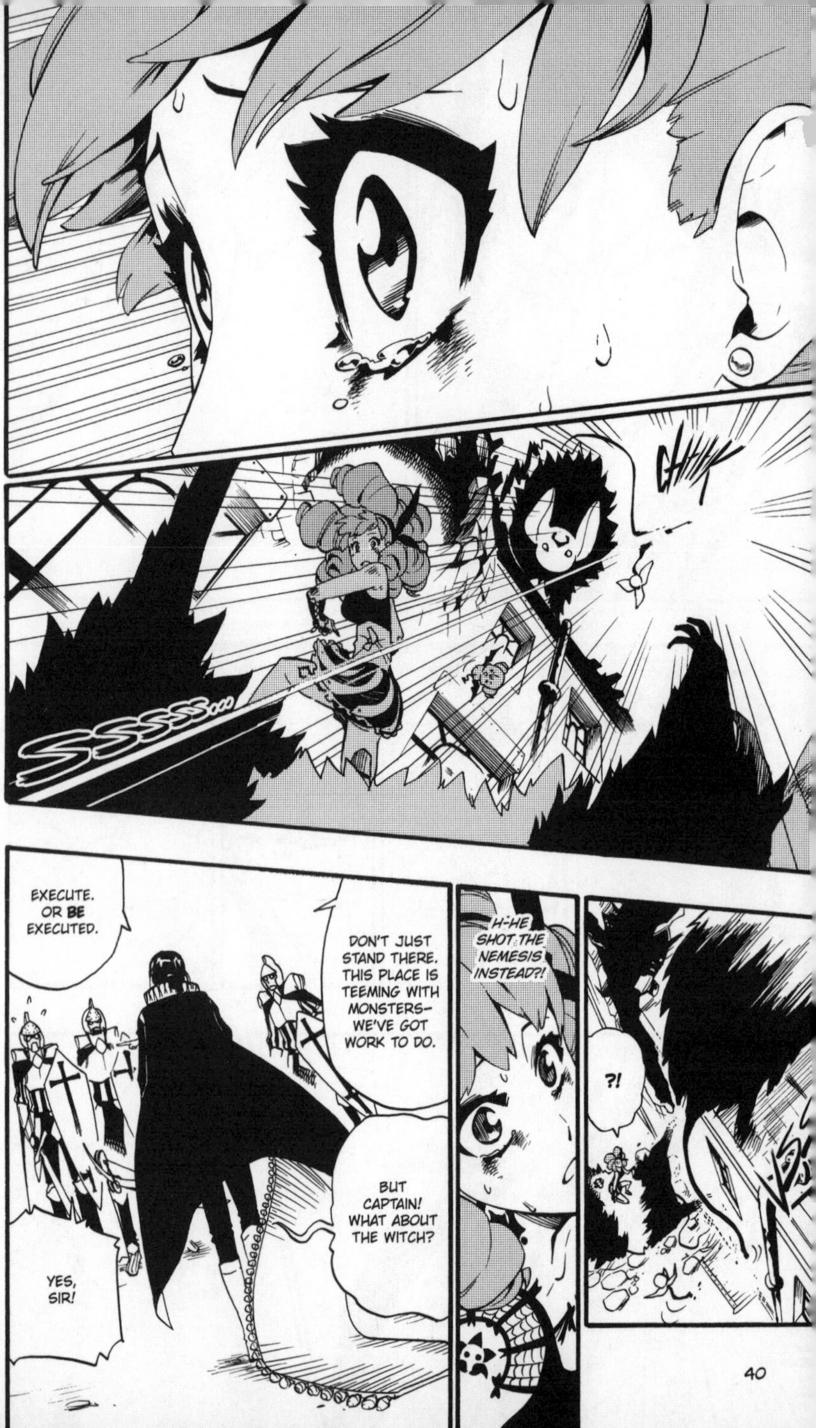
CHK
SSSSS...
?!
H-HE SHOT THE NEMESIS INSTEAD?!
BUT CAPTAIN! WHAT ABOUT THE WITCH?
DON'T JUST STAND THERE. THIS PLACE IS TEEMING WITH MONSTERS- WE'VE GOT WORK TO DO.
EXECUTE. OR BE EXECUTED.
YES, SIR!

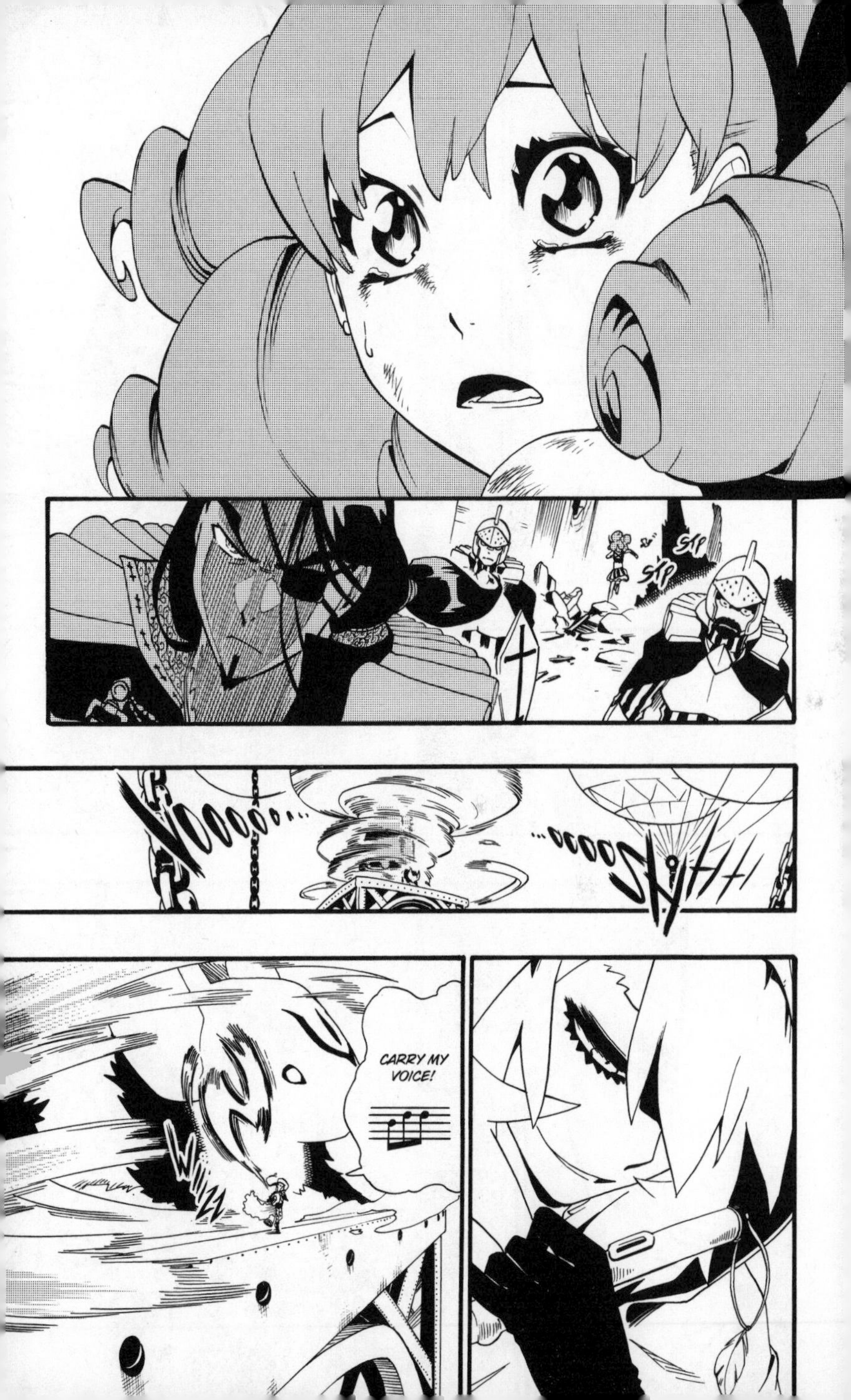
WOOOOO...
...OOOOSH!!!
CARRY MY VOICE!

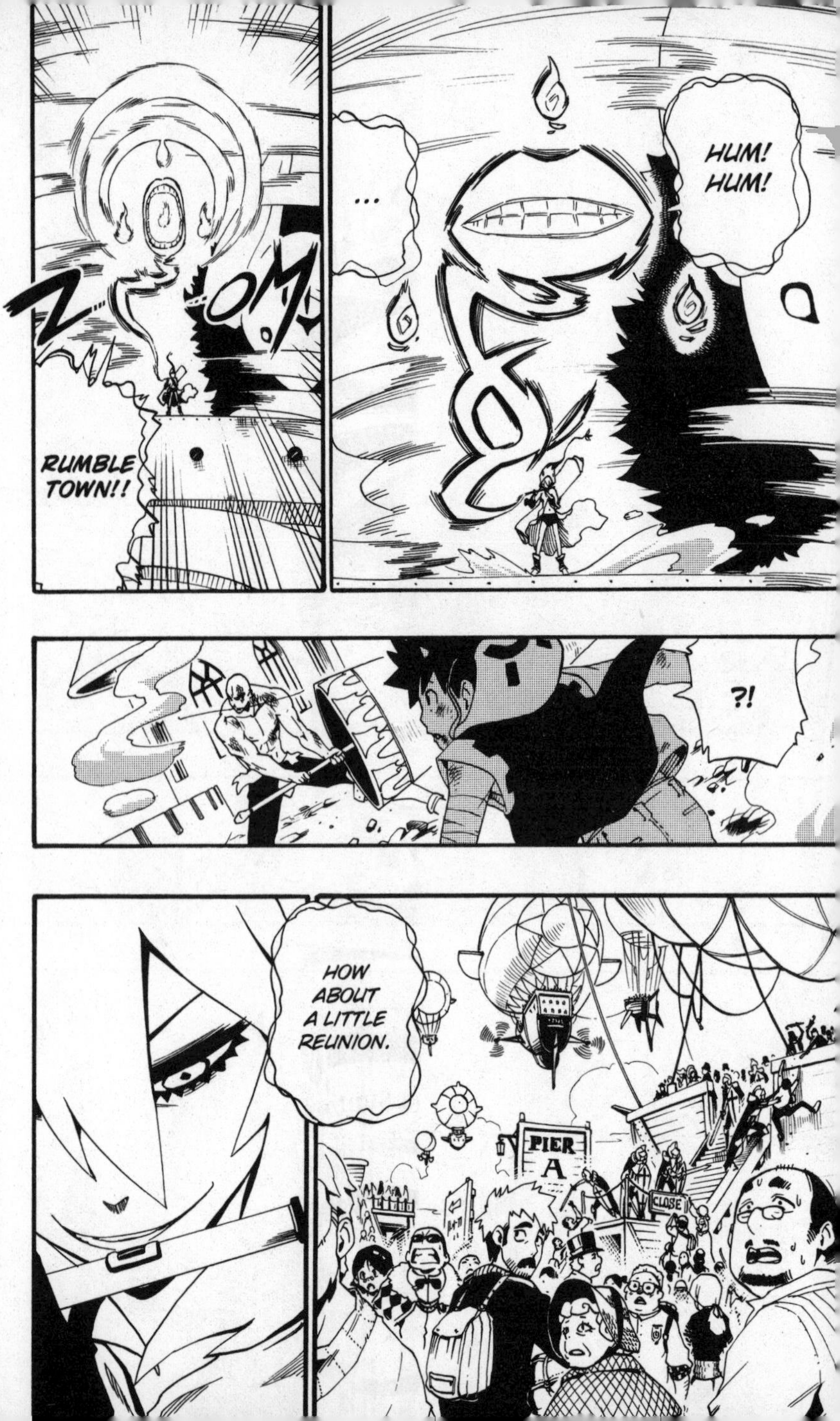
HUM!
HUM!
...
ZOOM!
RUMBLE
TOWN!!
?!
HOW
ABOUT
A LITTLE
REUNION.
PIER
A
CLOSE

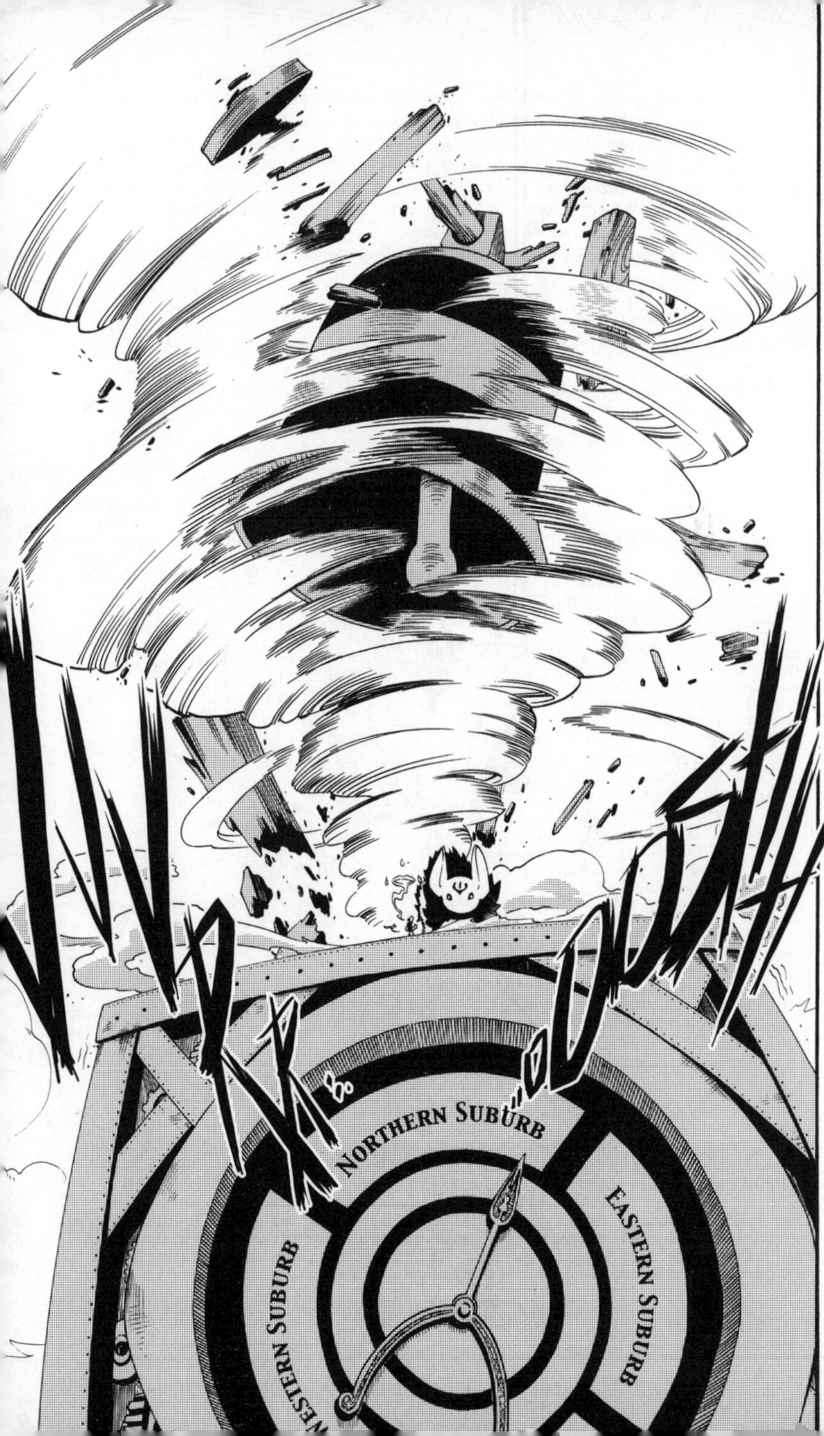
NORTHERN SUBURB
EASTERN SUBURB
ESTERN SUBURB

Hi there! I'm Tony Valente, the author of this manga! I've gotten a lot of questions from all of you about the world of *Radiant* during signing sessions and on social media, but haven't gotten the chance to answer them yet. So I decided to devote some space in this volume so everyone can take advantage of these answers. So without further ado, I present to you—The Readers' Mail Corner! Yaaay! Pop open dem bottles of Yoo-Hoo and let's go crazy!! But "readers' mail corner" is kind of a lame title, so I'm going to name it "TOUMSTAK!!!" instead. "TOUM," as in the sound of a question that comes rolling into my inbox, and "STAK," the sound of the crack of a whip!!

And since this is the first one, I'm handing out the first reader a credit of 6 *Toumstaks*. Off to you, reader!

Noah of Koko: Hi, I've got a few questions that I hope could get featured in the readers' question corner. Who knows…? Does the Artemis insignia have any specific meaning? (see chapter 6)

Tony Valente: Yes, it does. And I'm happy that you asked! Here's a little drawing to explain:

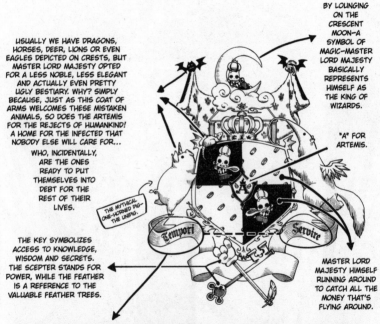

BY LOUNGING ON THE CRESCENT MOON—A SYMBOL OF MAGIC—MASTER LORD MAJESTY BASICALLY REPRESENTS HIMSELF AS THE KING OF WIZARDS.
USUALLY WE HAVE DRAGONS, HORSES, DEER, LIONS OR EVEN EAGLES DEPICTED ON CRESTS, BUT MASTER LORD MAJESTY OPTED FOR A LESS NOBLE, LESS ELEGANT AND ACTUALLY EVEN PRETTY UGLY BESTIARY. WHY? SIMPLY BECAUSE, JUST AS THIS COAT OF ARMS WELCOMES THESE MISTAKEN ANIMALS, SO DOES THE ARTEMIS FOR THE REJECTS OF HUMANKIND! A HOME FOR THE INFECTED THAT NOBODY ELSE WILL CARE FOR…
WHO, INCIDENTALLY, ARE THE ONES READY TO PUT THEMSELVES INTO DEBT FOR THE REST OF THEIR LIVES.
"A" FOR ARTEMIS.
THE MYTHICAL ONE-HORNED PIG—THE UNIPIG.
Tempori
Servire
THE KEY SYMBOLIZES ACCESS TO KNOWLEDGE, WISDOM AND SECRETS. THE SCEPTER STANDS FOR POWER, WHILE THE FEATHER IS A REFERENCE TO THE VALUABLE FEATHER TREES.
MASTER LORD MAJESTY HIMSELF RUNNING AROUND TO CATCH ALL THE MONEY THAT'S FLYING AROUND.

TEMPORI SERVIRE, THE MOTTO OF THE ARTEMIS, MEANS "TO ADAPT ONESELF TO CIRCUMSTANCES." THE INFECTED CONSTANTLY NEED TO ADAPT THEMSELVES. FIRST TO THEIR NEW WAY OF LIFE, THEN TO THE STONES THROWN AT THEM BY VILLAGERS AND FINALLY, TO THE INQUISITION'S SUDDEN STRONG INTEREST IN THEM. AND FOR THOSE WHO DECIDE TO HUNT NEMESES, THEY ALSO NEED TO ADAPT THEMSELVES TO HANDLING FANTASIA! THIS MOTTO WAS TAKEN FROM THE FAMOUS "SURVIVAL GUIDE FOR THE AMATEUR INFECTED," WRITTEN BY THE WIZARD MJÖLNGRKT THE LIGHT BEIGE. IN THIS BOOK, THERE'S A QUOTE THAT READS, "IF YOUR INFECTION IS VISIBLE, HIDE IT OR YOU'LL RISK GETTING HUNTED! IF YOUR BEHAVIOR CHANGES FROM ONE SECOND TO THE OTHER, BE SURE TO KEEP A BUDDY YOU CAN TRUST CLOSE BY WHO CAN HANDLE THE SITUATION DURING AN OUTBURST! IF YOU CAN ONLY HEAR THROUGH YOUR BUTT, DON'T EAT BEANS TO AVOID HAVING RINGING EARS! ADAPTING TO ALL KINDS OF CIRCUMSTANCES IS THE KEY TO A SUCCESSFUL INFECTED LIFE!"

(Questions corner to be continued after the next chapter…)

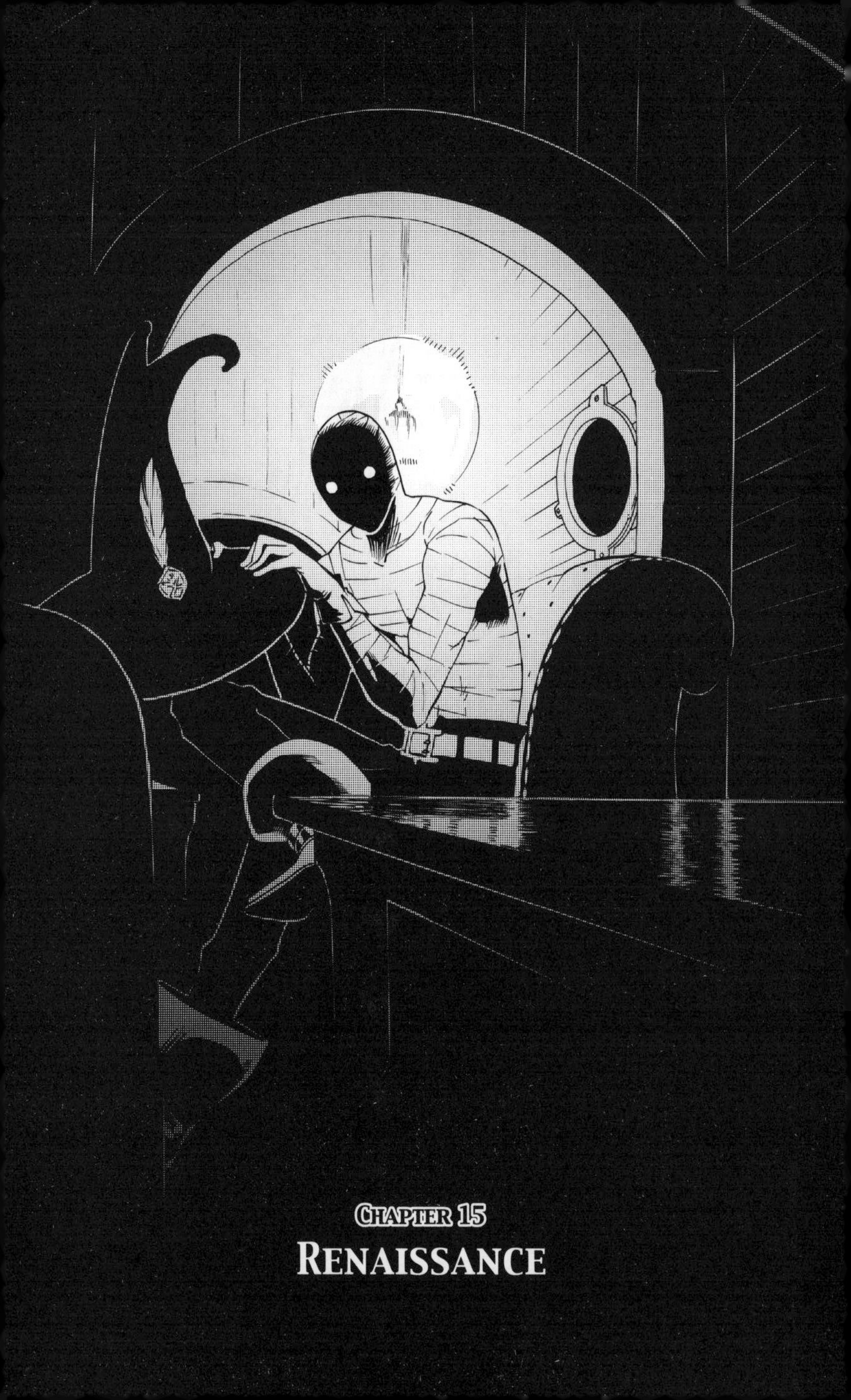

Chapter 15

Renaissance

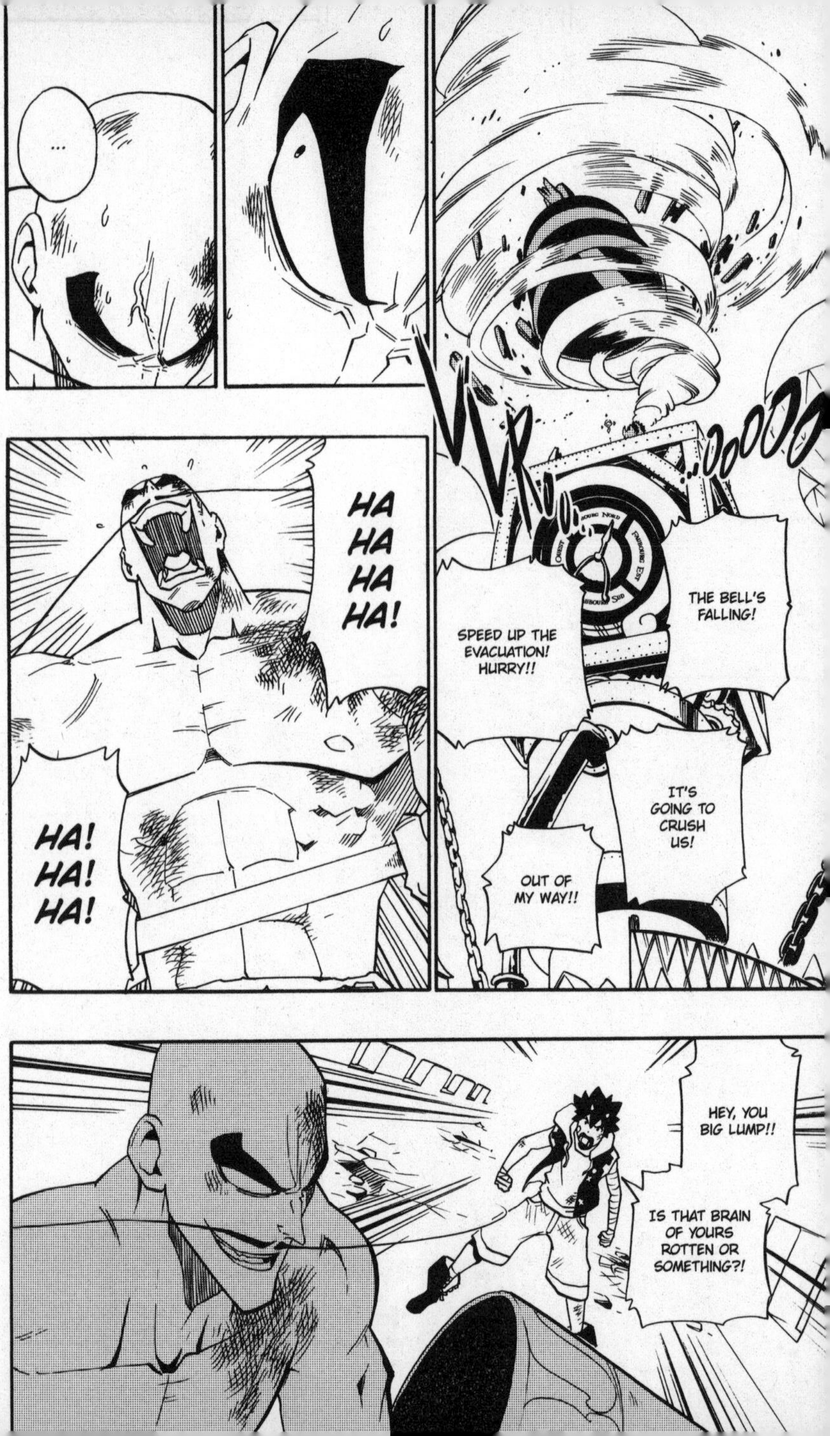
VRR...OOOOOO
THE BELL'S FALLING!
SPEED UP THE EVACUATION! HURRY!!
IT'S GOING TO CRUSH US!
OUT OF MY WAY!!
...
HA HA HA HA!
HA! HA! HA!
HEY, YOU BIG LUMP!!
IS THAT BRAIN OF YOURS ROTTEN OR SOMETHING?!

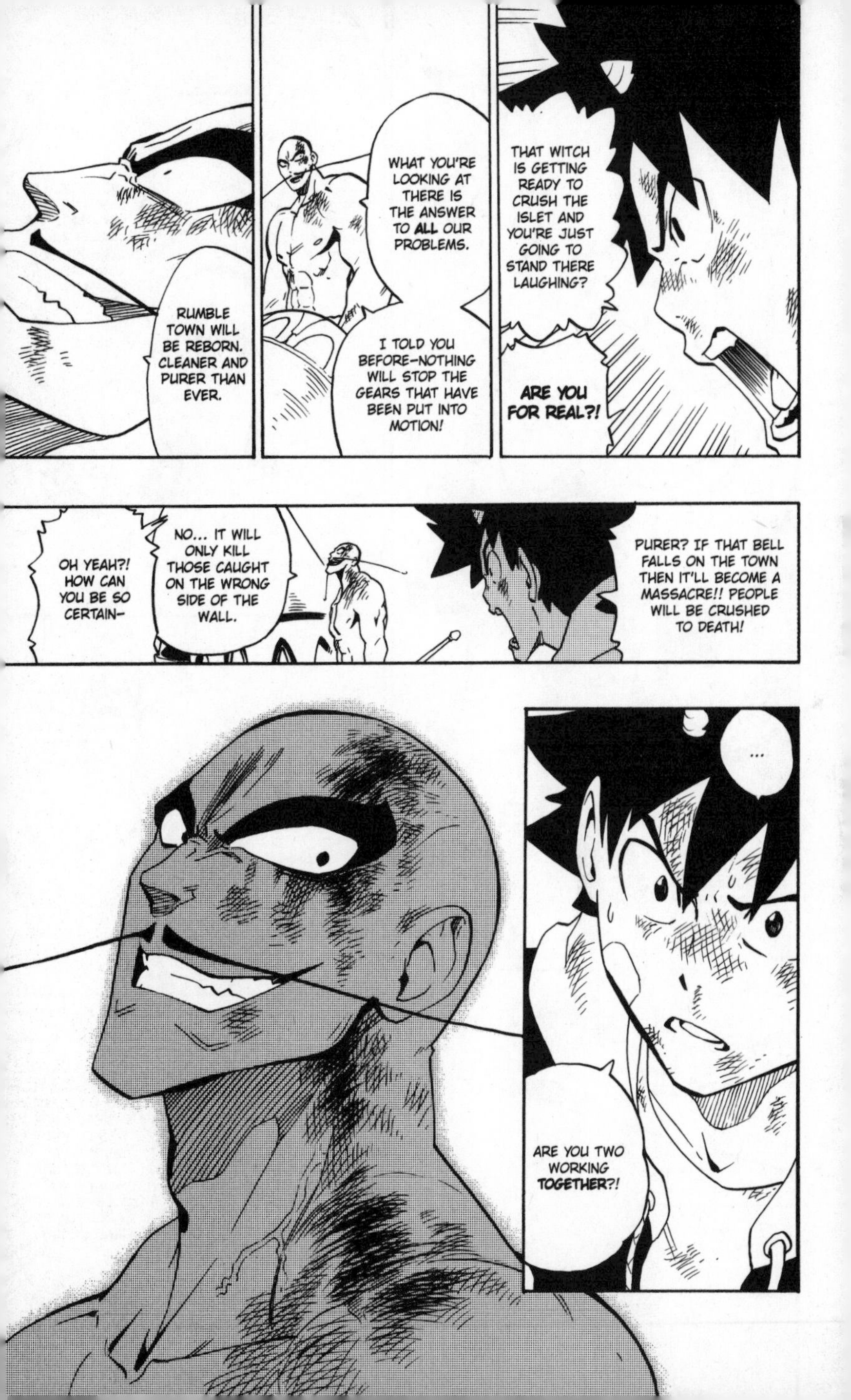
RUMBLE TOWN WILL BE REBORN. CLEANER AND PURER THAN EVER.
WHAT YOU'RE LOOKING AT THERE IS THE ANSWER TO ALL OUR PROBLEMS.
I TOLD YOU BEFORE—NOTHING WILL STOP THE GEARS THAT HAVE BEEN PUT INTO MOTION!
THAT WITCH IS GETTING READY TO CRUSH THE ISLET AND YOU'RE JUST GOING TO STAND THERE LAUGHING?
ARE YOU FOR REAL?!
PURER? IF THAT BELL FALLS ON THE TOWN THEN IT'LL BECOME A MASSACRE!! PEOPLE WILL BE CRUSHED TO DEATH!
NO... IT WILL ONLY KILL THOSE CAUGHT ON THE WRONG SIDE OF THE WALL.
OH YEAH?! HOW CAN YOU BE SO CERTAIN-
...
ARE YOU TWO WORKING TOGETHER?!

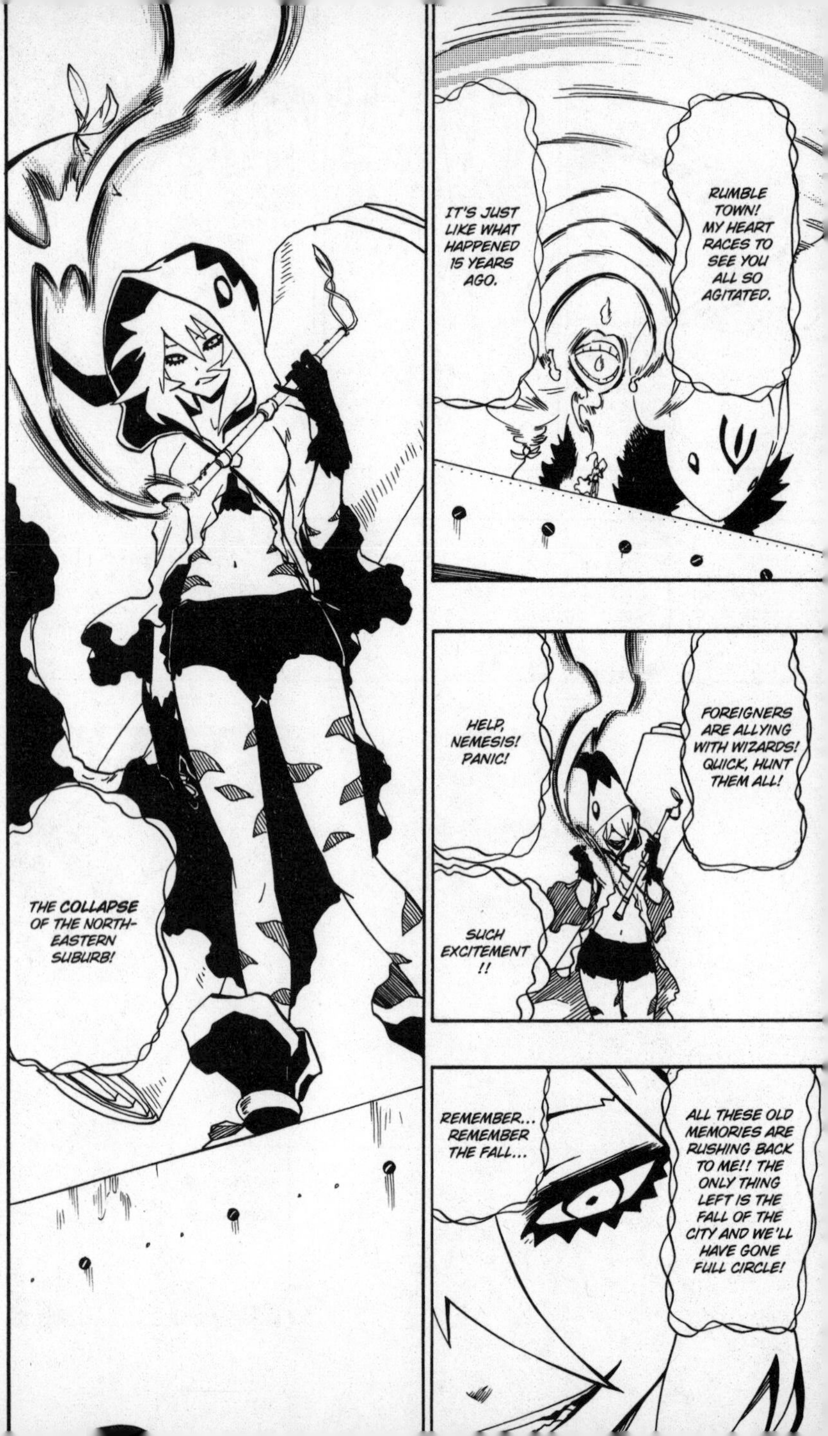
RUMBLE TOWN! MY HEART RACES TO SEE YOU ALL SO AGITATED.
IT'S JUST LIKE WHAT HAPPENED 15 YEARS AGO.
THE COLLAPSE OF THE NORTH-EASTERN SUBURB!
FOREIGNERS ARE ALLYING WITH WIZARDS! QUICK, HUNT THEM ALL!
HELP, NEMESIS! PANIC!
SUCH EXCITEMENT !!
ALL THESE OLD MEMORIES ARE RUSHING BACK TO ME!! THE ONLY THING LEFT IS THE FALL OF THE CITY AND WE'LL HAVE GONE FULL CIRCLE!
REMEMBER... REMEMBER THE FALL...

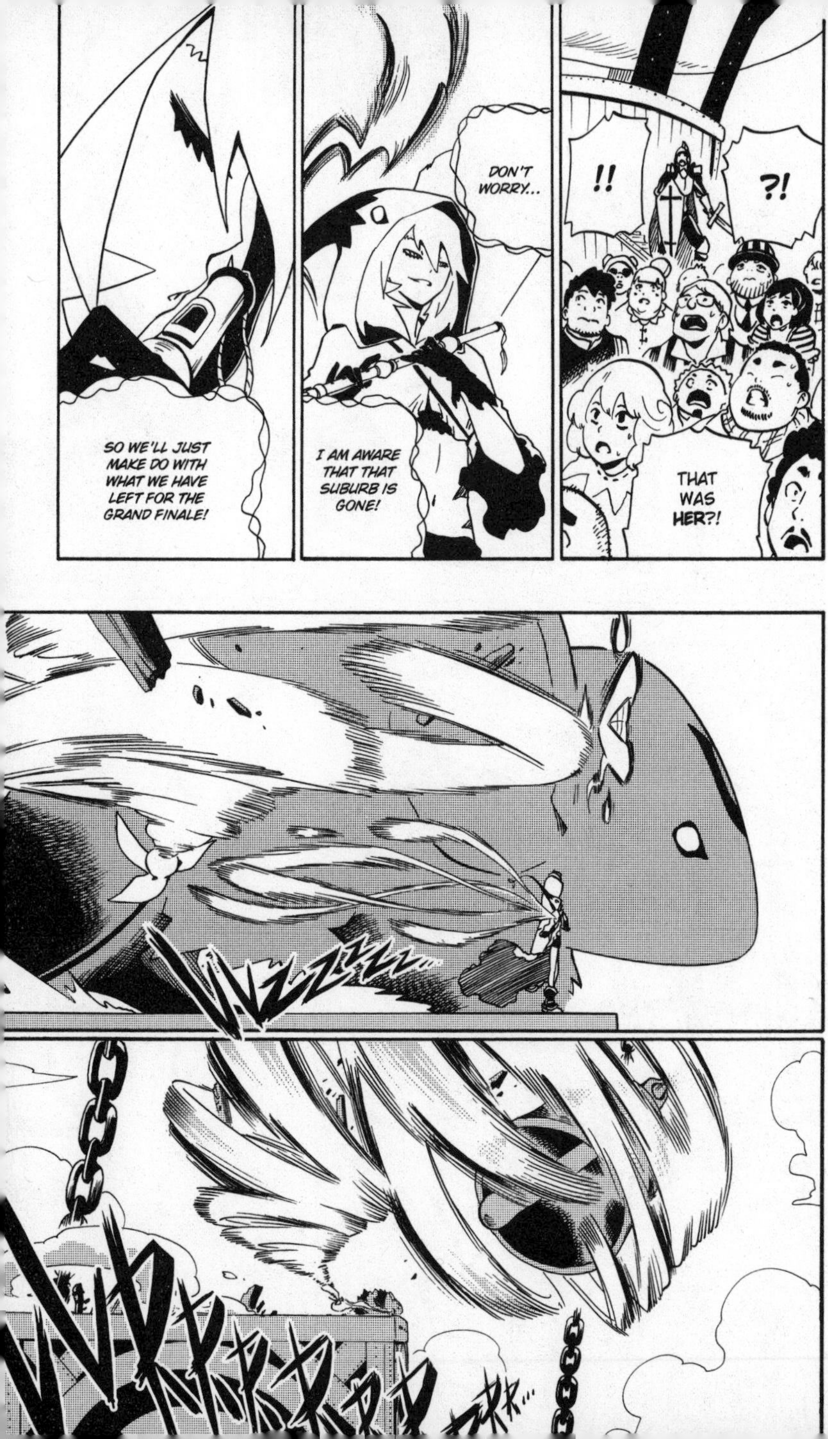
!!
?!
THAT WAS HER?!
DON'T WORRY...
I AM AWARE THAT THAT SUBURB IS GONE!
SO WE'LL JUST MAKE DO WITH WHAT WE HAVE LEFT FOR THE GRAND FINALE!
VWZZZZZZ...

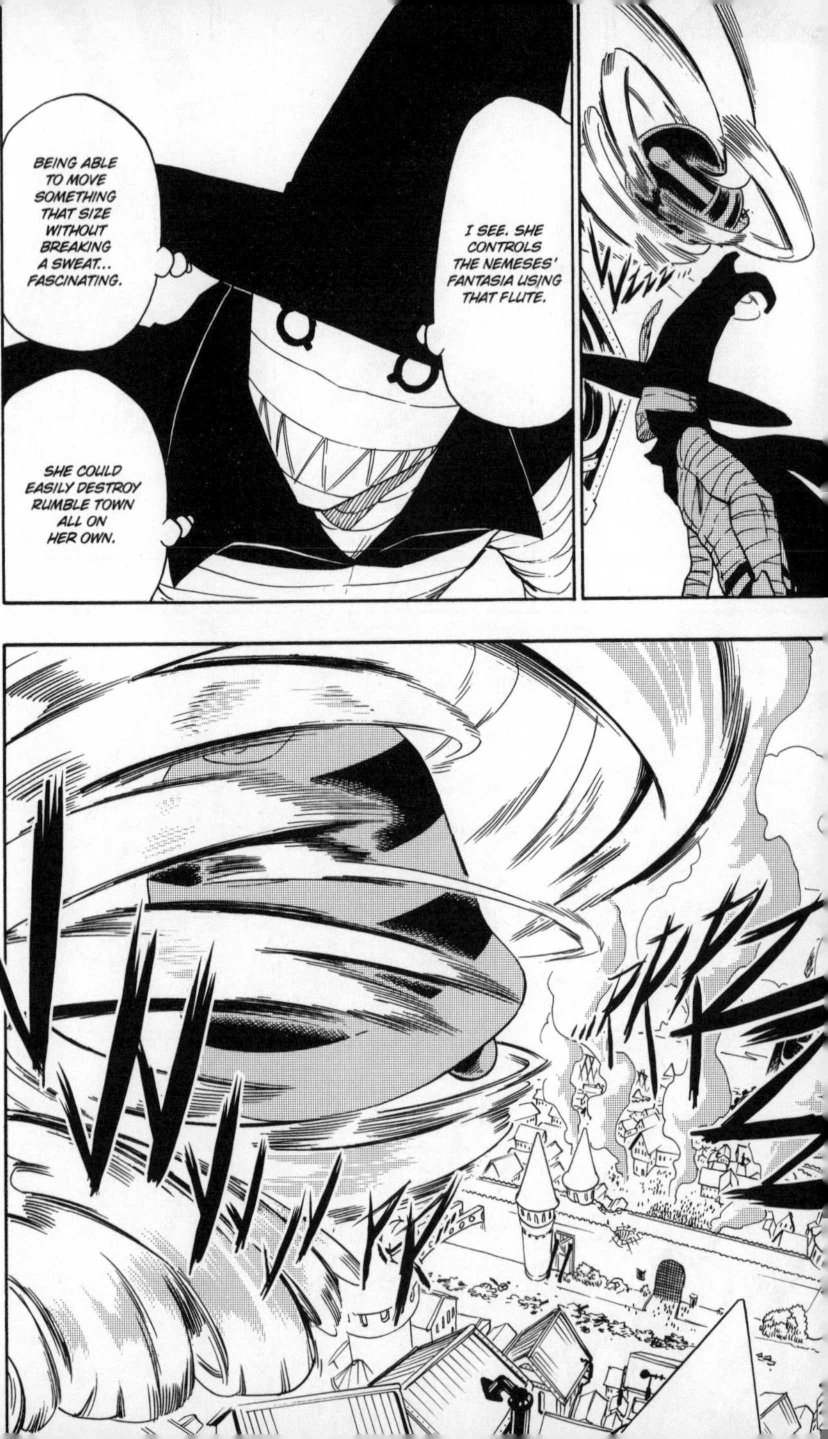
I SEE. SHE CONTROLS THE NEMESES' FANTASIA USING THAT FLUTE.
BEING ABLE TO MOVE SOMETHING THAT SIZE WITHOUT BREAKING A SWEAT... FASCINATING.
SHE COULD EASILY DESTROY RUMBLE TOWN ALL ON HER OWN.

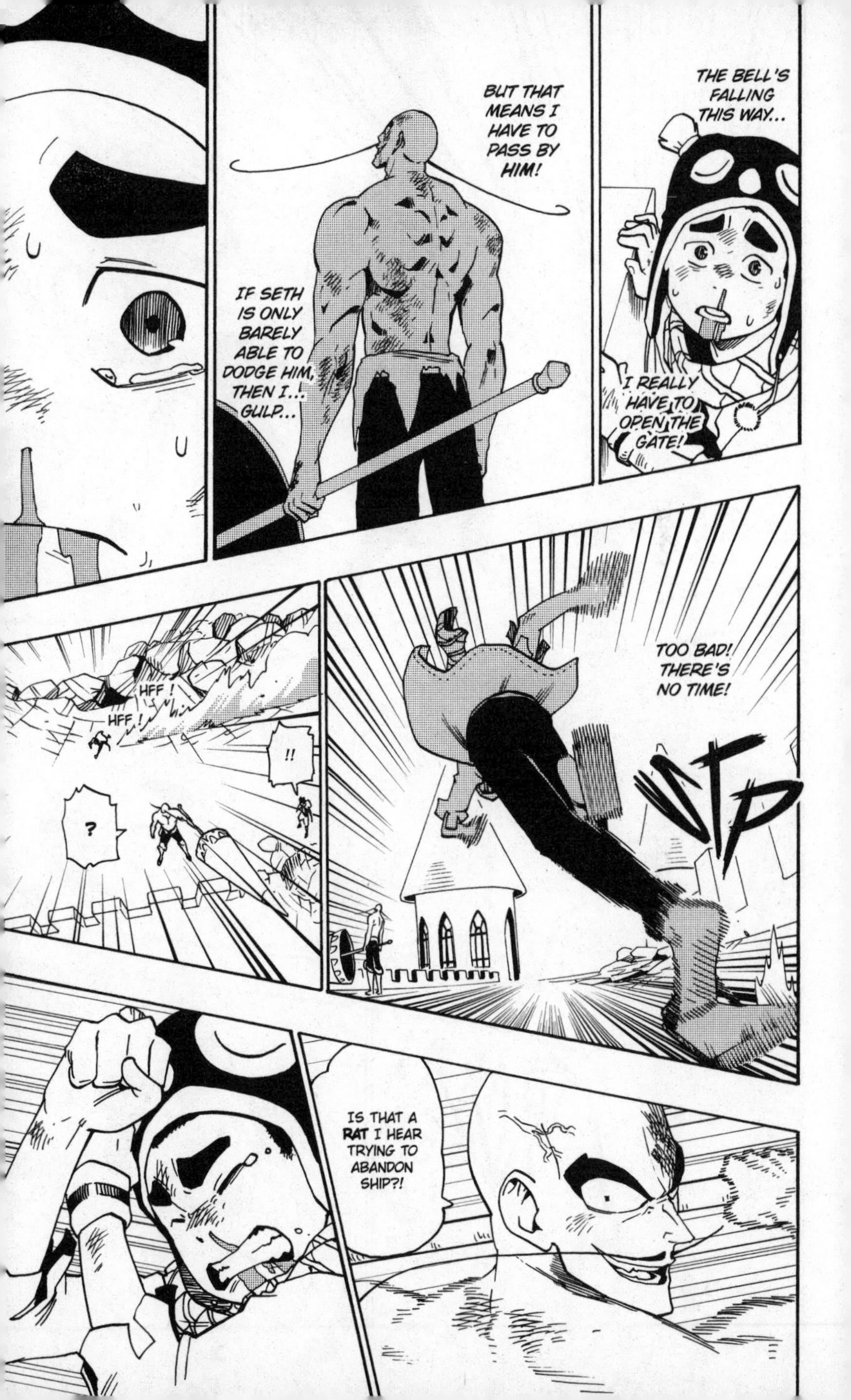
THE BELL'S FALLING THIS WAY...
I REALLY HAVE TO OPEN THE GATE!
BUT THAT MEANS I HAVE TO PASS BY HIM!
IF SETH IS ONLY BARELY ABLE TO DODGE HIM, THEN I... GULP...
TOO BAD! THERE'S NO TIME!
HFF! HFF!
!!
?
IS THAT A RAT I HEAR TRYING TO ABANDON SHIP?!

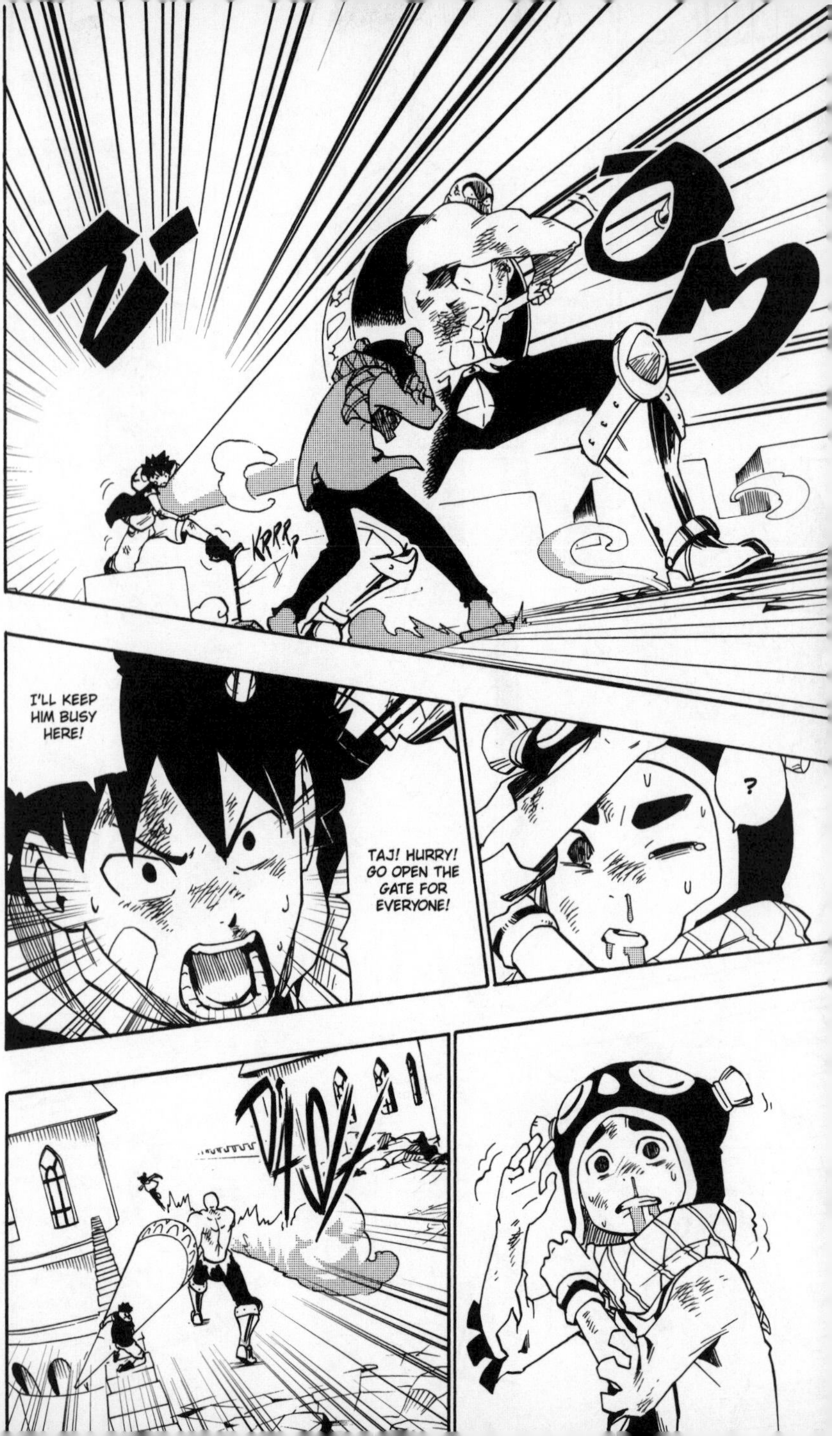
KRRR
I'LL KEEP HIM BUSY HERE!
TAJ! HURRY! GO OPEN THE GATE FOR EVERYONE!
?

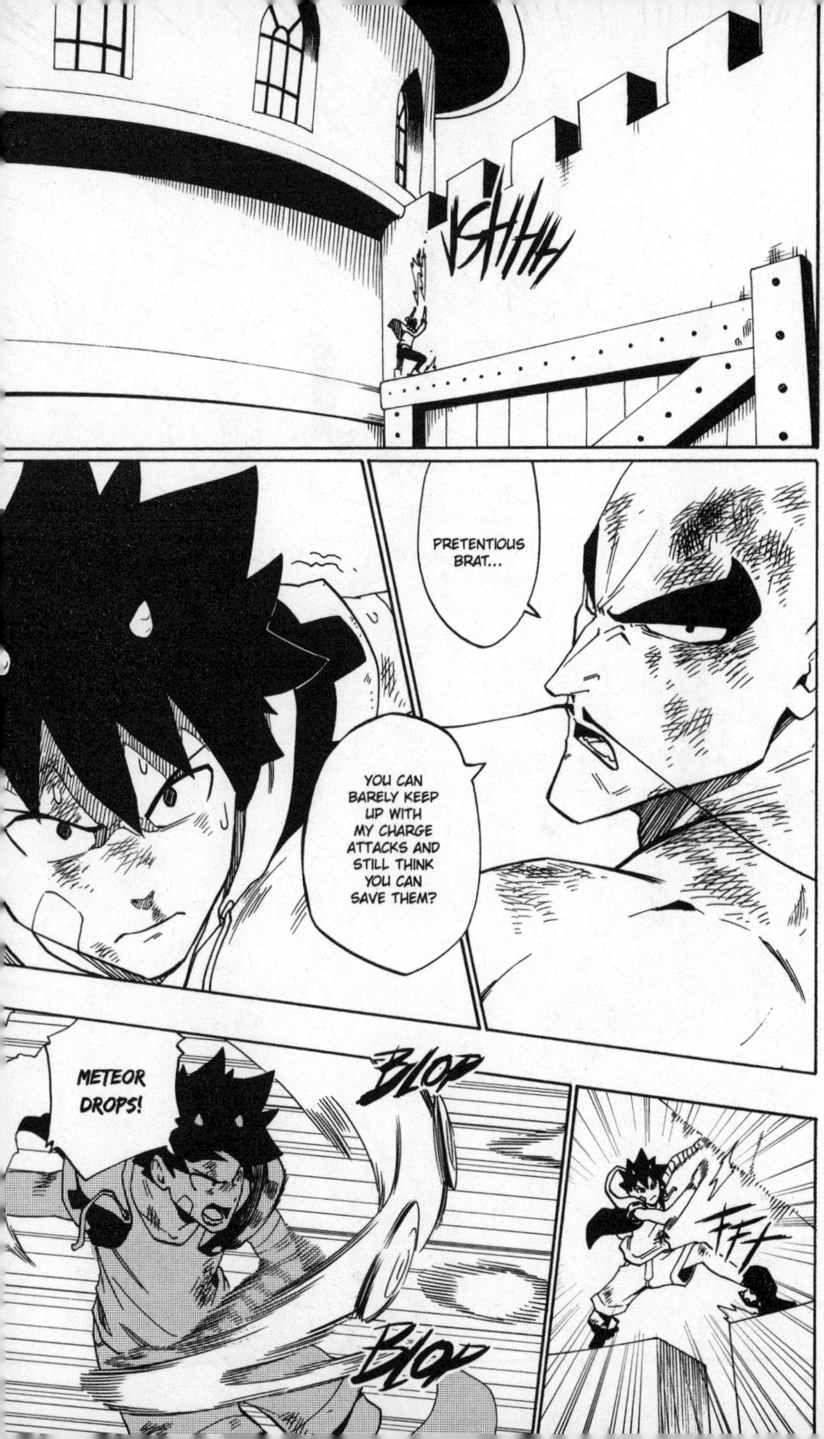
PRETENTIOUS BRAT...
YOU CAN BARELY KEEP UP WITH MY CHARGE ATTACKS AND STILL THINK YOU CAN SAVE THEM?
METEOR DROPS!
BLOP
BLOP
FFX

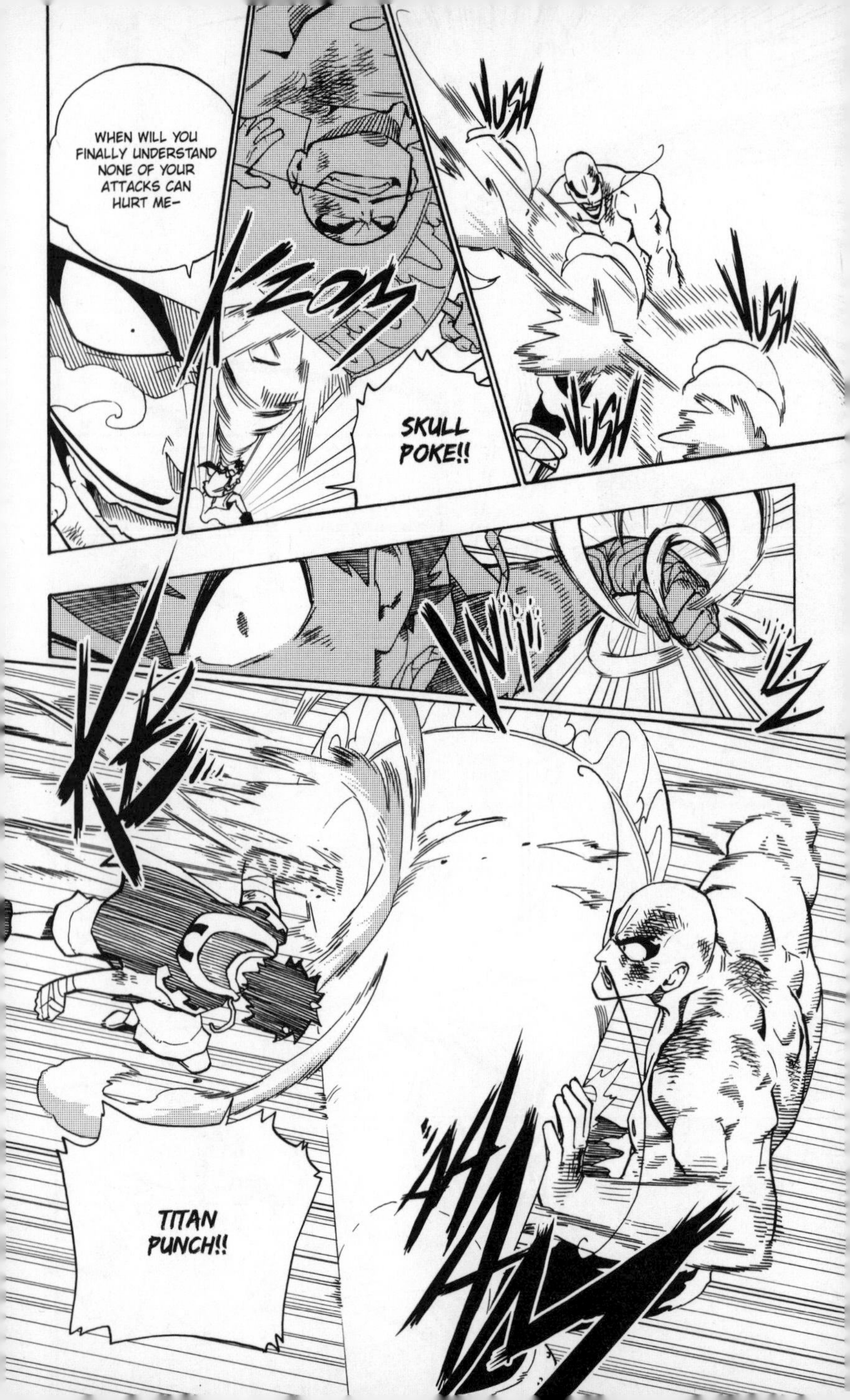

VUSH
VUSH
VUSH
WHEN WILL YOU FINALLY UNDERSTAND NONE OF YOUR ATTACKS CAN HURT ME-
ZOOM
SKULL POKE!!
TITAN PUNCH!!

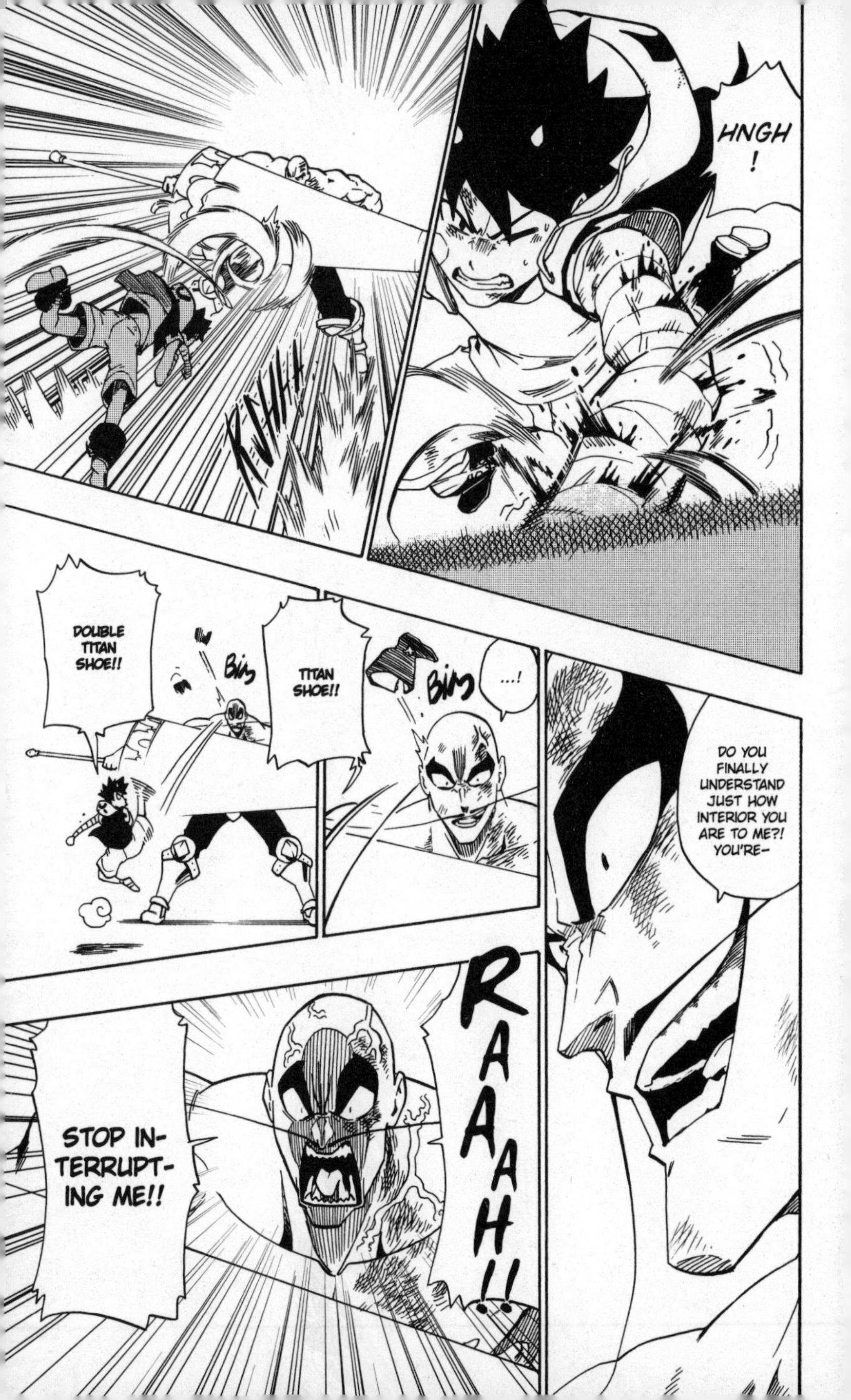
HNGH
!
DO YOU FINALLY UNDERSTAND JUST HOW INTERIOR YOU ARE TO ME?! YOU'RE–
...!
TITAN SHOE!!
DOUBLE TITAN SHOE!!
RAAAAH!!
STOP IN-TERRUPT-ING ME!!

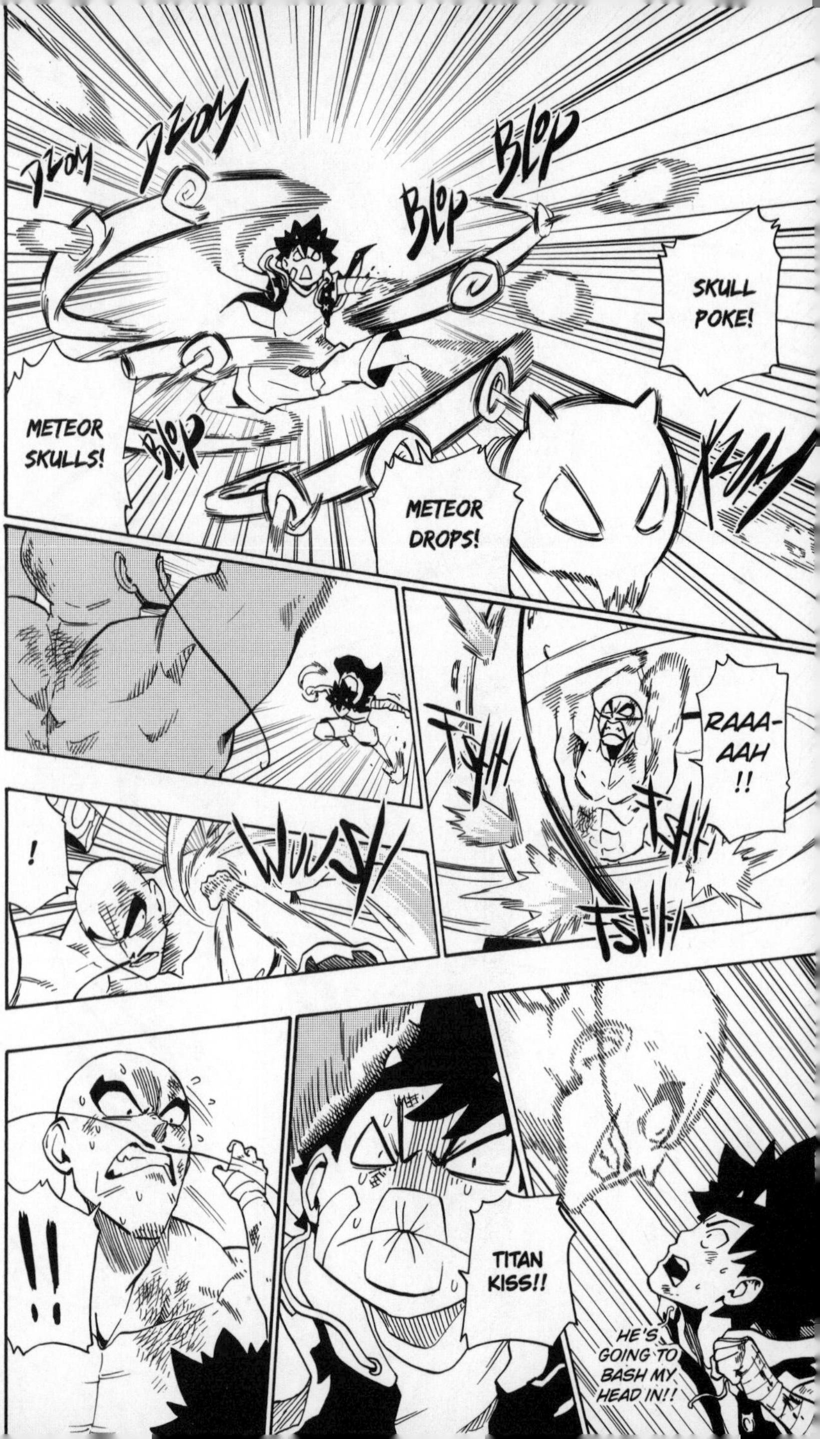
DZOY DZOY
BLOP BLOP
SKULL POKE!
METEOR DROPS!
METEOR SKULLS!
BLOP
RAAA-AAH!!
TSHH
TSHH
TSHH
WUUSH
!
HE'S GOING TO BASH MY HEAD IN!!
TITAN KISS!!
!!

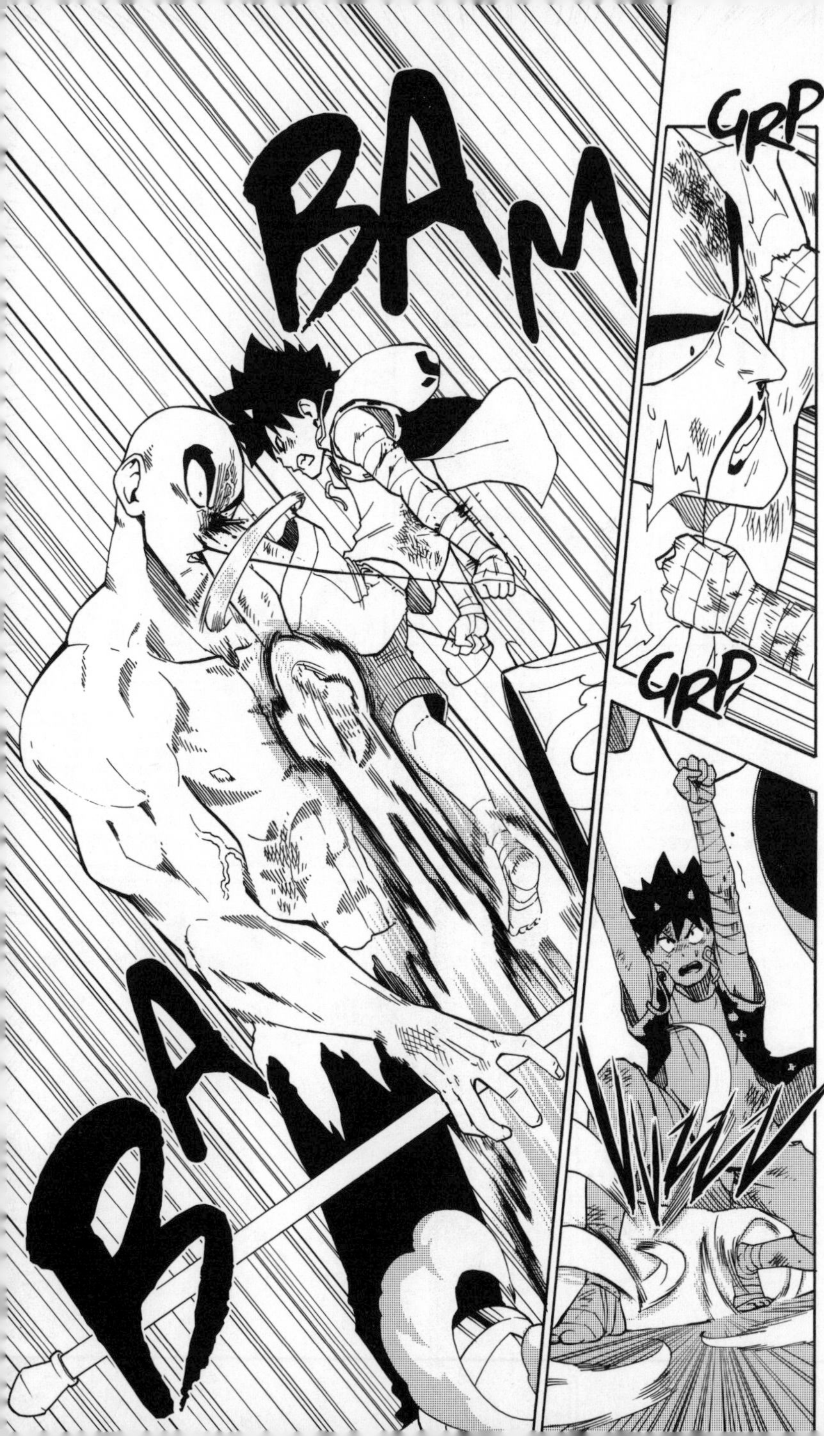
GRP
GRP
BAM
BAM

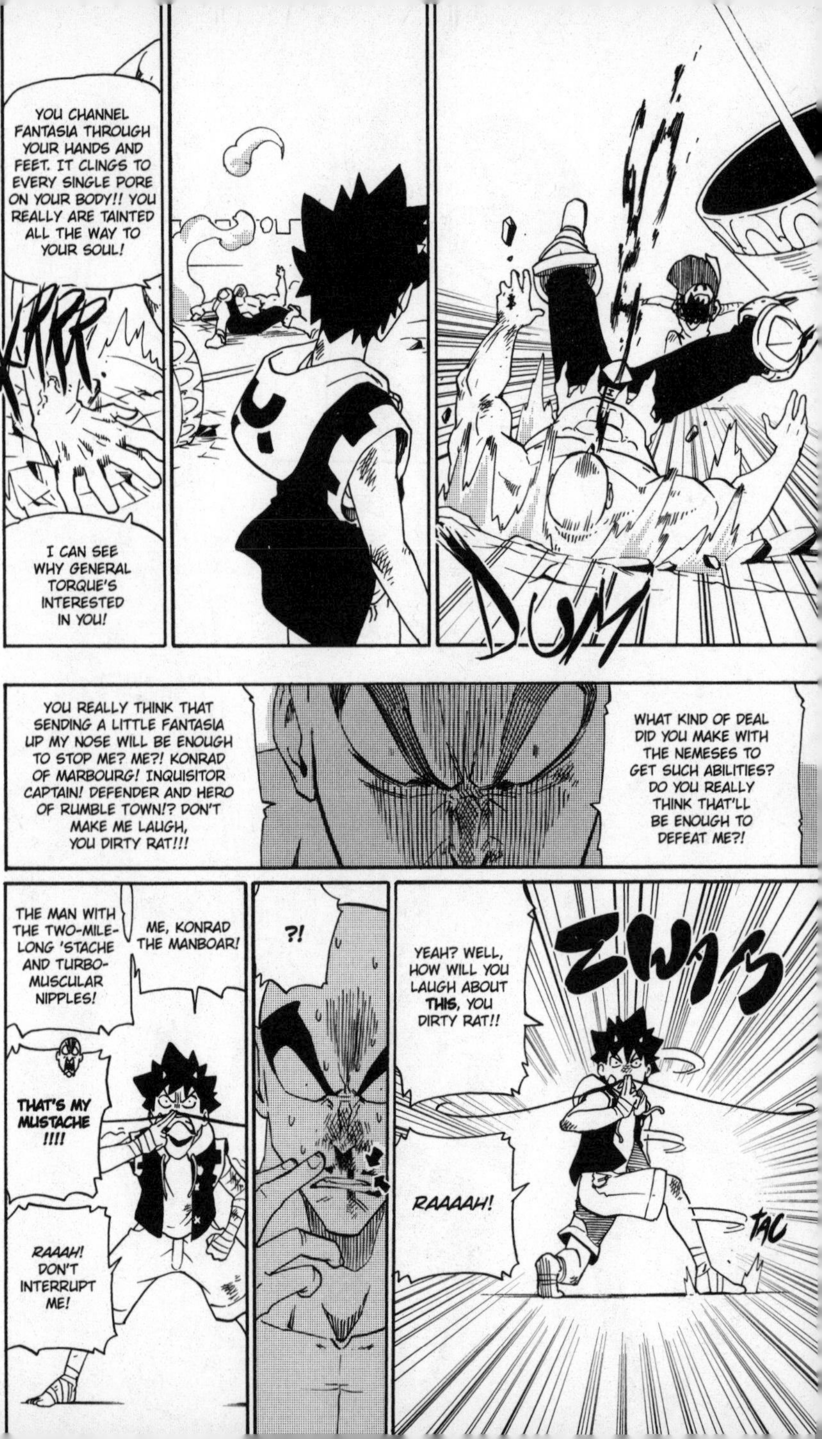
YOU CHANNEL FANTASIA THROUGH YOUR HANDS AND FEET. IT CLINGS TO EVERY SINGLE PORE ON YOUR BODY!! YOU REALLY ARE TAINTED ALL THE WAY TO YOUR SOUL!
KRRR
I CAN SEE WHY GENERAL TORQUE'S INTERESTED IN YOU!
DUM
YOU REALLY THINK THAT SENDING A LITTLE FANTASIA UP MY NOSE WILL BE ENOUGH TO STOP ME? ME?! KONRAD OF MARBOURG! INQUISITOR CAPTAIN! DEFENDER AND HERO OF RUMBLE TOWN!? DON'T MAKE ME LAUGH, YOU DIRTY RAT!!!
WHAT KIND OF DEAL DID YOU MAKE WITH THE NEMESES TO GET SUCH ABILITIES? DO YOU REALLY THINK THAT'LL BE ENOUGH TO DEFEAT ME?!
THE MAN WITH THE TWO-MILE-LONG 'STACHE AND TURBO-MUSCULAR NIPPLES!
ME, KONRAD THE MANBOAR!
THAT'S MY MUSTACHE!!!!
RAAAH! DON'T INTERRUPT ME!
?!
YEAH? WELL, HOW WILL YOU LAUGH ABOUT THIS, YOU DIRTY RAT!!
RAAAAH!
TAC

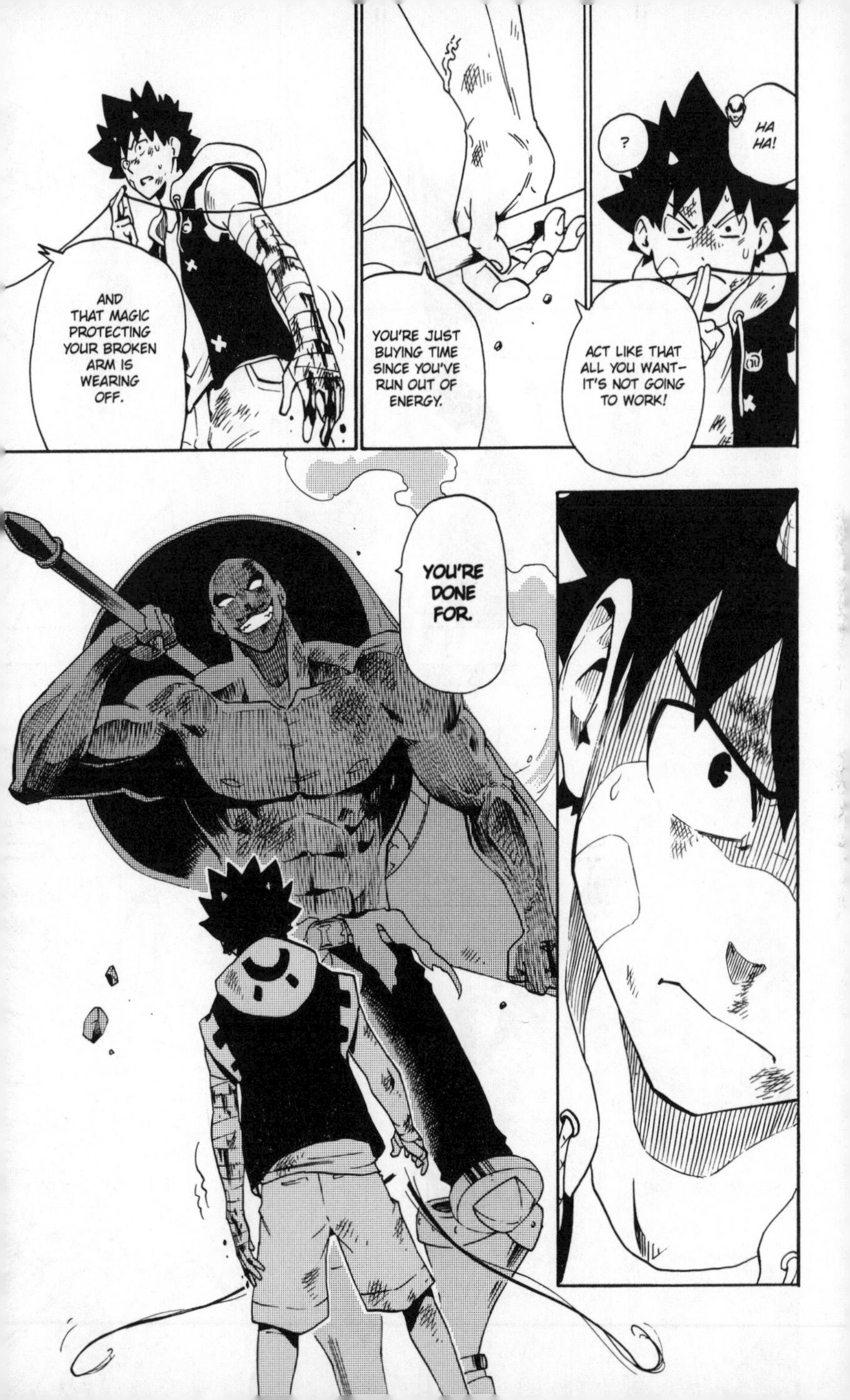

?
HA HA!
ACT LIKE THAT ALL YOU WANT—IT'S NOT GOING TO WORK!
YOU'RE JUST BUYING TIME SINCE YOU'VE RUN OUT OF ENERGY.
AND THAT MAGIC PROTECTING YOUR BROKEN ARM IS WEARING OFF.
YOU'RE DONE FOR.

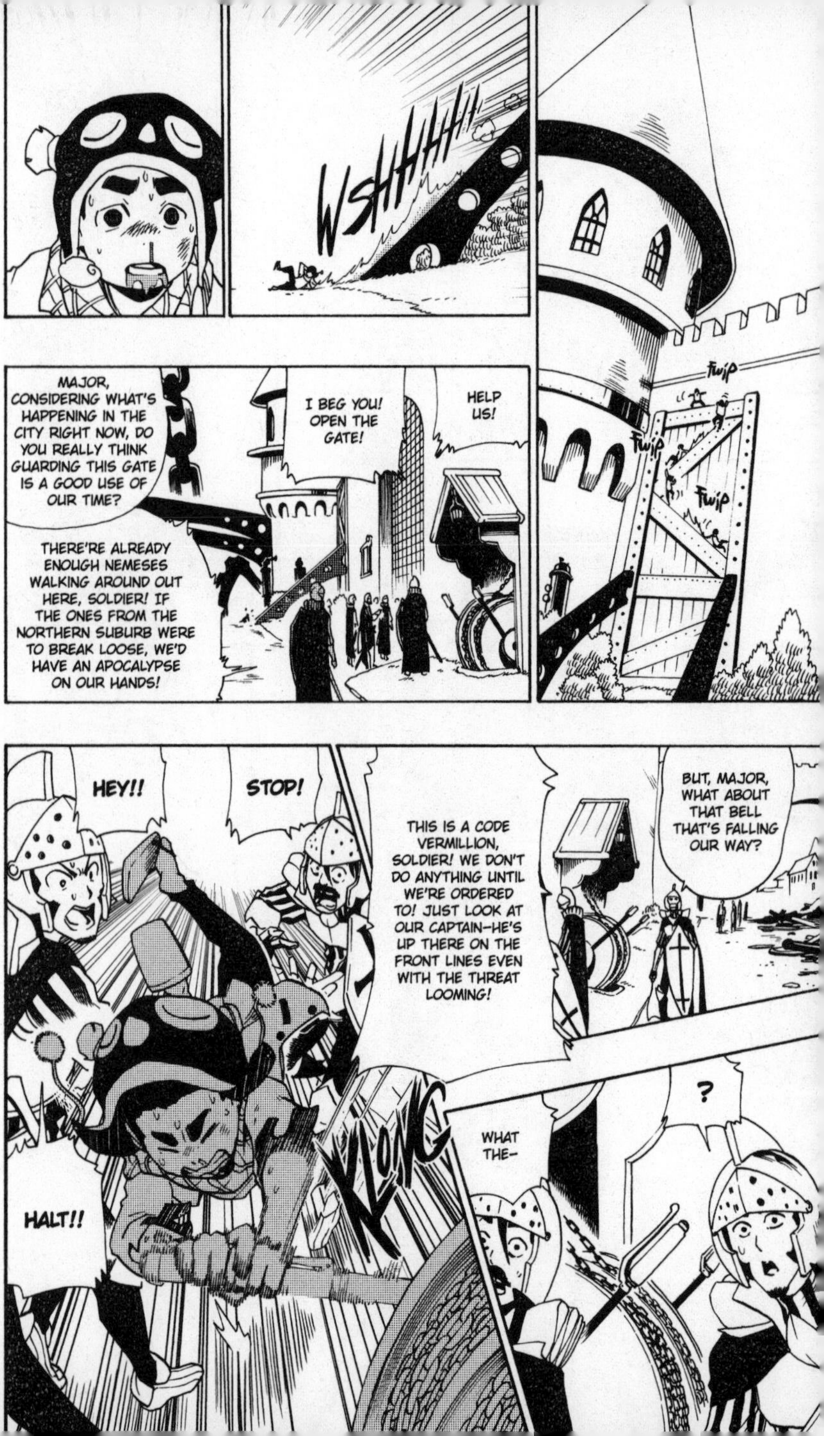
WSHHHHH!!
FWIP
FWIP
FWIP
HELP US!
I BEG YOU! OPEN THE GATE!
MAJOR, CONSIDERING WHAT'S HAPPENING IN THE CITY RIGHT NOW, DO YOU REALLY THINK GUARDING THIS GATE IS A GOOD USE OF OUR TIME?
THERE'RE ALREADY ENOUGH NEMESES WALKING AROUND OUT HERE, SOLDIER! IF THE ONES FROM THE NORTHERN SUBURB WERE TO BREAK LOOSE, WE'D HAVE AN APOCALYPSE ON OUR HANDS!
BUT, MAJOR, WHAT ABOUT THAT BELL THAT'S FALLING OUR WAY?
THIS IS A CODE VERMILLION, SOLDIER! WE DON'T DO ANYTHING UNTIL WE'RE ORDERED TO! JUST LOOK AT OUR CAPTAIN—HE'S UP THERE ON THE FRONT LINES EVEN WITH THE THREAT LOOMING!
?
WHAT THE-
KLONG
STOP!
HEY!!
HALT!!

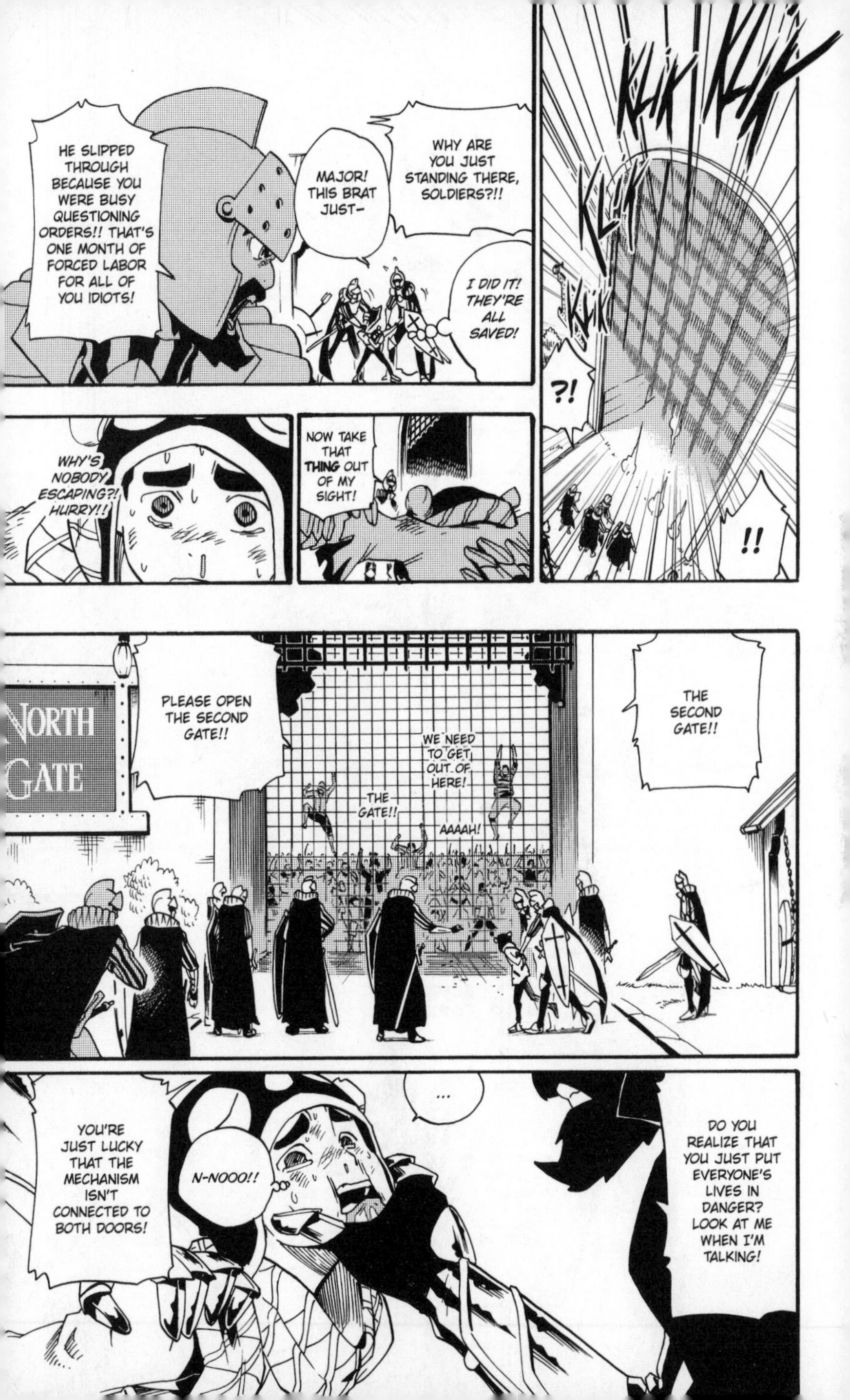
?!
!!
I DID IT! THEY'RE ALL SAVED!
WHY ARE YOU JUST STANDING THERE, SOLDIERS?!!
MAJOR! THIS BRAT JUST-
HE SLIPPED THROUGH BECAUSE YOU WERE BUSY QUESTIONING ORDERS!! THAT'S ONE MONTH OF FORCED LABOR FOR ALL OF YOU IDIOTS!
NOW TAKE THAT THING OUT OF MY SIGHT!
WHY'S NOBODY ESCAPING?! HURRY!!
THE SECOND GATE!!
WE NEED TO GET OUT OF HERE!
AAAAH!
THE GATE!!
PLEASE OPEN THE SECOND GATE!!
NORTH GATE
DO YOU REALIZE THAT YOU JUST PUT EVERYONE'S LIVES IN DANGER? LOOK AT ME WHEN I'M TALKING!
...
N-NOOO!!
YOU'RE JUST LUCKY THAT THE MECHANISM ISN'T CONNECTED TO BOTH DOORS!

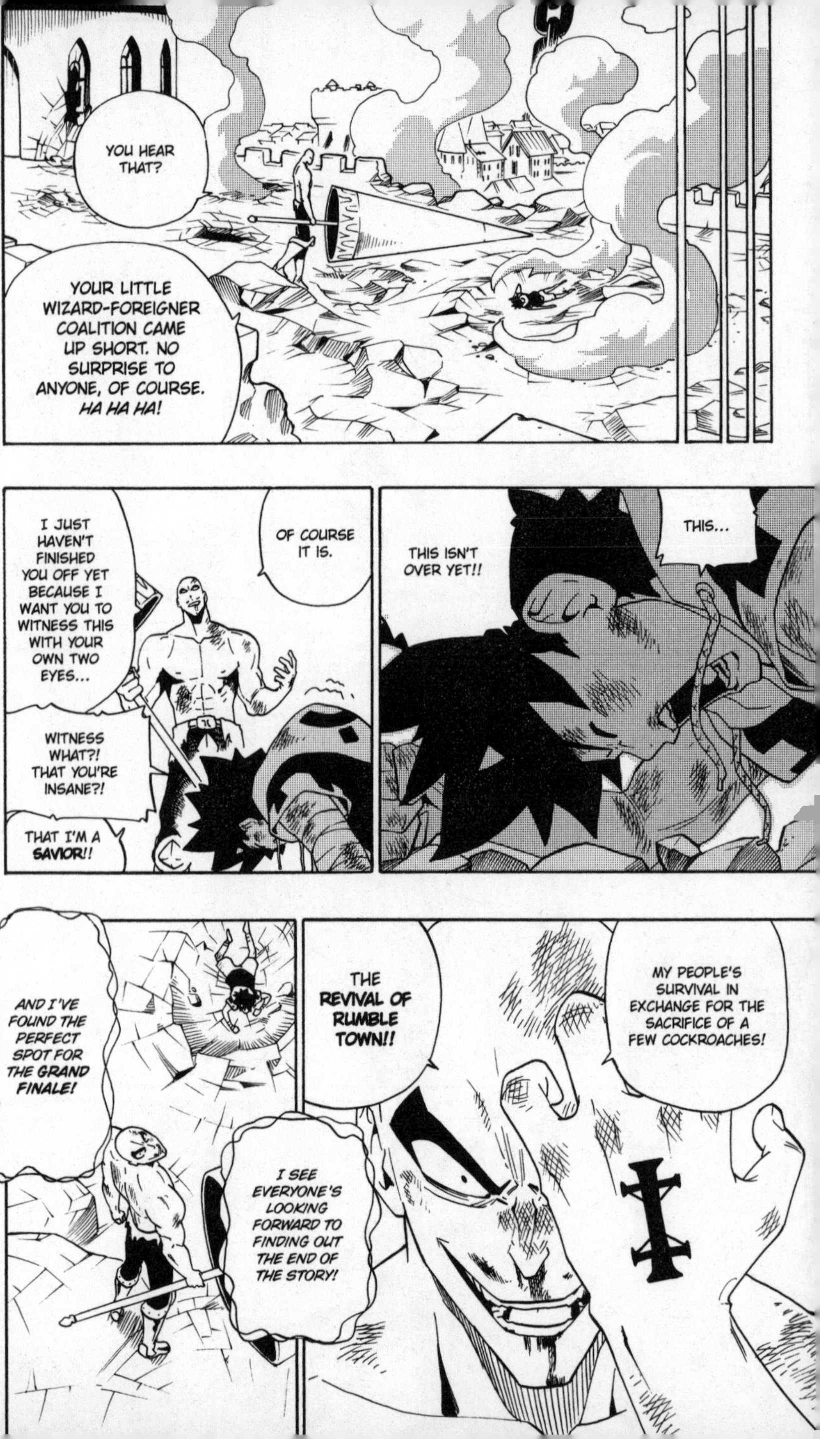
YOU HEAR THAT?
YOUR LITTLE WIZARD-FOREIGNER COALITION CAME UP SHORT. NO SURPRISE TO ANYONE, OF COURSE. HA HA HA!
THIS...
THIS ISN'T OVER YET!!
OF COURSE IT IS.
I JUST HAVEN'T FINISHED YOU OFF YET BECAUSE I WANT YOU TO WITNESS THIS WITH YOUR OWN TWO EYES...
WITNESS WHAT?! THAT YOU'RE INSANE?!
THAT I'M A SAVIOR!!
MY PEOPLE'S SURVIVAL IN EXCHANGE FOR THE SACRIFICE OF A FEW COCKROACHES!
THE REVIVAL OF RUMBLE TOWN!!
AND I'VE FOUND THE PERFECT SPOT FOR THE GRAND FINALE!
I SEE EVERYONE'S LOOKING FORWARD TO FINDING OUT THE END OF THE STORY!

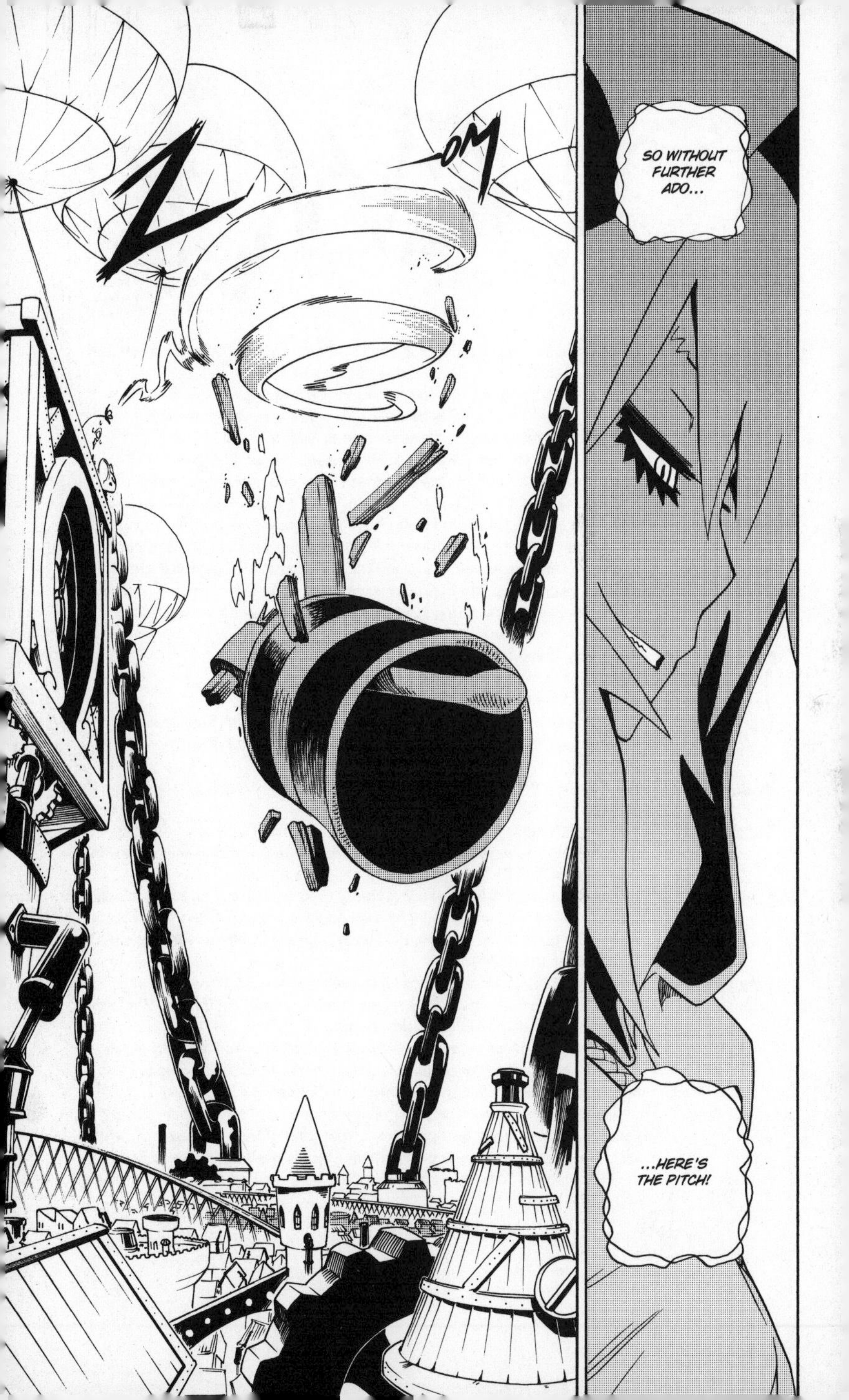

SO WITHOUT FURTHER ADO...
...HERE'S THE PITCH!

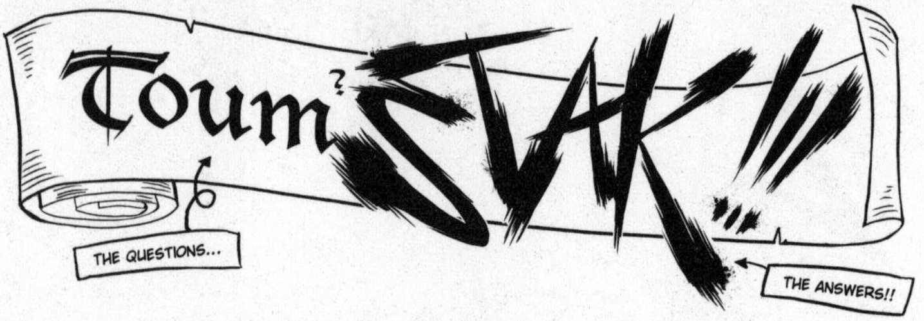
Toum? STAK!!
THE QUESTIONS...
THE ANSWERS!!

Noah of Koko: Could you tell us the meaning of the spells and the Latin phrases in the manga?

Tony Valente: For Seth: "Skull Poke" is a skull-shaped thrust attack.
For Yaga: "Meteor Drops" is because they're like little drops of falling meteors.
"Cauldron Crush" is because he's crushing his opponent with a cauldron.
For Mélie: "Gravem Carcerem" literally means "Heavy Prison."
For Grimm: "Veneficium Revelare" literally means "Reveal the Spell."
Other than that, the only phrase in Latin left is the one on the crest, which I explained earlier.

Noah of Koko: Could you tell us a little bit more about the Inquisition? Their internal organization, the different ranks, how and by whom it was founded, and how one can join.

Tony Valente: I'll use another bonus page to explain a bit about the Inquisition. But if someone wants to join, they would just need a resume and cover letter. One way you could start off that letter is by saying: "Ever since I can remember, I've always liked imprisoning people who are different..."

Noah of Koko: How many Thaumaturges are there?

Tony Valente: Roughly between five and 1,000.

Noah of Koko: What exactly is the Coven of Thirteen?

Tony Valente: An assembly of 13 exceptional wizards which Yaga is part of. Their role has never officially been defined, so other wizards only know that the Coven observes everything...

Noah of Koko: Will we ever get to see a map of the world of *Radiant*? What about some character profiles?

Tony Valente: Yes, I'm planning to make those! In volume 4 you'll have a glimpse of the huge area in which Seth's adventures take place. And the character profiles will be appearing over the next few volumes. Thank you for all the questions!

Alexandre P.: Hi there! I first wanted to tell you that I really liked volume 1 of *Radiant* and was looking forward to volume 2. After having bought and read it, I have to say volume 2 was just as good as the first one. But I have a question...why was there such a long wait between the volumes?

Tony Valente: *Hmm*... Well there's three reasons for the delay. First of all, I'm working all by myself. I tried to get help on some pages (thanks, Lucas!) but my way of working doesn't make it efficient to divide up the work.

The second reason is because of marketing. I often go to France for signing sessions, which allows for people to get to know the series and for me to get to know my readers, but that completely messes with my work schedule!

The third reason, well lemme tell ya'... It's because of my infection. Every time I sneeze, *bam*! I jump in the air. No joke! I lose days of work because of it, so it's a little annoying when planning out my work. Even if there's just a little bit of dust in the air, I go flying! Take my windowsill, for example... If I run over it with my finger, and I... *Ah-choooo*!!!!

Send your questions to: radiant@ankama.com

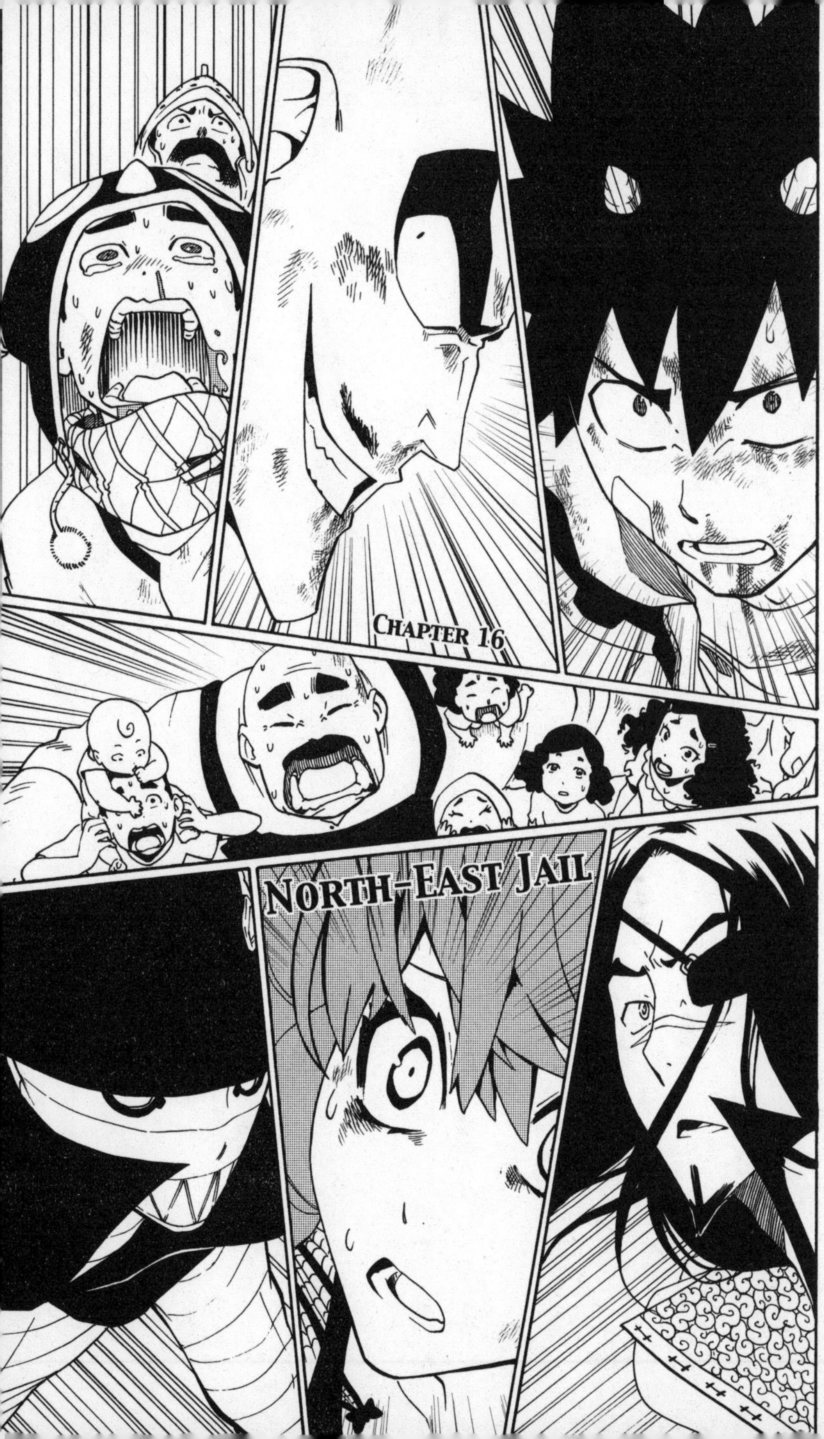
CHAPTER 16
NORTH-EAST JAIL

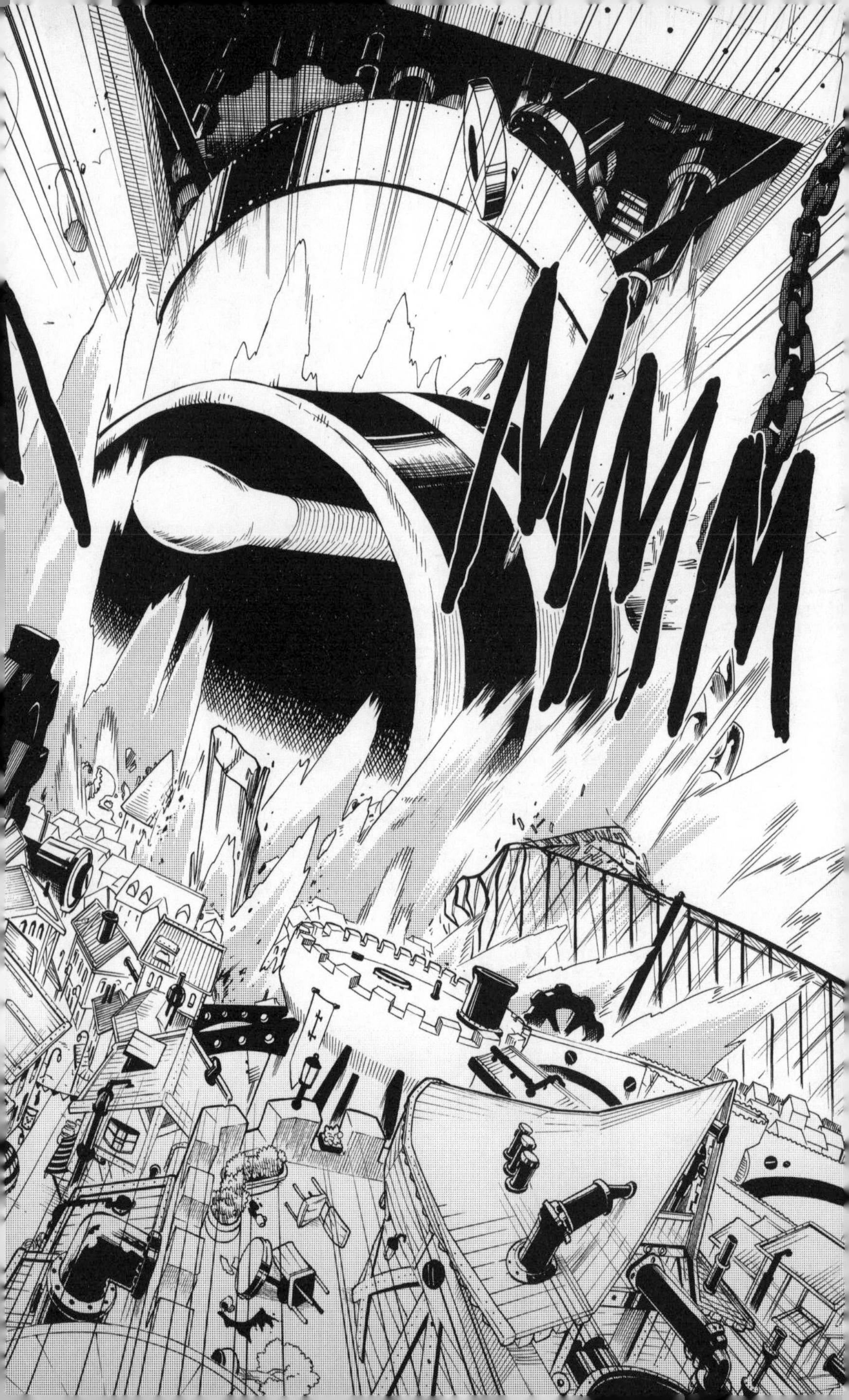
MMM

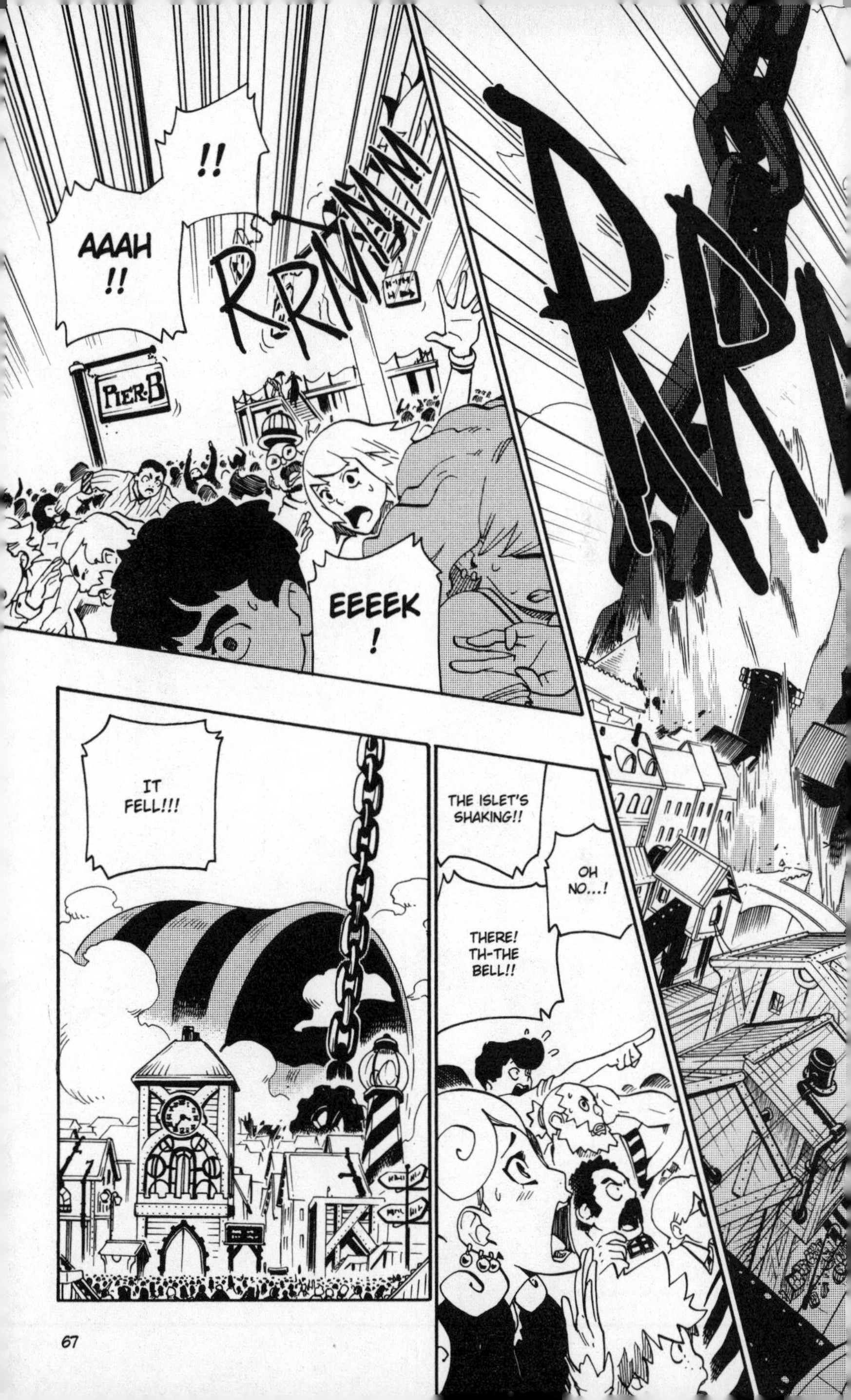

RRRMM
!!
AAAH !!
RRRMMM
PIER-B
EEEEK !
THE ISLET'S SHAKING!!
OH NO...!
THERE! TH-THE BELL!!
IT FELL!!!

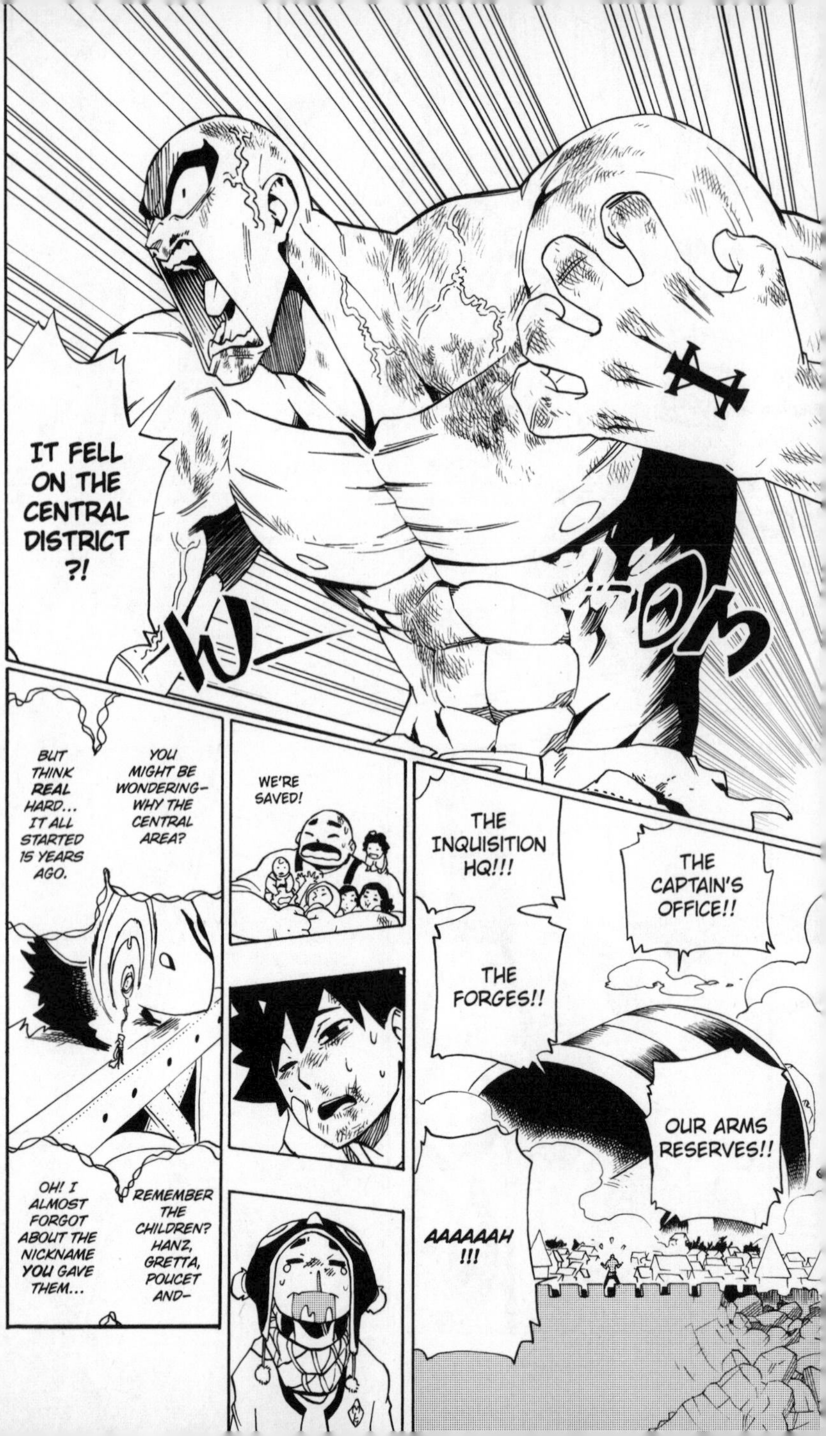
IT FELL ON THE CENTRAL DISTRICT ?!
THE CAPTAIN'S OFFICE!!
THE INQUISITION HQ!!!
THE FORGES!!
OUR ARMS RESERVES!!
AAAAAAH !!!
WE'RE SAVED!
YOU MIGHT BE WONDERING- WHY THE CENTRAL AREA?
BUT THINK REAL HARD... IT ALL STARTED 15 YEARS AGO.
REMEMBER THE CHILDREN? HANZ, GRETTA, POUCET AND-
OH! I ALMOST FORGOT ABOUT THE NICKNAME YOU GAVE THEM...

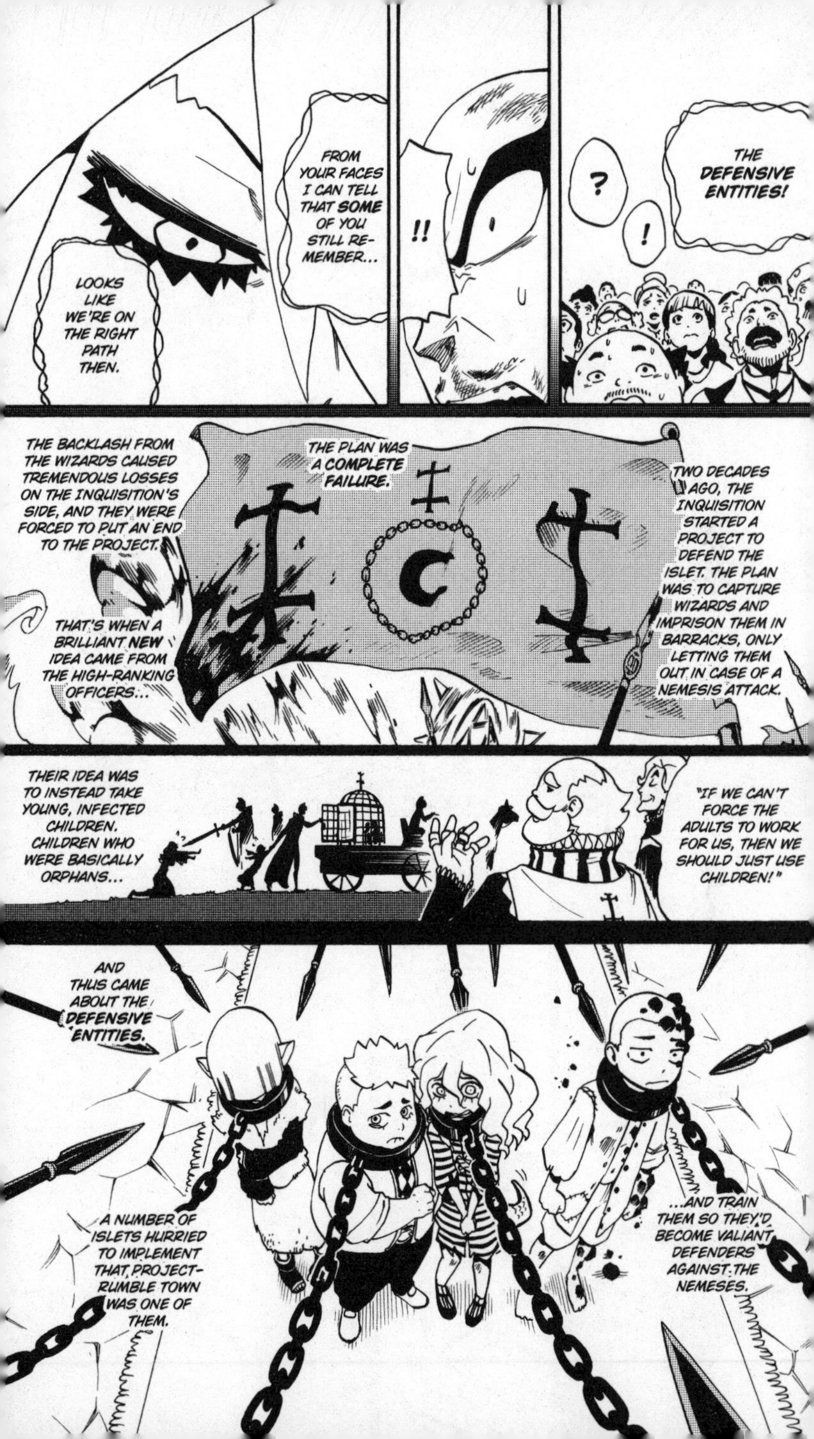

THE DEFENSIVE ENTITIES!
?
!
!!
FROM YOUR FACES I CAN TELL THAT SOME OF YOU STILL RE-MEMBER...
LOOKS LIKE WE'RE ON THE RIGHT PATH THEN.
TWO DECADES AGO, THE INQUISITION STARTED A PROJECT TO DEFEND THE ISLET. THE PLAN WAS TO CAPTURE WIZARDS AND IMPRISON THEM IN BARRACKS, ONLY LETTING THEM OUT IN CASE OF A NEMESIS ATTACK.
THE PLAN WAS A COMPLETE FAILURE.
THE BACKLASH FROM THE WIZARDS CAUSED TREMENDOUS LOSSES ON THE INQUISITION'S SIDE, AND THEY WERE FORCED TO PUT AN END TO THE PROJECT.
THAT'S WHEN A BRILLIANT NEW IDEA CAME FROM THE HIGH-RANKING OFFICERS...
"IF WE CAN'T FORCE THE ADULTS TO WORK FOR US, THEN WE SHOULD JUST USE CHILDREN!"
THEIR IDEA WAS TO INSTEAD TAKE YOUNG, INFECTED CHILDREN. CHILDREN WHO WERE BASICALLY ORPHANS...
...AND TRAIN THEM SO THEY'D BECOME VALIANT DEFENDERS AGAINST THE NEMESES.
AND THUS CAME ABOUT THE DEFENSIVE ENTITIES.
A NUMBER OF ISLETS HURRIED TO IMPLEMENT THAT PROJECT-RUMBLE TOWN WAS ONE OF THEM.

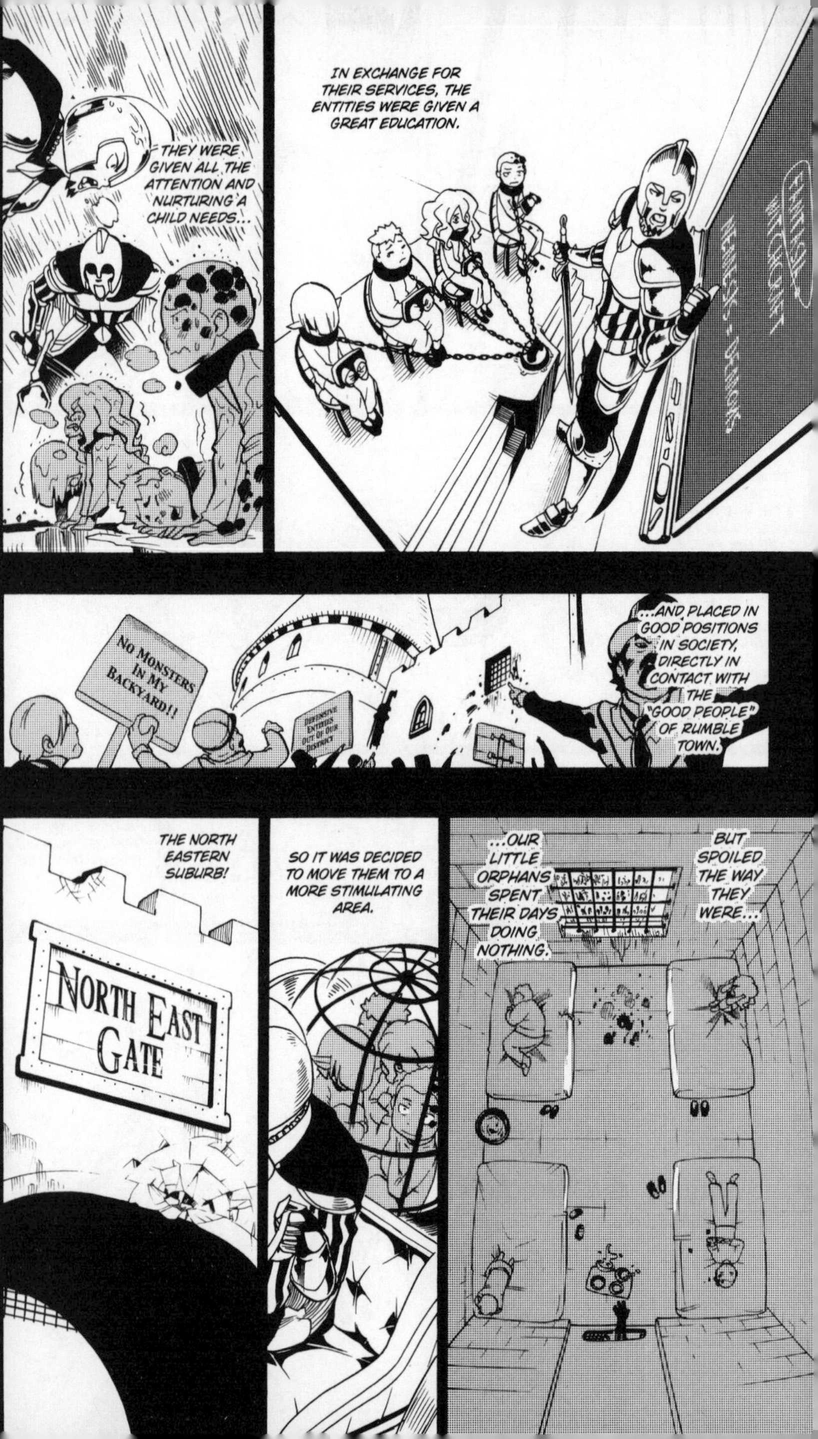
THEY WERE GIVEN ALL THE ATTENTION AND NURTURING A CHILD NEEDS...
IN EXCHANGE FOR THEIR SERVICES, THE ENTITIES WERE GIVEN A GREAT EDUCATION.
NO MONSTERS IN MY BACKYARD!!
...AND PLACED IN GOOD POSITIONS IN SOCIETY, DIRECTLY IN CONTACT WITH THE "GOOD PEOPLE" OF RUMBLE TOWN.
THE NORTH EASTERN SUBURB!
NORTH EAST GATE
SO IT WAS DECIDED TO MOVE THEM TO A MORE STIMULATING AREA.
BUT SPOILED THE WAY THEY WERE...
...OUR LITTLE ORPHANS SPENT THEIR DAYS DOING NOTHING.

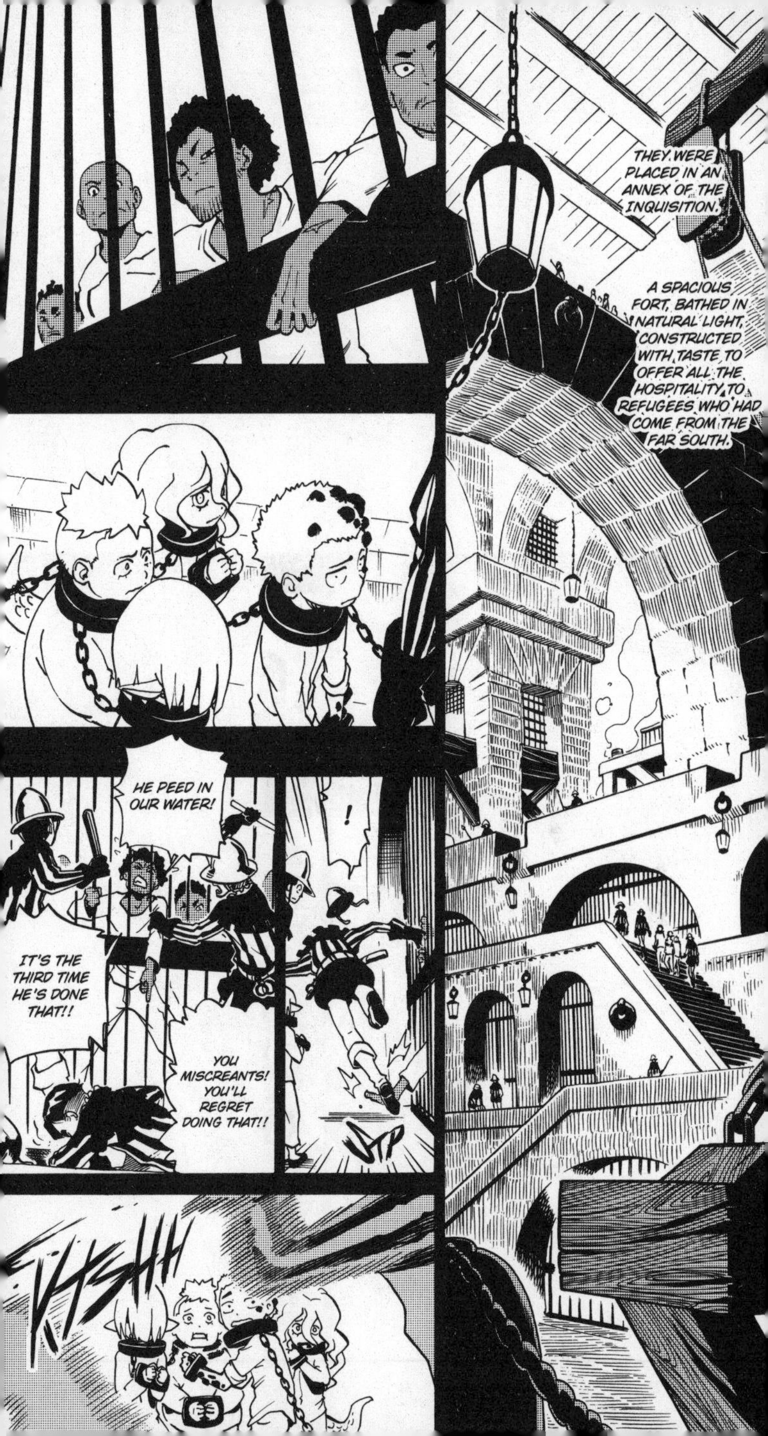
THEY WERE PLACED IN AN ANNEX OF THE INQUISITION.
A SPACIOUS FORT, BATHED IN NATURAL LIGHT, CONSTRUCTED WITH TASTE TO OFFER ALL THE HOSPITALITY TO REFUGEES WHO HAD COME FROM THE FAR SOUTH.
HE PEED IN OUR WATER!
IT'S THE THIRD TIME HE'S DONE THAT!!
!
YOU MISCREANTS! YOU'LL REGRET DOING THAT!!
STP
VSHHH

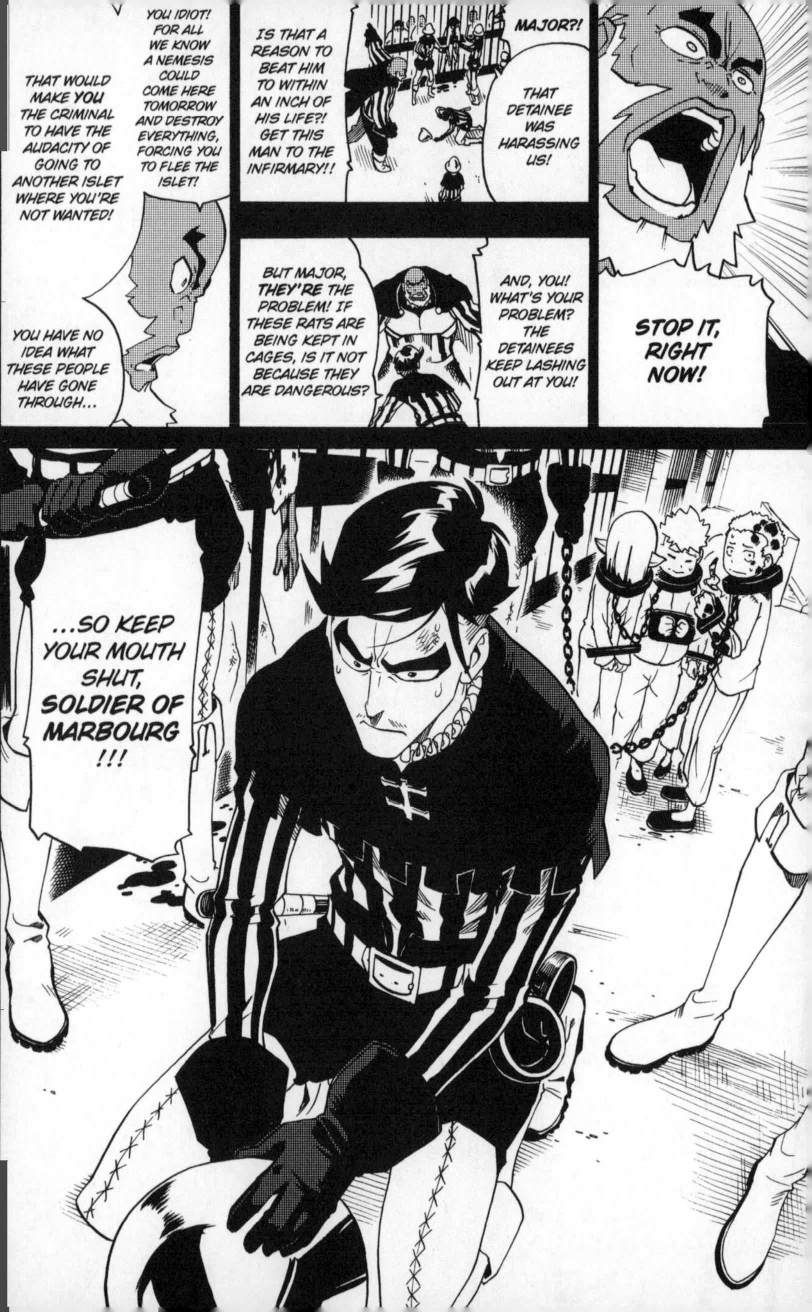
STOP IT, RIGHT NOW!
MAJOR?!
THAT DETAINEE WAS HARASSING US!
IS THAT A REASON TO BEAT HIM TO WITHIN AN INCH OF HIS LIFE?! GET THIS MAN TO THE INFIRMARY!!
AND, YOU! WHAT'S YOUR PROBLEM? THE DETAINEES KEEP LASHING OUT AT YOU!
BUT MAJOR, THEY'RE THE PROBLEM! IF THESE RATS ARE BEING KEPT IN CAGES, IS IT NOT BECAUSE THEY ARE DANGEROUS?
YOU IDIOT! FOR ALL WE KNOW A NEMESIS COULD COME HERE TOMORROW AND DESTROY EVERYTHING, FORCING YOU TO FLEE THE ISLET!
THAT WOULD MAKE YOU THE CRIMINAL TO HAVE THE AUDACITY OF GOING TO ANOTHER ISLET WHERE YOU'RE NOT WANTED!
YOU HAVE NO IDEA WHAT THESE PEOPLE HAVE GONE THROUGH...
...SO KEEP YOUR MOUTH SHUT, SOLDIER OF MARBOURG !!!

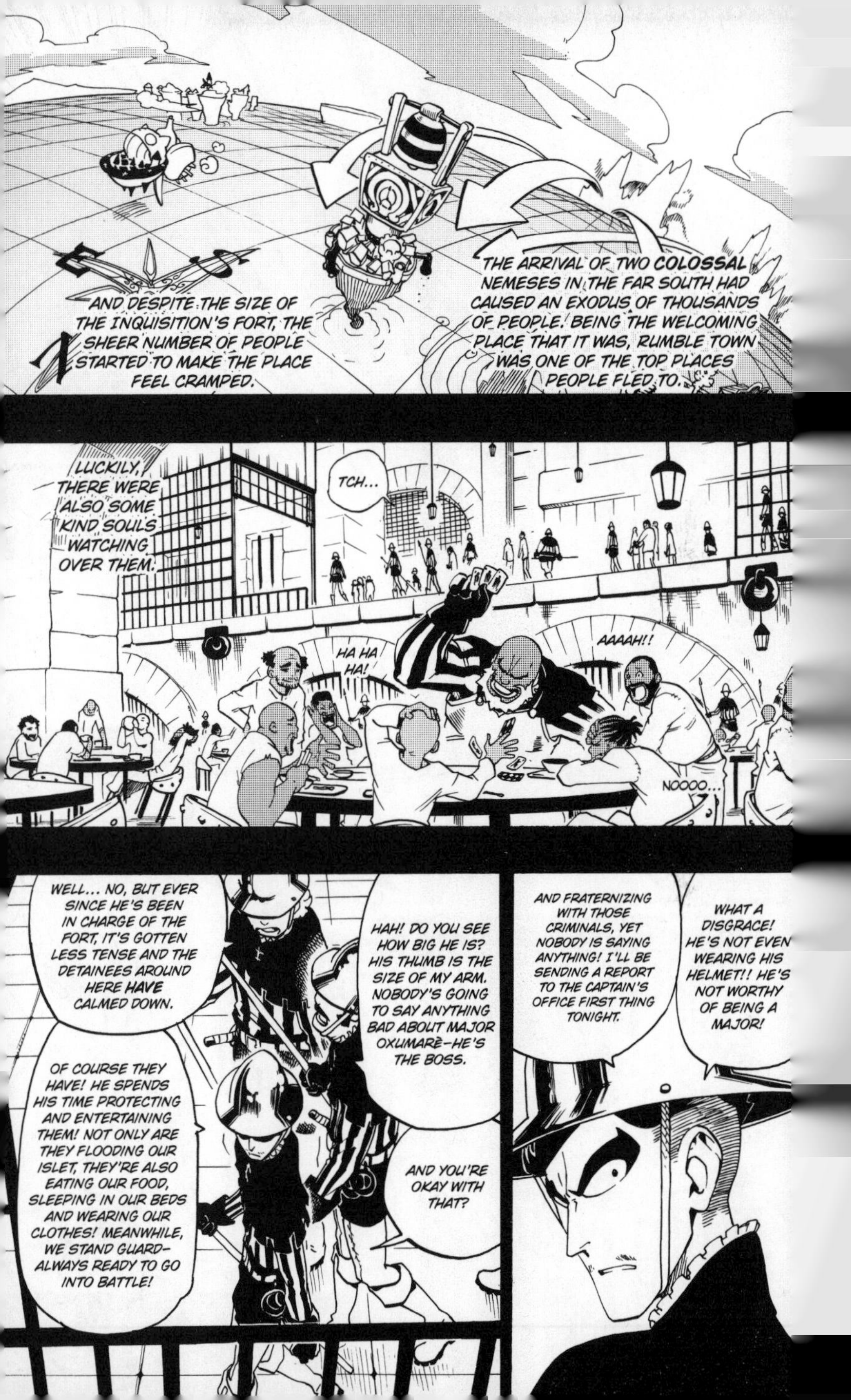
THE ARRIVAL OF TWO COLOSSAL NEMESES IN THE FAR SOUTH HAD CAUSED AN EXODUS OF THOUSANDS OF PEOPLE. BEING THE WELCOMING PLACE THAT IT WAS, RUMBLE TOWN WAS ONE OF THE TOP PLACES PEOPLE FLED TO.
AND DESPITE THE SIZE OF THE INQUISITION'S FORT, THE SHEER NUMBER OF PEOPLE STARTED TO MAKE THE PLACE FEEL CRAMPED.
LUCKILY, THERE WERE ALSO SOME KIND SOULS WATCHING OVER THEM.
TCH...
AAAAH!!
HA HA HA!
NOOOO...
WHAT A DISGRACE! HE'S NOT EVEN WEARING HIS HELMET!! HE'S NOT WORTHY OF BEING A MAJOR!
AND FRATERNIZING WITH THOSE CRIMINALS, YET NOBODY IS SAYING ANYTHING! I'LL BE SENDING A REPORT TO THE CAPTAIN'S OFFICE FIRST THING TONIGHT.
HAH! DO YOU SEE HOW BIG HE IS? HIS THUMB IS THE SIZE OF MY ARM. NOBODY'S GOING TO SAY ANYTHING BAD ABOUT MAJOR OXUMARÈ—HE'S THE BOSS.
WELL... NO, BUT EVER SINCE HE'S BEEN IN CHARGE OF THE FORT, IT'S GOTTEN LESS TENSE AND THE DETAINEES AROUND HERE HAVE CALMED DOWN.
AND YOU'RE OKAY WITH THAT?
OF COURSE THEY HAVE! HE SPENDS HIS TIME PROTECTING AND ENTERTAINING THEM! NOT ONLY ARE THEY FLOODING OUR ISLET, THEY'RE ALSO EATING OUR FOOD, SLEEPING IN OUR BEDS AND WEARING OUR CLOTHES! MEANWHILE, WE STAND GUARD—ALWAYS READY TO GO INTO BATTLE!

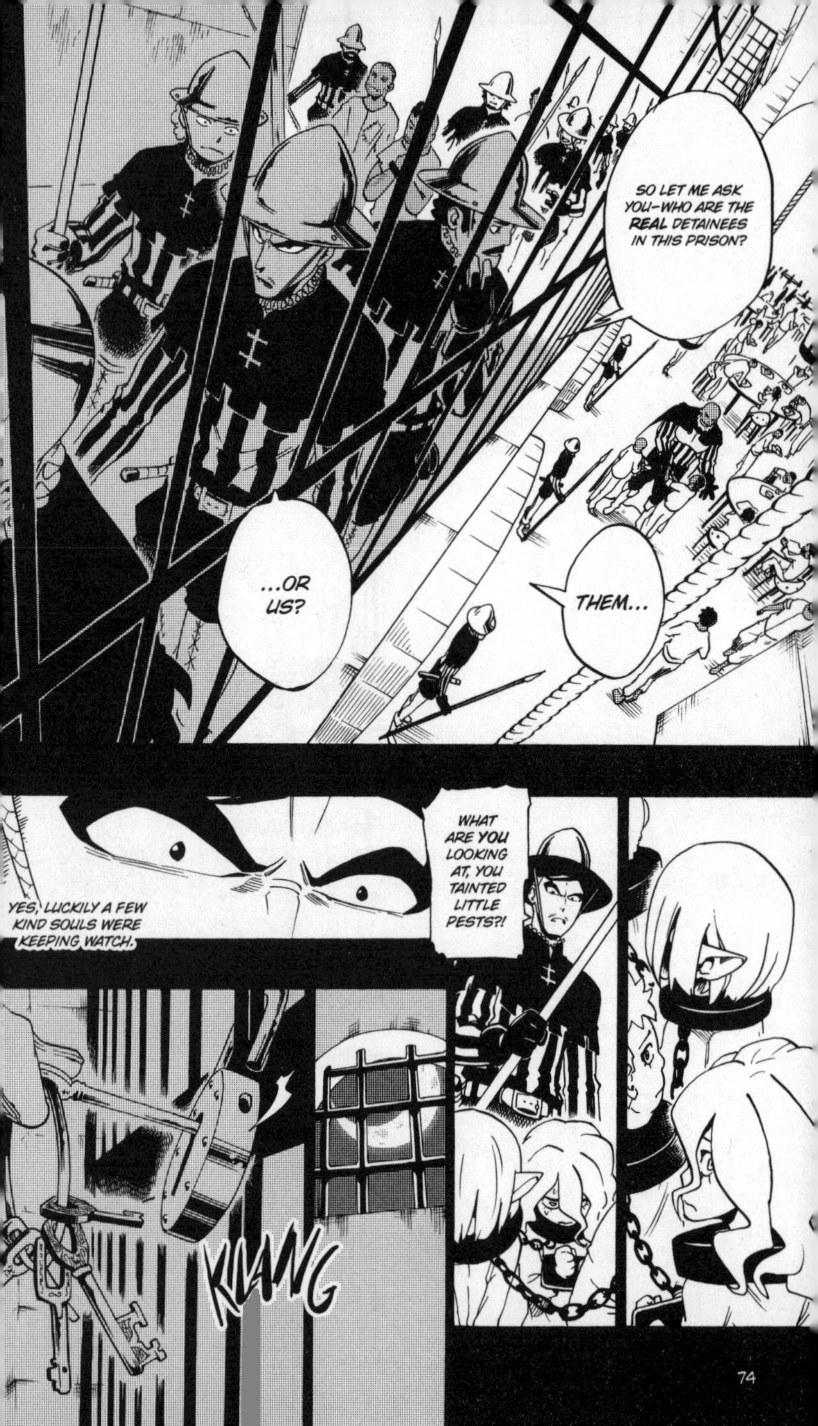
SO LET ME ASK YOU—WHO ARE THE REAL DETAINEES IN THIS PRISON?
THEM...
...OR US?
WHAT ARE YOU LOOKING AT, YOU TAINTED LITTLE PESTS?!
YES, LUCKILY A FEW KIND SOULS WERE KEEPING WATCH.
KLANG

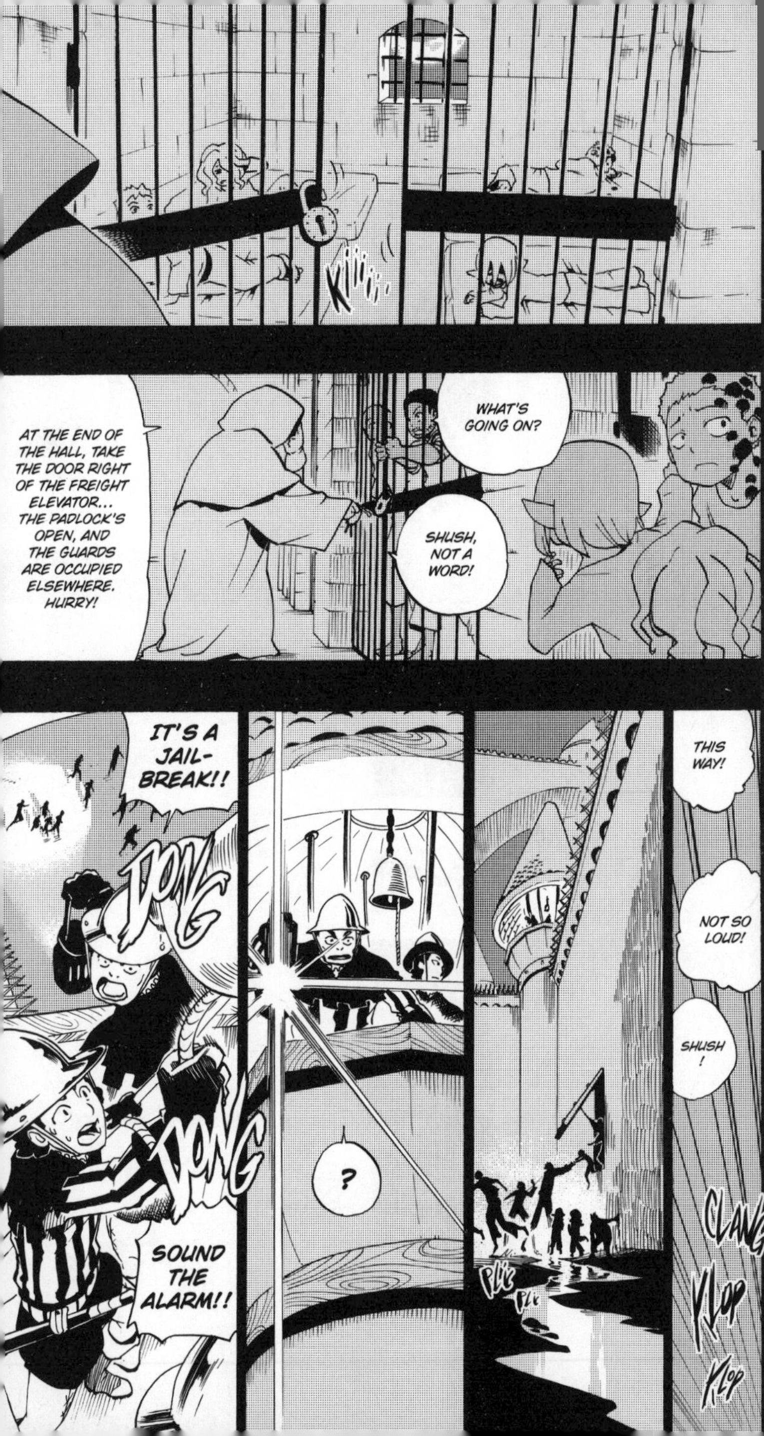
KIIIII...
WHAT'S GOING ON?
SHUSH, NOT A WORD!
AT THE END OF THE HALL, TAKE THE DOOR RIGHT OF THE FREIGHT ELEVATOR... THE PADLOCK'S OPEN, AND THE GUARDS ARE OCCUPIED ELSEWHERE. HURRY!
THIS WAY!
NOT SO LOUD!
SHUSH!
CLANG
KLOP
KLOP
PLIC
PLIC
?
IT'S A JAIL-BREAK!!
DONG
DONG
SOUND THE ALARM!!

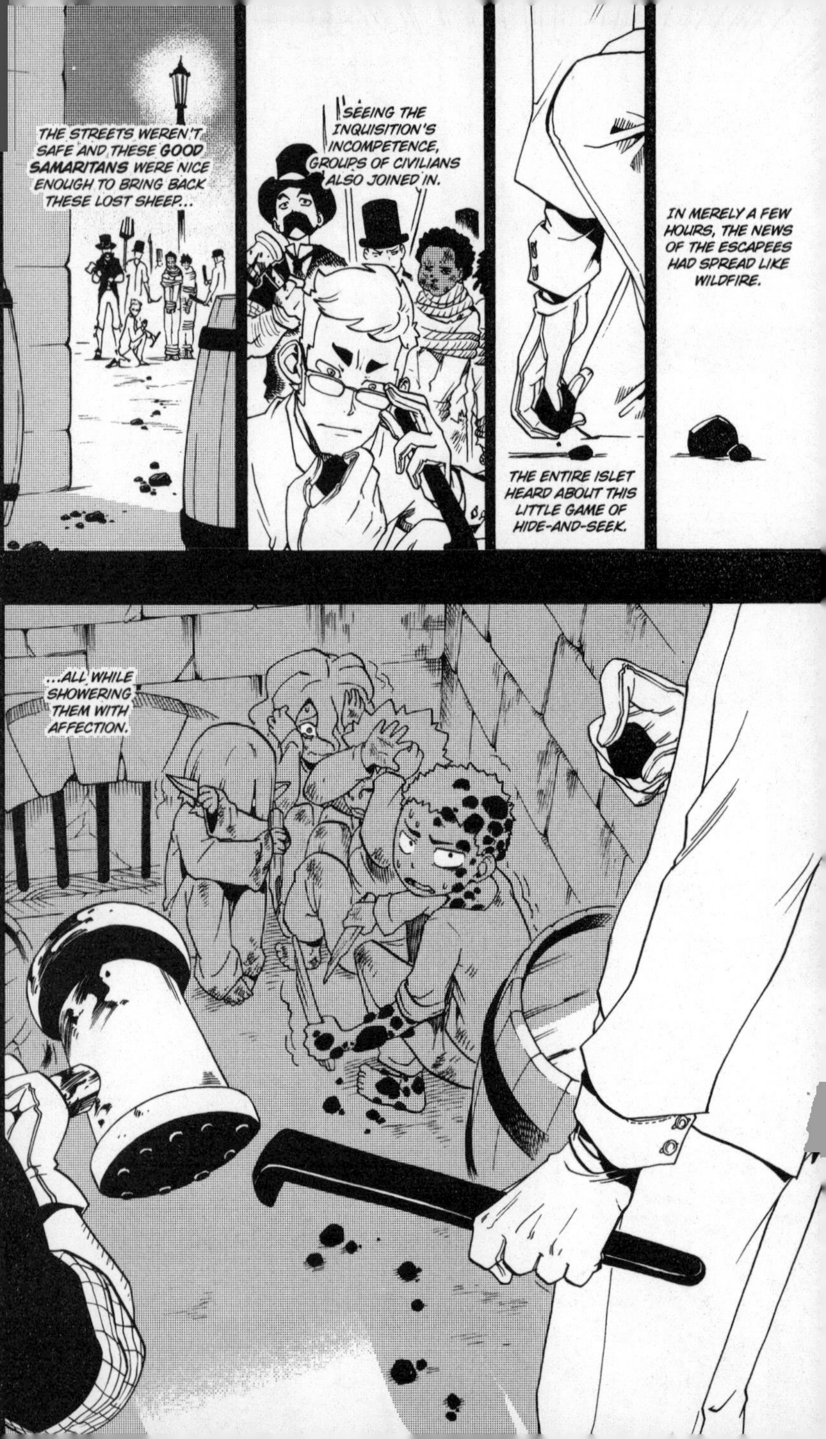
IN MERELY A FEW HOURS, THE NEWS OF THE ESCAPEES HAD SPREAD LIKE WILDFIRE.
THE ENTIRE ISLET HEARD ABOUT THIS LITTLE GAME OF HIDE-AND-SEEK.
SEEING THE INQUISITION'S INCOMPETENCE, GROUPS OF CIVILIANS ALSO JOINED IN.
THE STREETS WEREN'T SAFE AND THESE GOOD SAMARITANS WERE NICE ENOUGH TO BRING BACK THESE LOST SHEEP...
...ALL WHILE SHOWERING THEM WITH AFFECTION.

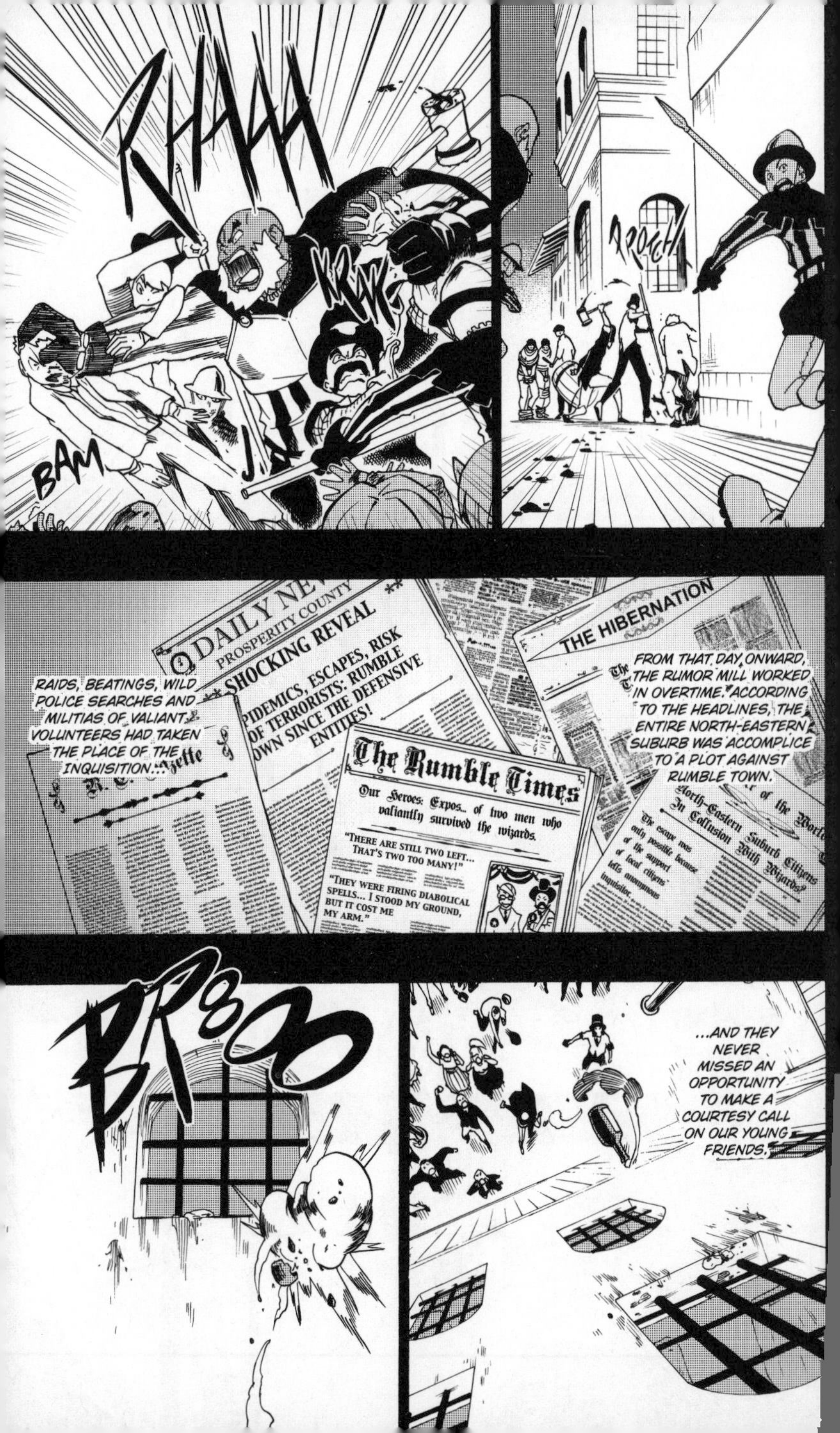
RHAAA
KRAK
BAM
RAIDS, BEATINGS, WILD POLICE SEARCHES AND MILITIAS OF VALIANT VOLUNTEERS HAD TAKEN THE PLACE OF THE INQUISITION...
DAILY NE
PROSPERITY COUNTY
SHOCKING REVEAL
PIDEMICS, ESCAPES, RISK OF TERRORISTS: RUMBLE OWN SINCE THE DEFENSIVE ENTITIES!
The Rumble Times
Our Heroes: Expos... of two men who valiantly survived the wizards.
"THERE ARE STILL TWO LEFT... THAT'S TWO TOO MANY!"
"THEY WERE FIRING DIABOLICAL SPELLS... I STOOD MY GROUND, BUT IT COST ME MY ARM."
THE HIBERNATION
FROM THAT DAY ONWARD, THE RUMOR MILL WORKED IN OVERTIME. ACCORDING TO THE HEADLINES, THE ENTIRE NORTH-EASTERN SUBURB WAS ACCOMPLICE TO A PLOT AGAINST RUMBLE TOWN.
North-Eastern Suburb Citizens In Collusion With Wizards?
The escape was only possible because of the support of local citizens' tells anonymous inquisitor.
...AND THEY NEVER MISSED AN OPPORTUNITY TO MAKE A COURTESY CALL ON OUR YOUNG FRIENDS.

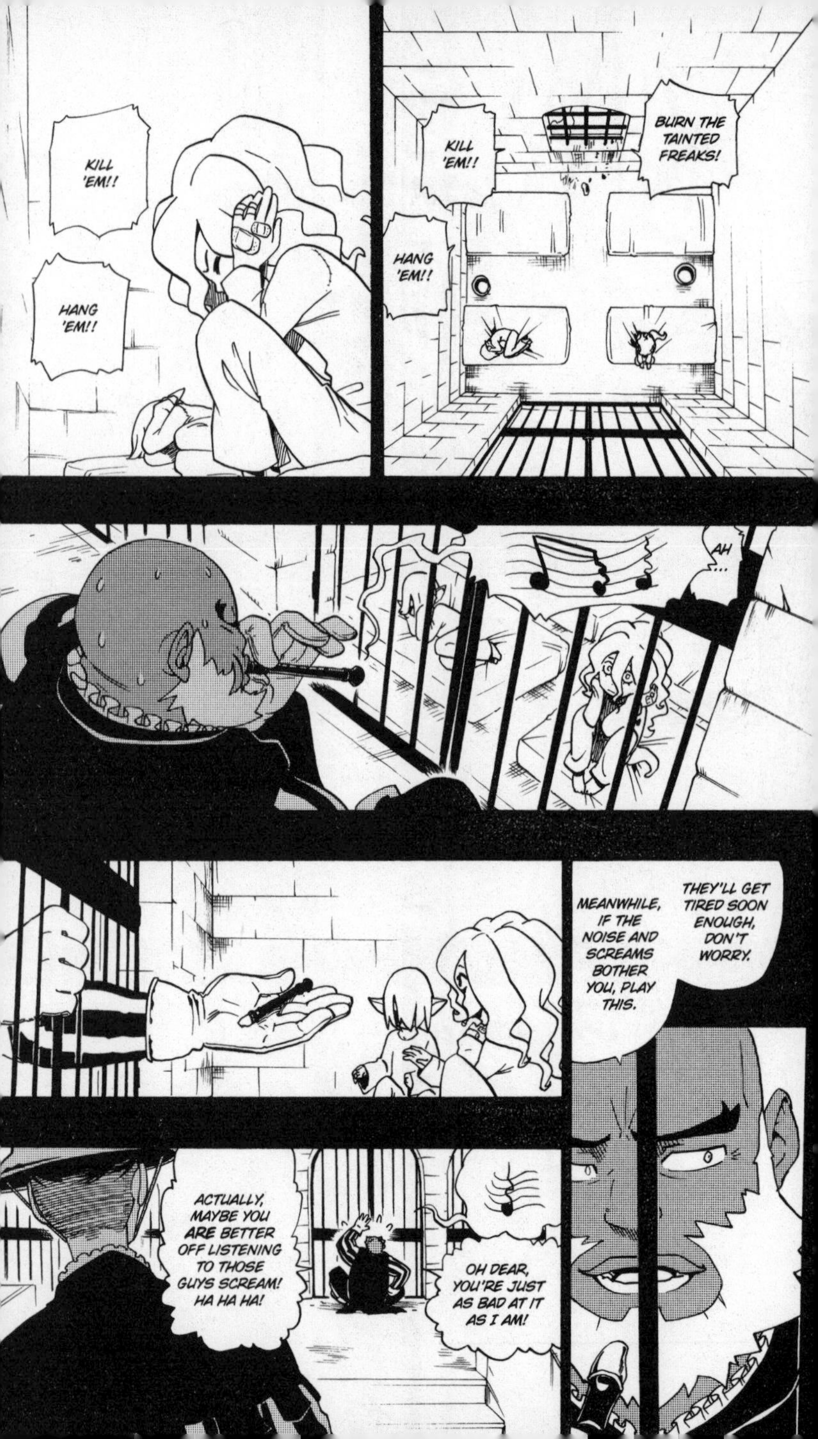
BURN THE TAINTED FREAKS!
KILL 'EM!!
HANG 'EM!!
KILL 'EM!!
HANG 'EM!!
AH ...
THEY'LL GET TIRED SOON ENOUGH, DON'T WORRY.
MEANWHILE, IF THE NOISE AND SCREAMS BOTHER YOU, PLAY THIS.
OH DEAR, YOU'RE JUST AS BAD AT IT AS I AM!
ACTUALLY, MAYBE YOU ARE BETTER OFF LISTENING TO THOSE GUYS SCREAM! HA HA HA!

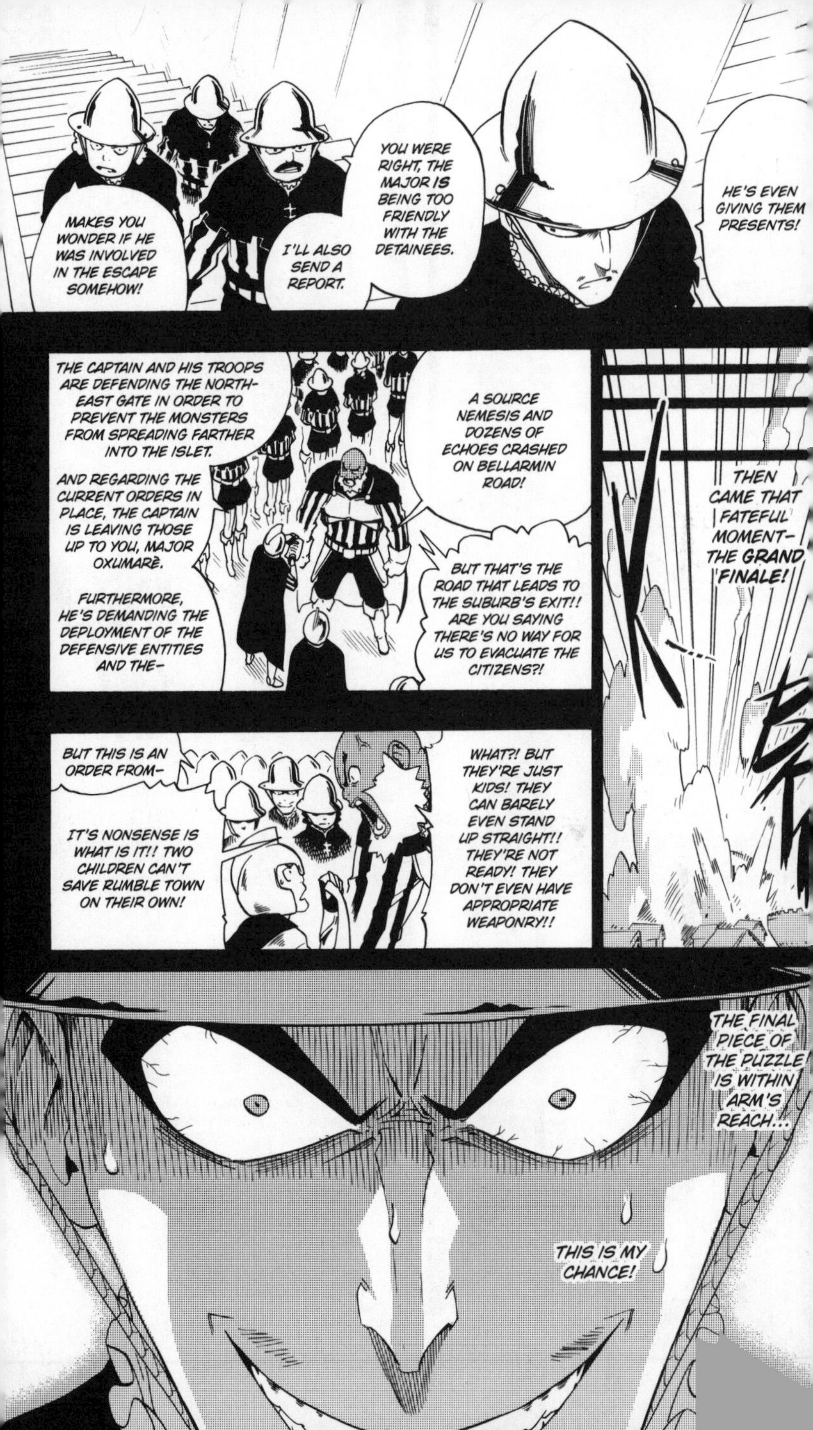
HE'S EVEN GIVING THEM PRESENTS!
YOU WERE RIGHT, THE MAJOR IS BEING TOO FRIENDLY WITH THE DETAINEES.
I'LL ALSO SEND A REPORT.
MAKES YOU WONDER IF HE WAS INVOLVED IN THE ESCAPE SOMEHOW!
THEN CAME THAT FATEFUL MOMENT– THE GRAND FINALE!
A SOURCE NEMESIS AND DOZENS OF ECHOES CRASHED ON BELLARMIN ROAD!
BUT THAT'S THE ROAD THAT LEADS TO THE SUBURB'S EXIT!! ARE YOU SAYING THERE'S NO WAY FOR US TO EVACUATE THE CITIZENS?!
THE CAPTAIN AND HIS TROOPS ARE DEFENDING THE NORTH-EAST GATE IN ORDER TO PREVENT THE MONSTERS FROM SPREADING FARTHER INTO THE ISLET.
AND REGARDING THE CURRENT ORDERS IN PLACE, THE CAPTAIN IS LEAVING THOSE UP TO YOU, MAJOR OXUMARÈ.
FURTHERMORE, HE'S DEMANDING THE DEPLOYMENT OF THE DEFENSIVE ENTITIES AND THE–
WHAT?! BUT THEY'RE JUST KIDS! THEY CAN BARELY EVEN STAND UP STRAIGHT!! THEY'RE NOT READY! THEY DON'T EVEN HAVE APPROPRIATE WEAPONRY!!
BUT THIS IS AN ORDER FROM–
IT'S NONSENSE IS WHAT IS IT!! TWO CHILDREN CAN'T SAVE RUMBLE TOWN ON THEIR OWN!
THE FINAL PIECE OF THE PUZZLE IS WITHIN ARM'S REACH...
THIS IS MY CHANCE!

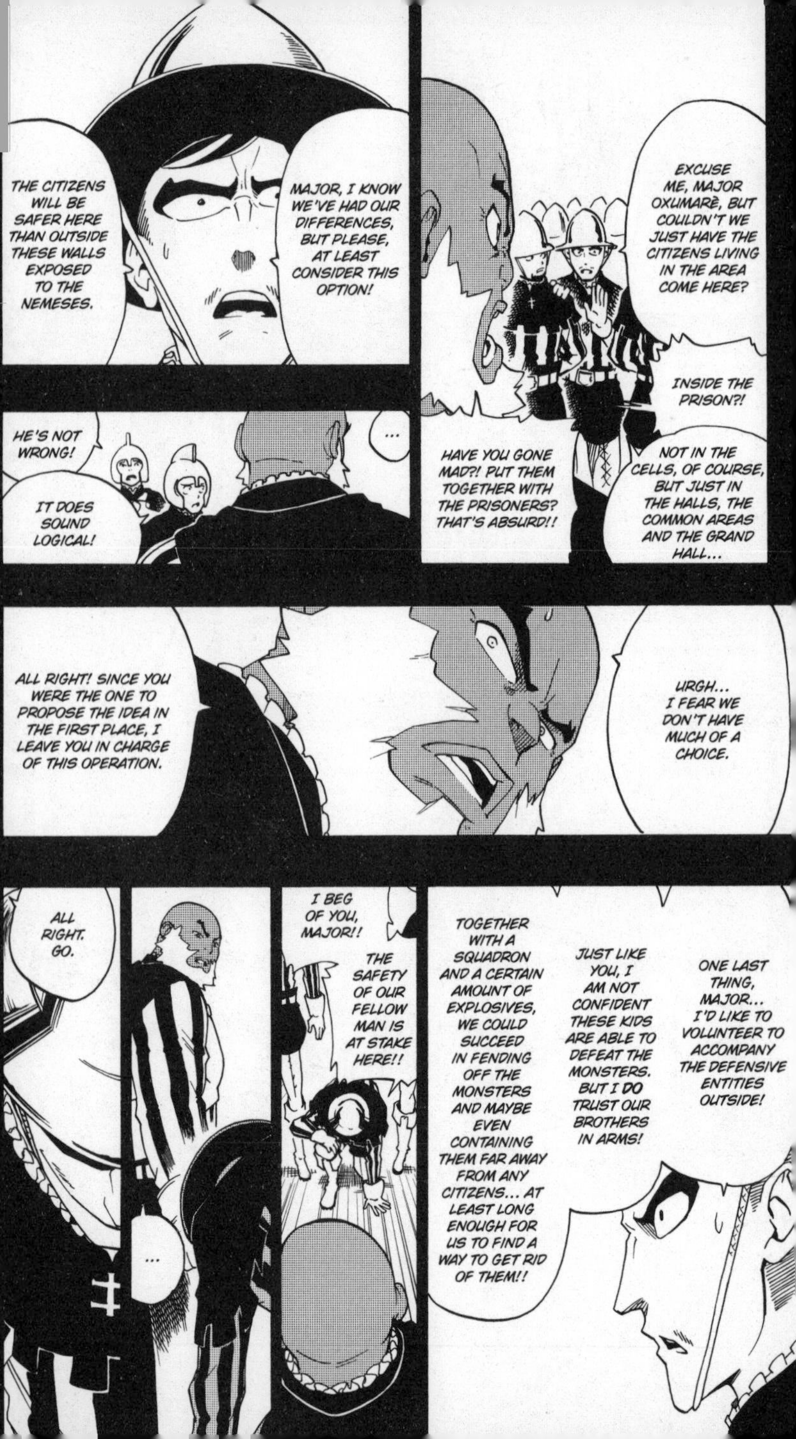
EXCUSE ME, MAJOR OXUMARÈ, BUT COULDN'T WE JUST HAVE THE CITIZENS LIVING IN THE AREA COME HERE?
INSIDE THE PRISON?!
HAVE YOU GONE MAD?! PUT THEM TOGETHER WITH THE PRISONERS? THAT'S ABSURD!!
NOT IN THE CELLS, OF COURSE, BUT JUST IN THE HALLS, THE COMMON AREAS AND THE GRAND HALL...
MAJOR, I KNOW WE'VE HAD OUR DIFFERENCES, BUT PLEASE, AT LEAST CONSIDER THIS OPTION!
THE CITIZENS WILL BE SAFER HERE THAN OUTSIDE THESE WALLS EXPOSED TO THE NEMESES.
...
HE'S NOT WRONG!
IT DOES SOUND LOGICAL!
URGH... I FEAR WE DON'T HAVE MUCH OF A CHOICE.
ALL RIGHT! SINCE YOU WERE THE ONE TO PROPOSE THE IDEA IN THE FIRST PLACE, I LEAVE YOU IN CHARGE OF THIS OPERATION.
ONE LAST THING, MAJOR... I'D LIKE TO VOLUNTEER TO ACCOMPANY THE DEFENSIVE ENTITIES OUTSIDE!
JUST LIKE YOU, I AM NOT CONFIDENT THESE KIDS ARE ABLE TO DEFEAT THE MONSTERS. BUT I DO TRUST OUR BROTHERS IN ARMS!
TOGETHER WITH A SQUADRON AND A CERTAIN AMOUNT OF EXPLOSIVES, WE COULD SUCCEED IN FENDING OFF THE MONSTERS AND MAYBE EVEN CONTAINING THEM FAR AWAY FROM ANY CITIZENS... AT LEAST LONG ENOUGH FOR US TO FIND A WAY TO GET RID OF THEM!!
I BEG OF YOU, MAJOR!!
THE SAFETY OF OUR FELLOW MAN IS AT STAKE HERE!!
...
ALL RIGHT. GO.

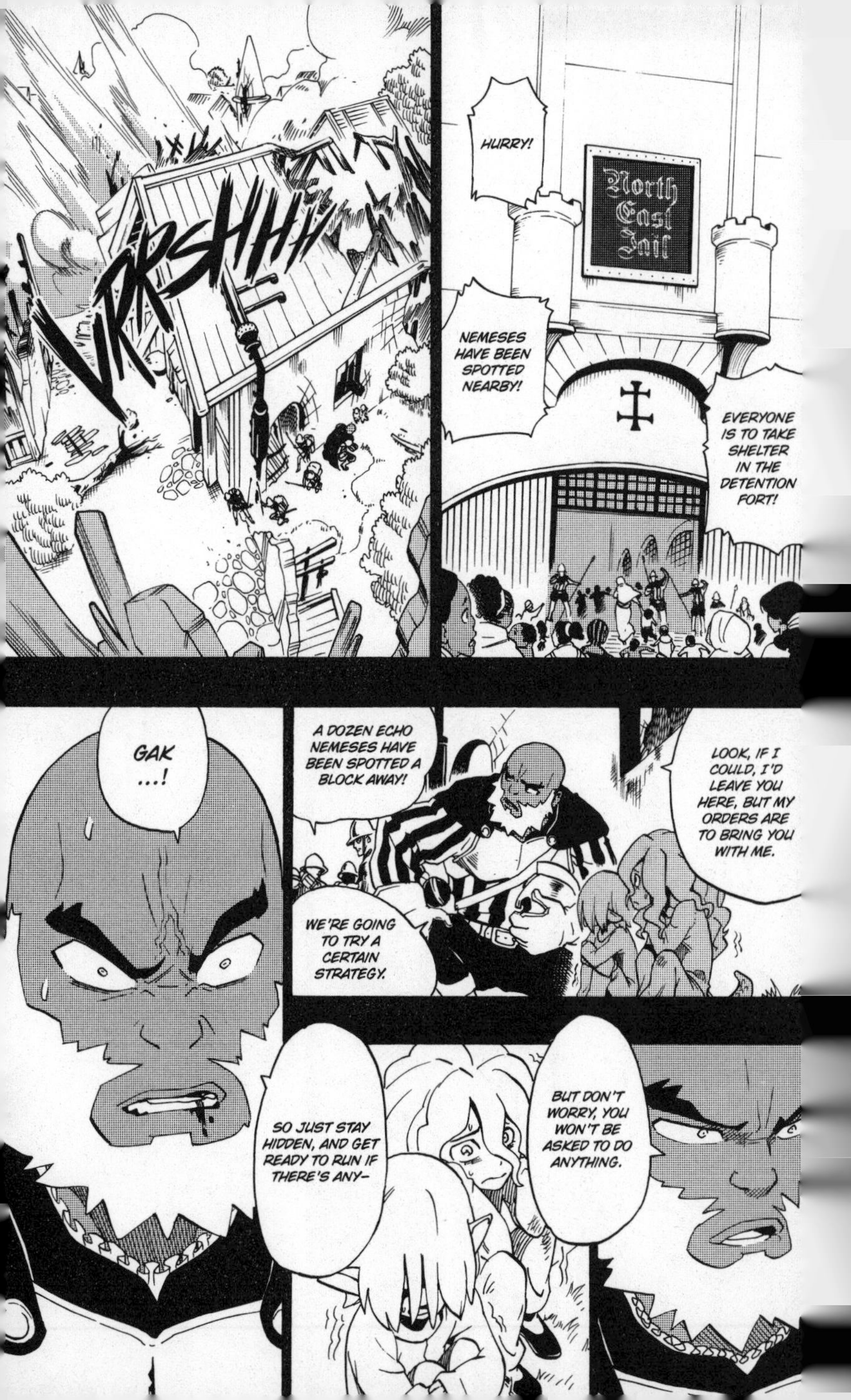

VRRSHHHH
HURRY!
NEMESES HAVE BEEN SPOTTED NEARBY!
North East Jail
EVERYONE IS TO TAKE SHELTER IN THE DETENTION FORT!
GAK ...!
A DOZEN ECHO NEMESES HAVE BEEN SPOTTED A BLOCK AWAY!
LOOK, IF I COULD, I'D LEAVE YOU HERE, BUT MY ORDERS ARE TO BRING YOU WITH ME.
WE'RE GOING TO TRY A CERTAIN STRATEGY.
BUT DON'T WORRY, YOU WON'T BE ASKED TO DO ANYTHING.
SO JUST STAY HIDDEN, AND GET READY TO RUN IF THERE'S ANY—

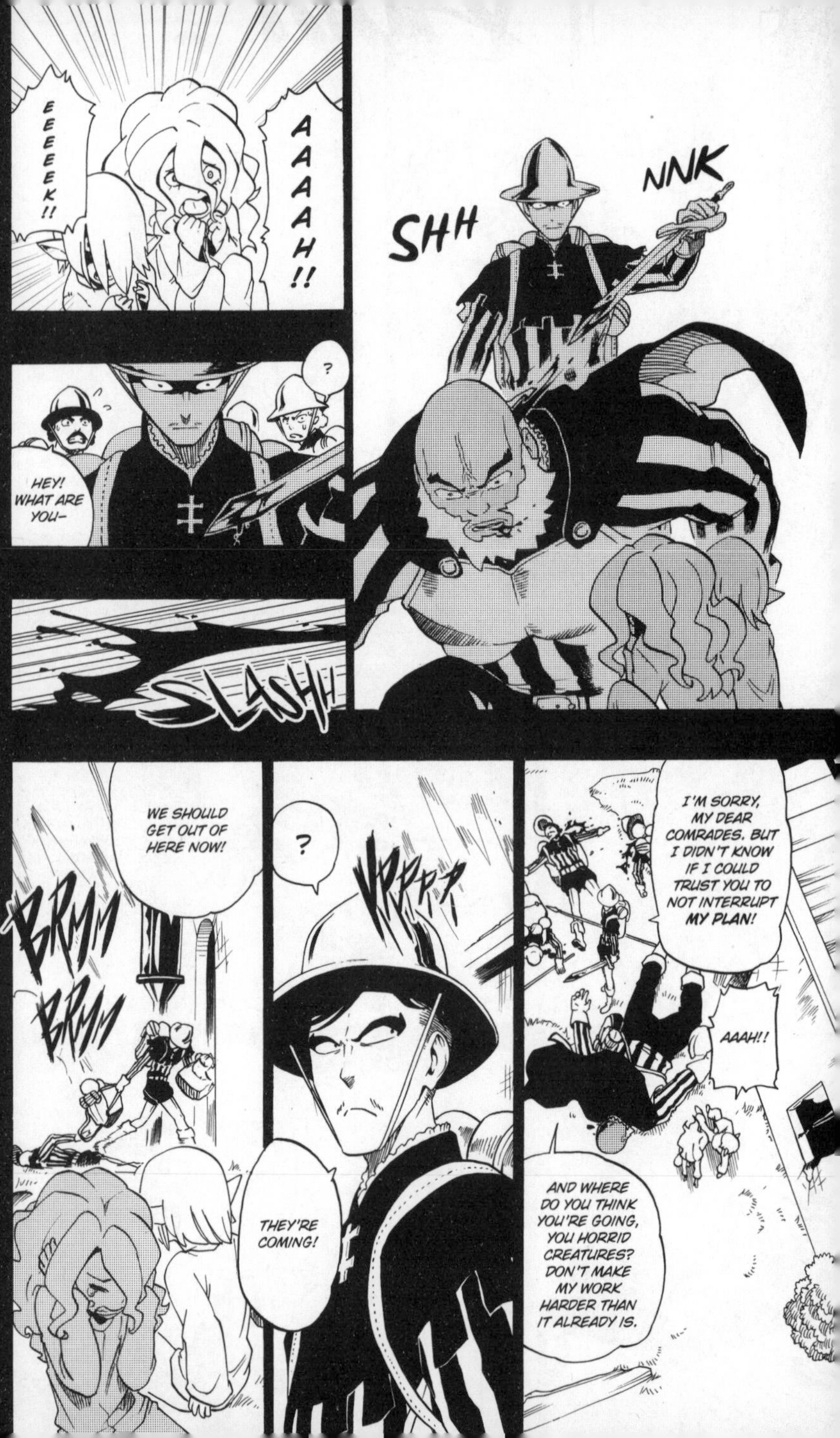
EEEEEK!!
AAAAAH!!
SHH
NNK
HEY! WHAT ARE YOU-
?
SLASH
WE SHOULD GET OUT OF HERE NOW!
BRMM
BRMM
?
VRRRR
THEY'RE COMING!
I'M SORRY, MY DEAR COMRADES. BUT I DIDN'T KNOW IF I COULD TRUST YOU TO NOT INTERRUPT MY PLAN!
AAAH!!
AND WHERE DO YOU THINK YOU'RE GOING, YOU HORRID CREATURES? DON'T MAKE MY WORK HARDER THAN IT ALREADY IS.

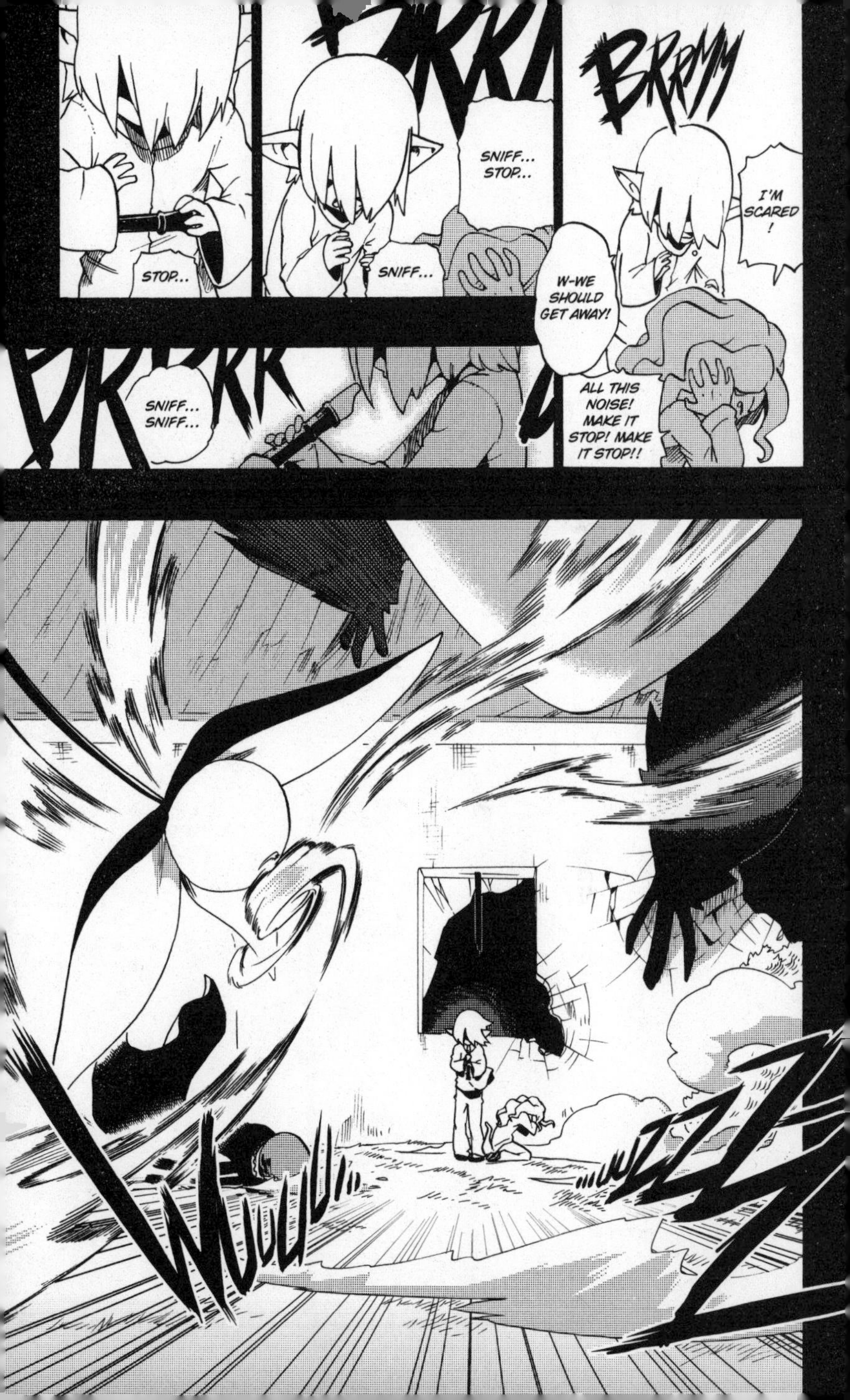
BRRMM
I'M SCARED!
DRRRR
SNIFF... STOP...
SNIFF...
STOP...
W-WE SHOULD GET AWAY!
ALL THIS NOISE! MAKE IT STOP! MAKE IT STOP!!
SNIFF... SNIFF...
DRRRK
...WZZZ
WUUU...

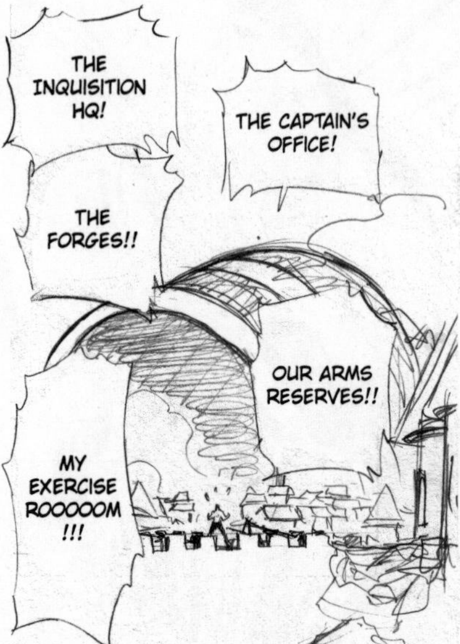
THE INQUISITION HQ!
THE CAPTAIN'S OFFICE!
THE FORGES!!
OUR ARMS RESERVES!!
MY EXERCISE ROOOOOM !!!

Chapter 17

THE FALL

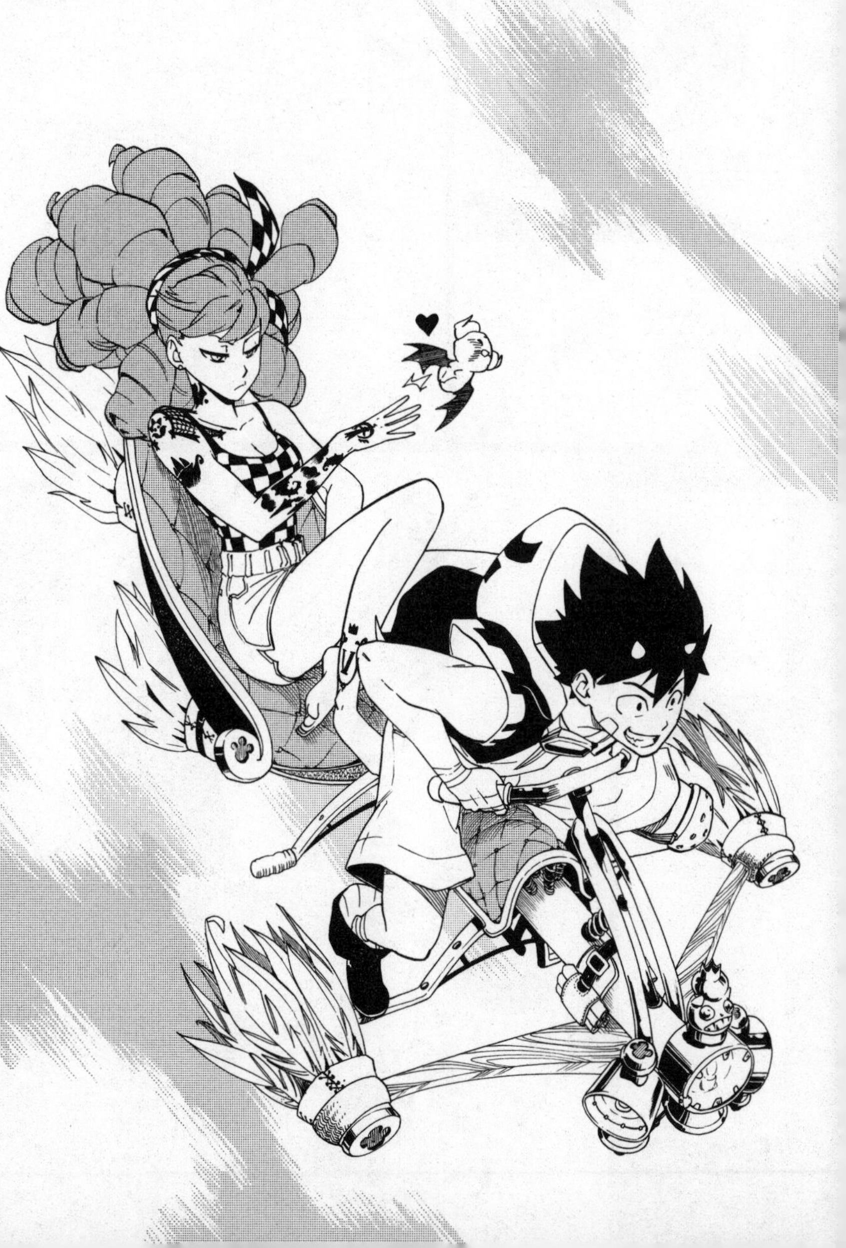

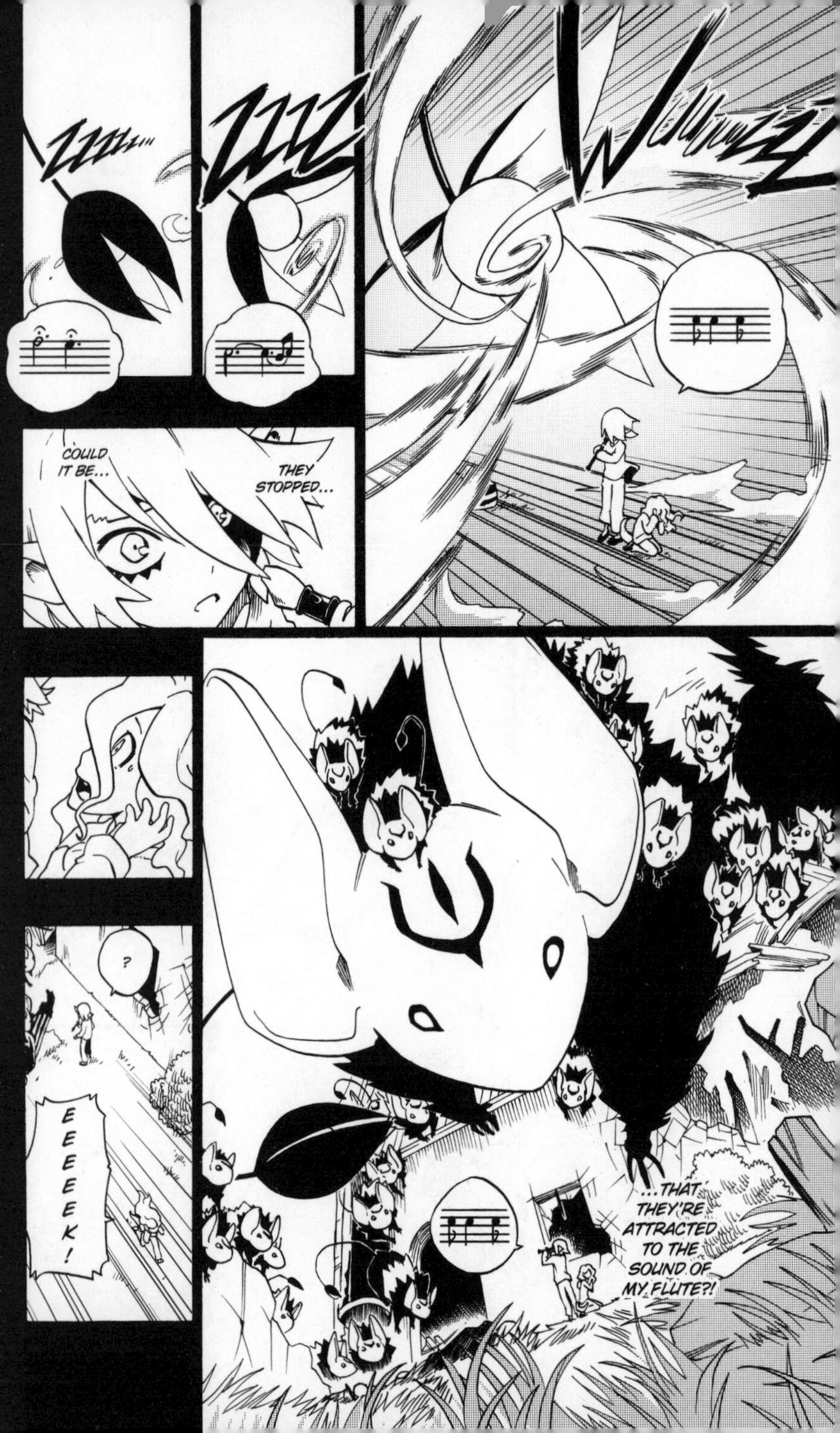

WHUMP
ZZZZ
ZZZZ...
THEY STOPPED...
COULD IT BE...
?
...THAT THEY'RE ATTRACTED TO THE SOUND OF MY FLUTE?!
EEEEEEK!

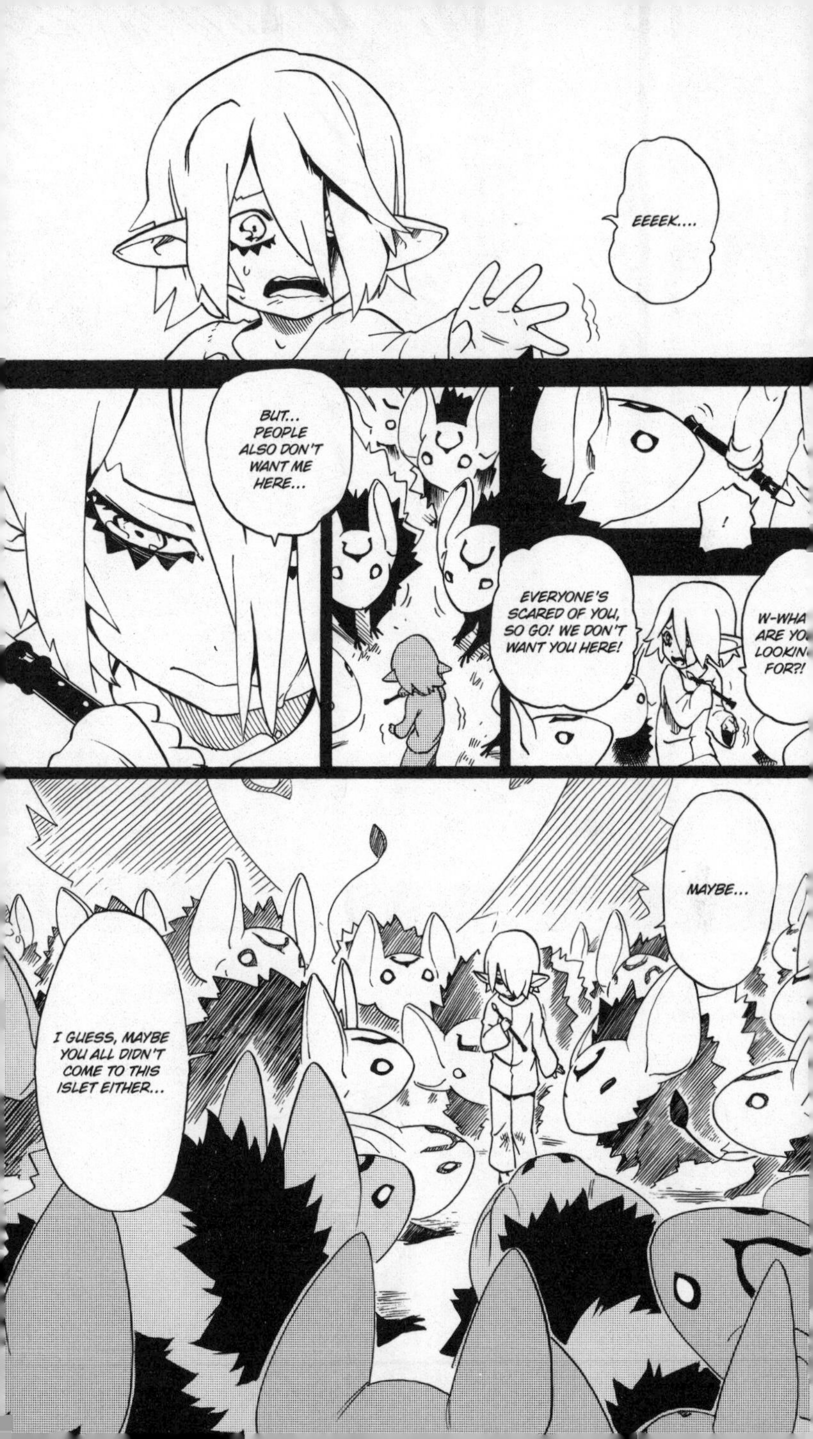
EEEEK....
!
W-WHA ARE YO LOOKIN FOR?!
EVERYONE'S SCARED OF YOU, SO GO! WE DON'T WANT YOU HERE!
BUT... PEOPLE ALSO DON'T WANT ME HERE...
MAYBE...
I GUESS, MAYBE YOU ALL DIDN'T COME TO THIS ISLET EITHER...

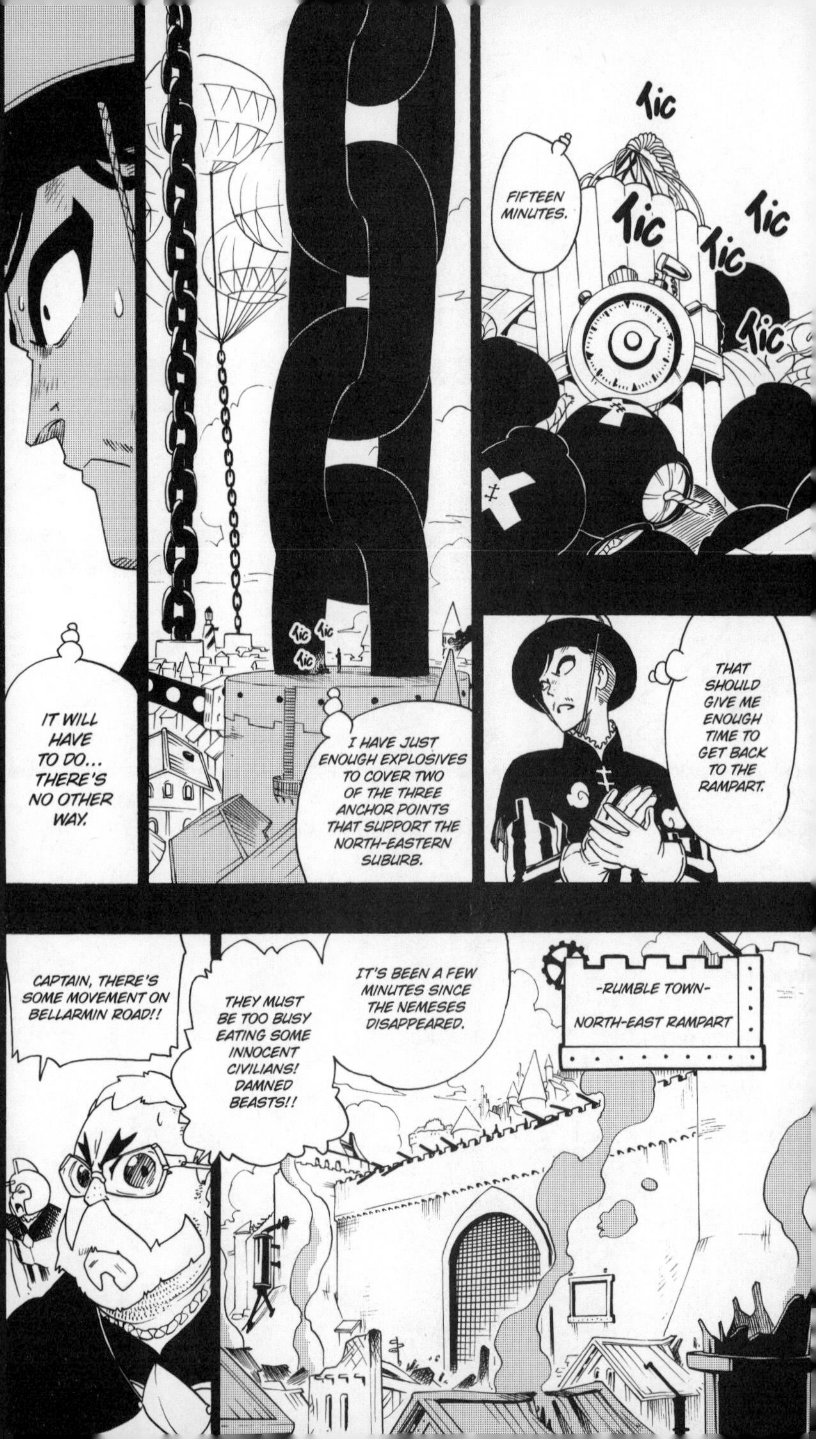

TIC
FIFTEEN MINUTES.
TIC
TIC
TIC
TIC
IT WILL HAVE TO DO... THERE'S NO OTHER WAY.
TIC TIC TIC
I HAVE JUST ENOUGH EXPLOSIVES TO COVER TWO OF THE THREE ANCHOR POINTS THAT SUPPORT THE NORTH-EASTERN SUBURB.
THAT SHOULD GIVE ME ENOUGH TIME TO GET BACK TO THE RAMPART.
-RUMBLE TOWN-
NORTH-EAST RAMPART
CAPTAIN, THERE'S SOME MOVEMENT ON BELLARMIN ROAD!!
IT'S BEEN A FEW MINUTES SINCE THE NEMESES DISAPPEARED.
THEY MUST BE TOO BUSY EATING SOME INNOCENT CIVILIANS! DAMNED BEASTS!!

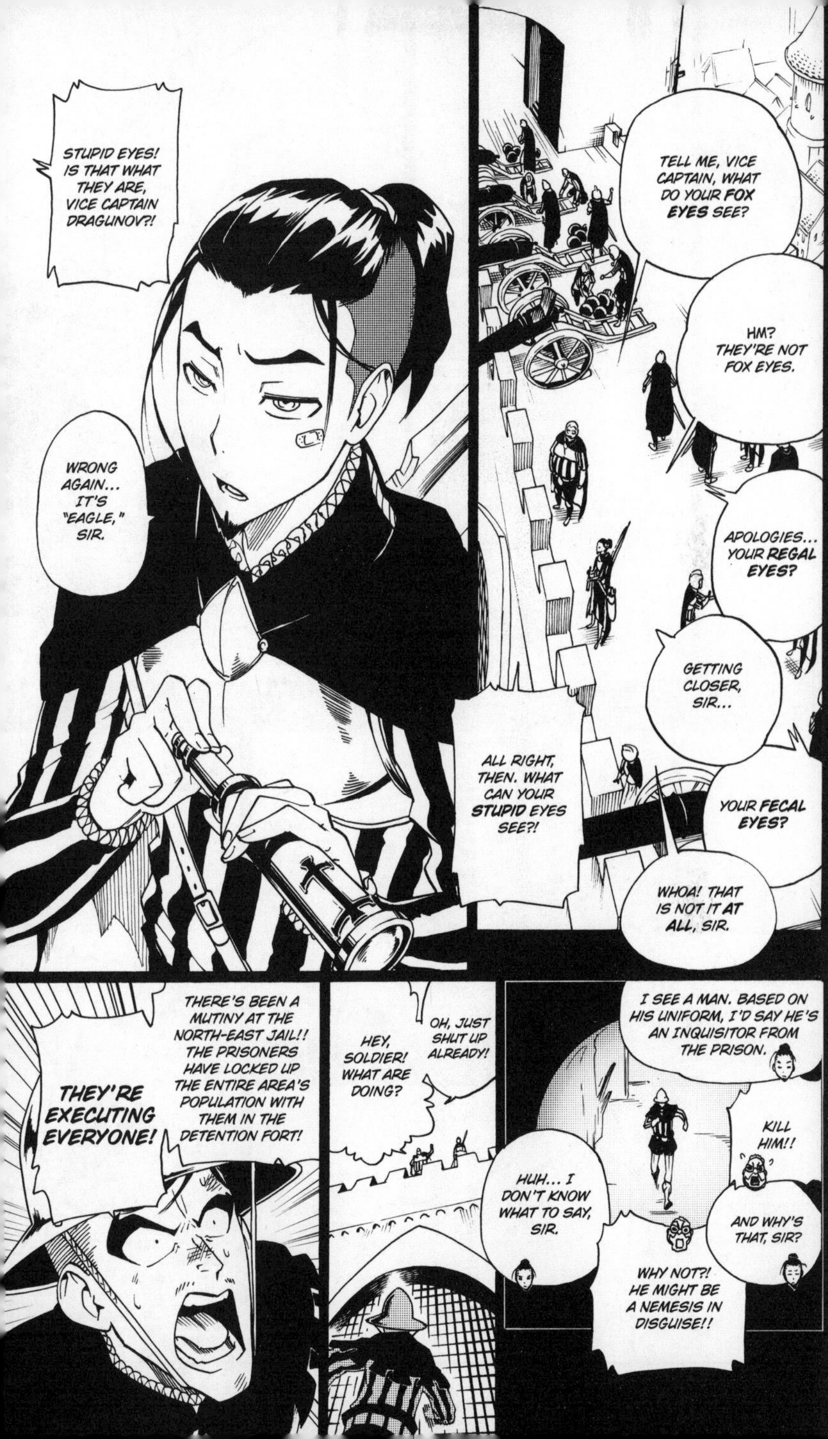

TELL ME, VICE CAPTAIN, WHAT DO YOUR FOX EYES SEE?
HM? THEY'RE NOT FOX EYES.
APOLOGIES... YOUR REGAL EYES?
GETTING CLOSER, SIR...
YOUR FECAL EYES?
WHOA! THAT IS NOT IT AT ALL, SIR.
ALL RIGHT, THEN. WHAT CAN YOUR STUPID EYES SEE?!
STUPID EYES! IS THAT WHAT THEY ARE, VICE CAPTAIN DRAGUNOV?!
WRONG AGAIN... IT'S "EAGLE," SIR.
I SEE A MAN. BASED ON HIS UNIFORM, I'D SAY HE'S AN INQUISITOR FROM THE PRISON.
KILL HIM!!
AND WHY'S THAT, SIR?
WHY NOT?! HE MIGHT BE A NEMESIS IN DISGUISE!!
HUH... I DON'T KNOW WHAT TO SAY, SIR.
HEY, SOLDIER! WHAT ARE DOING?
OH, JUST SHUT UP ALREADY!
THERE'S BEEN A MUTINY AT THE NORTH-EAST JAIL!! THE PRISONERS HAVE LOCKED UP THE ENTIRE AREA'S POPULATION WITH THEM IN THE DETENTION FORT!
THEY'RE EXECUTING EVERYONE!

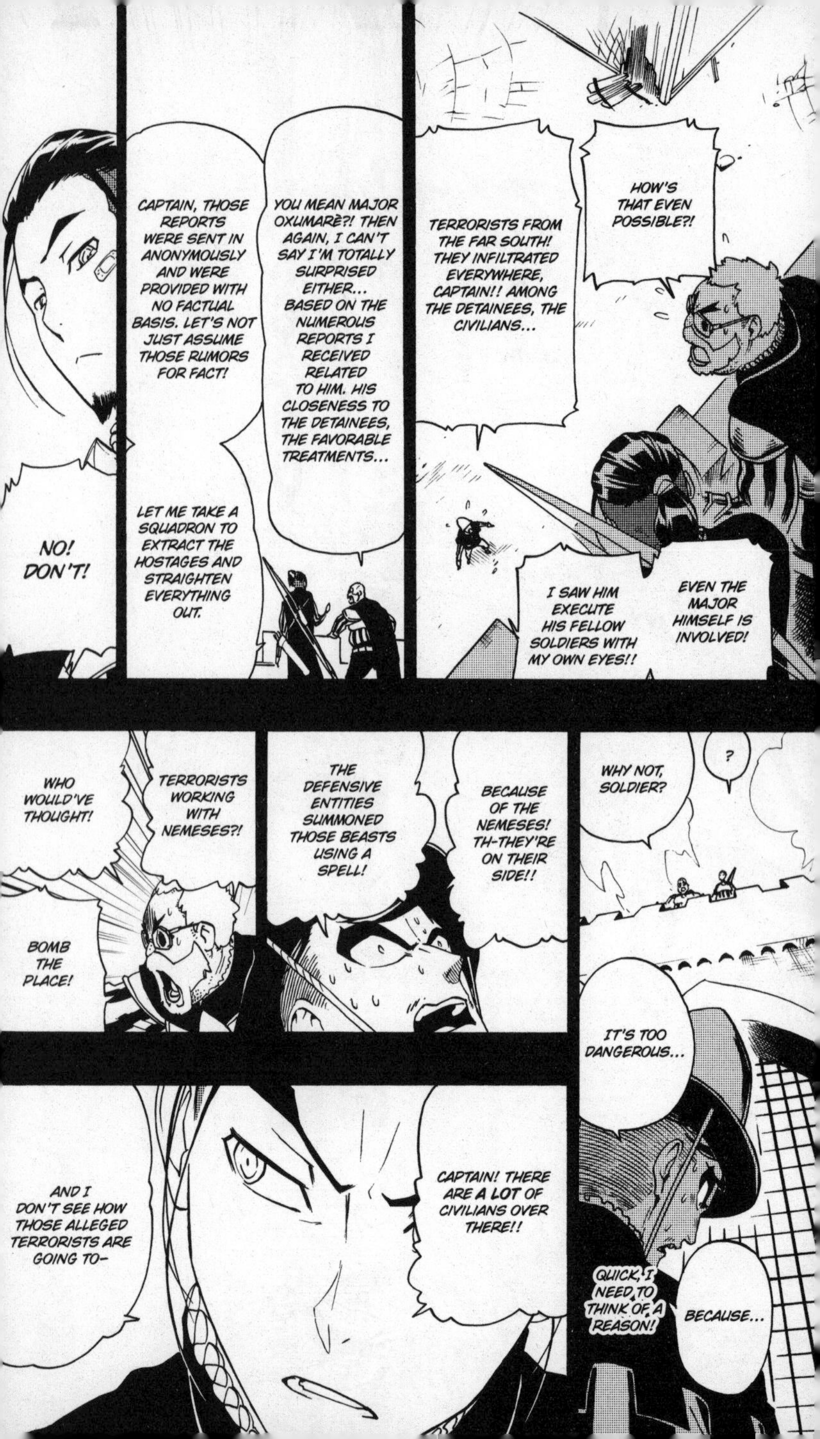
HOW'S THAT EVEN POSSIBLE?!
TERRORISTS FROM THE FAR SOUTH! THEY INFILTRATED EVERYWHERE, CAPTAIN!! AMONG THE DETAINEES, THE CIVILIANS...
EVEN THE MAJOR HIMSELF IS INVOLVED!
I SAW HIM EXECUTE HIS FELLOW SOLDIERS WITH MY OWN EYES!!
YOU MEAN MAJOR OXUMARÈ?! THEN AGAIN, I CAN'T SAY I'M TOTALLY SURPRISED EITHER... BASED ON THE NUMEROUS REPORTS I RECEIVED RELATED TO HIM. HIS CLOSENESS TO THE DETAINEES, THE FAVORABLE TREATMENTS...
CAPTAIN, THOSE REPORTS WERE SENT IN ANONYMOUSLY AND WERE PROVIDED WITH NO FACTUAL BASIS. LET'S NOT JUST ASSUME THOSE RUMORS FOR FACT!
LET ME TAKE A SQUADRON TO EXTRACT THE HOSTAGES AND STRAIGHTEN EVERYTHING OUT.
NO! DON'T!
WHY NOT, SOLDIER?
?
BECAUSE OF THE NEMESES! TH-THEY'RE ON THEIR SIDE!!
THE DEFENSIVE ENTITIES SUMMONED THOSE BEASTS USING A SPELL!
TERRORISTS WORKING WITH NEMESES?!
WHO WOULD'VE THOUGHT!
BOMB THE PLACE!
IT'S TOO DANGEROUS...
QUICK, I NEED TO THINK OF A REASON!
BECAUSE...
CAPTAIN! THERE ARE A LOT OF CIVILIANS OVER THERE!!
AND I DON'T SEE HOW THOSE ALLEGED TERRORISTS ARE GOING TO-

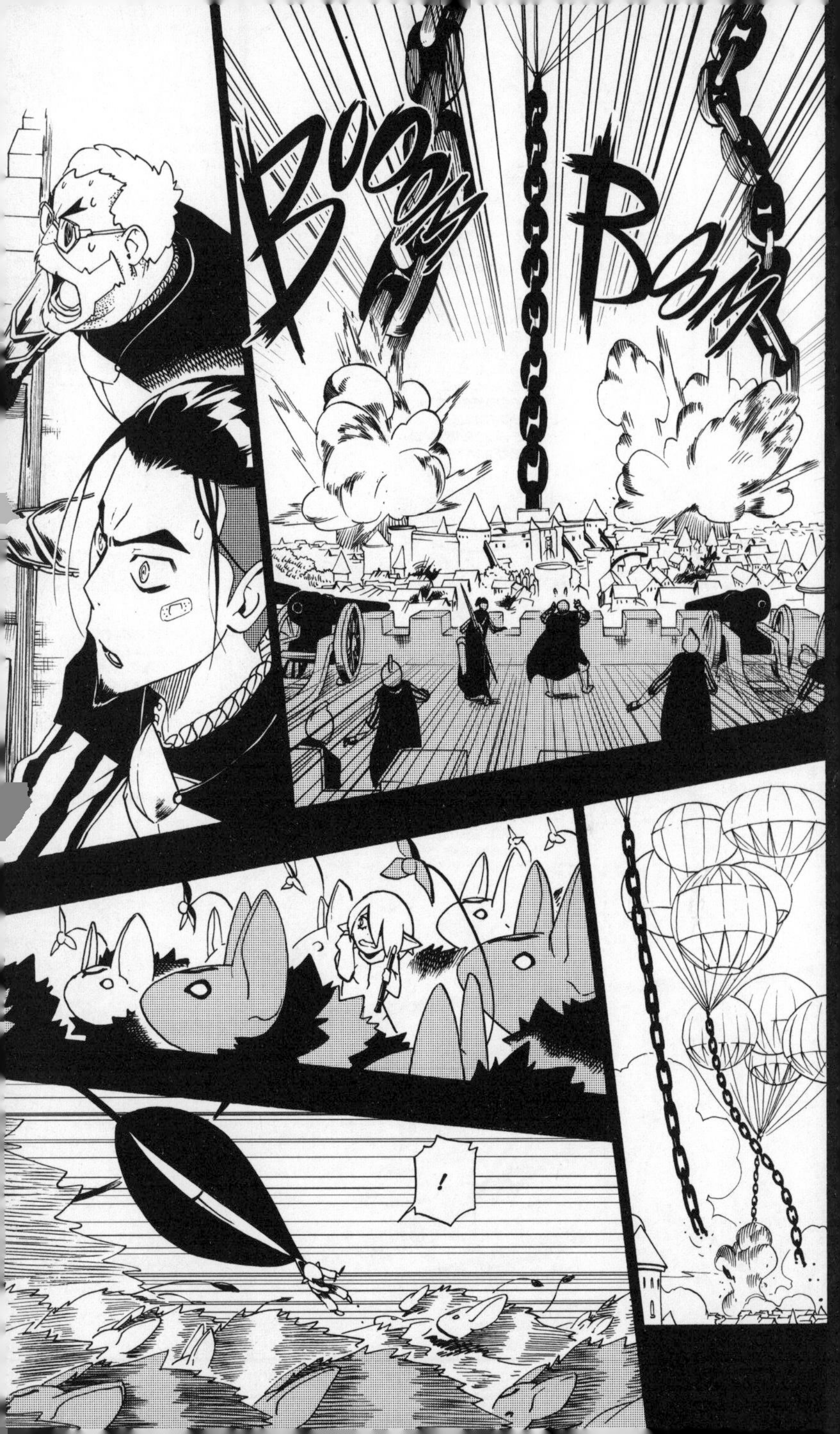
BOOOM
BOOM
!

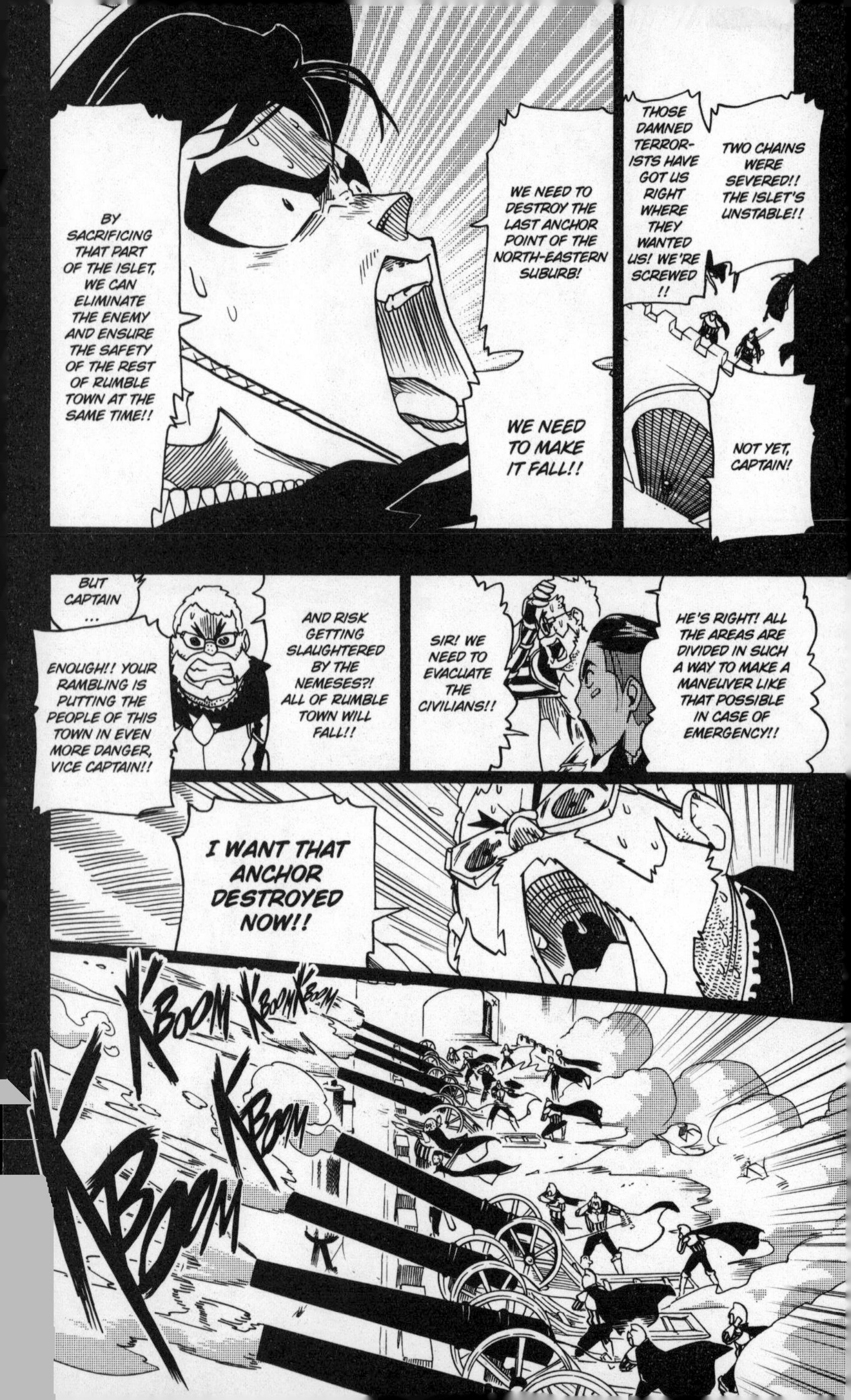

TWO CHAINS WERE SEVERED!! THE ISLET'S UNSTABLE!!
THOSE DAMNED TERROR-ISTS HAVE GOT US RIGHT WHERE THEY WANTED US! WE'RE SCREWED!!
NOT YET, CAPTAIN!
WE NEED TO MAKE IT FALL!!
WE NEED TO DESTROY THE LAST ANCHOR POINT OF THE NORTH-EASTERN SUBURB!
BY SACRIFICING THAT PART OF THE ISLET, WE CAN ELIMINATE THE ENEMY AND ENSURE THE SAFETY OF THE REST OF RUMBLE TOWN AT THE SAME TIME!!
HE'S RIGHT! ALL THE AREAS ARE DIVIDED IN SUCH A WAY TO MAKE A MANEUVER LIKE THAT POSSIBLE IN CASE OF EMERGENCY!!
SIR! WE NEED TO EVACUATE THE CIVILIANS!!
AND RISK GETTING SLAUGHTERED BY THE NEMESES?! ALL OF RUMBLE TOWN WILL FALL!!
BUT CAPTAIN...
ENOUGH!! YOUR RAMBLING IS PUTTING THE PEOPLE OF THIS TOWN IN EVEN MORE DANGER, VICE CAPTAIN!!
I WANT THAT ANCHOR DESTROYED NOW!!
KBOOM KBOOM KBOOM
KBOOM
KBOOM

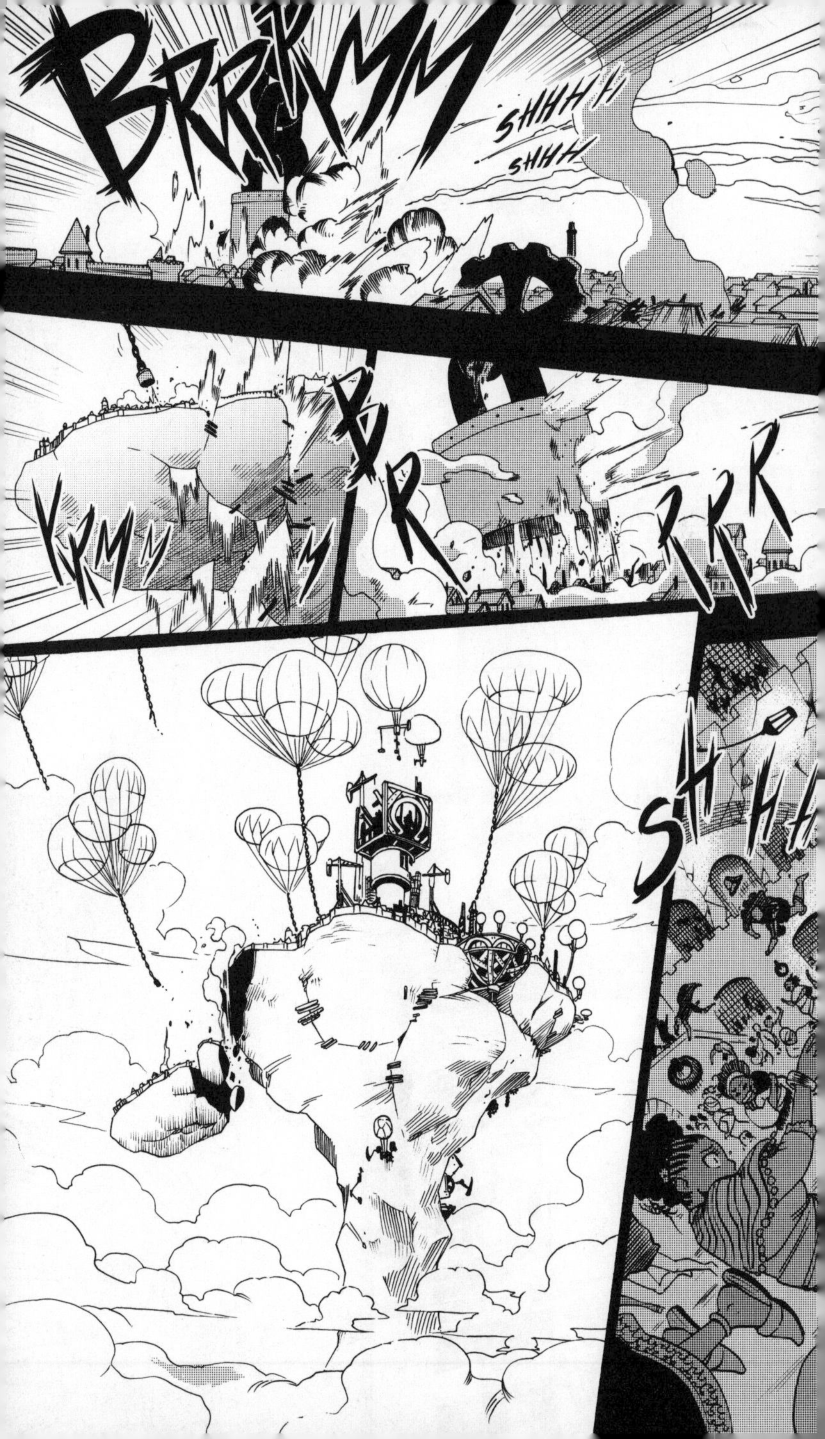
BRRMM
SHHHH
SHHH
KRMM
BR
RRR
SHH

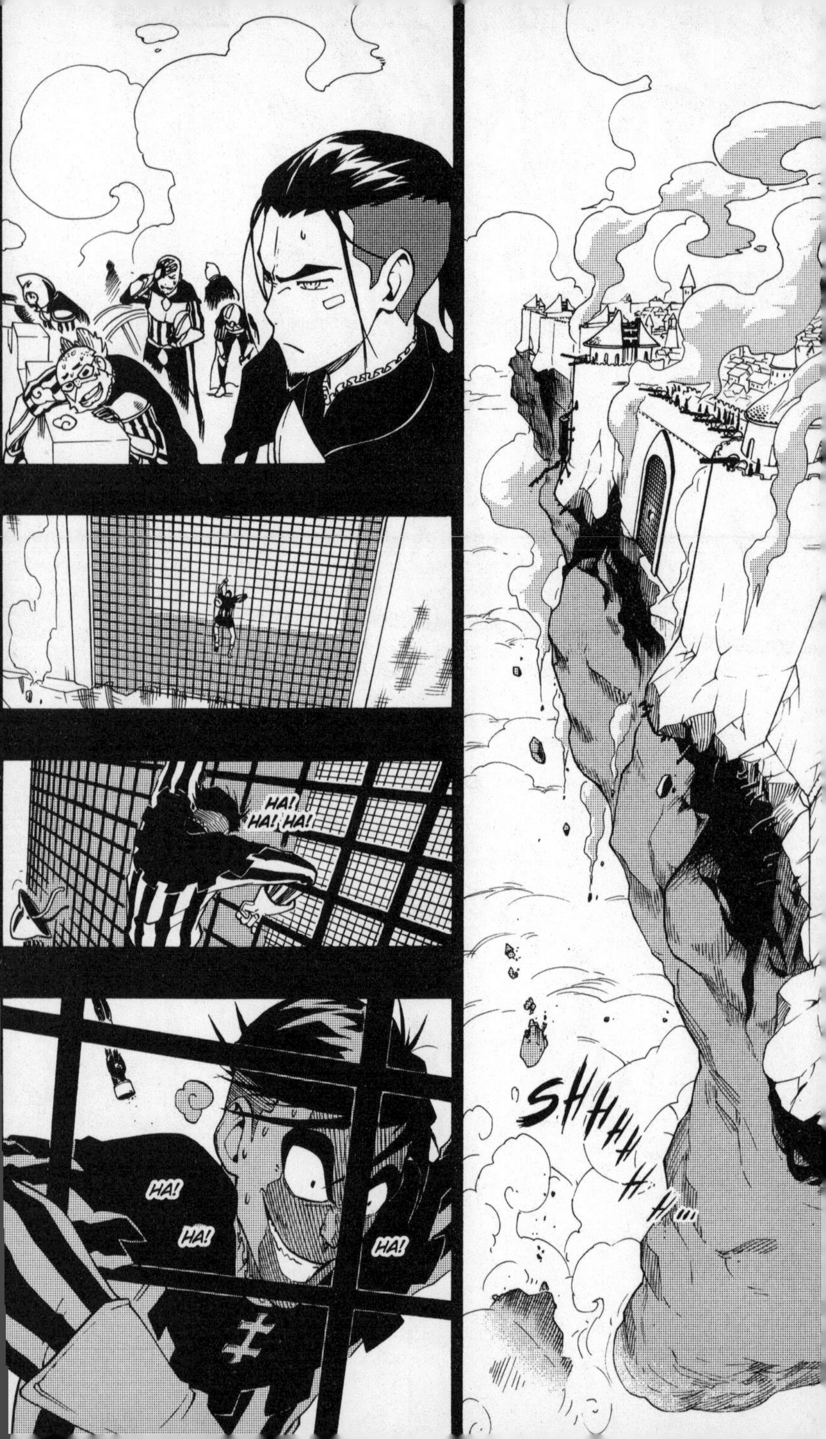
SHHHHHH...
HA! HA! HA!
HA!
HA!
HA!

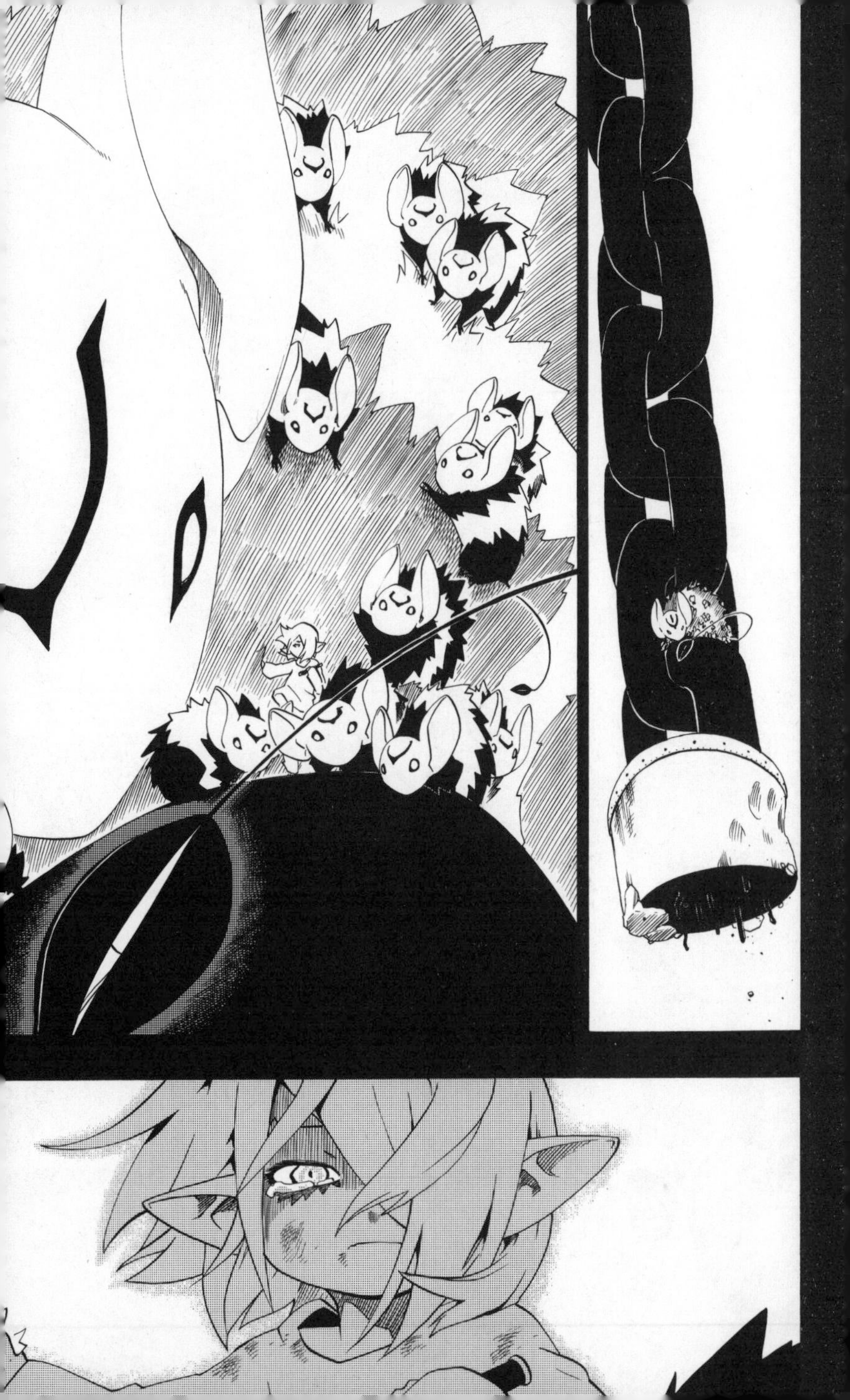

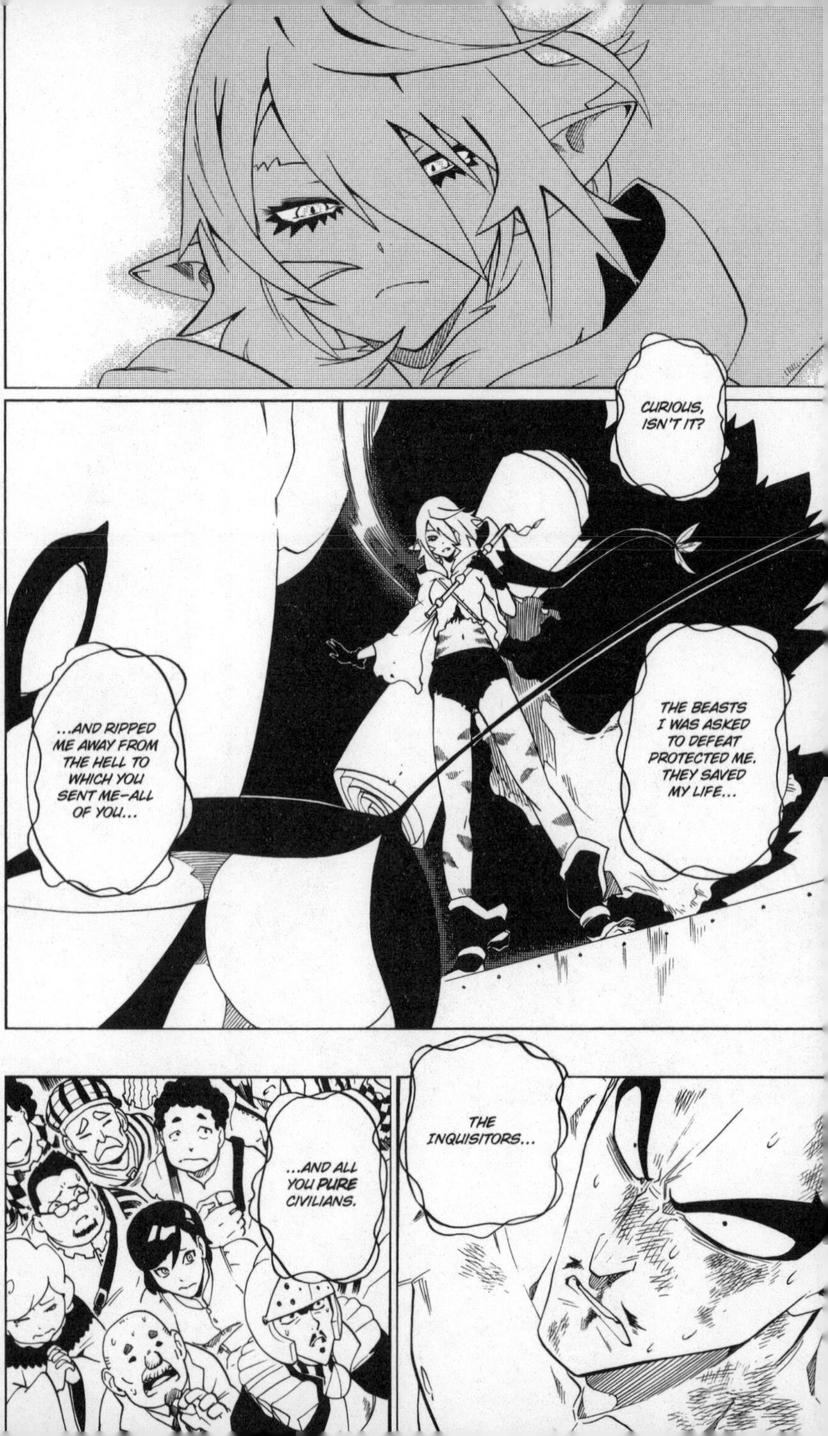
CURIOUS, ISN'T IT?
THE BEASTS I WAS ASKED TO DEFEAT PROTECTED ME. THEY SAVED MY LIFE...
...AND RIPPED ME AWAY FROM THE HELL TO WHICH YOU SENT ME-ALL OF YOU...
THE INQUISITORS...
...AND ALL YOU PURE CIVILIANS.

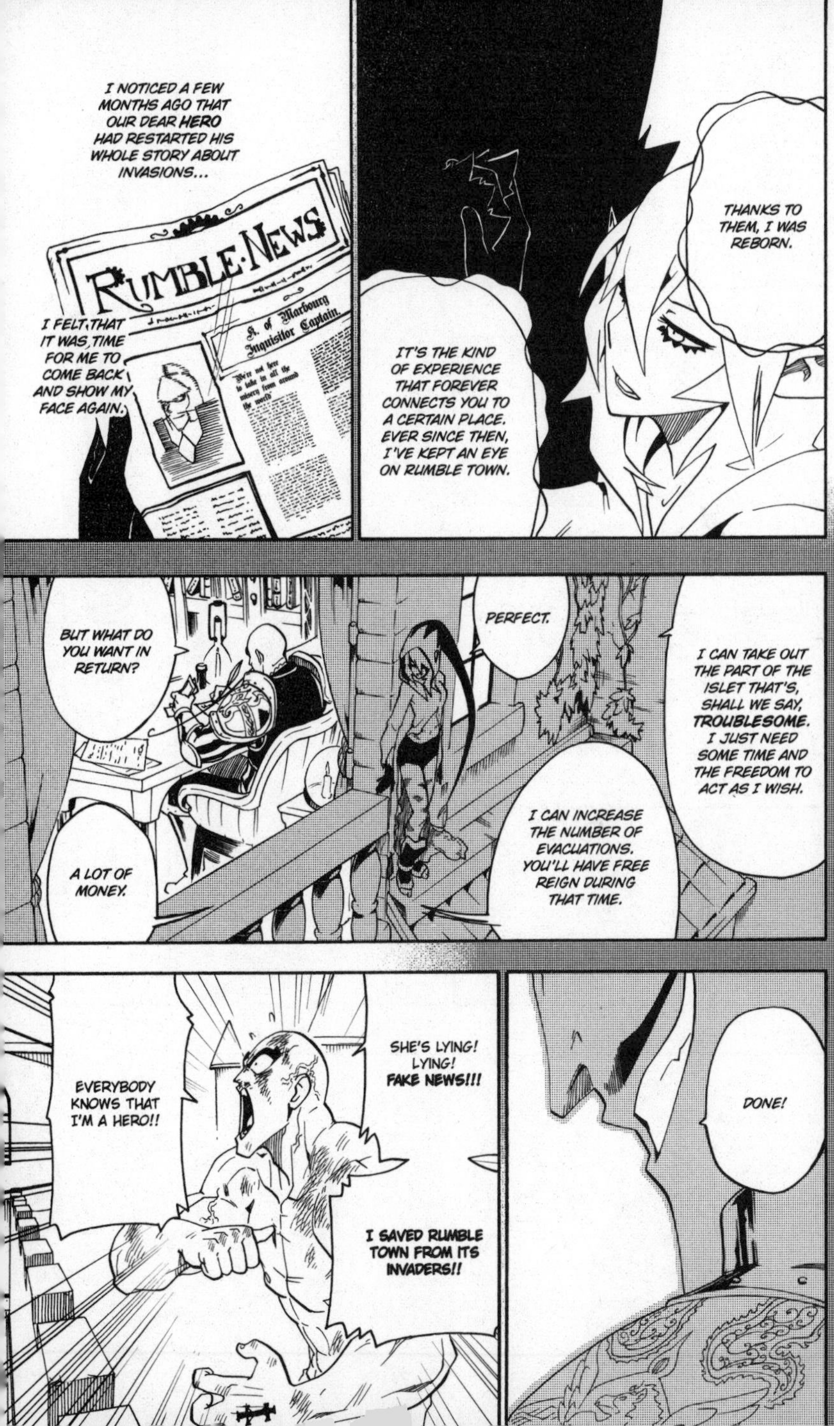
I NOTICED A FEW MONTHS AGO THAT OUR DEAR HERO HAD RESTARTED HIS WHOLE STORY ABOUT INVASIONS...
RUMBLE·NEWS
Inquisitor Captain.
I FELT THAT IT WAS TIME FOR ME TO COME BACK AND SHOW MY FACE AGAIN.
IT'S THE KIND OF EXPERIENCE THAT FOREVER CONNECTS YOU TO A CERTAIN PLACE. EVER SINCE THEN, I'VE KEPT AN EYE ON RUMBLE TOWN.
THANKS TO THEM, I WAS REBORN.
BUT WHAT DO YOU WANT IN RETURN?
A LOT OF MONEY.
PERFECT.
I CAN INCREASE THE NUMBER OF EVACUATIONS. YOU'LL HAVE FREE REIGN DURING THAT TIME.
I CAN TAKE OUT THE PART OF THE ISLET THAT'S, SHALL WE SAY, TROUBLESOME. I JUST NEED SOME TIME AND THE FREEDOM TO ACT AS I WISH.
EVERYBODY KNOWS THAT I'M A HERO!!
SHE'S LYING! LYING! FAKE NEWS!!!
I SAVED RUMBLE TOWN FROM ITS INVADERS!!
DONE!

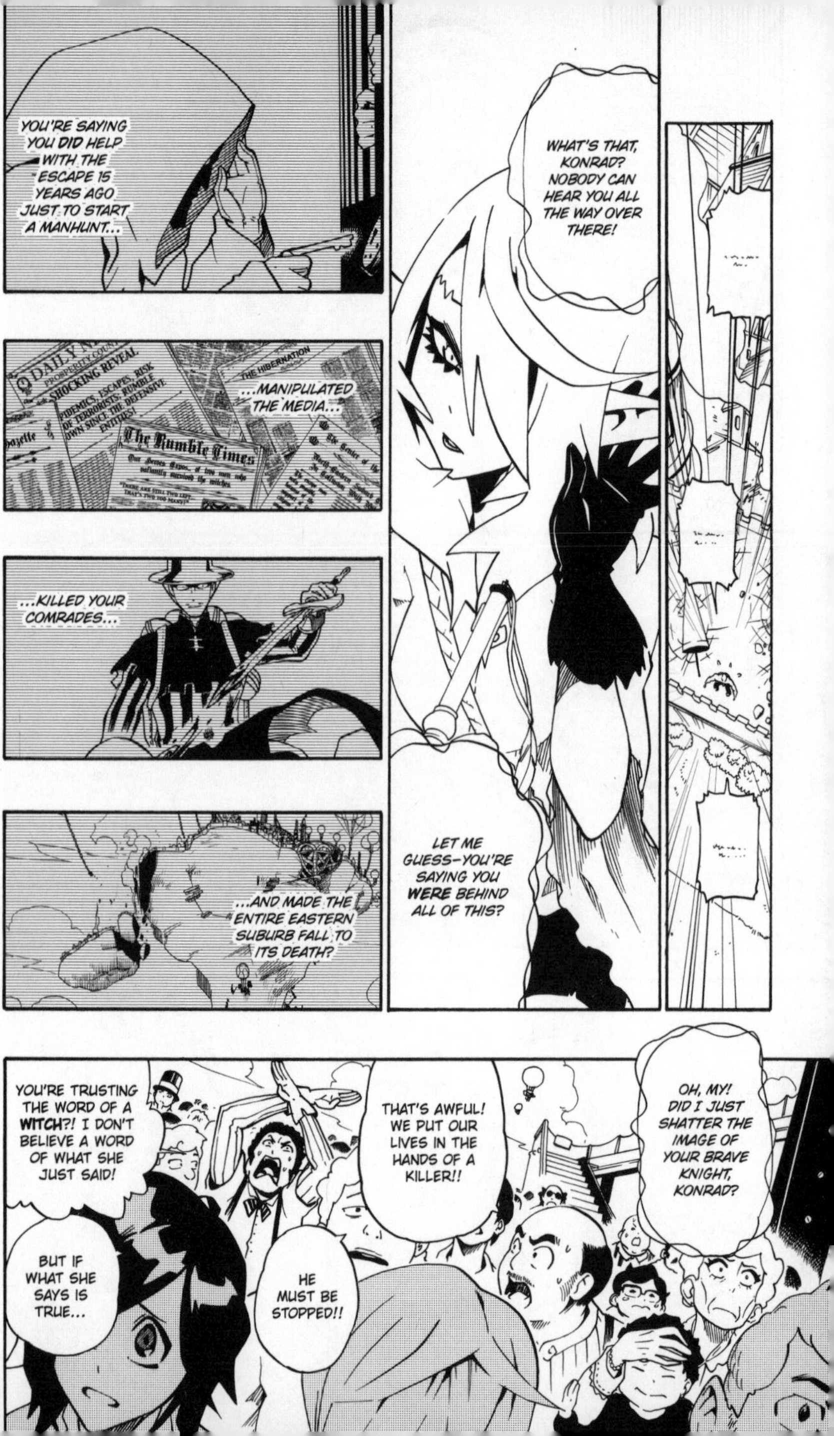
WHAT'S THAT, KONRAD? NOBODY CAN HEAR YOU ALL THE WAY OVER THERE!
LET ME GUESS—YOU'RE SAYING YOU WERE BEHIND ALL OF THIS?
YOU'RE SAYING YOU DID HELP WITH THE ESCAPE 15 YEARS AGO JUST TO START A MANHUNT...
SHOCKING REVEAL
THE HIBERNATION
The Rumble Times
...MANIPULATED THE MEDIA...
...KILLED YOUR COMRADES...
...AND MADE THE ENTIRE EASTERN SUBURB FALL TO ITS DEATH?
OH, MY! DID I JUST SHATTER THE IMAGE OF YOUR BRAVE KNIGHT, KONRAD?
THAT'S AWFUL! WE PUT OUR LIVES IN THE HANDS OF A KILLER!!
YOU'RE TRUSTING THE WORD OF A WITCH?! I DON'T BELIEVE A WORD OF WHAT SHE JUST SAID!
HE MUST BE STOPPED!!
BUT IF WHAT SHE SAYS IS TRUE...

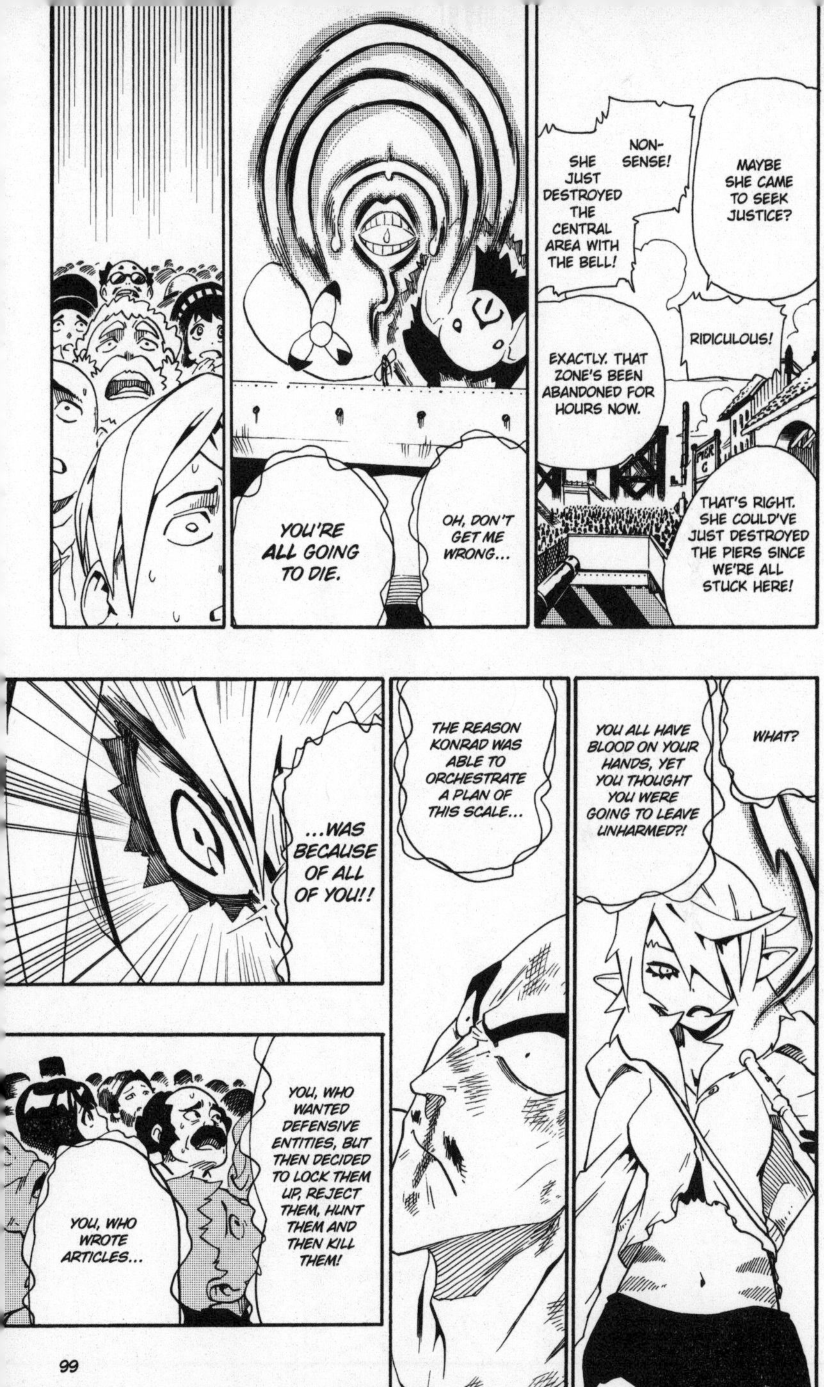
MAYBE SHE CAME TO SEEK JUSTICE?
NON-SENSE!
SHE JUST DESTROYED THE CENTRAL AREA WITH THE BELL!
RIDICULOUS!
EXACTLY. THAT ZONE'S BEEN ABANDONED FOR HOURS NOW.
THAT'S RIGHT. SHE COULD'VE JUST DESTROYED THE PIERS SINCE WE'RE ALL STUCK HERE!
PIER C
OH, DON'T GET ME WRONG...
YOU'RE ALL GOING TO DIE.
WHAT?
YOU ALL HAVE BLOOD ON YOUR HANDS, YET YOU THOUGHT YOU WERE GOING TO LEAVE UNHARMED?!
THE REASON KONRAD WAS ABLE TO ORCHESTRATE A PLAN OF THIS SCALE...
...WAS BECAUSE OF ALL OF YOU!!
YOU, WHO WANTED DEFENSIVE ENTITIES, BUT THEN DECIDED TO LOCK THEM UP, REJECT THEM, HUNT THEM AND THEN KILL THEM!
YOU, WHO WROTE ARTICLES...

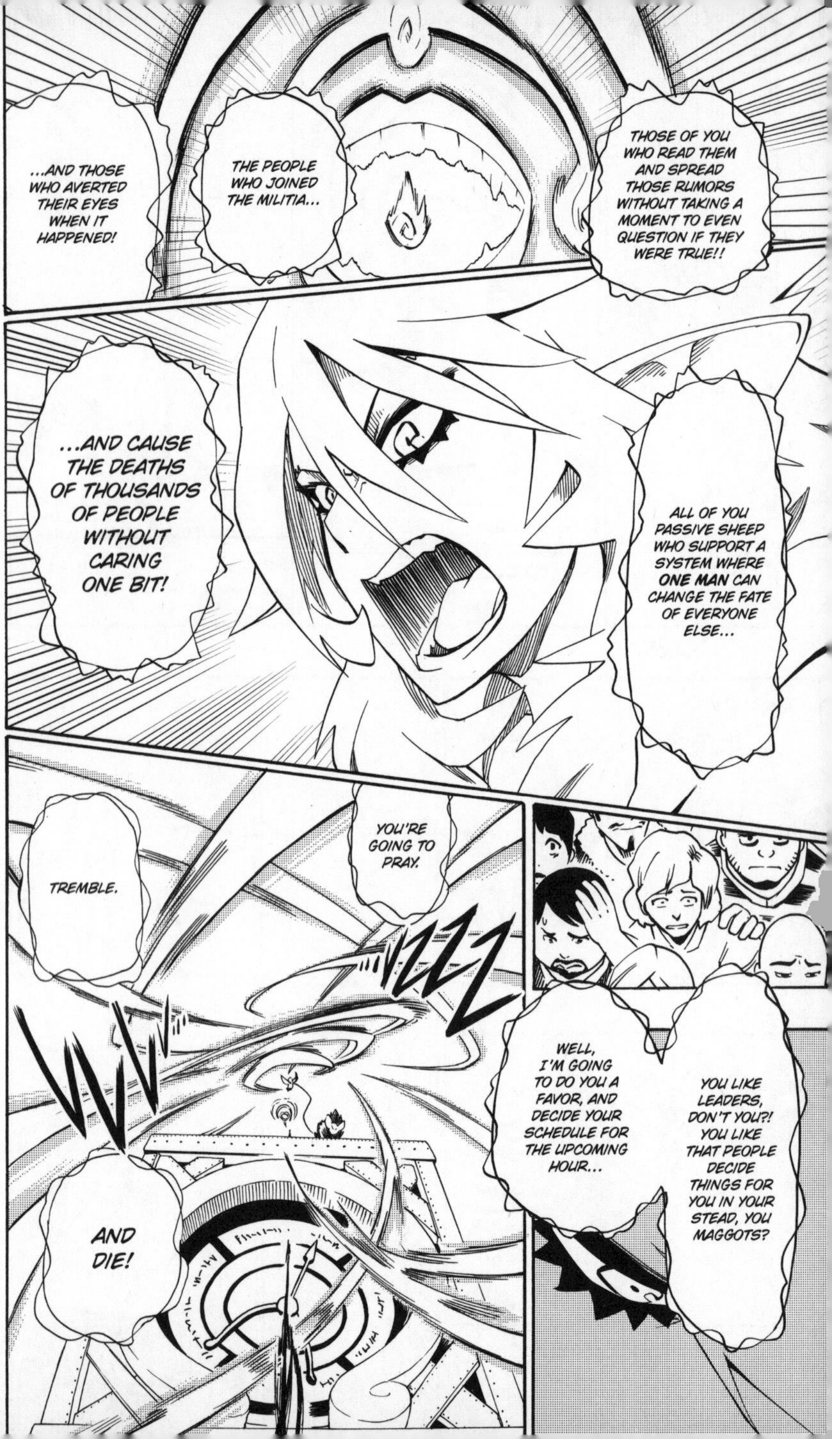
THOSE OF YOU WHO READ THEM AND SPREAD THOSE RUMORS WITHOUT TAKING A MOMENT TO EVEN QUESTION IF THEY WERE TRUE!!
THE PEOPLE WHO JOINED THE MILITIA...
...AND THOSE WHO AVERTED THEIR EYES WHEN IT HAPPENED!
ALL OF YOU PASSIVE SHEEP WHO SUPPORT A SYSTEM WHERE **ONE MAN** CAN CHANGE THE FATE OF EVERYONE ELSE...
...AND CAUSE THE DEATHS OF THOUSANDS OF PEOPLE WITHOUT CARING ONE BIT!
YOU LIKE LEADERS, DON'T YOU?! YOU LIKE THAT PEOPLE DECIDE THINGS FOR YOU IN YOUR STEAD, YOU MAGGOTS?
WELL, I'M GOING TO DO YOU A FAVOR, AND DECIDE YOUR SCHEDULE FOR THE UPCOMING HOUR...
YOU'RE GOING TO PRAY.
TREMBLE.
AND DIE!

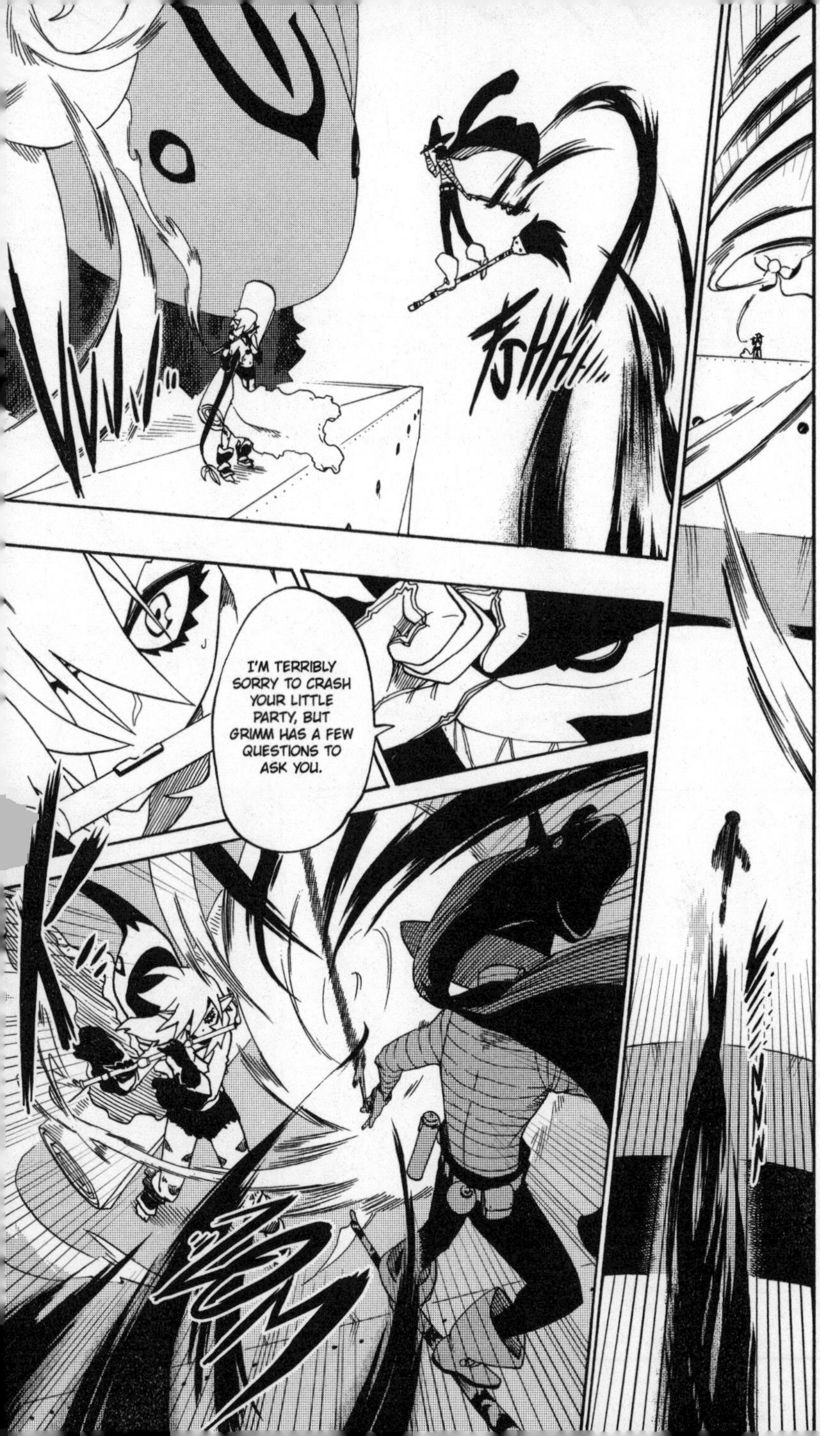
FSHHH...
I'M TERRIBLY SORRY TO CRASH YOUR LITTLE PARTY, BUT GRIMM HAS A FEW QUESTIONS TO ASK YOU.

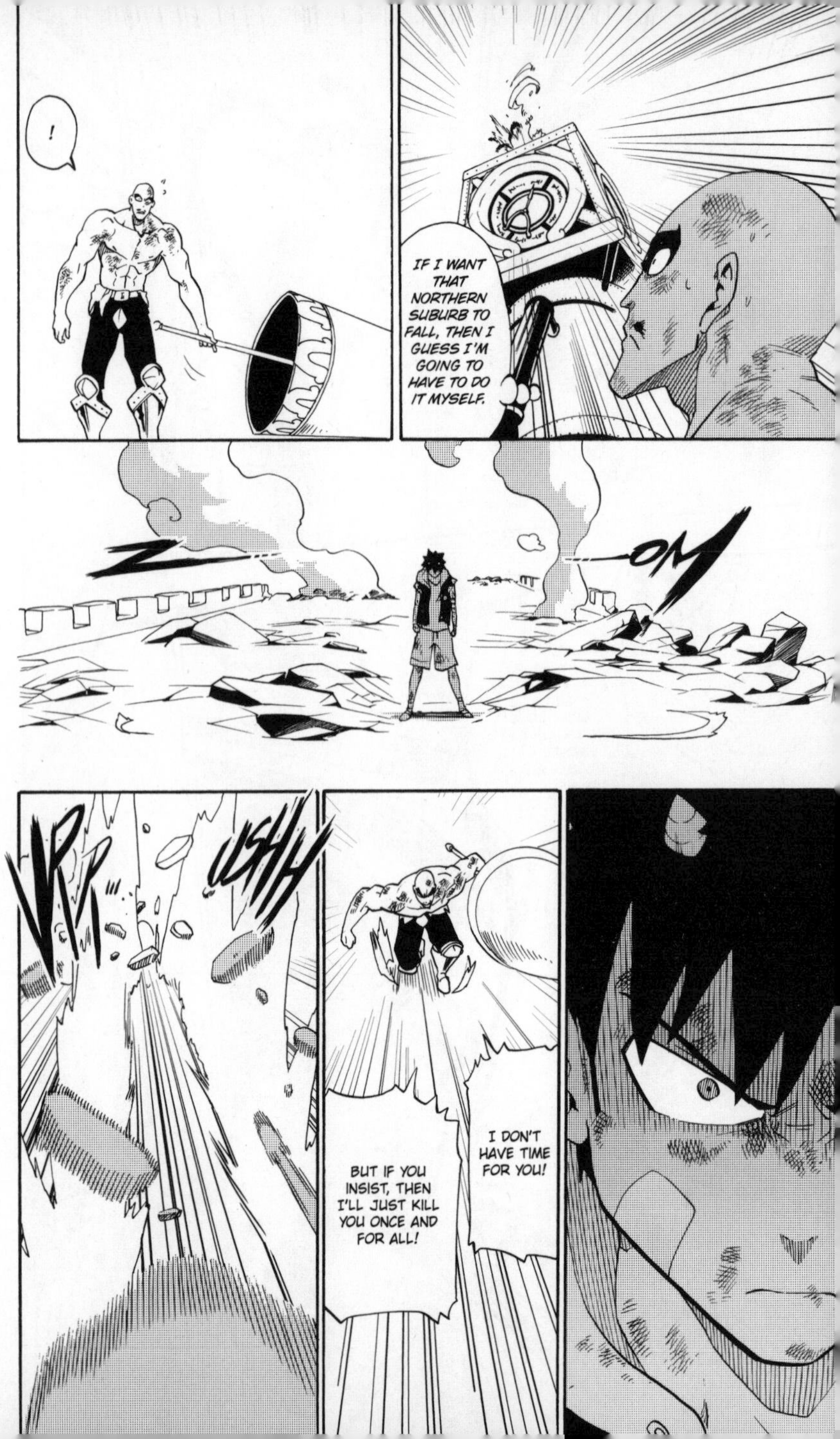
IF I WANT THAT NORTHERN SUBURB TO FALL, THEN I GUESS I'M GOING TO HAVE TO DO IT MYSELF.
!
Z
OM
I DON'T HAVE TIME FOR YOU!
BUT IF YOU INSIST, THEN I'LL JUST KILL YOU ONCE AND FOR ALL!
VRR
USHH

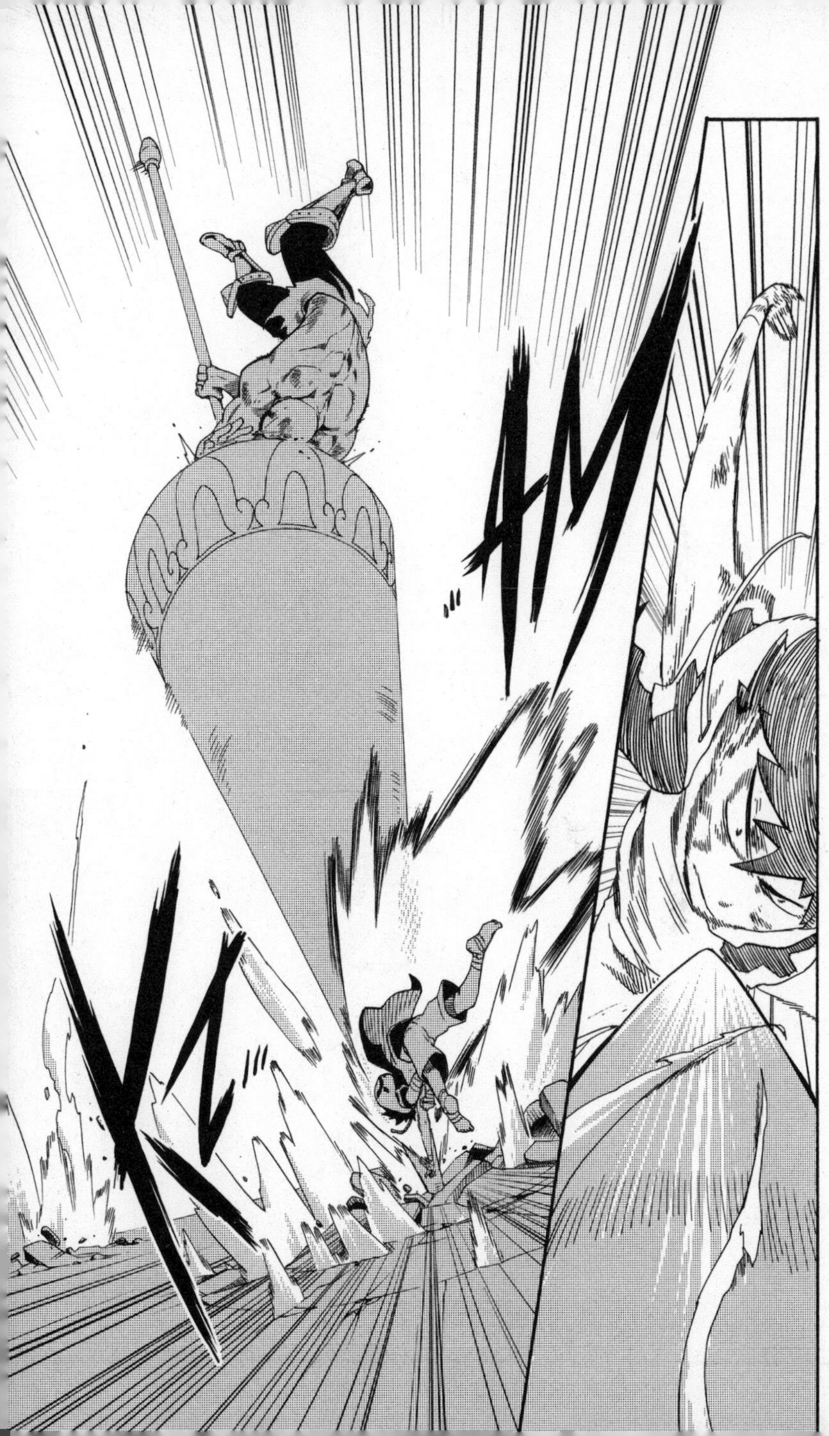

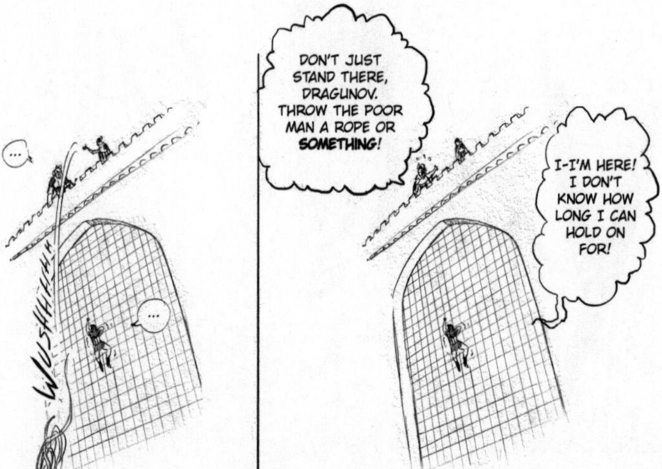
DON'T JUST STAND THERE, DRAGUNOV. THROW THE POOR MAN A ROPE OR **SOMETHING**!
I-I'M HERE! I DON'T KNOW HOW LONG I CAN HOLD ON FOR!
...
WUSHHHH
...

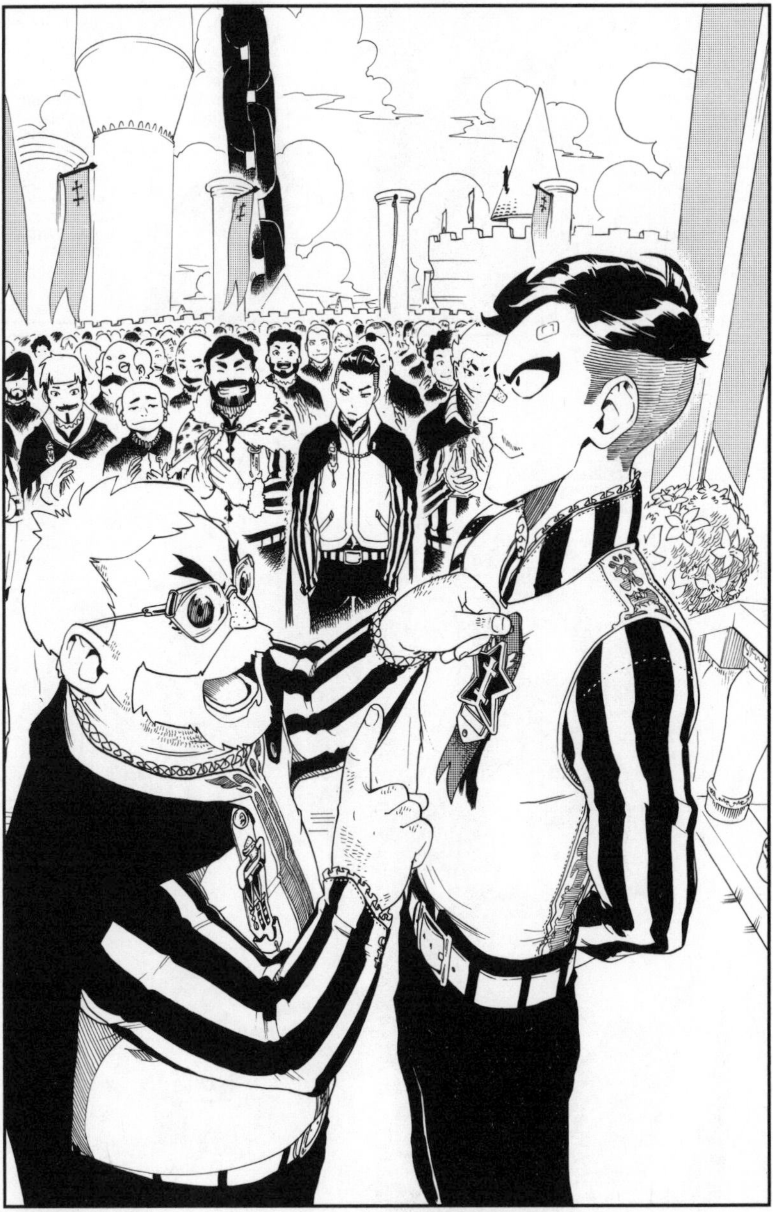

Chapter 18

THAUMATURGES

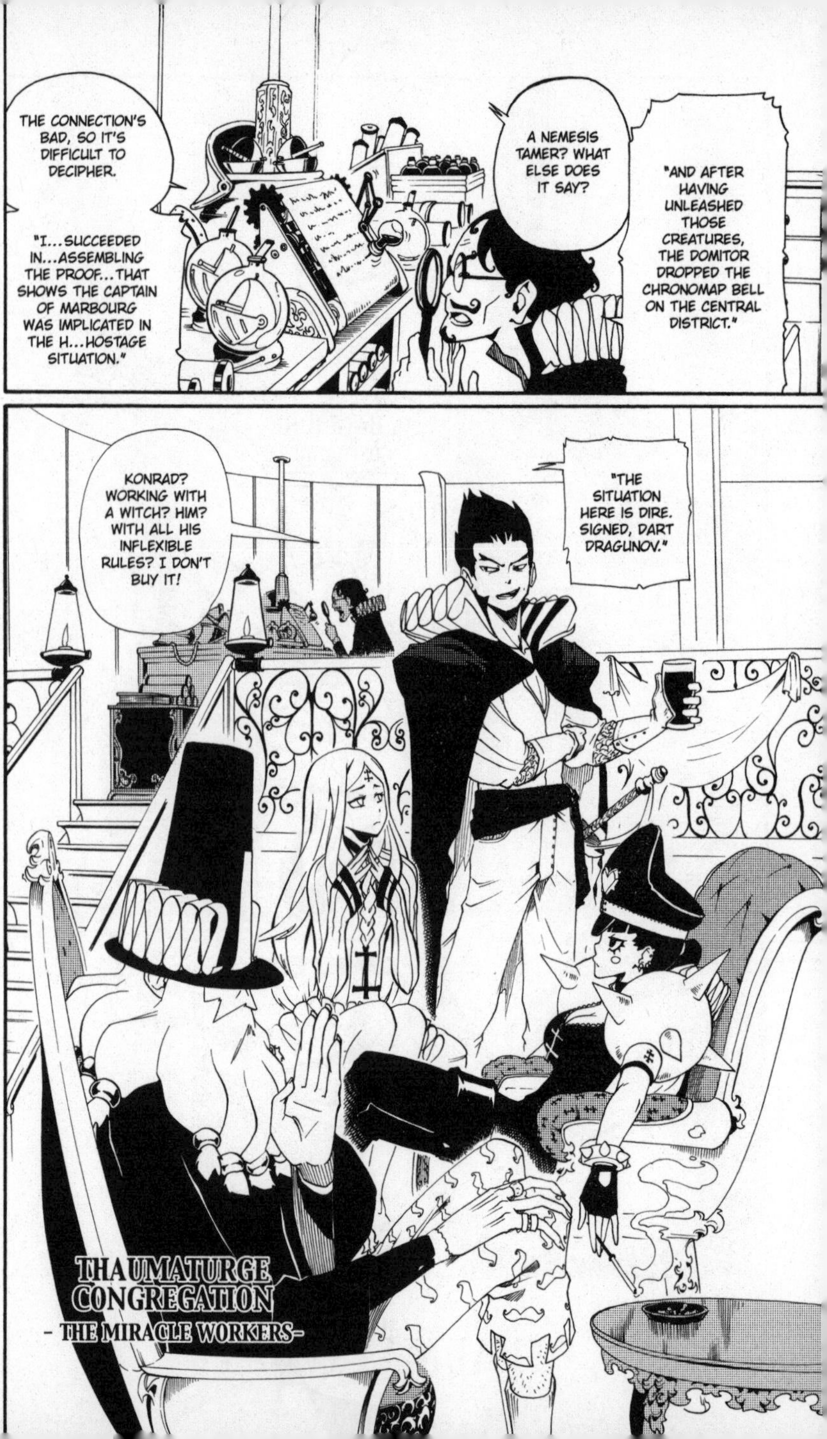
A NEMESIS TAMER? WHAT ELSE DOES IT SAY?
THE CONNECTION'S BAD, SO IT'S DIFFICULT TO DECIPHER.
"I... SUCCEEDED IN... ASSEMBLING THE PROOF... THAT SHOWS THE CAPTAIN OF MARBOURG WAS IMPLICATED IN THE H... HOSTAGE SITUATION."
"AND AFTER HAVING UNLEASHED THOSE CREATURES, THE DOMITOR DROPPED THE CHRONOMAP BELL ON THE CENTRAL DISTRICT."
"THE SITUATION HERE IS DIRE. SIGNED, DART DRAGUNOV."
KONRAD? WORKING WITH A WITCH? HIM? WITH ALL HIS INFLEXIBLE RULES? I DON'T BUY IT!
THAUMATURGE CONGREGATION
-THE MIRACLE WORKERS-

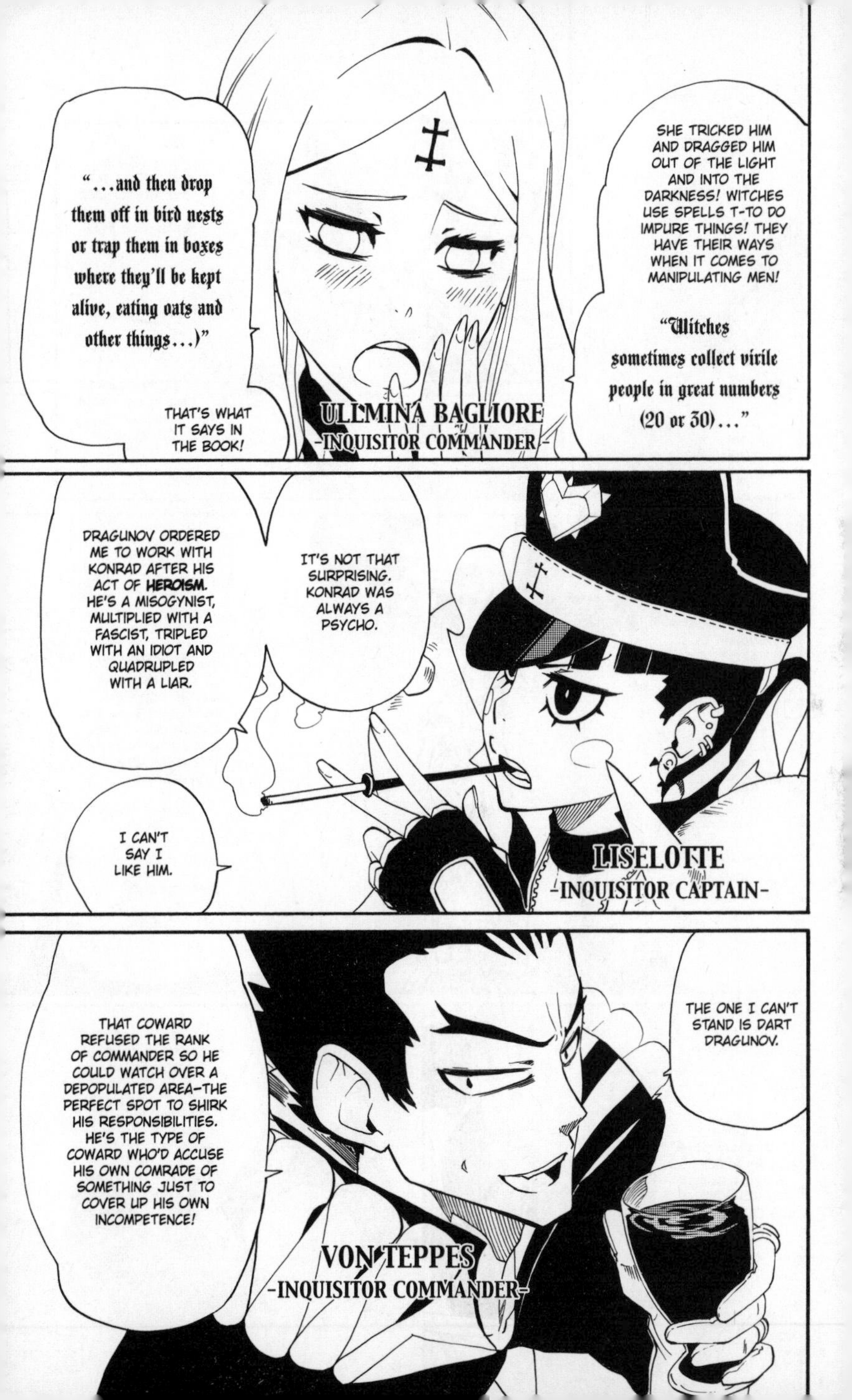

SHE TRICKED HIM AND DRAGGED HIM OUT OF THE LIGHT AND INTO THE DARKNESS! WITCHES USE SPELLS T-TO DO IMPURE THINGS! THEY HAVE THEIR WAYS WHEN IT COMES TO MANIPULATING MEN!
"Witches sometimes collect virile people in great numbers (20 or 30)..."
"...and then drop them off in bird nests or trap them in boxes where they'll be kept alive, eating oats and other things...)"
THAT'S WHAT IT SAYS IN THE BOOK!
ULLMINA BAGLIORE
-INQUISITOR COMMANDER-
IT'S NOT THAT SURPRISING. KONRAD WAS ALWAYS A PSYCHO.
DRAGUNOV ORDERED ME TO WORK WITH KONRAD AFTER HIS ACT OF HEROISM. HE'S A MISOGYNIST, MULTIPLIED WITH A FASCIST, TRIPLED WITH AN IDIOT AND QUADRUPLED WITH A LIAR.
I CAN'T SAY I LIKE HIM.
LISELOTTE
-INQUISITOR CAPTAIN-
THE ONE I CAN'T STAND IS DART DRAGUNOV.
THAT COWARD REFUSED THE RANK OF COMMANDER SO HE COULD WATCH OVER A DEPOPULATED AREA—THE PERFECT SPOT TO SHIRK HIS RESPONSIBILITIES. HE'S THE TYPE OF COWARD WHO'D ACCUSE HIS OWN COMRADE OF SOMETHING JUST TO COVER UP HIS OWN INCOMPETENCE!
VON TEPPES
-INQUISITOR COMMANDER-

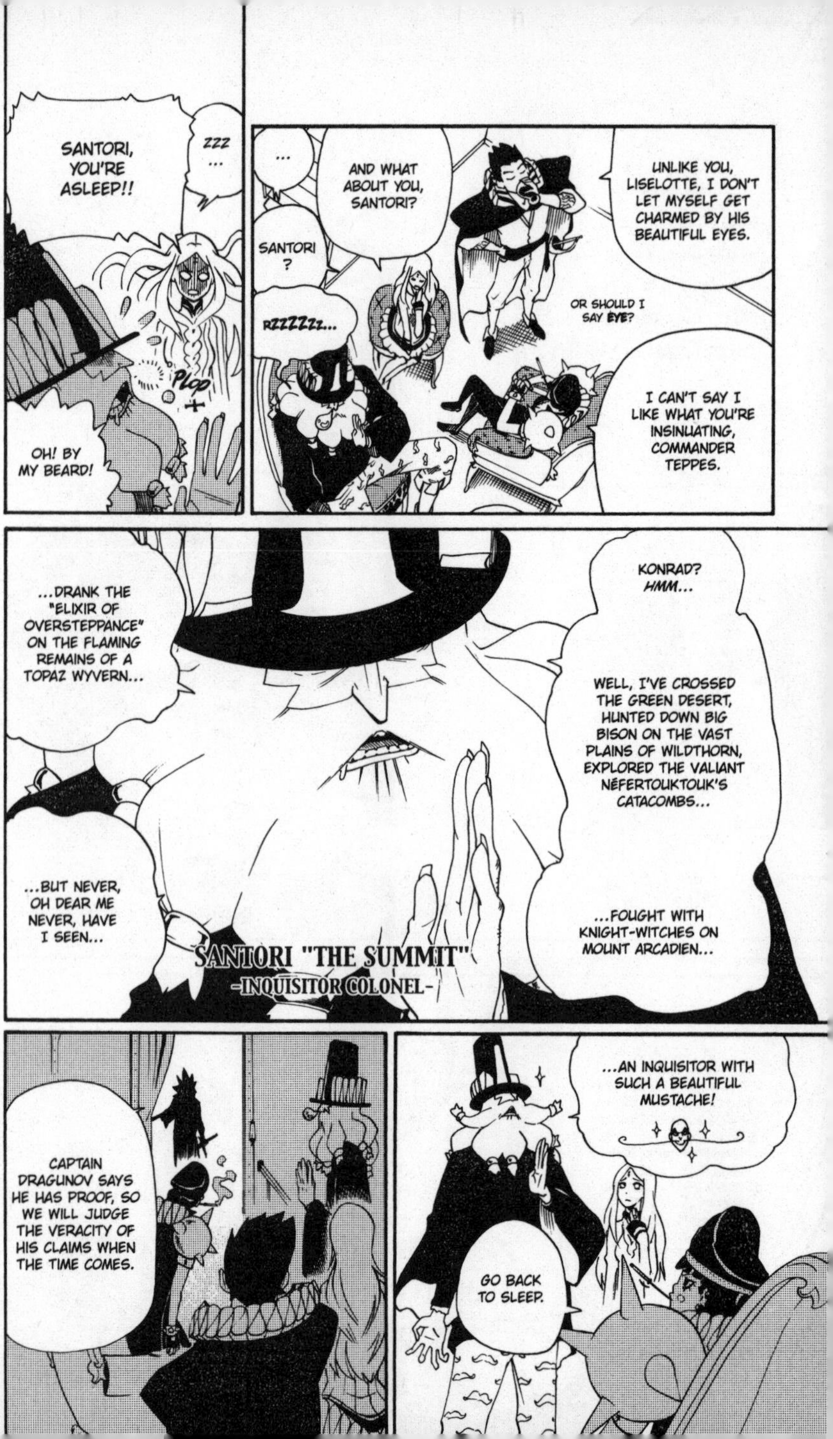
SANTORI, YOU'RE ASLEEP!!
ZZZ ...
PLOP
OH! BY MY BEARD!
...
AND WHAT ABOUT YOU, SANTORI?
SANTORI ?
RZZZZZZ...
UNLIKE YOU, LISELOTTE, I DON'T LET MYSELF GET CHARMED BY HIS BEAUTIFUL EYES.
OR SHOULD I SAY EYE?
I CAN'T SAY I LIKE WHAT YOU'RE INSINUATING, COMMANDER TEPPES.
KONRAD? HMM...
WELL, I'VE CROSSED THE GREEN DESERT, HUNTED DOWN BIG BISON ON THE VAST PLAINS OF WILDTHORN, EXPLORED THE VALIANT NÉFERTOUKTOUK'S CATACOMBS...
...FOUGHT WITH KNIGHT-WITCHES ON MOUNT ARCADIEN...
...DRANK THE "ELIXIR OF OVERSTEPPANCE" ON THE FLAMING REMAINS OF A TOPAZ WYVERN...
...BUT NEVER, OH DEAR ME NEVER, HAVE I SEEN...
SANTORI "THE SUMMIT"
-INQUISITOR COLONEL-
CAPTAIN DRAGUNOV SAYS HE HAS PROOF, SO WE WILL JUDGE THE VERACITY OF HIS CLAIMS WHEN THE TIME COMES.
...AN INQUISITOR WITH SUCH A BEAUTIFUL MUSTACHE!
GO BACK TO SLEEP.

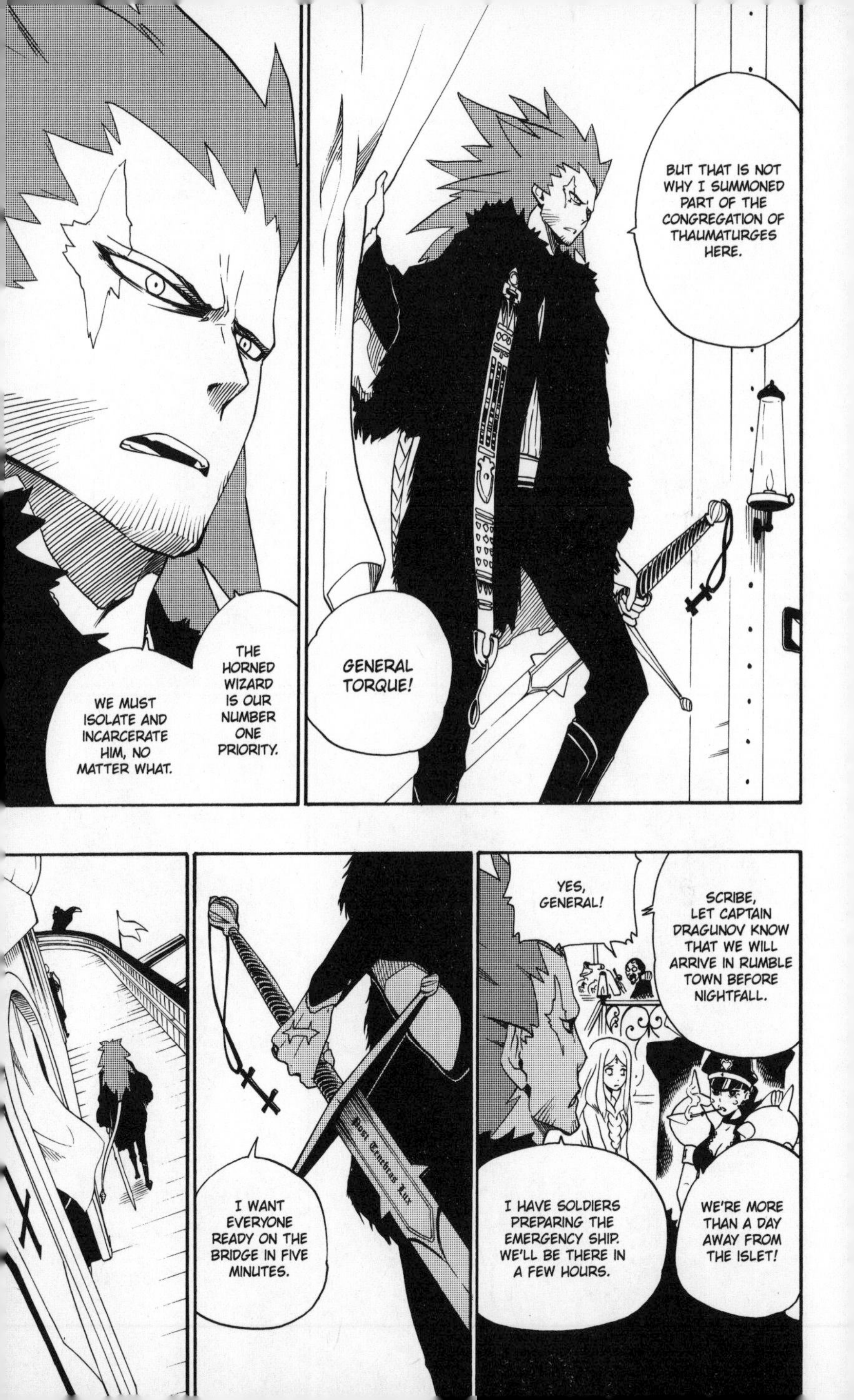
BUT THAT IS NOT WHY I SUMMONED PART OF THE CONGREGATION OF THAUMATURGES HERE.
GENERAL TORQUE!
THE HORNED WIZARD IS OUR NUMBER ONE PRIORITY.
WE MUST ISOLATE AND INCARCERATE HIM, NO MATTER WHAT.
SCRIBE, LET CAPTAIN DRAGUNOV KNOW THAT WE WILL ARRIVE IN RUMBLE TOWN BEFORE NIGHTFALL.
YES, GENERAL!
WE'RE MORE THAN A DAY AWAY FROM THE ISLET!
I HAVE SOLDIERS PREPARING THE EMERGENCY SHIP. WE'LL BE THERE IN A FEW HOURS.
Post Tenebras Lux
I WANT EVERYONE READY ON THE BRIDGE IN FIVE MINUTES.

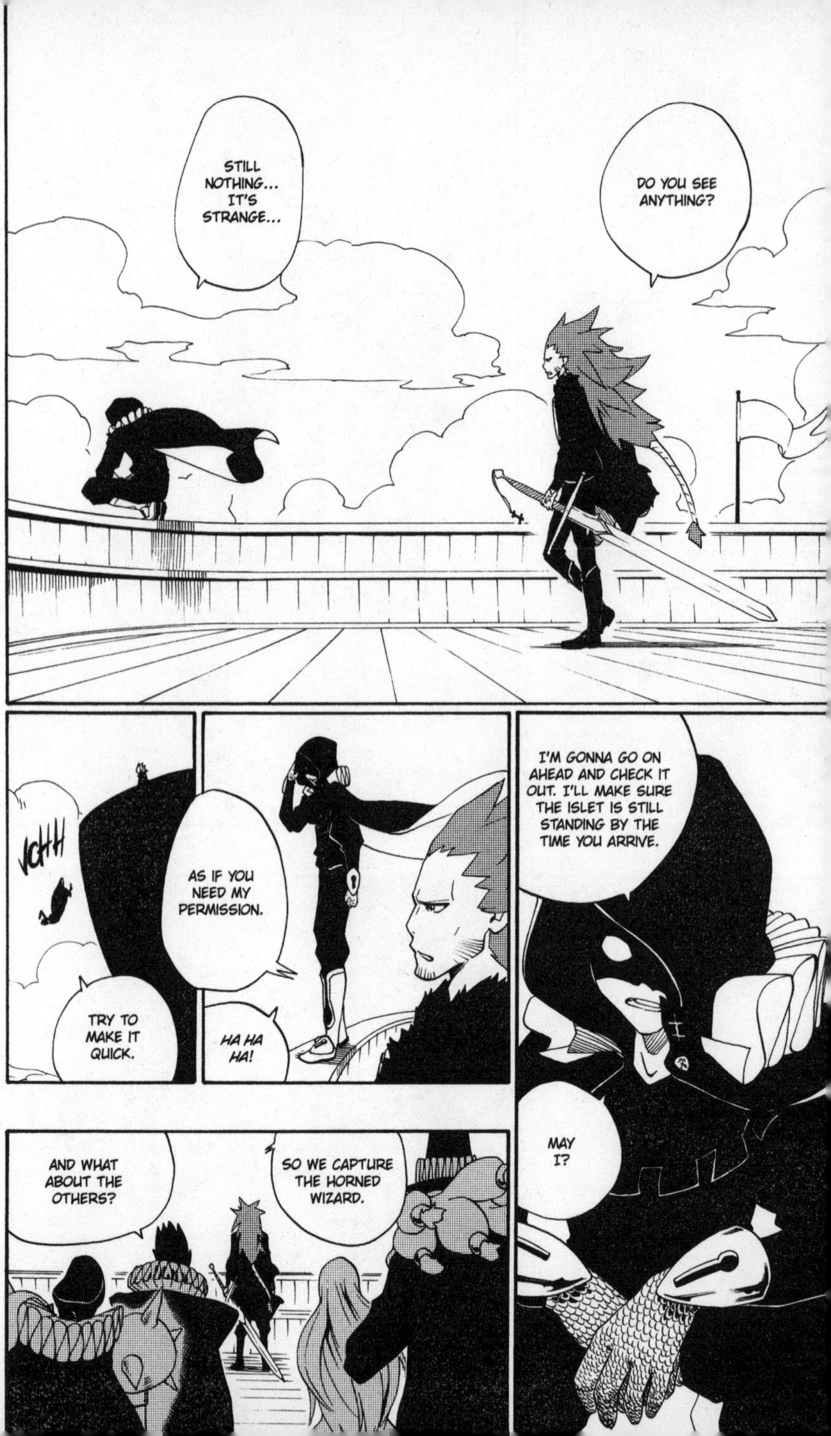
DO YOU SEE ANYTHING?
STILL NOTHING... IT'S STRANGE...
I'M GONNA GO ON AHEAD AND CHECK IT OUT. I'LL MAKE SURE THE ISLET IS STILL STANDING BY THE TIME YOU ARRIVE.
MAY I?
AS IF YOU NEED MY PERMISSION.
HA HA HA!
VCHH
TRY TO MAKE IT QUICK.
SO WE CAPTURE THE HORNED WIZARD.
AND WHAT ABOUT THE OTHERS?

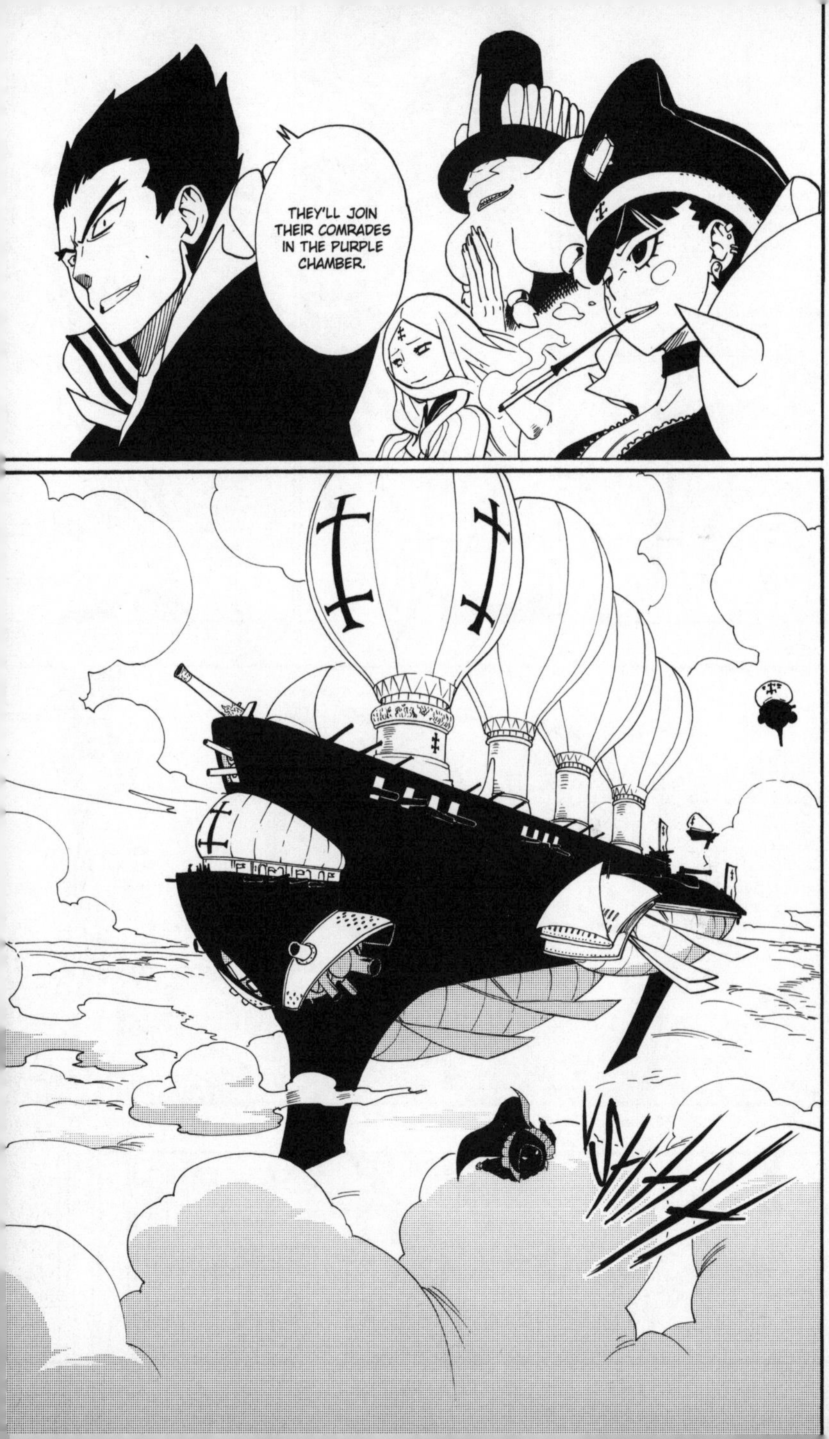
THEY'LL JOIN THEIR COMRADES IN THE PURPLE CHAMBER.
VSHHH

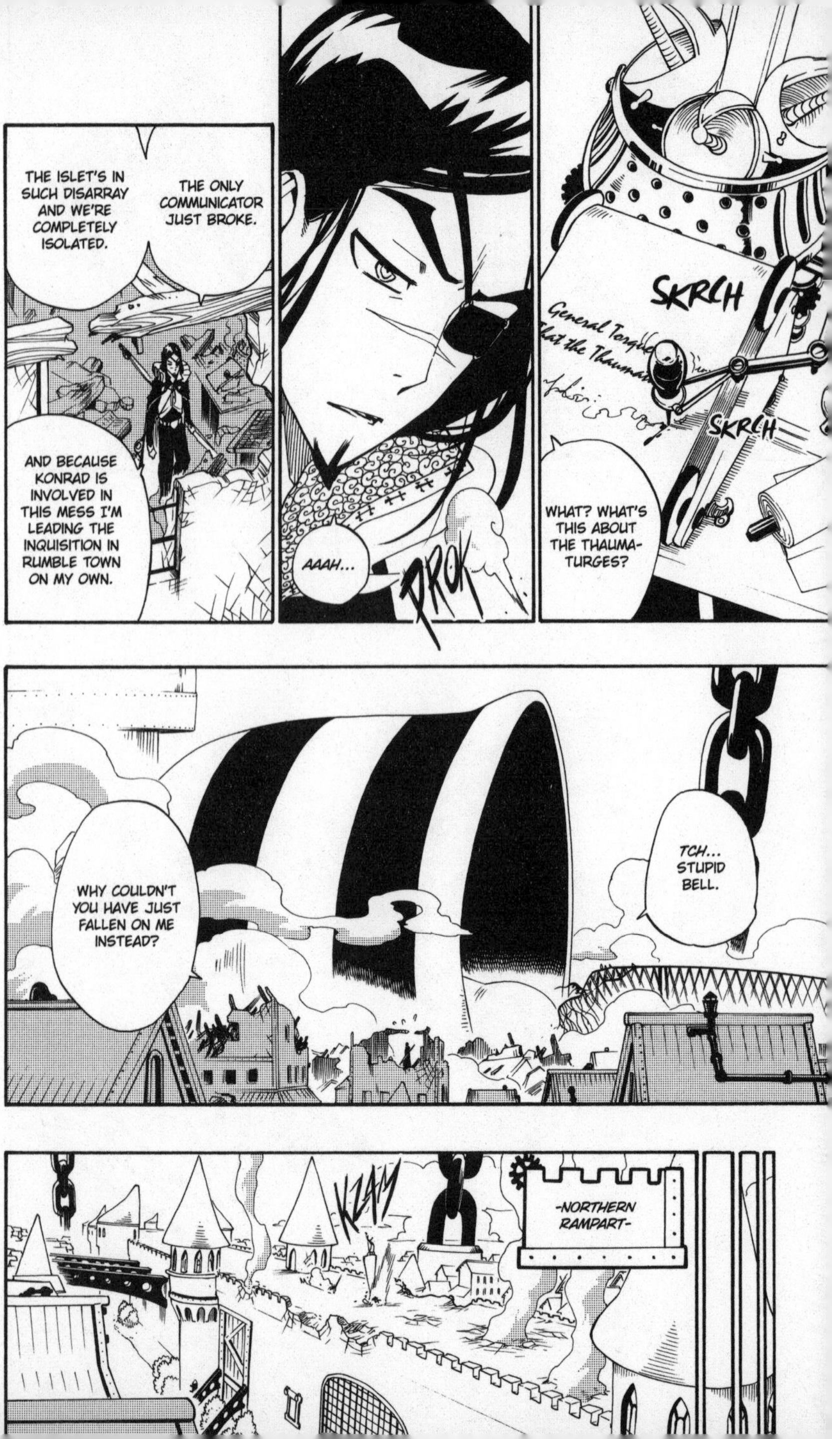
THE ISLET'S IN SUCH DISARRAY AND WE'RE COMPLETELY ISOLATED.
THE ONLY COMMUNICATOR JUST BROKE.
AND BECAUSE KONRAD IS INVOLVED IN THIS MESS I'M LEADING THE INQUISITION IN RUMBLE TOWN ON MY OWN.
AAAH...
DROK
SKRCH
SKRCH
WHAT? WHAT'S THIS ABOUT THE THAUMA-TURGES?
WHY COULDN'T YOU HAVE JUST FALLEN ON ME INSTEAD?
TCH... STUPID BELL.
KZAM
-NORTHERN RAMPART-

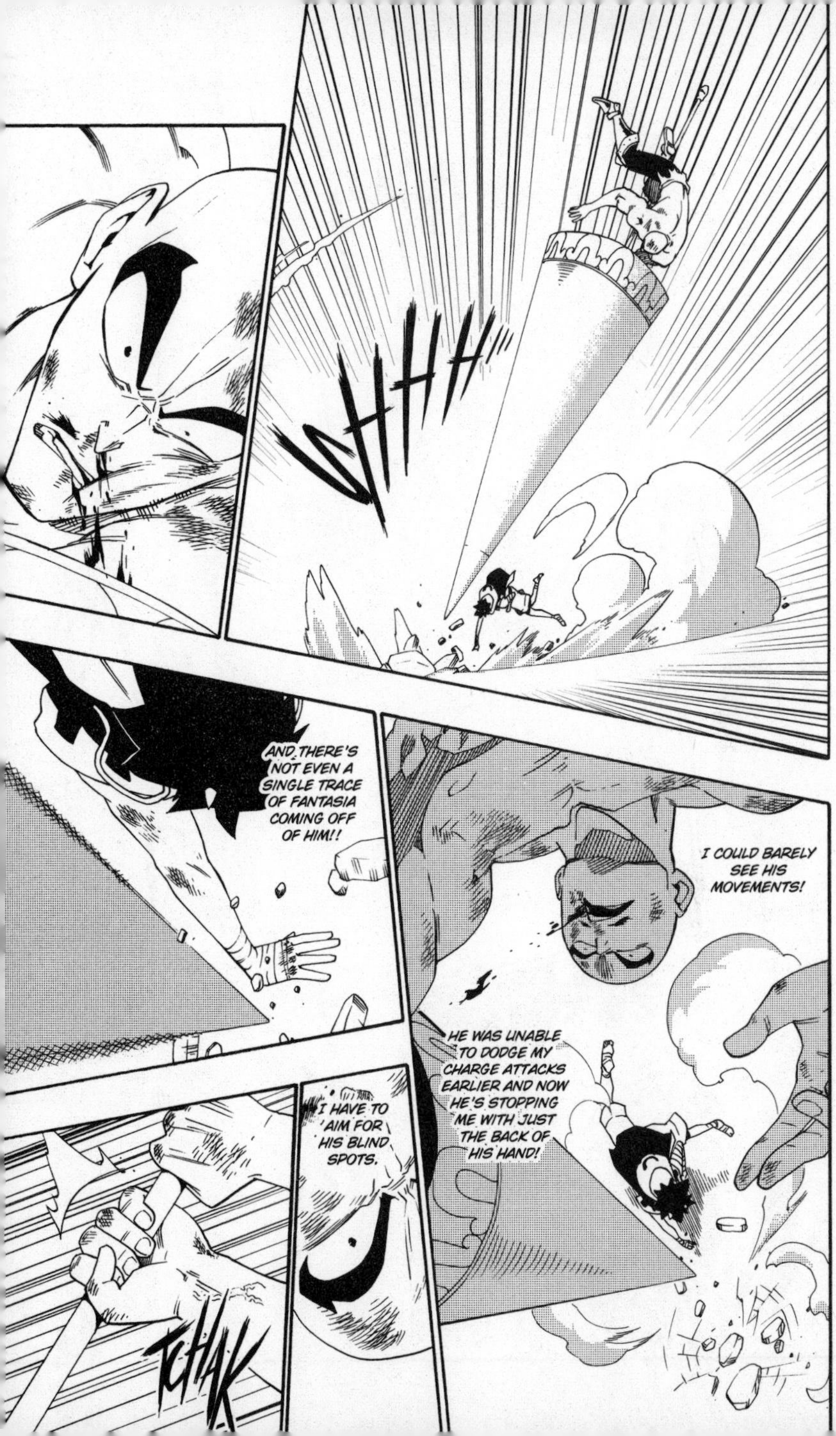
I COULD BARELY SEE HIS MOVEMENTS!
HE WAS UNABLE TO DODGE MY CHARGE ATTACKS EARLIER AND NOW HE'S STOPPING ME WITH JUST THE BACK OF HIS HAND!
AND THERE'S NOT EVEN A SINGLE TRACE OF FANTASIA COMING OFF OF HIM!!
I HAVE TO AIM FOR HIS BLIND SPOTS.
TCHAK

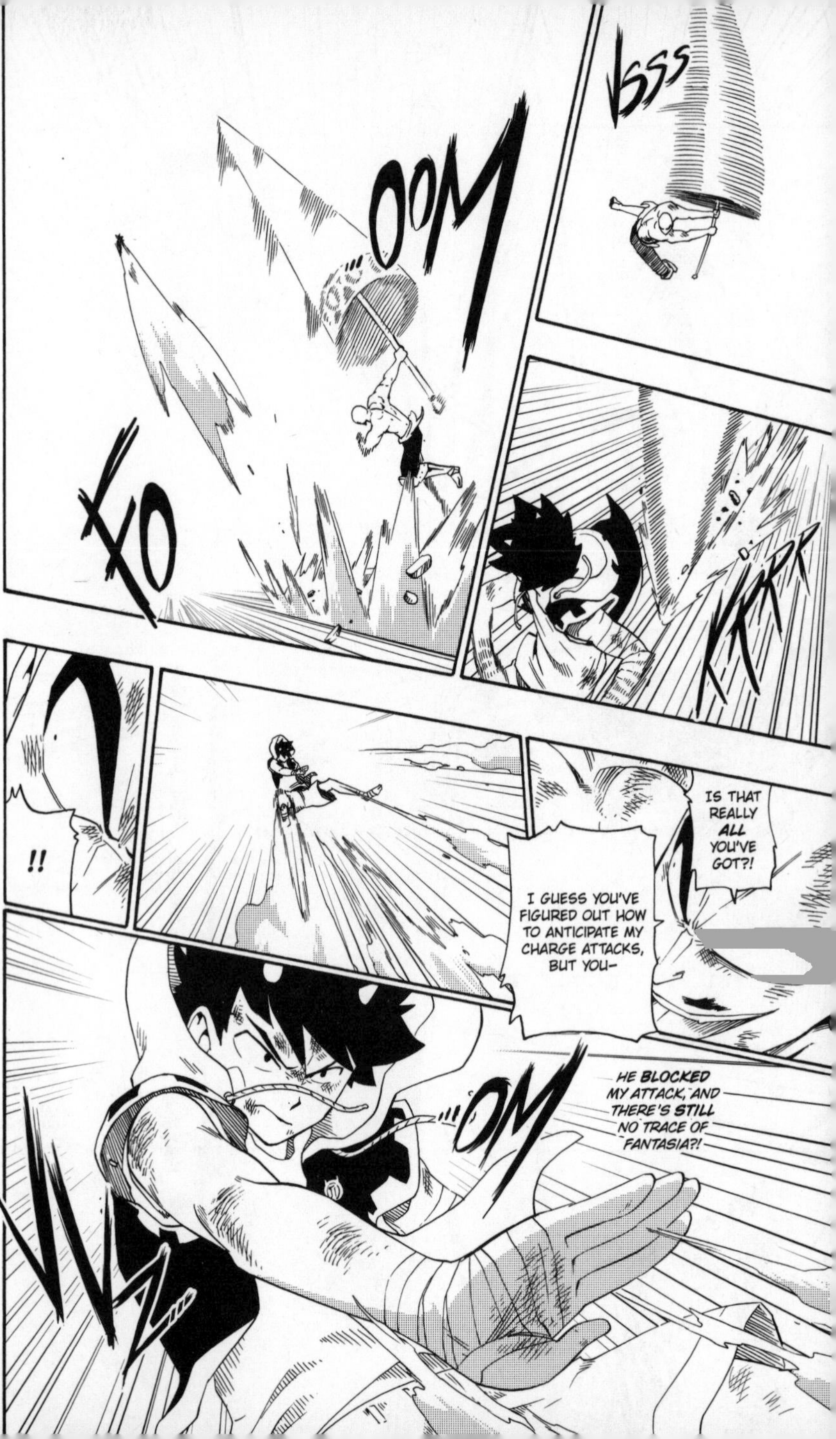
VSSS
OOM
KO
KRRRR
!!
IS THAT REALLY ALL YOU'VE GOT?!
I GUESS YOU'VE FIGURED OUT HOW TO ANTICIPATE MY CHARGE ATTACKS, BUT YOU–
HE BLOCKED MY ATTACK, AND THERE'S STILL NO TRACE OF FANTASIA?!
OM

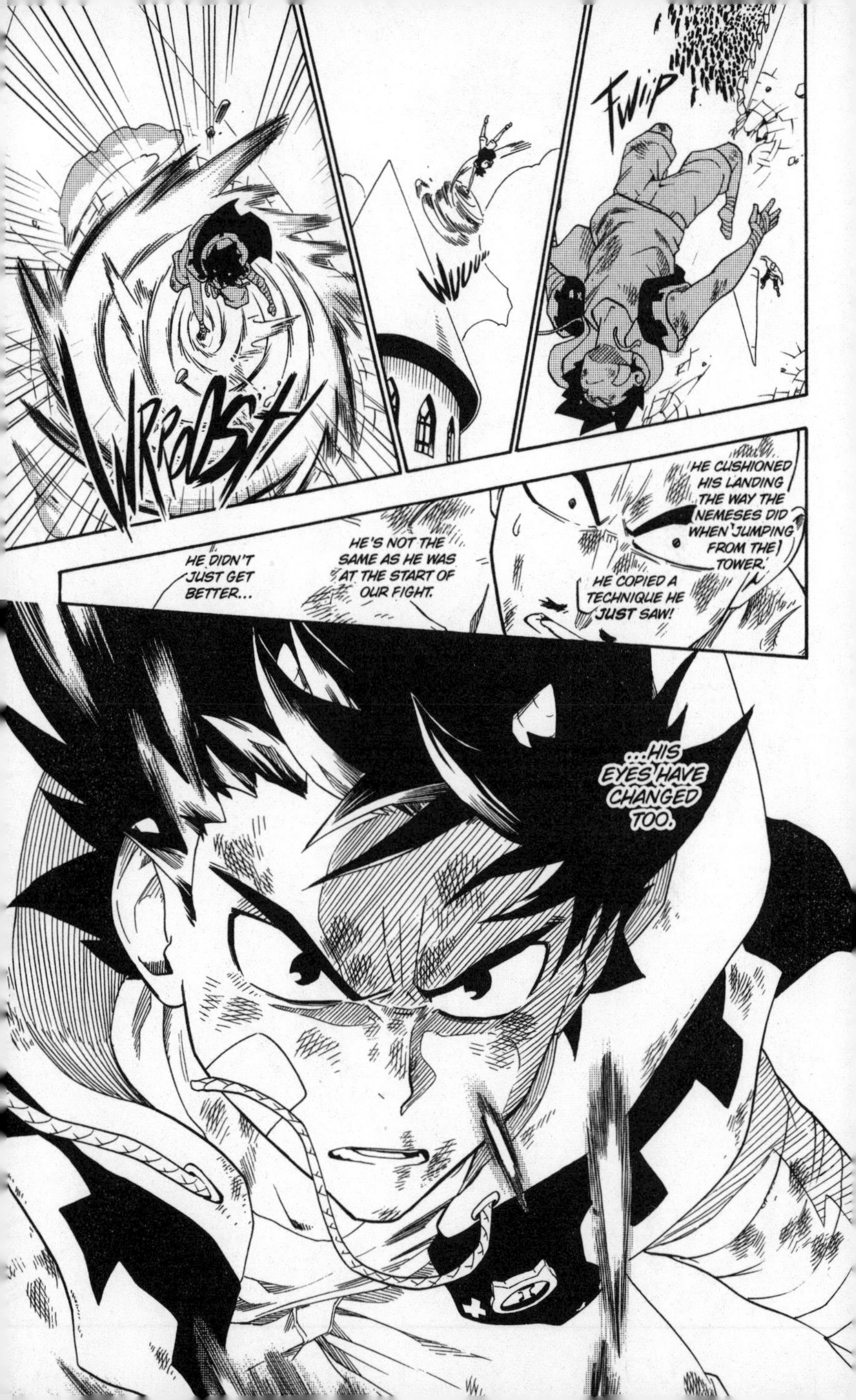
FWIP
WUUU
WRROOSH
HE CUSHIONED HIS LANDING THE WAY THE NEMESES DID WHEN JUMPING FROM THE TOWER.
HE COPIED A TECHNIQUE HE JUST SAW!
HE'S NOT THE SAME AS HE WAS AT THE START OF OUR FIGHT.
HE DIDN'T JUST GET BETTER...
...HIS EYES HAVE CHANGED TOO.

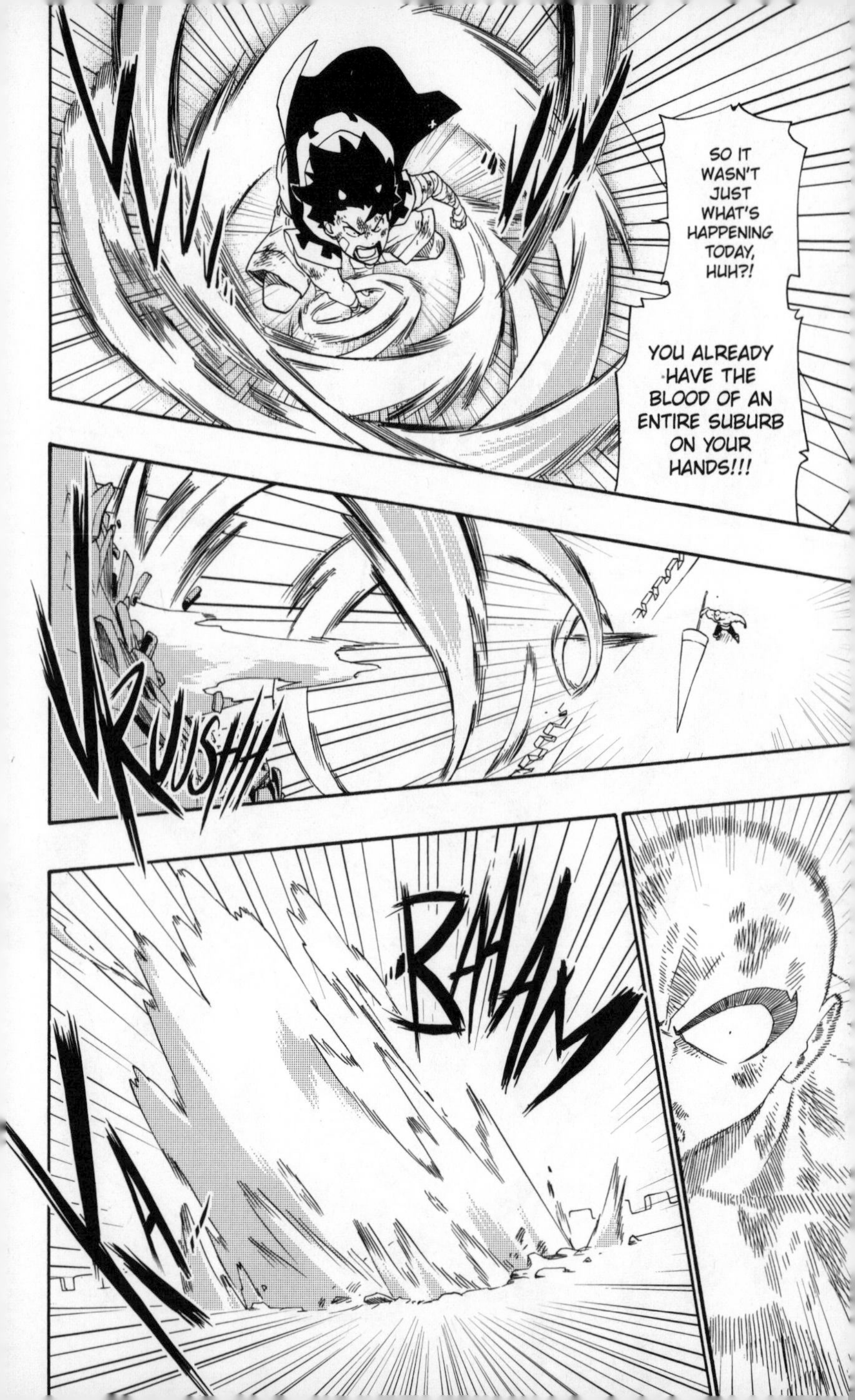
SO IT WASN'T JUST WHAT'S HAPPENING TODAY, HUH?!
YOU ALREADY HAVE THE BLOOD OF AN ENTIRE SUBURB ON YOUR HANDS!!!
VRUUSHH
BAAAM

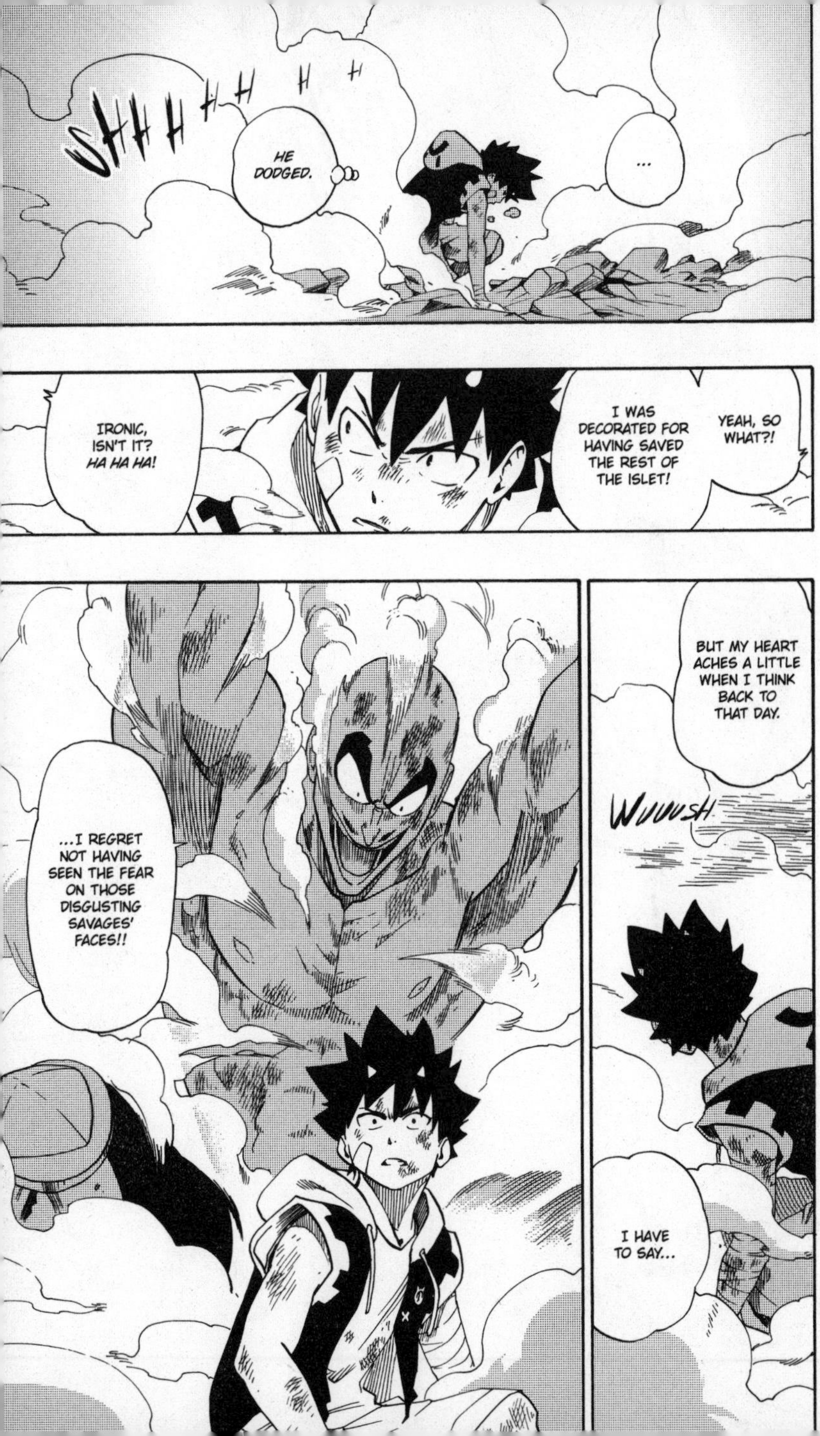
...
HE DODGED.
SHHHHHHH
YEAH, SO WHAT?!
I WAS DECORATED FOR HAVING SAVED THE REST OF THE ISLET!
IRONIC, ISN'T IT? HA HA HA!
BUT MY HEART ACHES A LITTLE WHEN I THINK BACK TO THAT DAY.
WUUUSH
I HAVE TO SAY...
...I REGRET NOT HAVING SEEN THE FEAR ON THOSE DISGUSTING SAVAGES' FACES!!

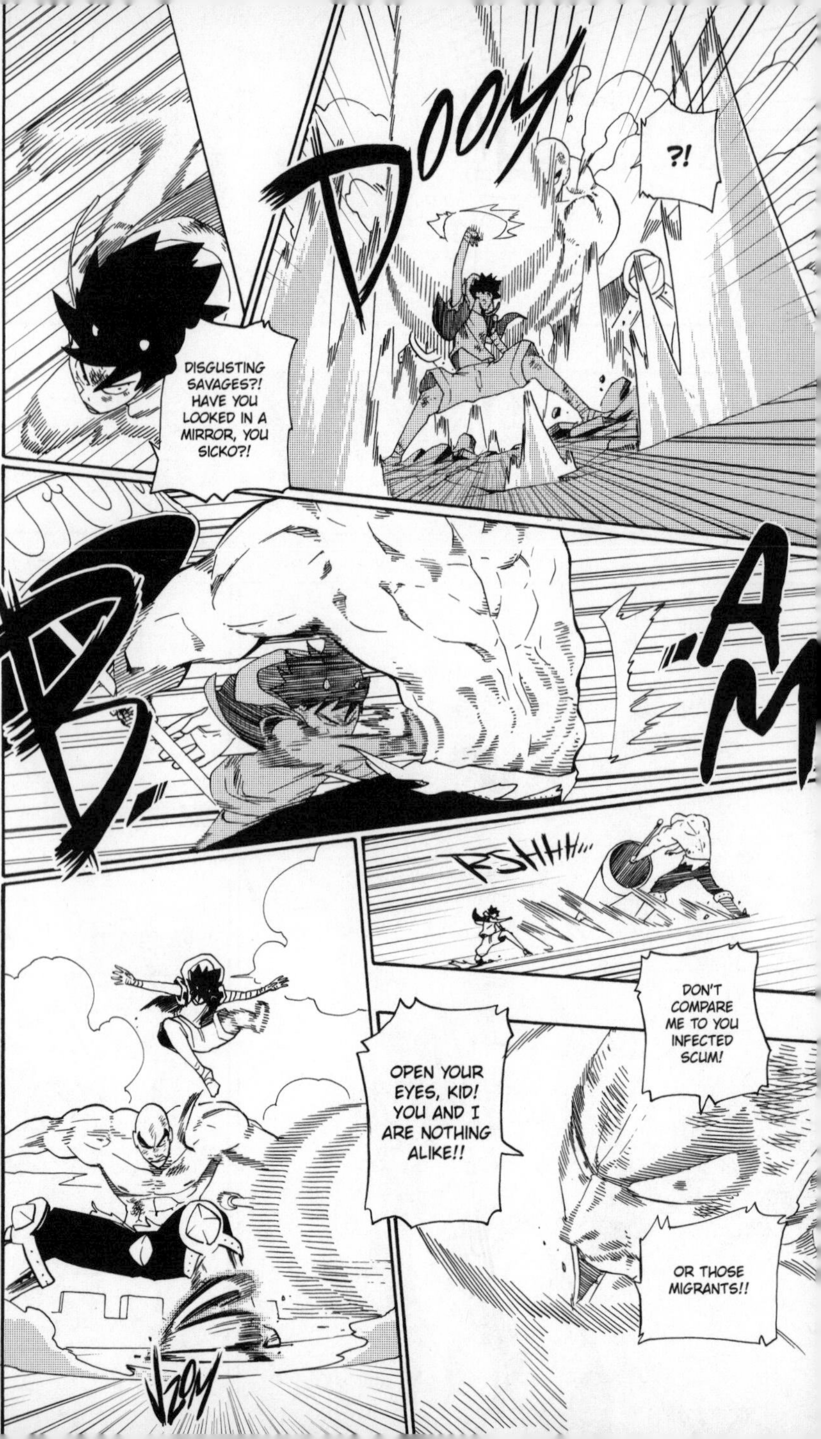

?!
DOOM
DISGUSTING SAVAGES?! HAVE YOU LOOKED IN A MIRROR, YOU SICKO?!
B..AM
RSHHH...
DON'T COMPARE ME TO YOU INFECTED SCUM!
OPEN YOUR EYES, KID! YOU AND I ARE NOTHING ALIKE!!
OR THOSE MIGRANTS!!
VZOOM

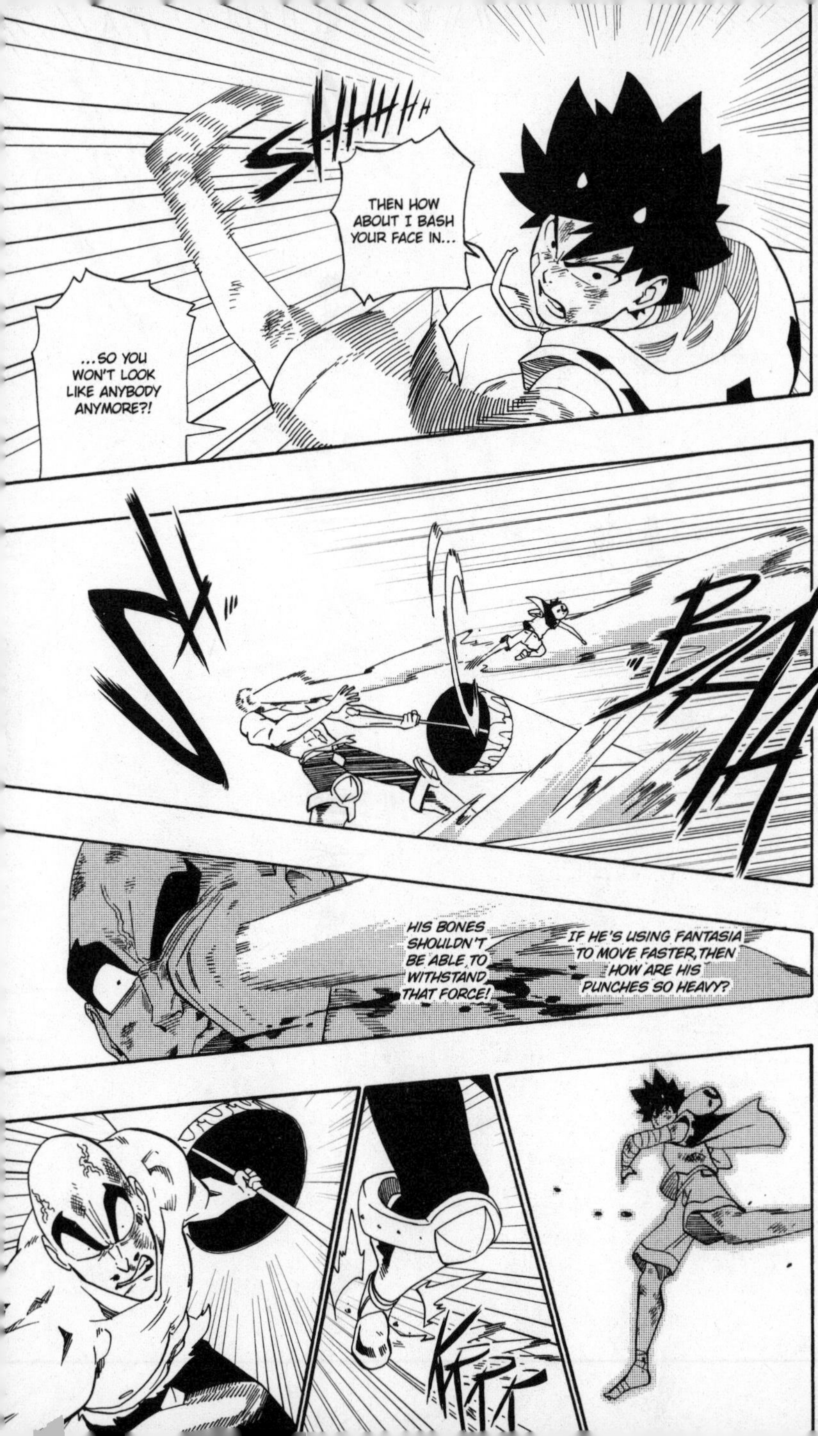
THEN HOW ABOUT I BASH YOUR FACE IN...
...SO YOU WON'T LOOK LIKE ANYBODY ANYMORE?!
IF HE'S USING FANTASIA TO MOVE FASTER, THEN HOW ARE HIS PUNCHES SO HEAVY?
HIS BONES SHOULDN'T BE ABLE TO WITHSTAND THAT FORCE!

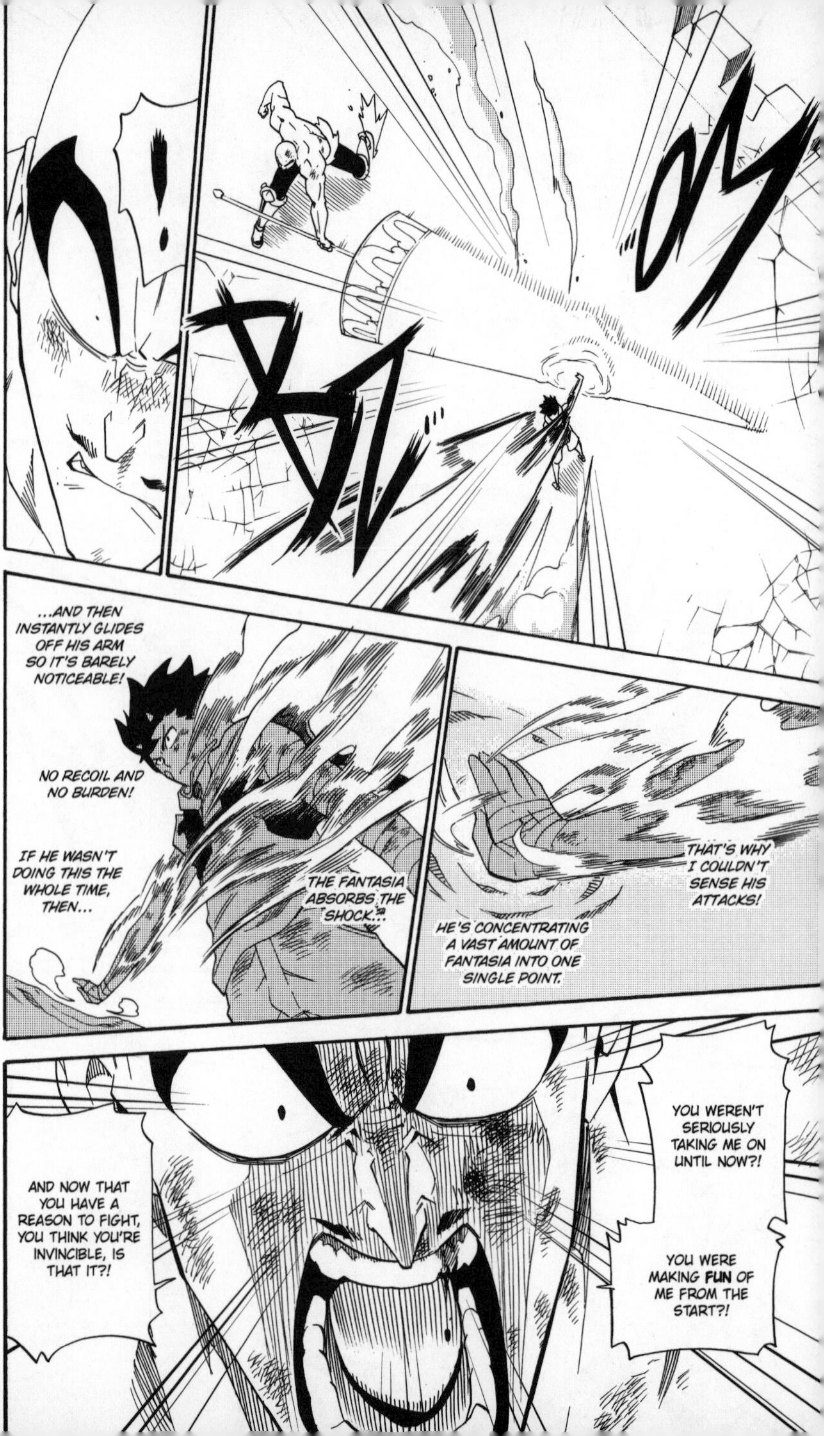
!
HE'S CONCENTRATING A VAST AMOUNT OF FANTASIA INTO ONE SINGLE POINT.
THAT'S WHY I COULDN'T SENSE HIS ATTACKS!
THE FANTASIA ABSORBS THE SHOCK...
...AND THEN INSTANTLY GLIDES OFF HIS ARM SO IT'S BARELY NOTICEABLE!
NO RECOIL AND NO BURDEN!
IF HE WASN'T DOING THIS THE WHOLE TIME, THEN...
YOU WEREN'T SERIOUSLY TAKING ME ON UNTIL NOW?!
YOU WERE MAKING **FUN** OF ME FROM THE START?!
AND NOW THAT YOU HAVE A REASON TO FIGHT, YOU THINK YOU'RE INVINCIBLE, IS THAT IT?!

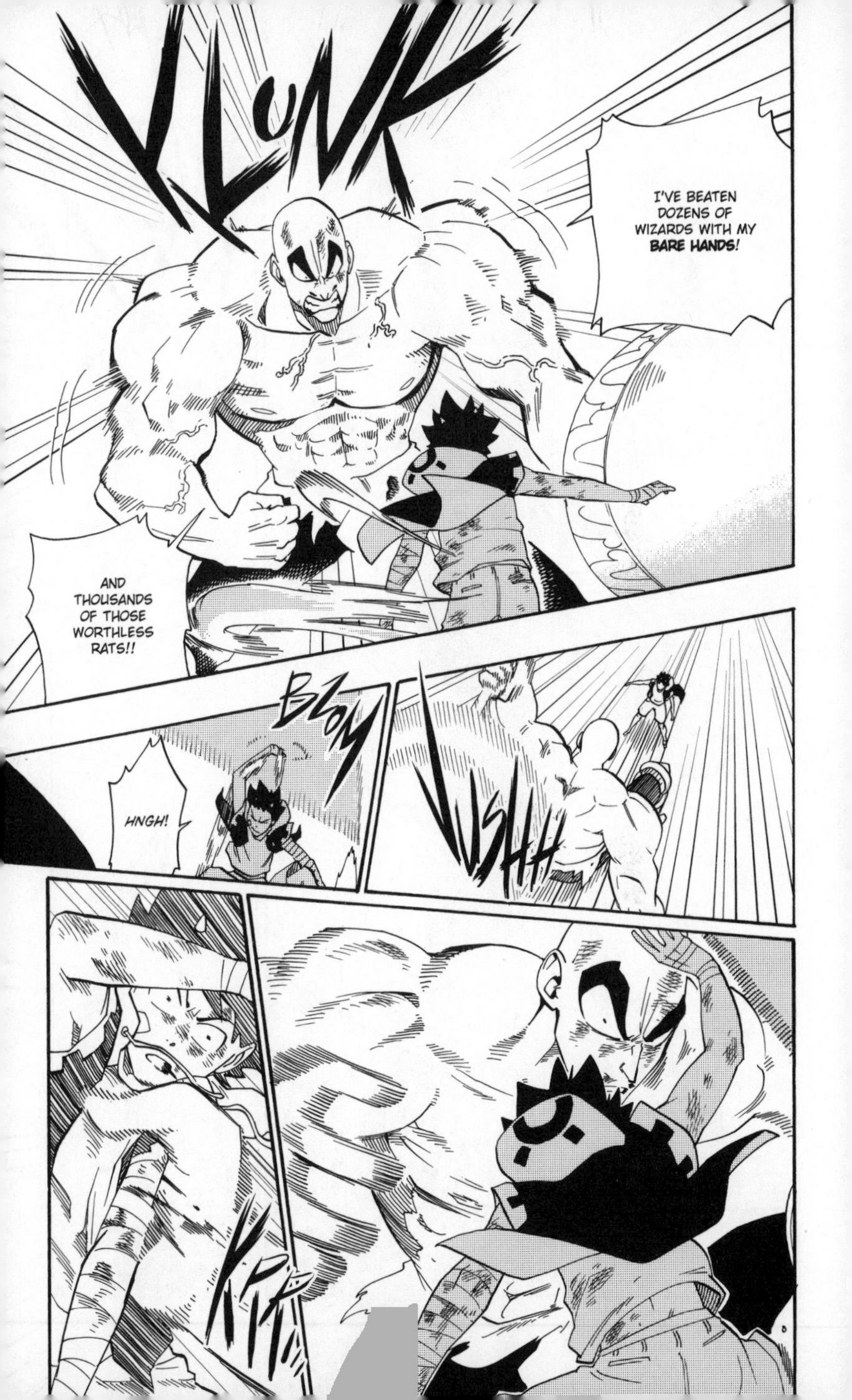
KLUNK
I'VE BEATEN DOZENS OF WIZARDS WITH MY **BARE HANDS!**
AND THOUSANDS OF THOSE WORTHLESS RATS!!
BLOW
HNGH!
VUSHH

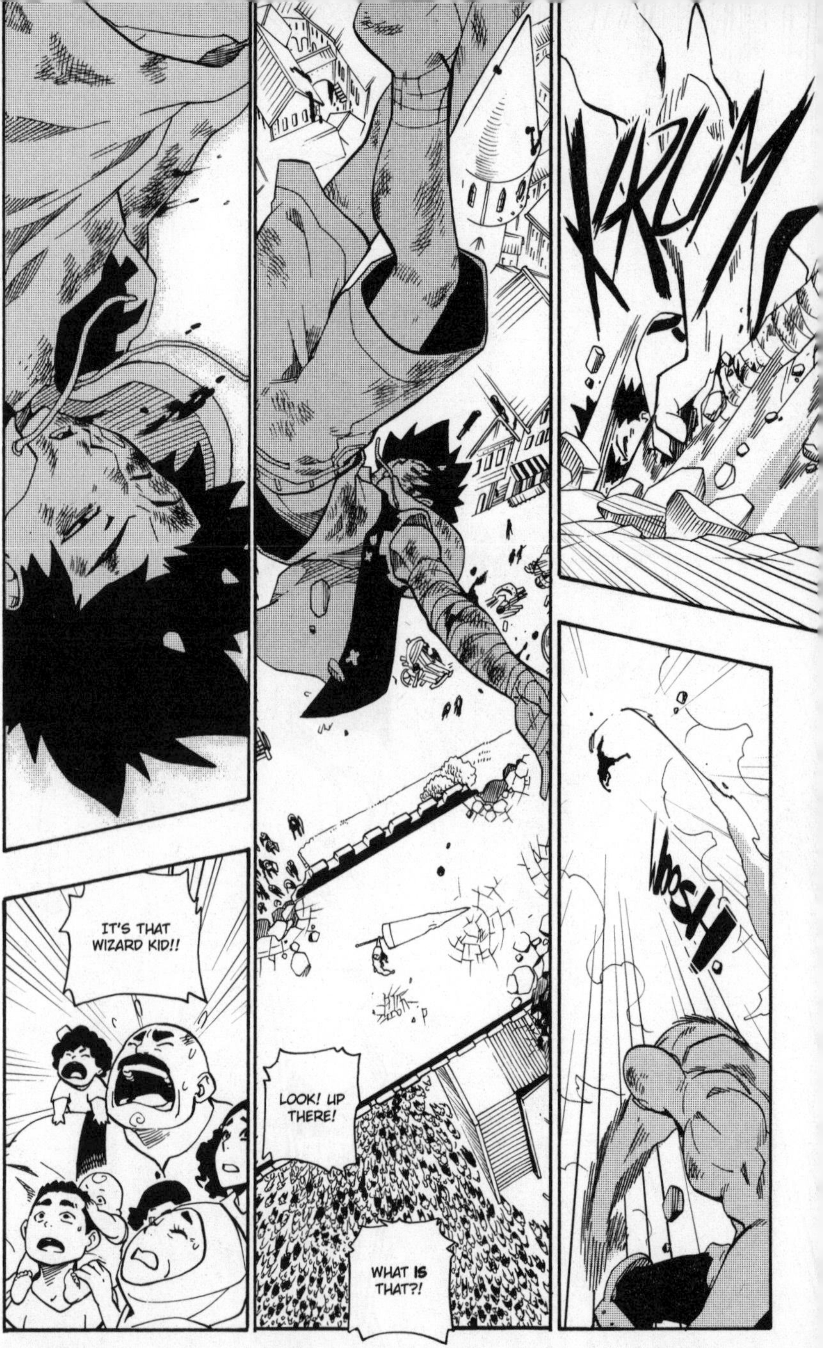
KRUM
IT'S THAT WIZARD KID!!
LOOK! UP THERE!
WHAT IS THAT?!
WHOOSH!

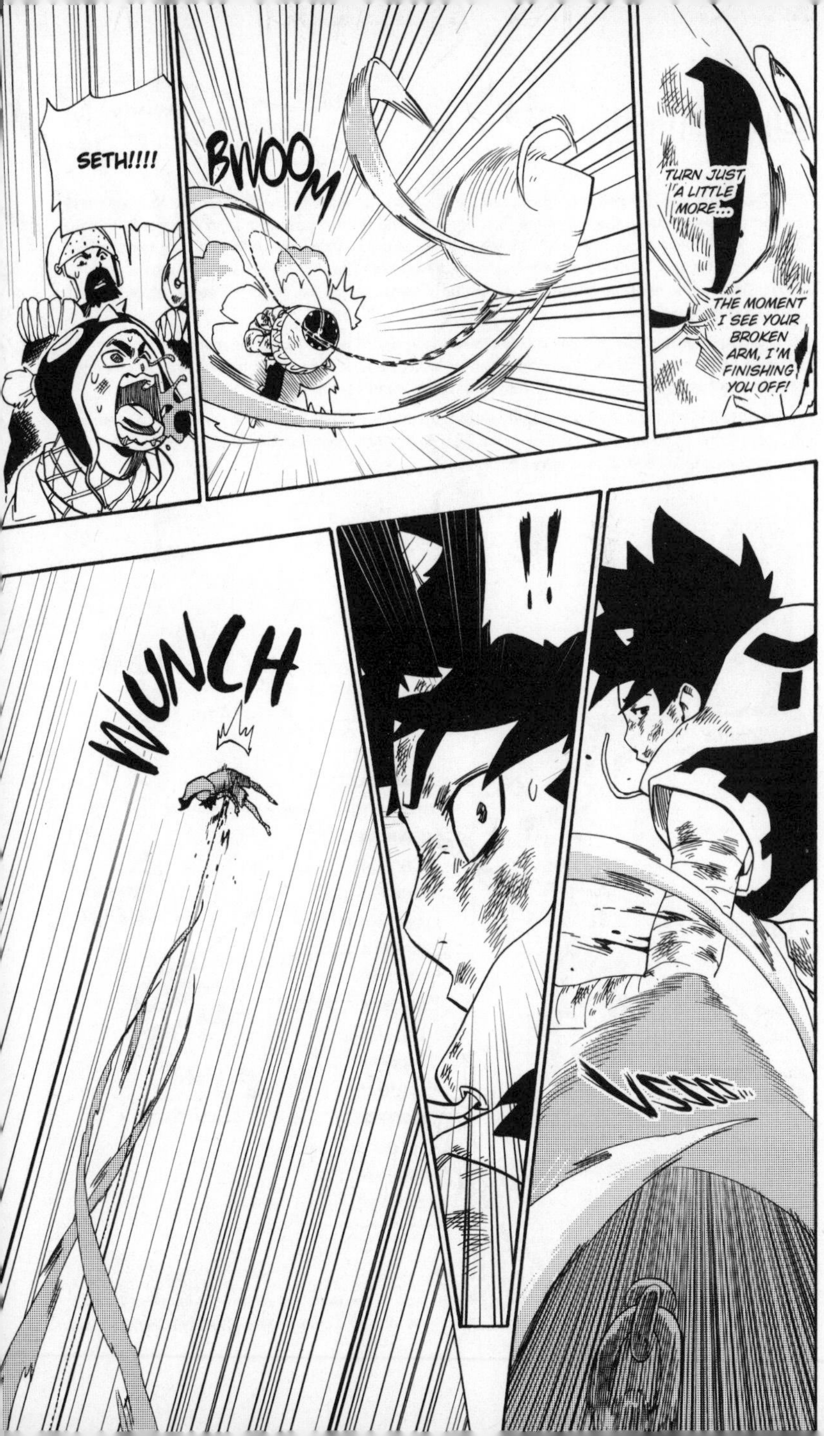
TURN JUST A LITTLE MORE...
THE MOMENT I SEE YOUR BROKEN ARM, I'M FINISHING YOU OFF!
BWOOM
SETH!!!!
VSSSS...
!!
WUNCH

The Inquisition ☩

-The World of Radiant-

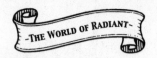

The Inquisition is a military organization. Its inception is dated to shortly after the Nemeses first started appearing during the era of the First Wizards. The original goal of the Inquisition was to fight against magic, and it was the only bulwark against certain Infected criminals who had become too powerful. Nowadays, despite the exemplary work of Nemeses Hunters, the Inquisition is also very much responsible for the negative image of the Infected Wizards, which has become deeply rooted into the people's collective subconscious.

The role of the Inquisition has diversified over the years. In recent years, the management of magic affairs is not its sole assignment anymore. The Inquisition is now somewhat integrated into all branches of power and exercises its influence across most of the world's territories.

On certain islets, Inquisitors are simple agents responsible for the safety of the community. On others, the Inquisition has become a substitute for the local government and exercises its power with an iron fist, going even as far as banning wizardry entirely.

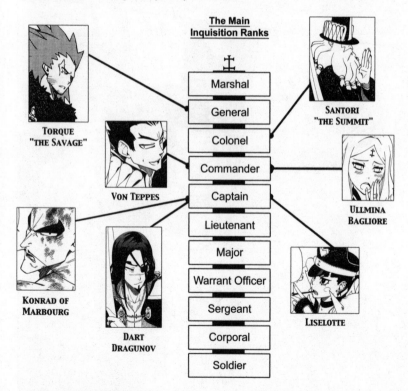

The Main Inquisition Ranks
Marshal
General
Colonel
Commander
Captain
Lieutenant
Major
Warrant Officer
Sergeant
Corporal
Soldier
Torque "The Savage"
Santori "The Summit"
Von Teppes
Ullmina Bagliore
Konrad of Marbourg
Dart Dragunov
Liselotte

The Congregation of Thaumaturges:

Founded by General Torque, this elite group is made up of Inquisitors of all ranks commandeered for certain, often confidential, missions. They are called "The Miracle Workers" because of their extraordinary abilities gained after their initiation ceremony...

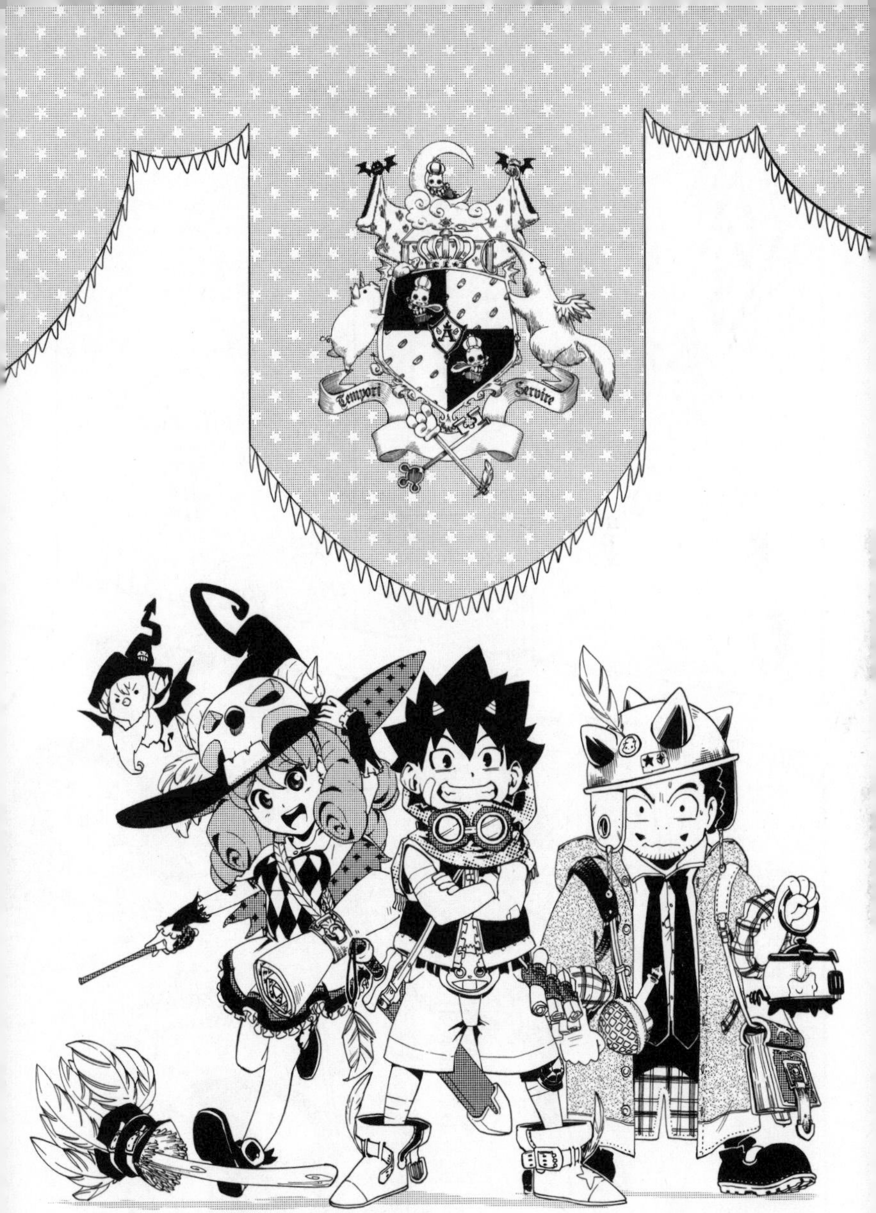
Tempori Servire

CHAPTER 19
THE RAMPART

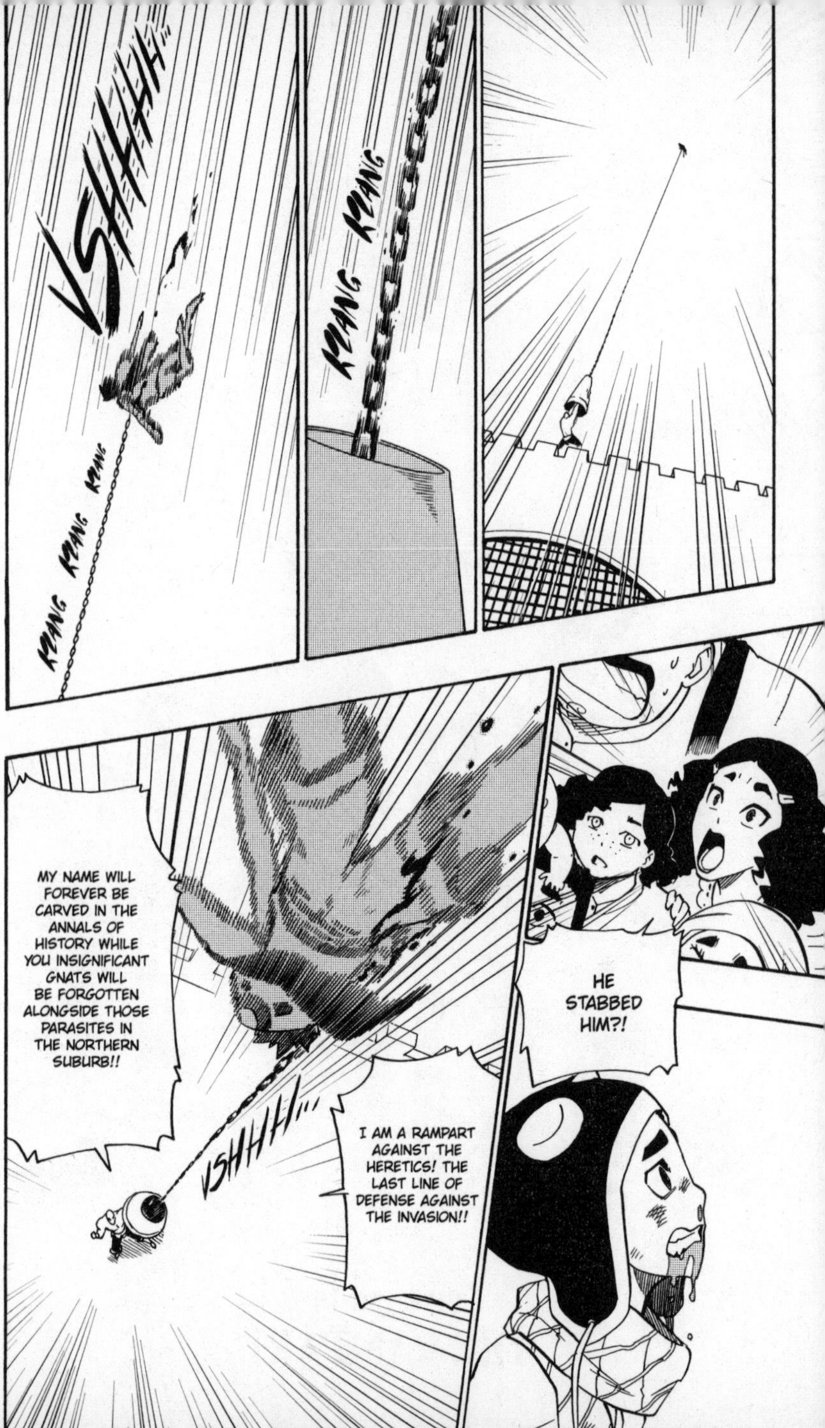

KRANG KRANG
VSHHHH...
KRANG KRANG KRANG
HE STABBED HIM?!
I AM A RAMPART AGAINST THE HERETICS! THE LAST LINE OF DEFENSE AGAINST THE INVASION!!
MY NAME WILL FOREVER BE CARVED IN THE ANNALS OF HISTORY WHILE YOU INSIGNIFICANT GNATS WILL BE FORGOTTEN ALONGSIDE THOSE PARASITES IN THE NORTHERN SUBURB!!
VSHHH...

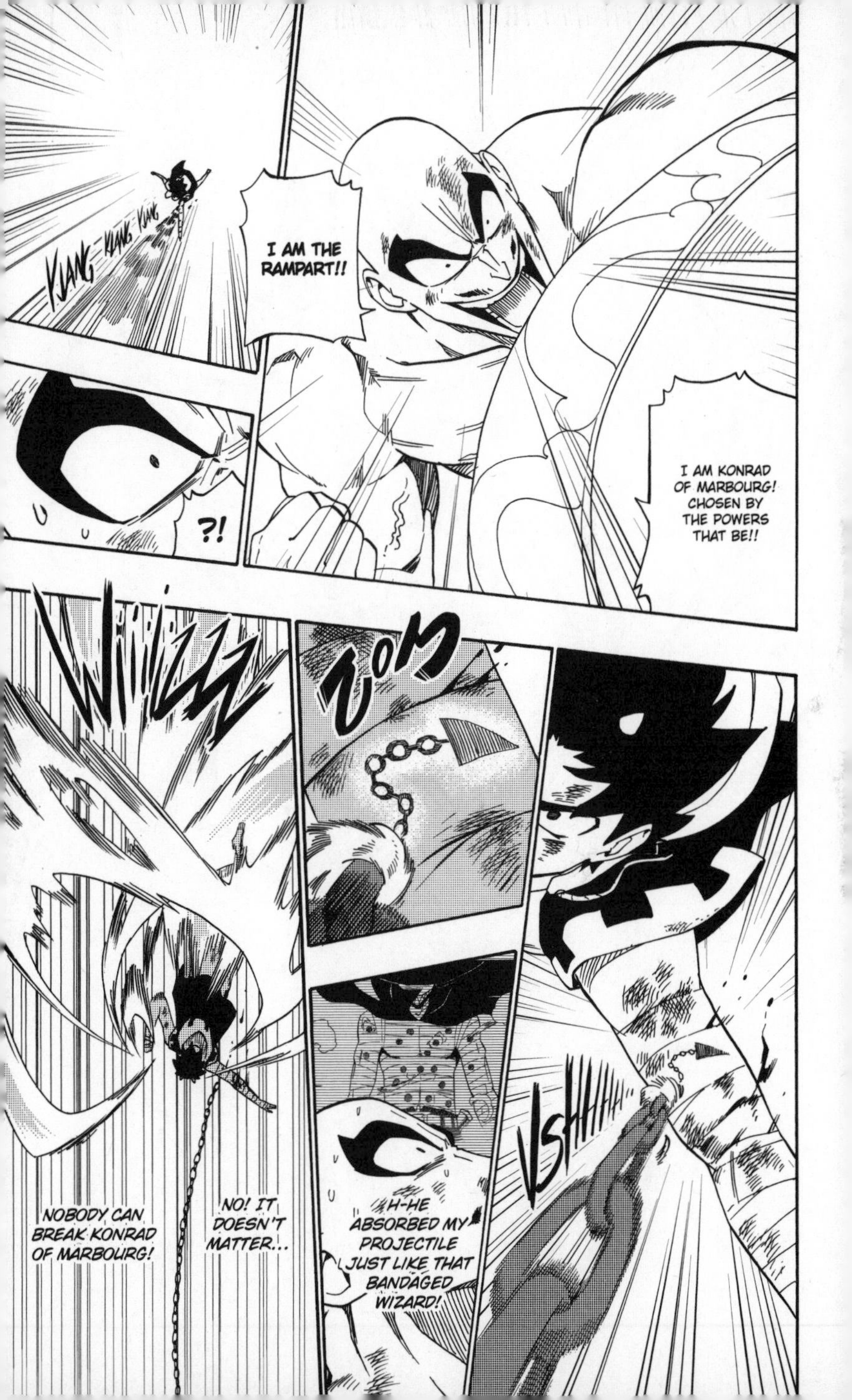
I AM KONRAD OF MARBOURG! CHOSEN BY THE POWERS THAT BE!!
I AM THE RAMPART!!
KLANG KLANG KLANG
?!
H-HE ABSORBED MY PROJECTILE JUST LIKE THAT BANDAGED WIZARD!
ZOOM
NO! IT DOESN'T MATTER...
NOBODY CAN BREAK KONRAD OF MARBOURG!

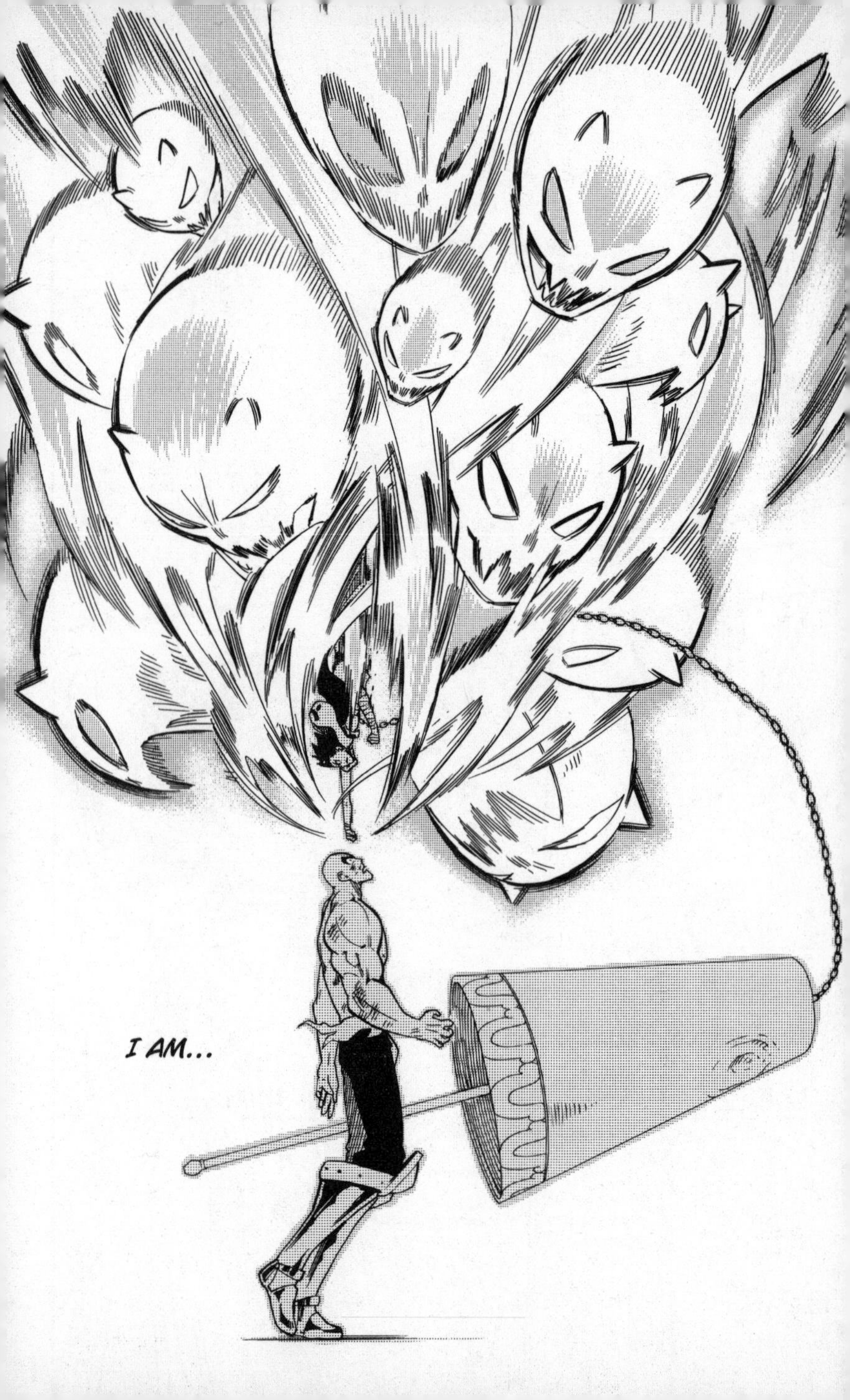
I AM...

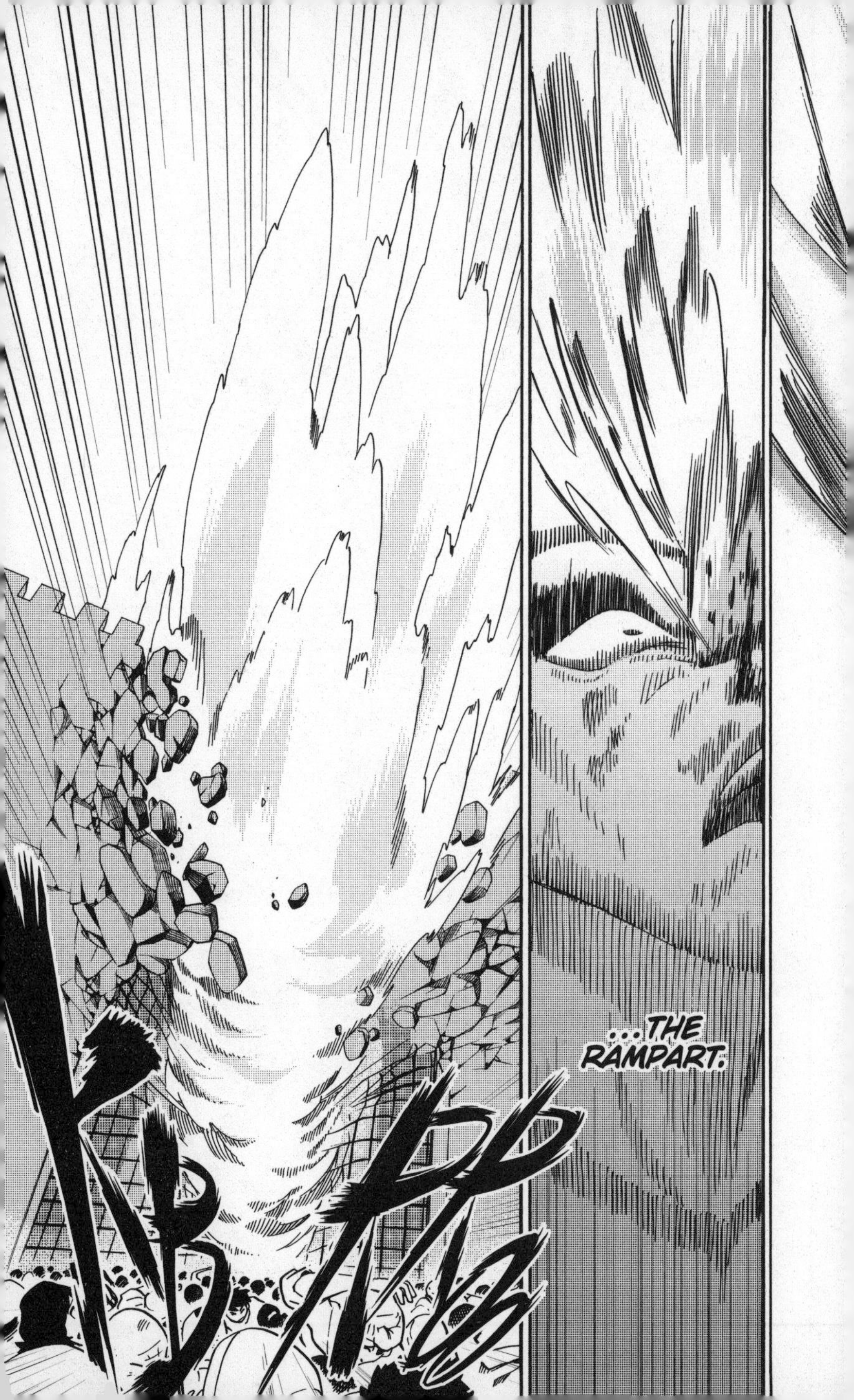
...THE RAMPART.

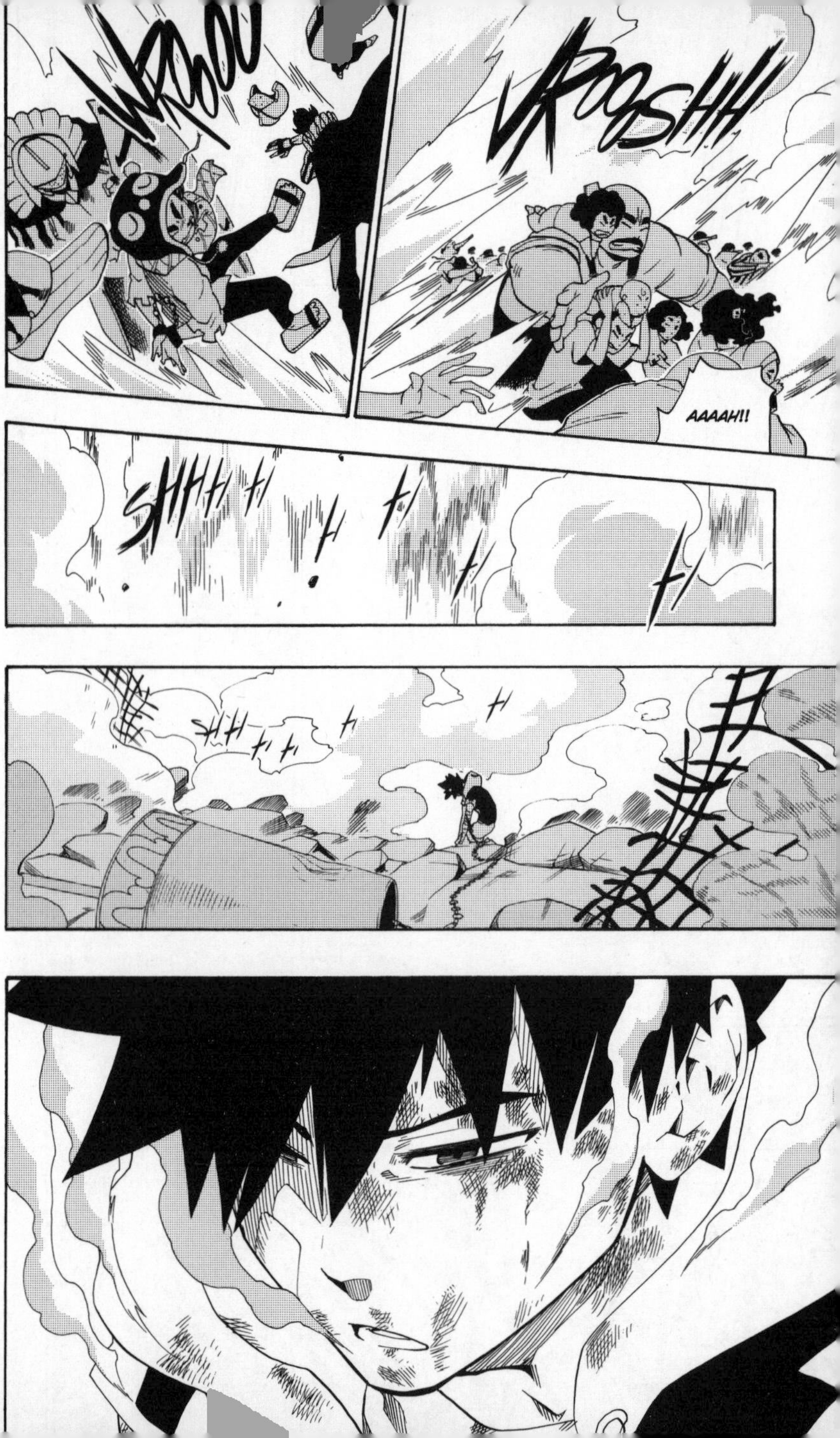
VROOSHH
AAAAH!!

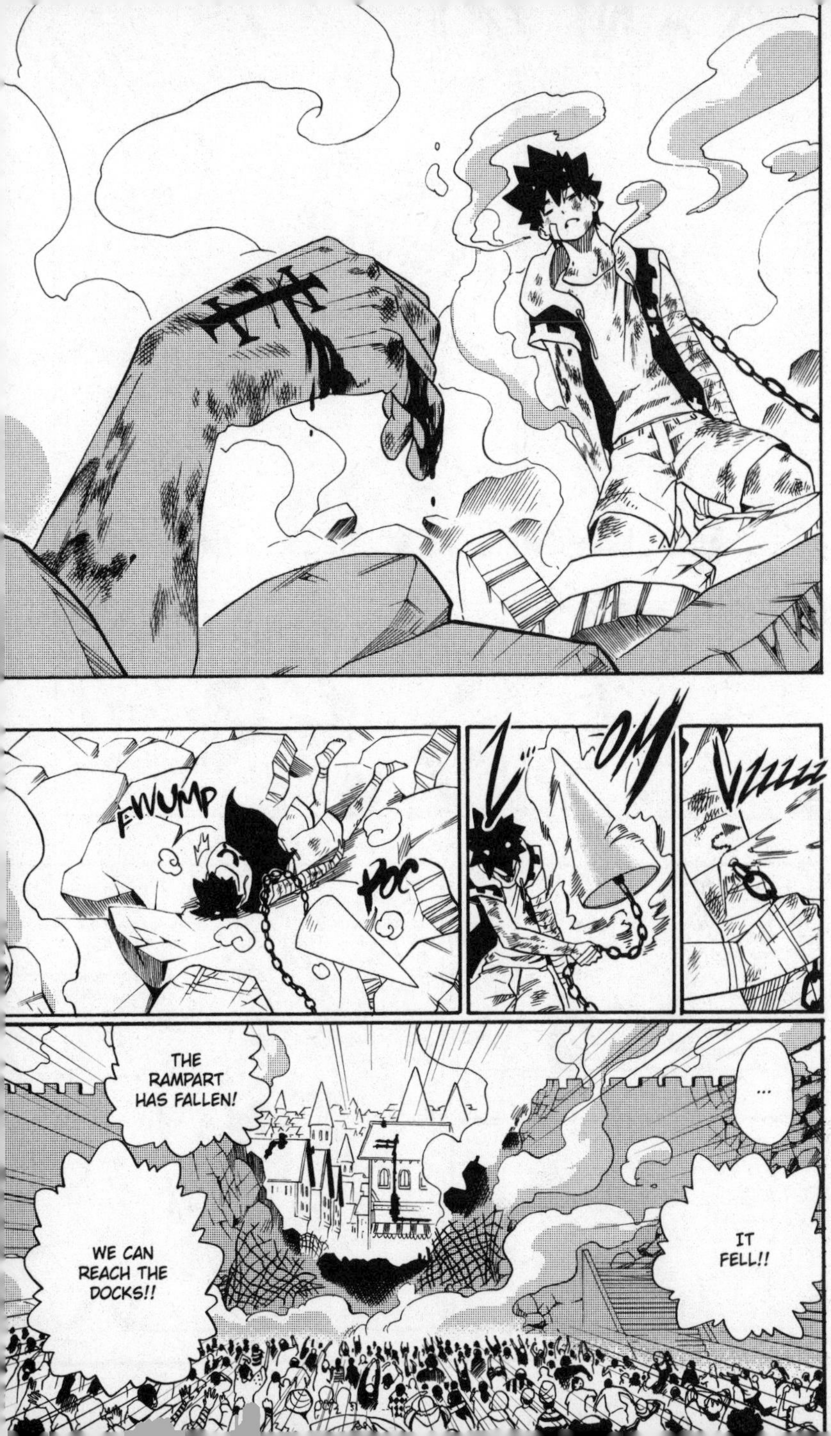

FWUMP
POC
ZOM
VZZZZZ
...
THE RAMPART HAS FALLEN!
IT FELL!!
WE CAN REACH THE DOCKS!!

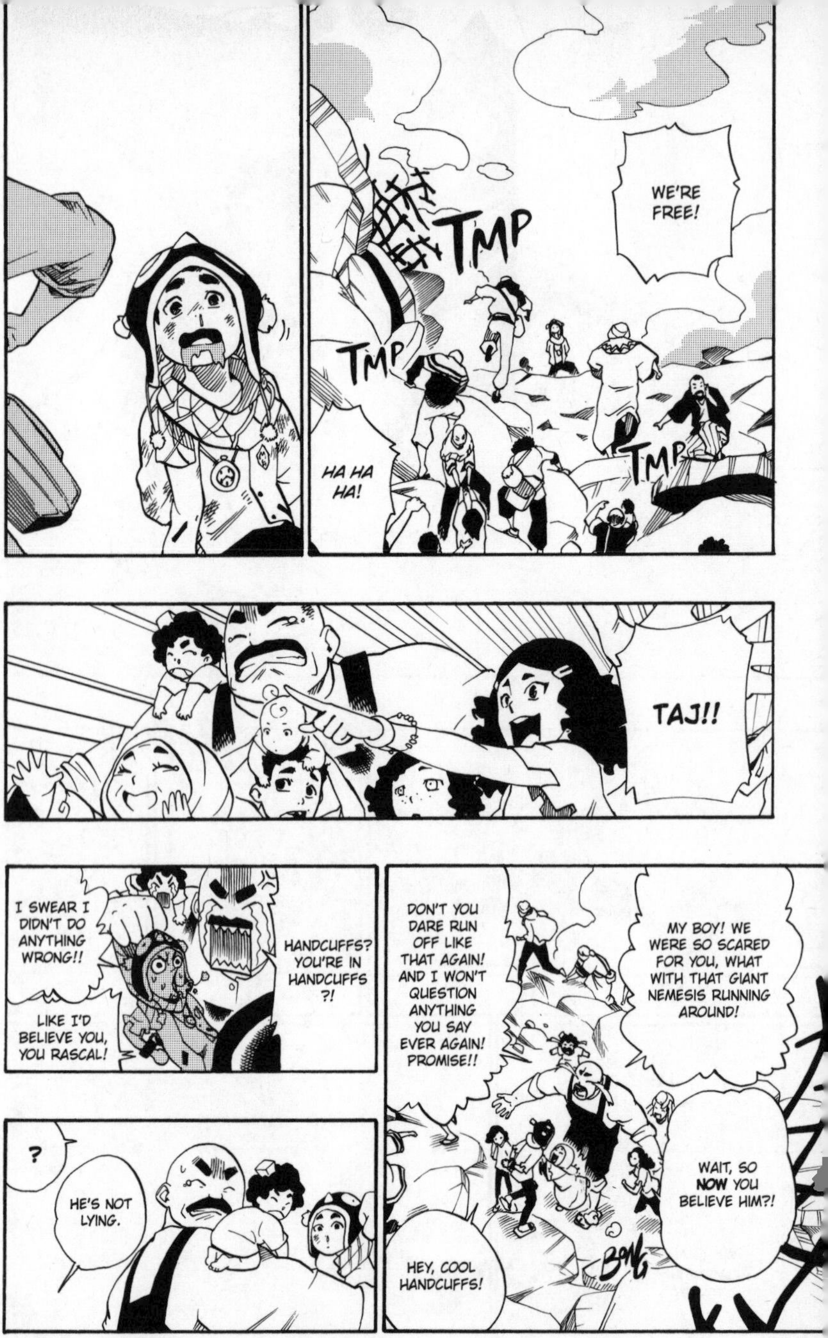

TMP
WE'RE FREE!
TMP
TMP
HA HA HA!
TAJ!!
I SWEAR I DIDN'T DO ANYTHING WRONG!!
LIKE I'D BELIEVE YOU, YOU RASCAL!
HANDCUFFS? YOU'RE IN HANDCUFFS?!
DON'T YOU DARE RUN OFF LIKE THAT AGAIN! AND I WON'T QUESTION ANYTHING YOU SAY EVER AGAIN! PROMISE!!
MY BOY! WE WERE SO SCARED FOR YOU, WHAT WITH THAT GIANT NEMESIS RUNNING AROUND!
?
HE'S NOT LYING.
HEY, COOL HANDCUFFS!
WAIT, SO NOW YOU BELIEVE HIM?!
BONG

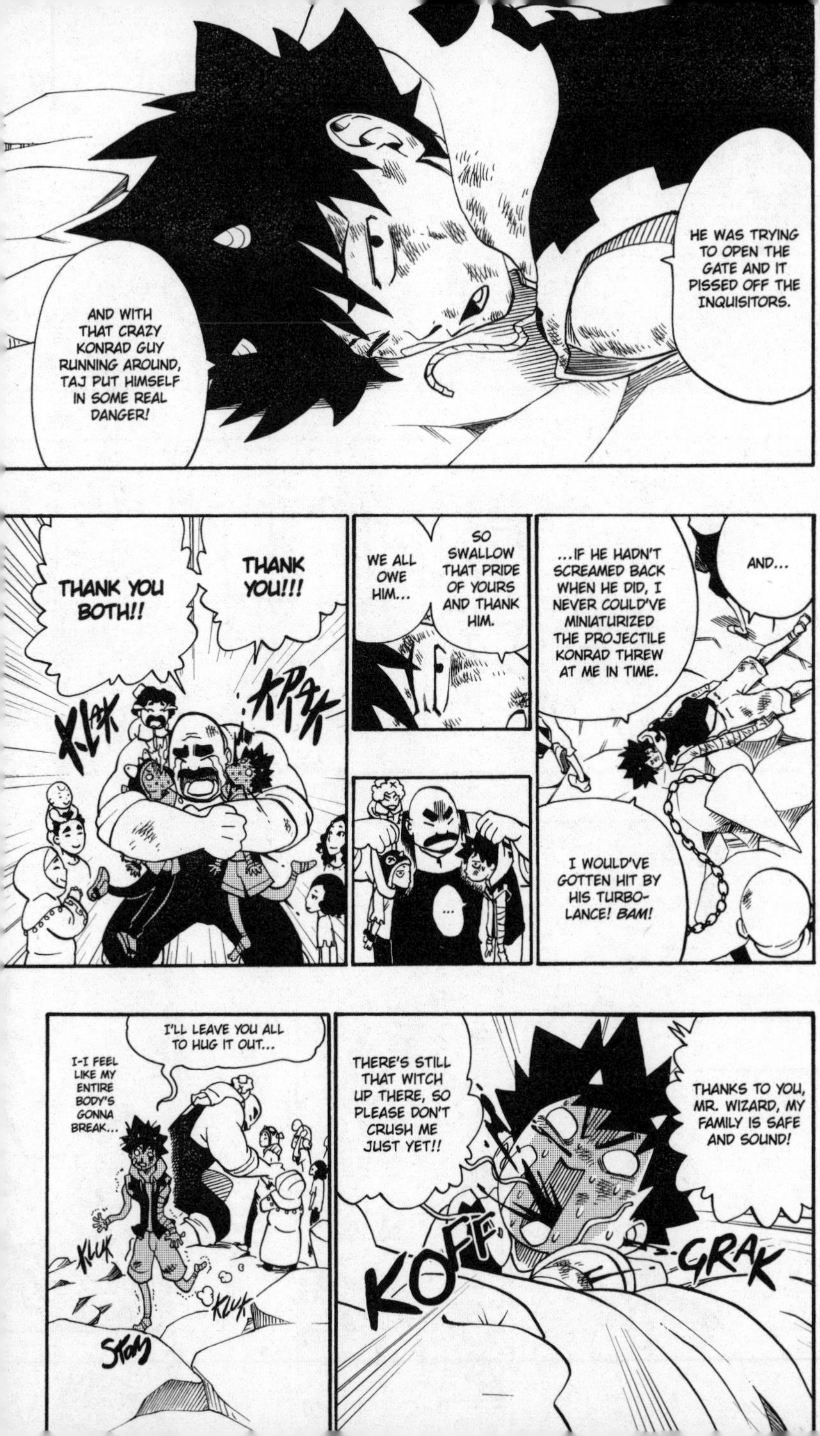
HE WAS TRYING TO OPEN THE GATE AND IT PISSED OFF THE INQUISITORS.
AND WITH THAT CRAZY KONRAD GUY RUNNING AROUND, TAJ PUT HIMSELF IN SOME REAL DANGER!
AND...
...IF HE HADN'T SCREAMED BACK WHEN HE DID, I NEVER COULD'VE MINIATURIZED THE PROJECTILE KONRAD THREW AT ME IN TIME.
I WOULD'VE GOTTEN HIT BY HIS TURBO-LANCE! BAM!
SO SWALLOW THAT PRIDE OF YOURS AND THANK HIM.
WE ALL OWE HIM...
...
THANK YOU!!!
THANK YOU BOTH!!
KRAK
KLAK
THANKS TO YOU, MR. WIZARD, MY FAMILY IS SAFE AND SOUND!
THERE'S STILL THAT WITCH UP THERE, SO PLEASE DON'T CRUSH ME JUST YET!!
KOFF
GRAK
I'LL LEAVE YOU ALL TO HUG IT OUT...
I-I FEEL LIKE MY ENTIRE BODY'S GONNA BREAK...
KLUK
KLUK
STOM

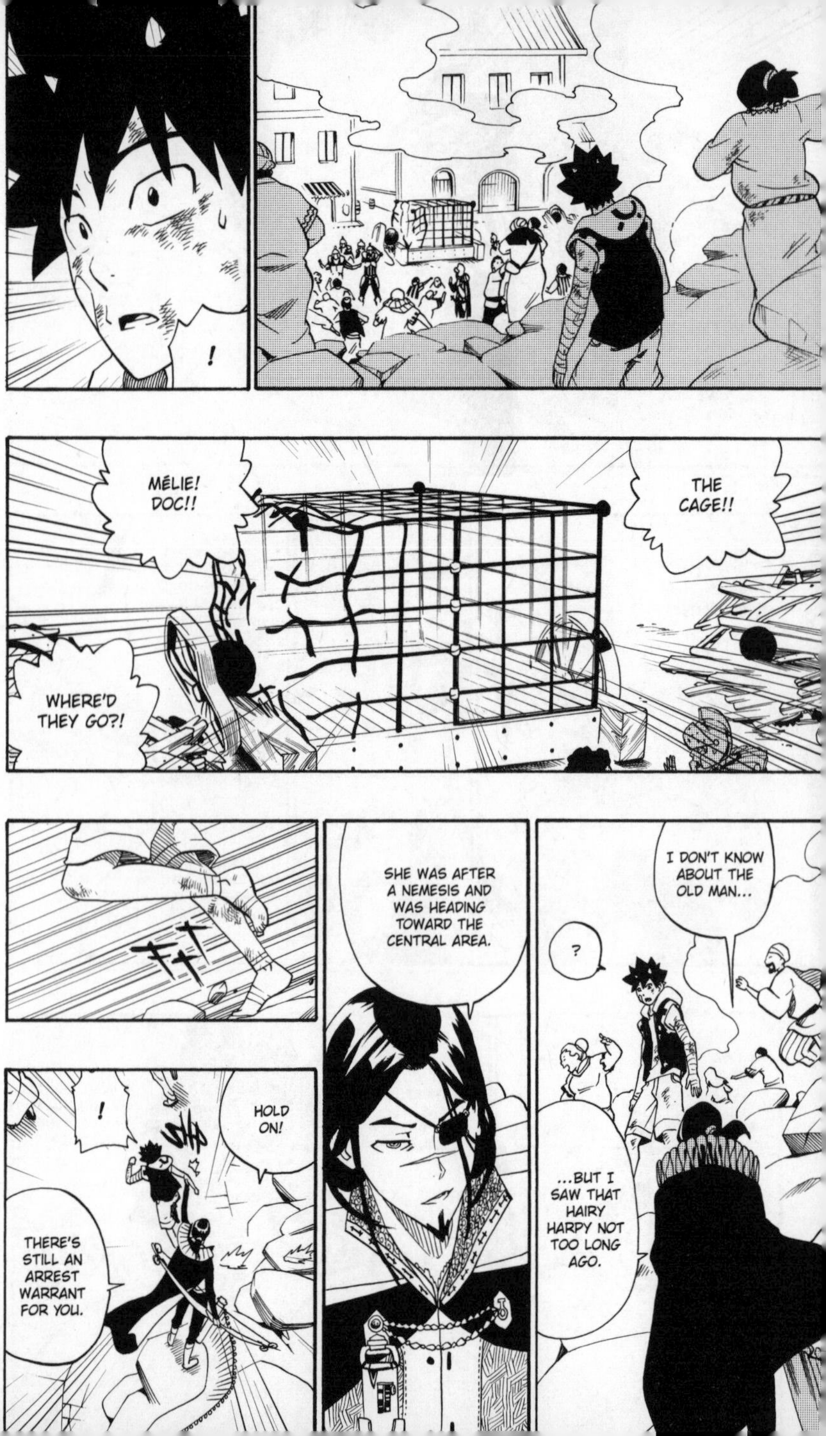
!
THE CAGE!!
MÉLIE! DOC!!
WHERE'D THEY GO?!
I DON'T KNOW ABOUT THE OLD MAN...
?
...BUT I SAW THAT HAIRY HARPY NOT TOO LONG AGO.
SHE WAS AFTER A NEMESIS AND WAS HEADING TOWARD THE CENTRAL AREA.
HOLD ON!
SHP
!
THERE'S STILL AN ARREST WARRANT FOR YOU.

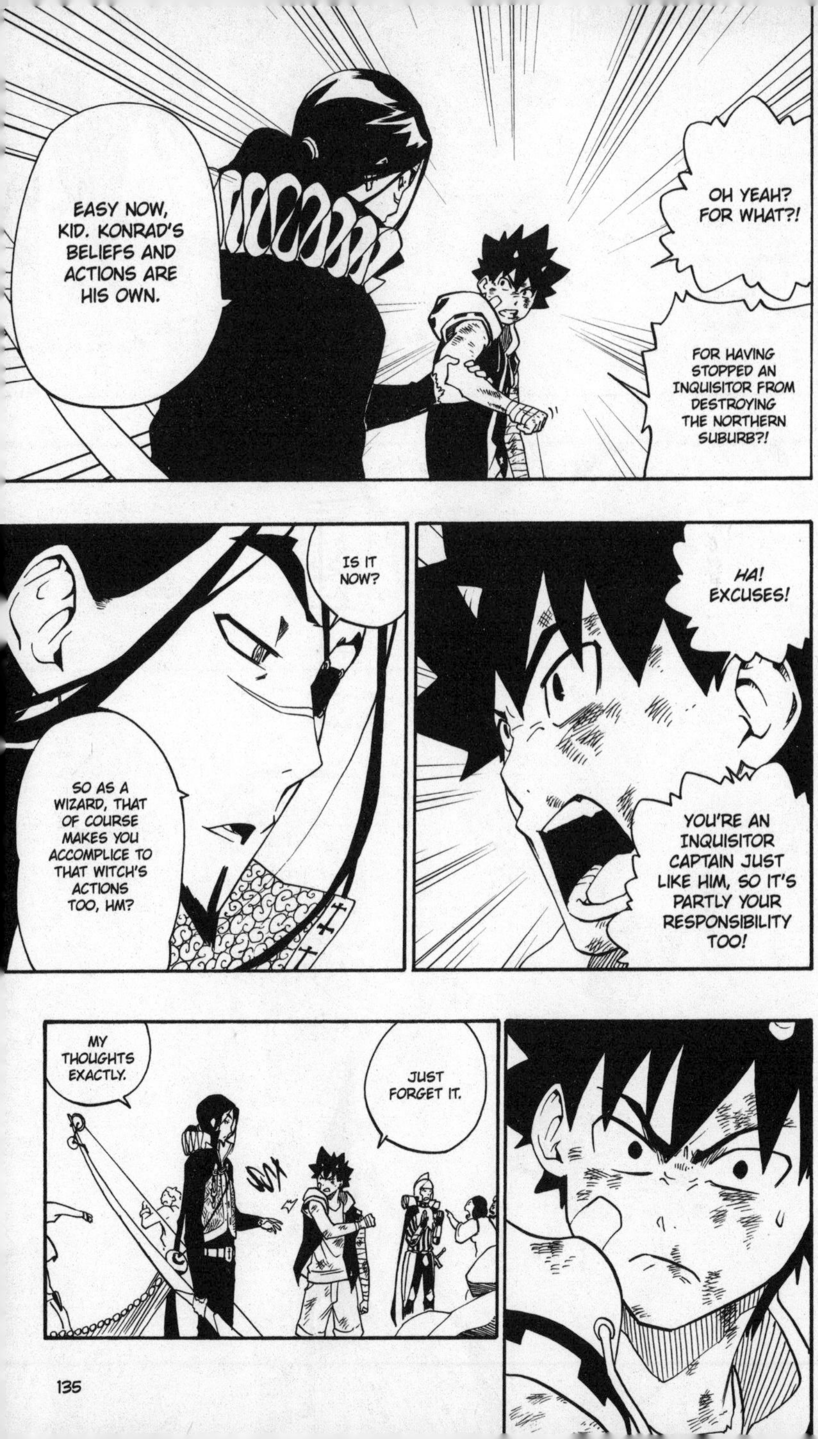
OH YEAH? FOR WHAT?!
FOR HAVING STOPPED AN INQUISITOR FROM DESTROYING THE NORTHERN SUBURB?!
EASY NOW, KID. KONRAD'S BELIEFS AND ACTIONS ARE HIS OWN.
HA! EXCUSES!
YOU'RE AN INQUISITOR CAPTAIN JUST LIKE HIM, SO IT'S PARTLY YOUR RESPONSIBILITY TOO!
IS IT NOW?
SO AS A WIZARD, THAT OF COURSE MAKES YOU ACCOMPLICE TO THAT WITCH'S ACTIONS TOO, HM?
JUST FORGET IT.
MY THOUGHTS EXACTLY.

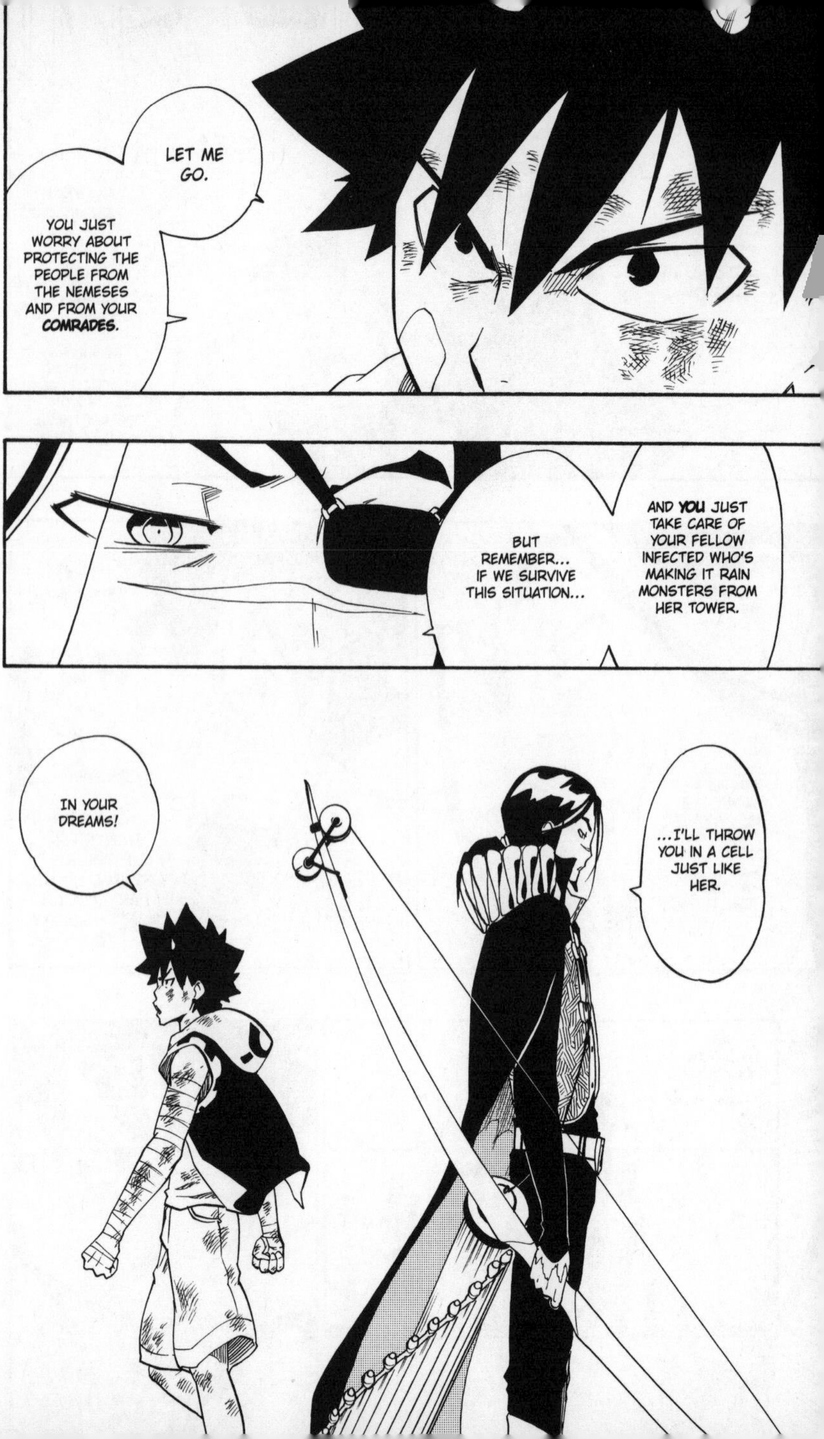
LET ME GO.
YOU JUST WORRY ABOUT PROTECTING THE PEOPLE FROM THE NEMESES AND FROM YOUR COMRADES.
AND YOU JUST TAKE CARE OF YOUR FELLOW INFECTED WHO'S MAKING IT RAIN MONSTERS FROM HER TOWER.
BUT REMEMBER... IF WE SURVIVE THIS SITUATION...
...I'LL THROW YOU IN A CELL JUST LIKE HER.
IN YOUR DREAMS!

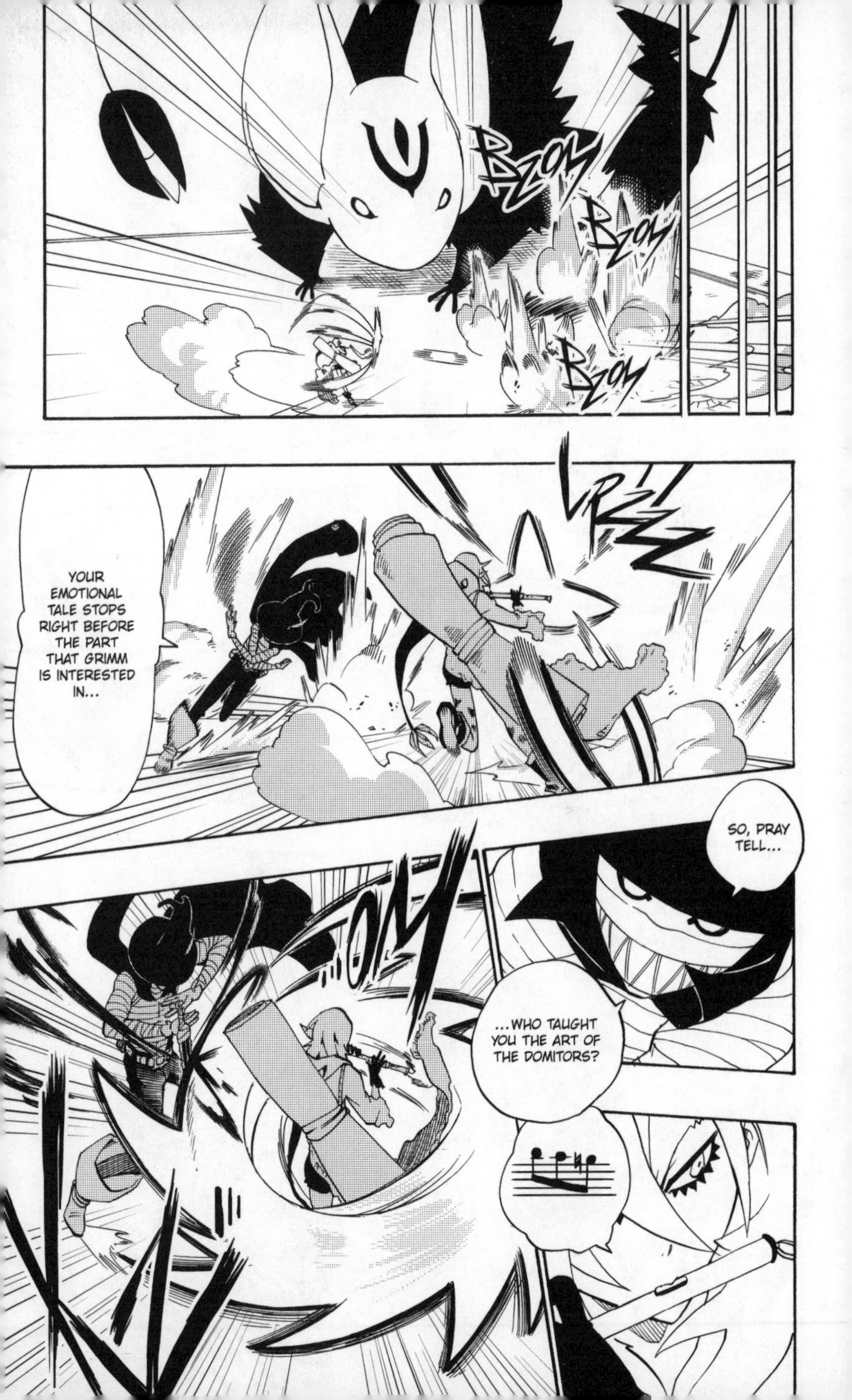
BZOM
BZOM
BZOM
VRZZZ
YOUR EMOTIONAL TALE STOPS RIGHT BEFORE THE PART THAT GRIMM IS INTERESTED IN...
SO, PRAY TELL...
...WHO TAUGHT YOU THE ART OF THE DOMITORS?
FOOM

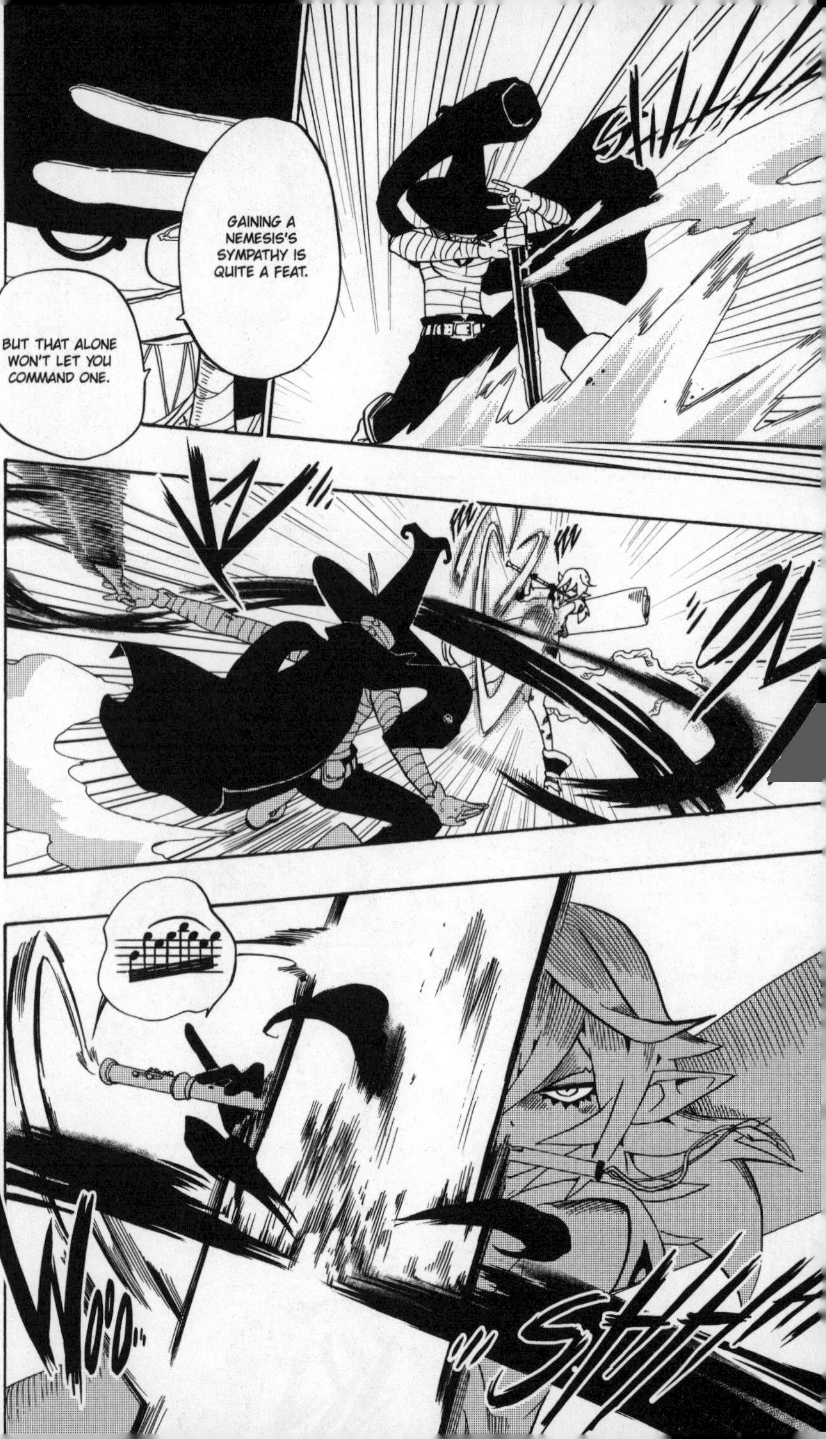

GAINING A NEMESIS'S SYMPATHY IS QUITE A FEAT.
BUT THAT ALONE WON'T LET YOU COMMAND ONE.

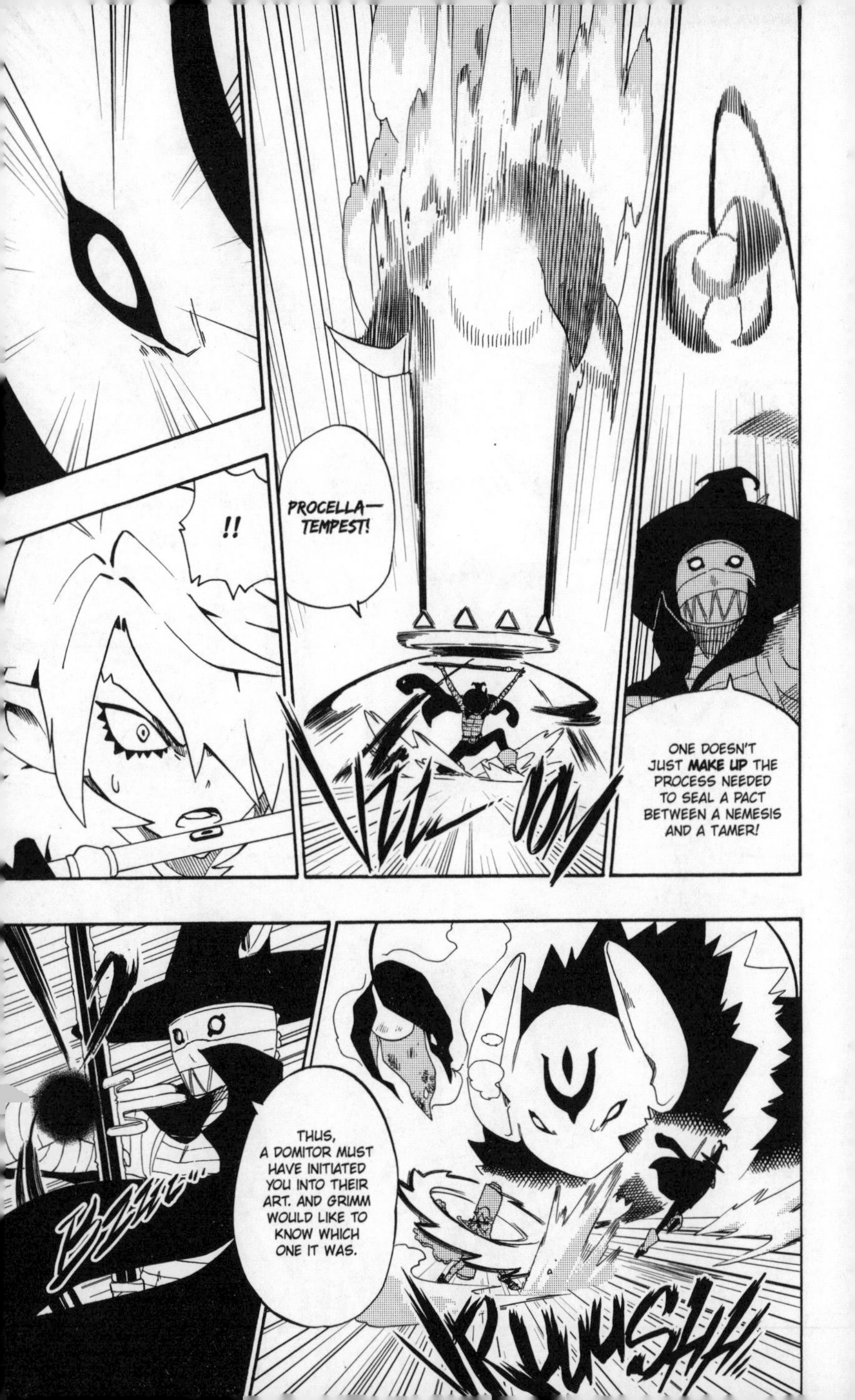
ONE DOESN'T JUST **MAKE UP** THE PROCESS NEEDED TO SEAL A PACT BETWEEN A NEMESIS AND A TAMER!
PROCELLA—TEMPEST!
!!
THUS, A DOMITOR MUST HAVE INITIATED YOU INTO THEIR ART. AND GRIMM WOULD LIKE TO KNOW WHICH ONE IT WAS.

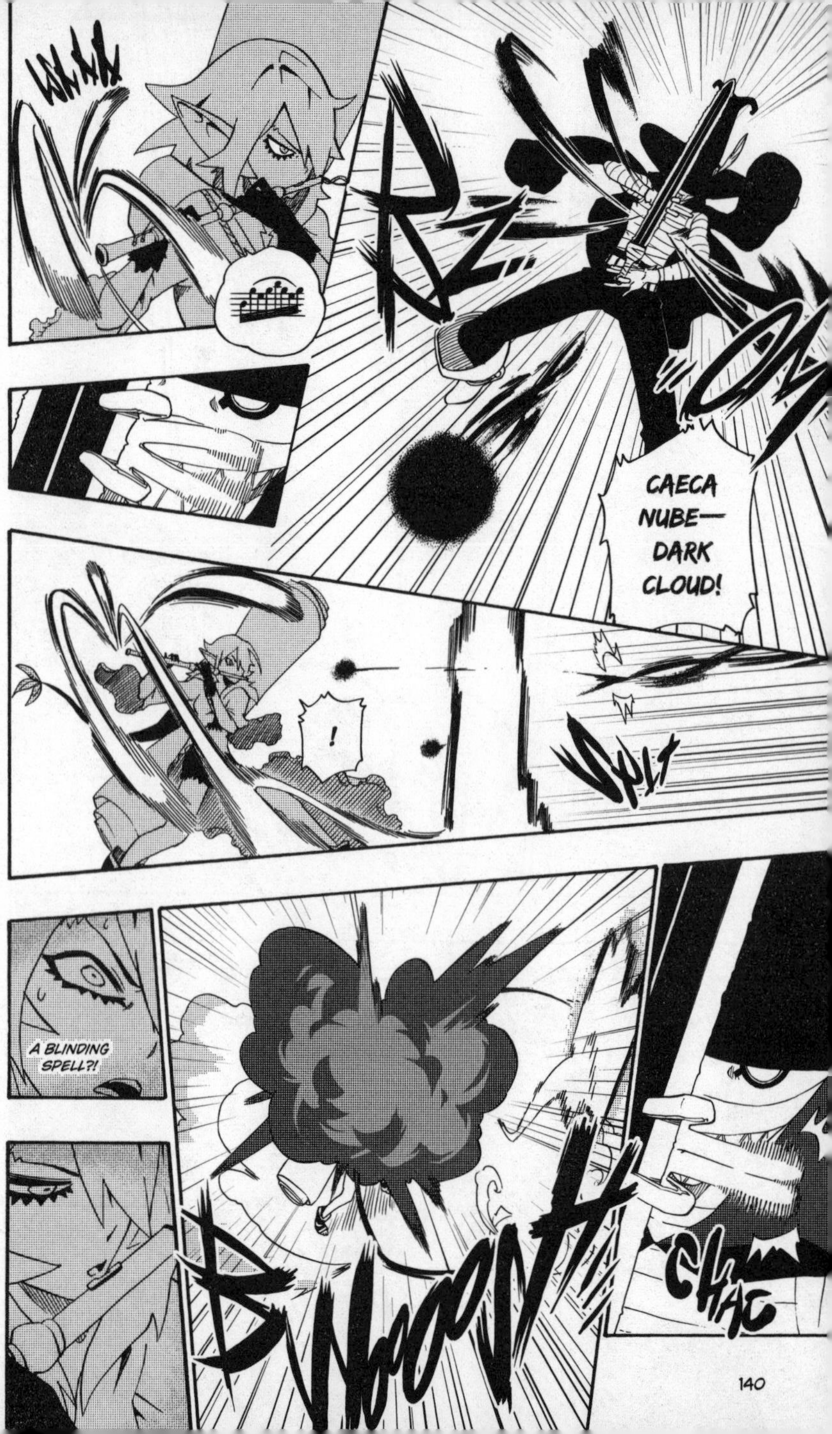
CAECA NUBE—DARK CLOUD!
!
A BLINDING SPELL?!

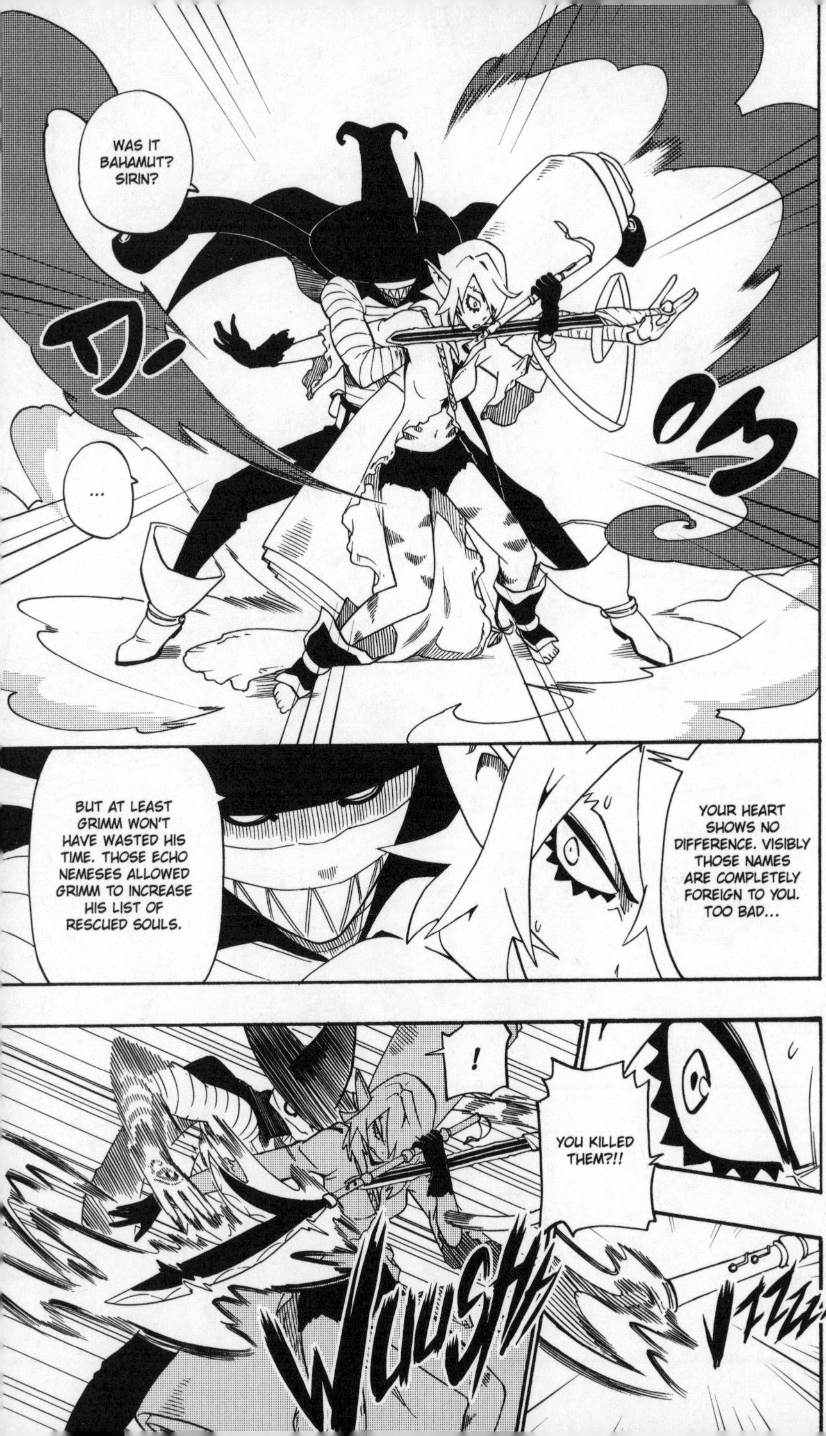
WAS IT BAHAMUT? SIRIN?
...
YOUR HEART SHOWS NO DIFFERENCE. VISIBLY THOSE NAMES ARE COMPLETELY FOREIGN TO YOU. TOO BAD...
BUT AT LEAST GRIMM WON'T HAVE WASTED HIS TIME. THOSE ECHO NEMESES ALLOWED GRIMM TO INCREASE HIS LIST OF RESCUED SOULS.
!
YOU KILLED THEM?!!

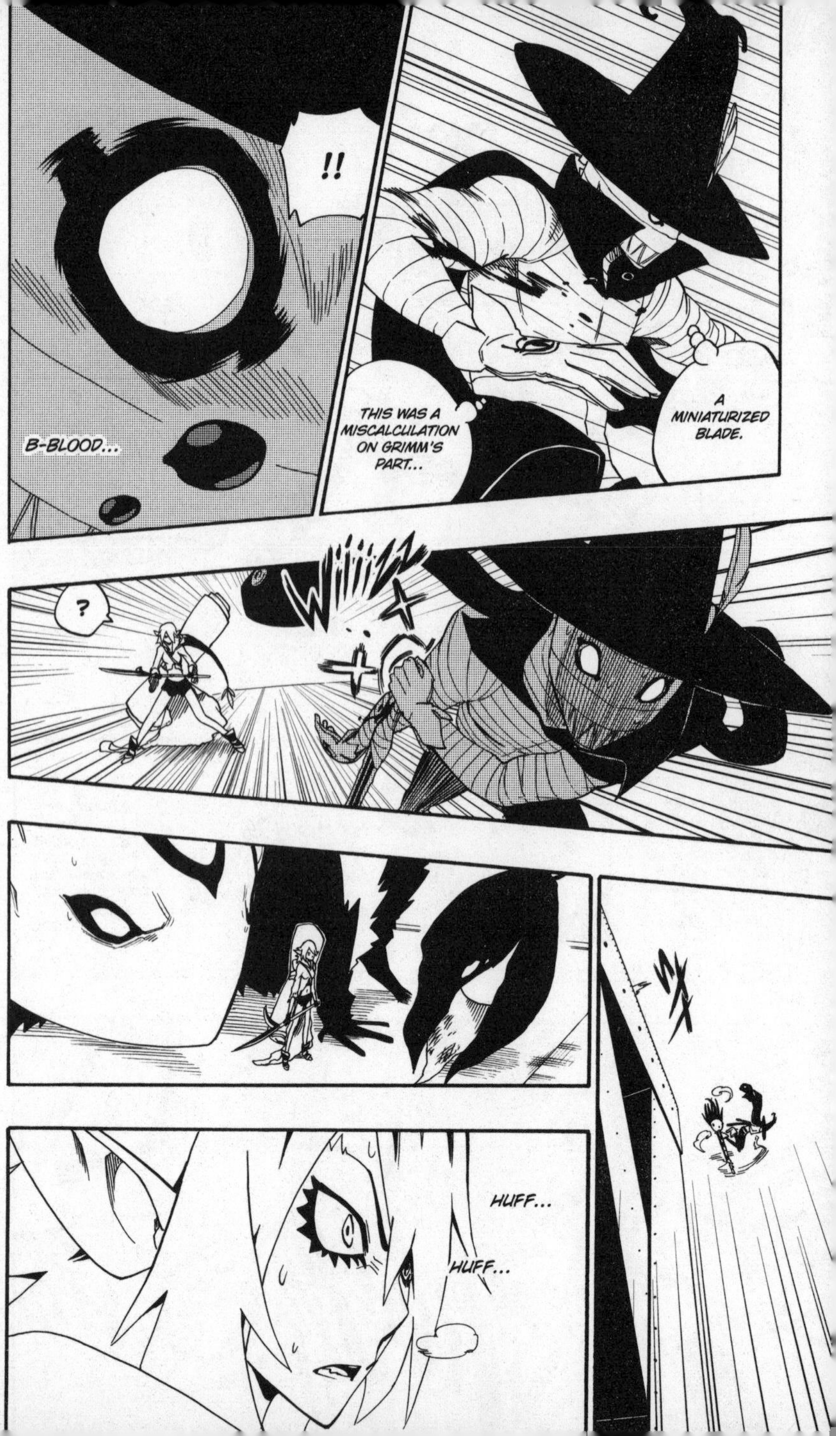
!!
A MINIATURIZED BLADE.
THIS WAS A MISCALCULATION ON GRIMM'S PART...
B-BLOOD...
WIIIZZ
?
SKT
HUFF...
HUFF...

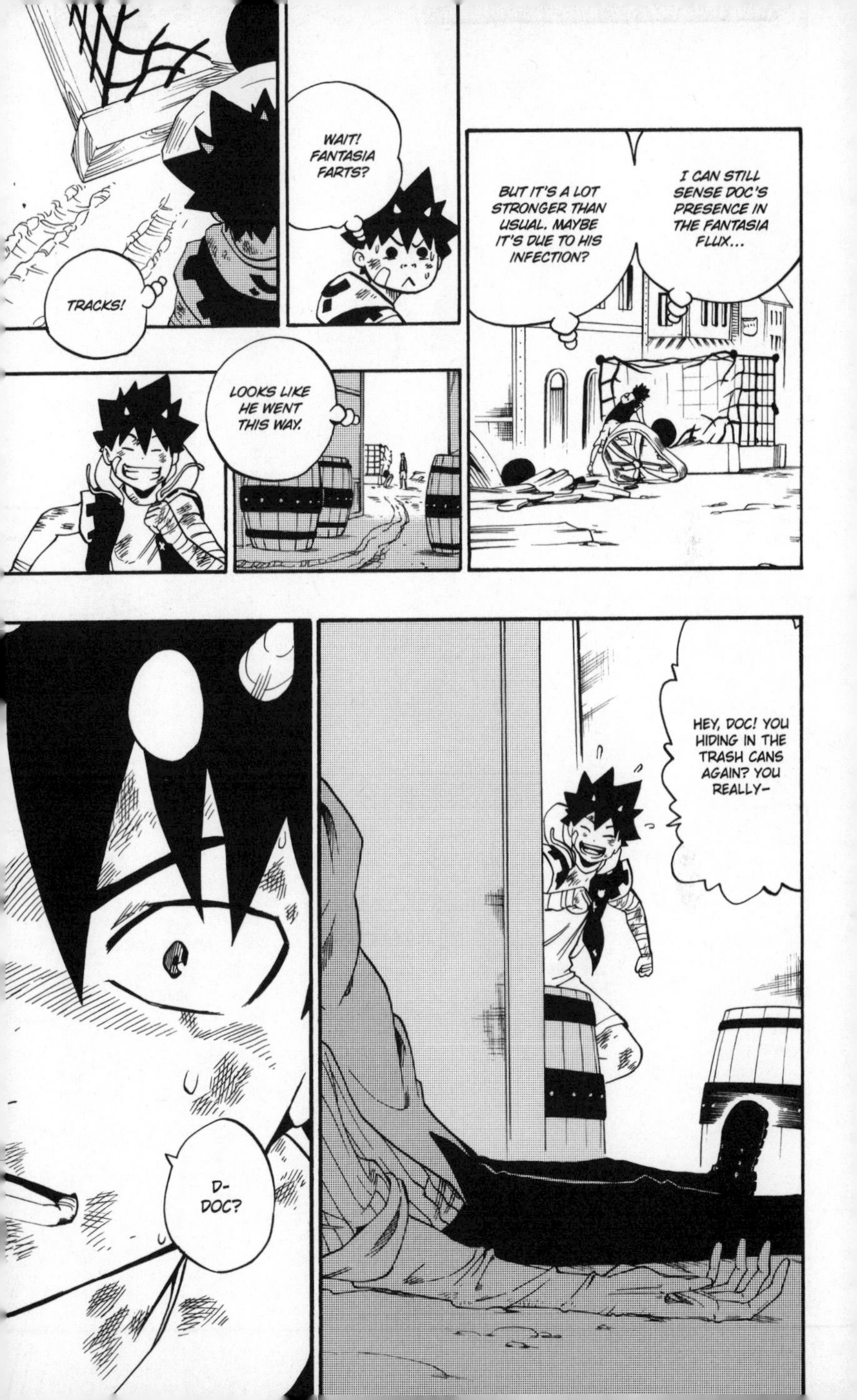
WAIT! FANTASIA FARTS?
TRACKS!
I CAN STILL SENSE DOC'S PRESENCE IN THE FANTASIA FLUX...
BUT IT'S A LOT STRONGER THAN USUAL. MAYBE IT'S DUE TO HIS INFECTION?
LOOKS LIKE HE WENT THIS WAY.
HEY, DOC! YOU HIDING IN THE TRASH CANS AGAIN? YOU REALLY-
D- DOC?

MEANWHILE ON THE DOCKS...

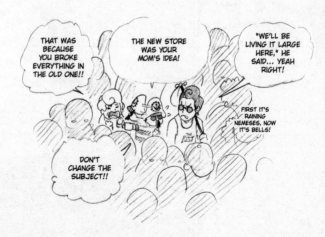

"WE'LL BE LIVING IT LARGE HERE," HE SAID... YEAH RIGHT!
FIRST IT'S RAINING NEMESES, NOW IT'S BELLS!
THE NEW STORE WAS YOUR MOM'S IDEA!
THAT WAS BECAUSE YOU BROKE EVERYTHING IN THE OLD ONE!!
DON'T CHANGE THE SUBJECT!!

Chapter 20
A Coffin for Doc

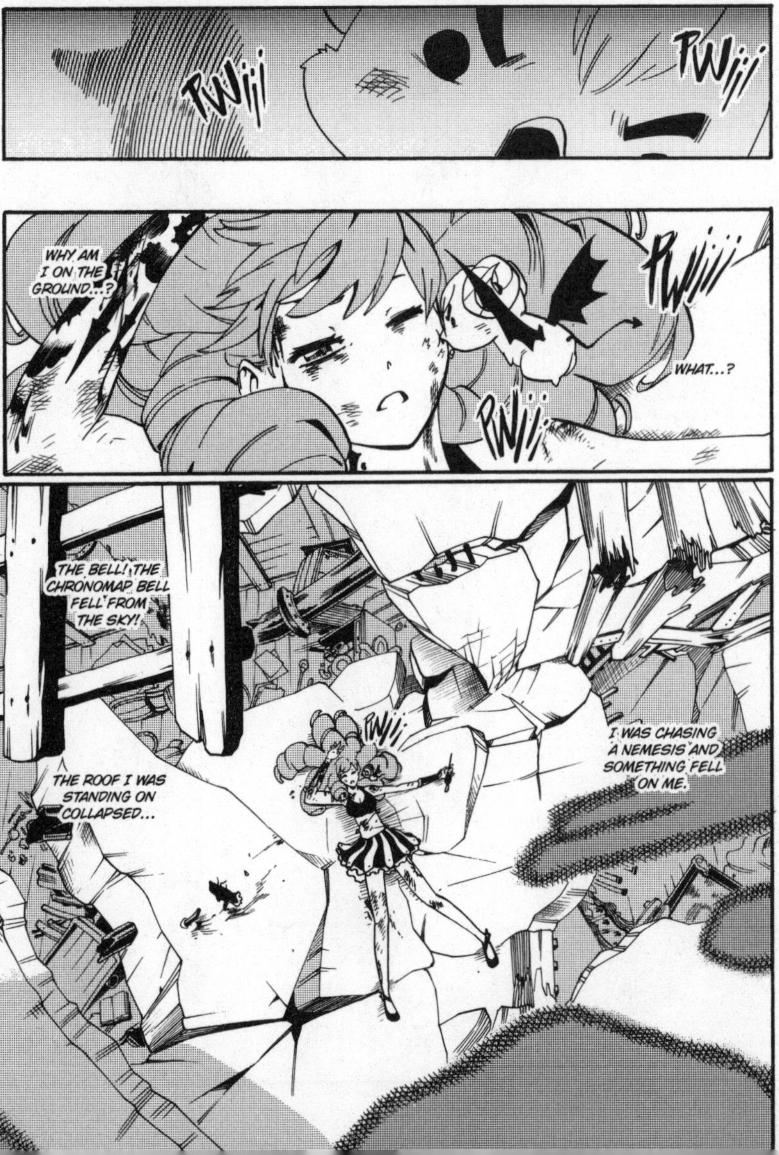
PWiii
PWiii
PWiii
WHAT...?
PWiii
WHY AM I ON THE GROUND...?
I WAS CHASING A NEMESIS AND SOMETHING FELL ON ME.
PWiii
THE ROOF I WAS STANDING ON COLLAPSED...
THE BELL! THE CHRONOMAP BELL FELL FROM THE SKY!

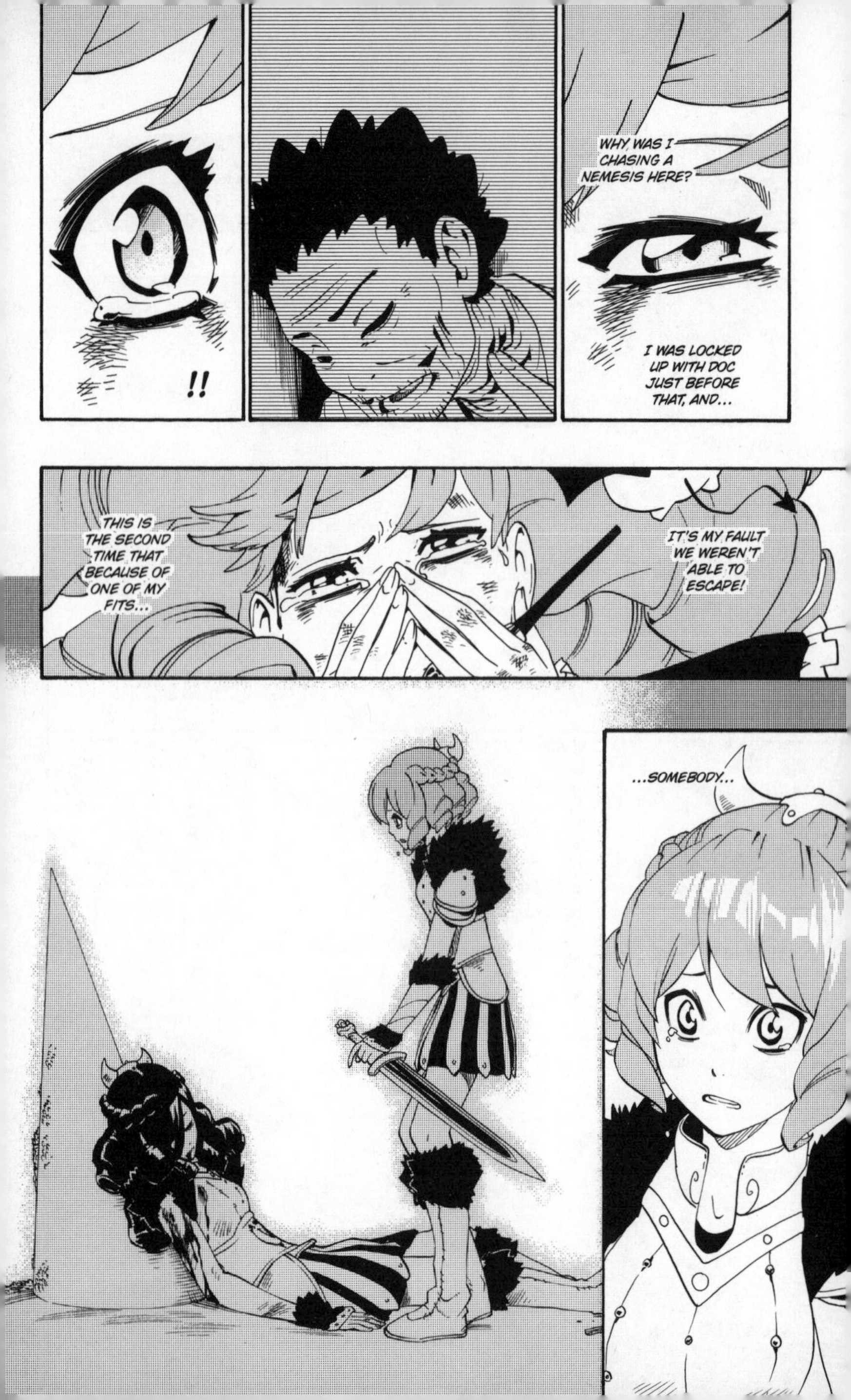
WHY WAS I CHASING A NEMESIS HERE?
I WAS LOCKED UP WITH DOC JUST BEFORE THAT, AND...
!!
THIS IS THE SECOND TIME THAT BECAUSE OF ONE OF MY FITS...
IT'S MY FAULT WE WEREN'T ABLE TO ESCAPE!
...SOMEBODY...

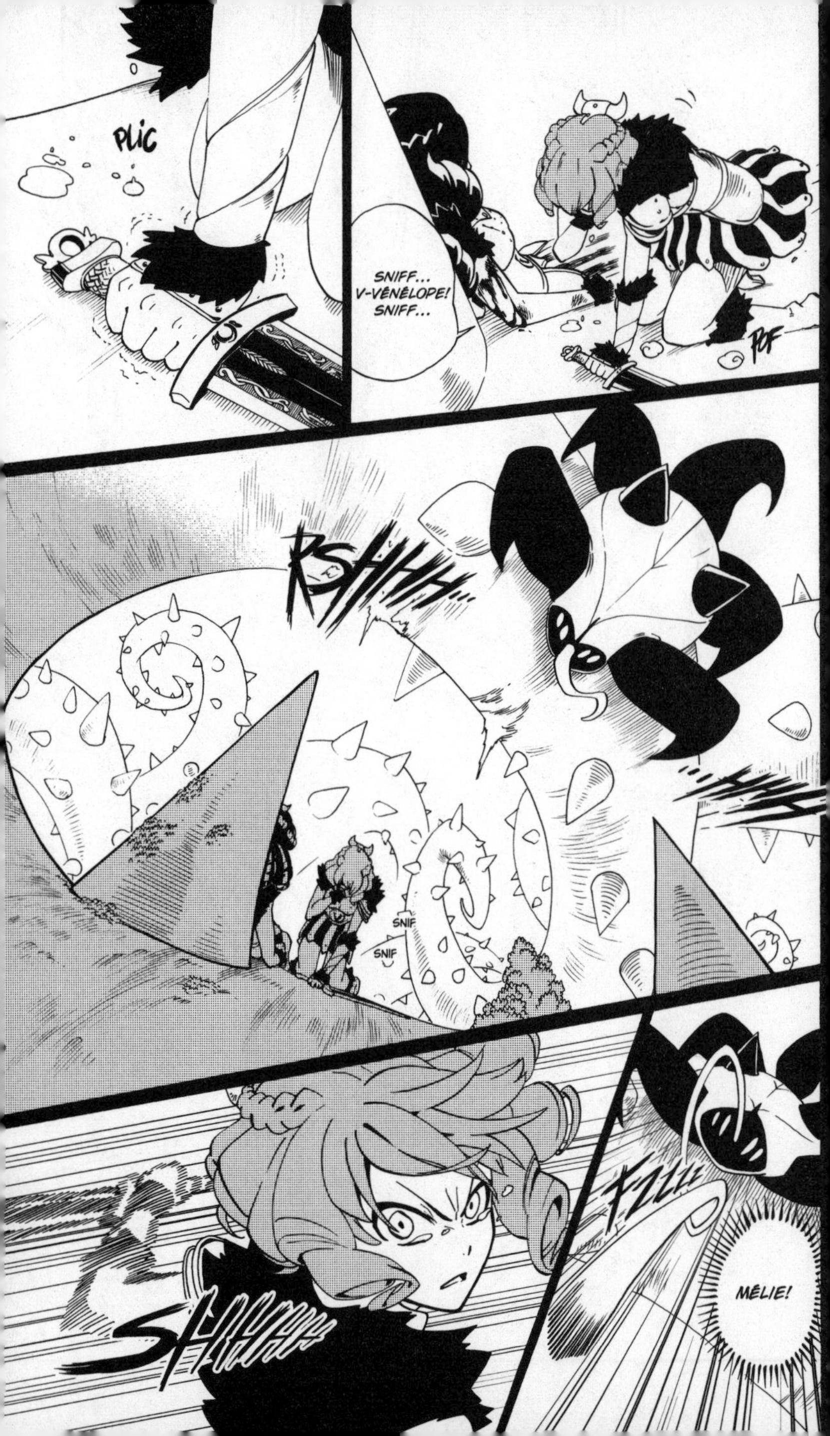
SNIFF... V-VÉNÉLOPE! SNIFF...
POF
PLIC
RSHHHH...
SNIF
SNIF
MÉLIE!

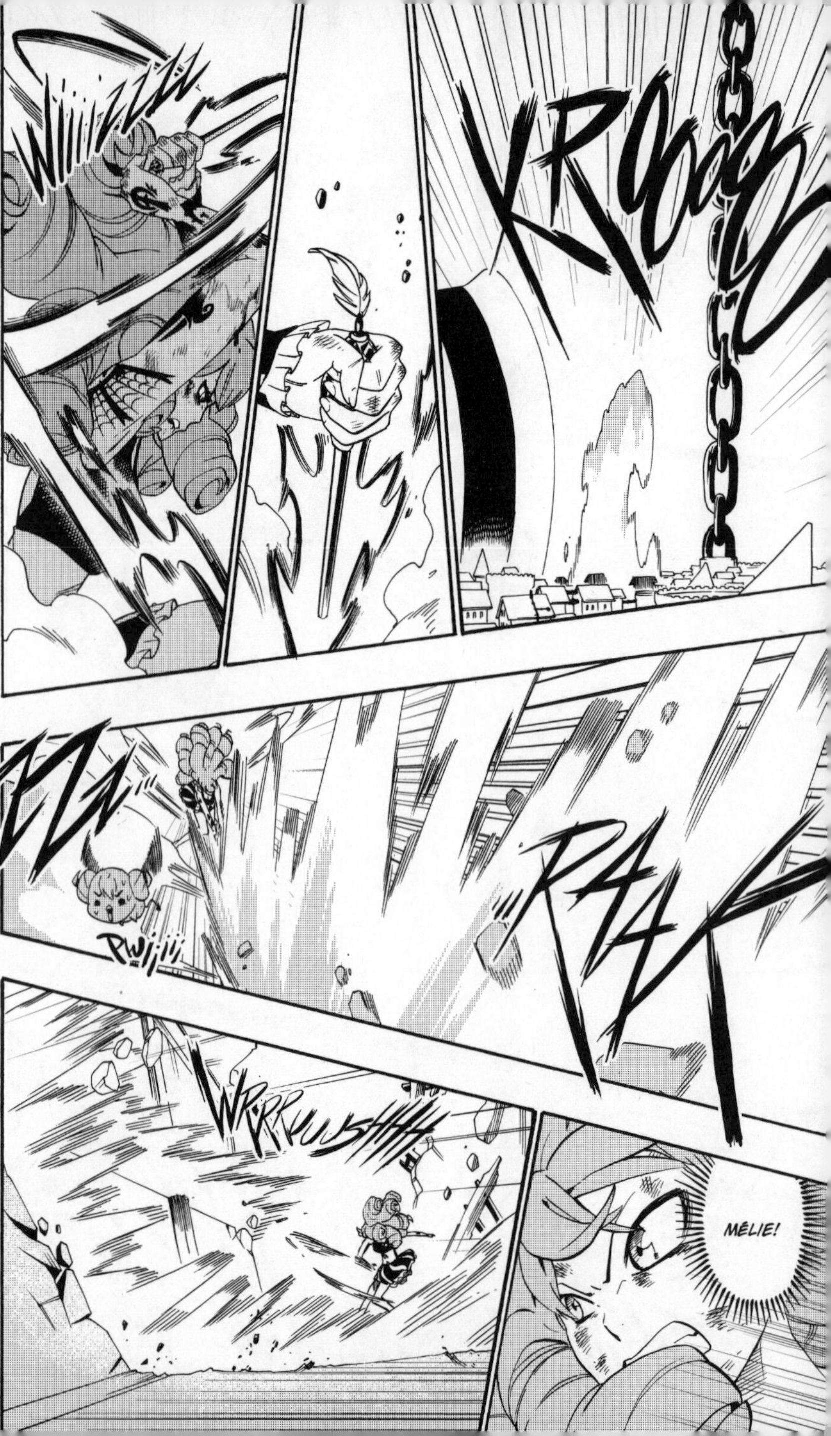
MÊLIE!

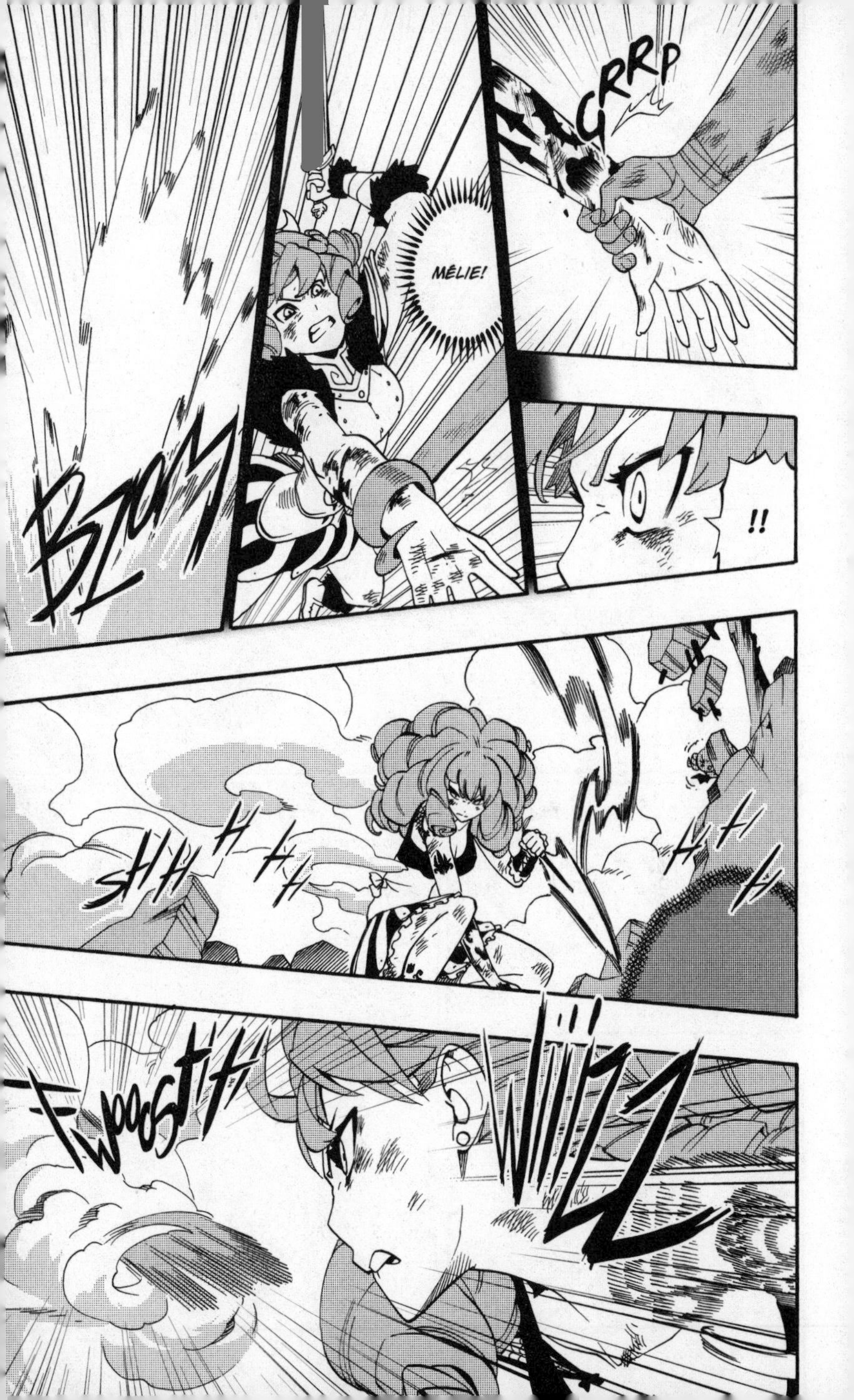
GRRP
MÉLIE!
BZOOM
!!
SHHHH
WHIZZ
FWOOSHH

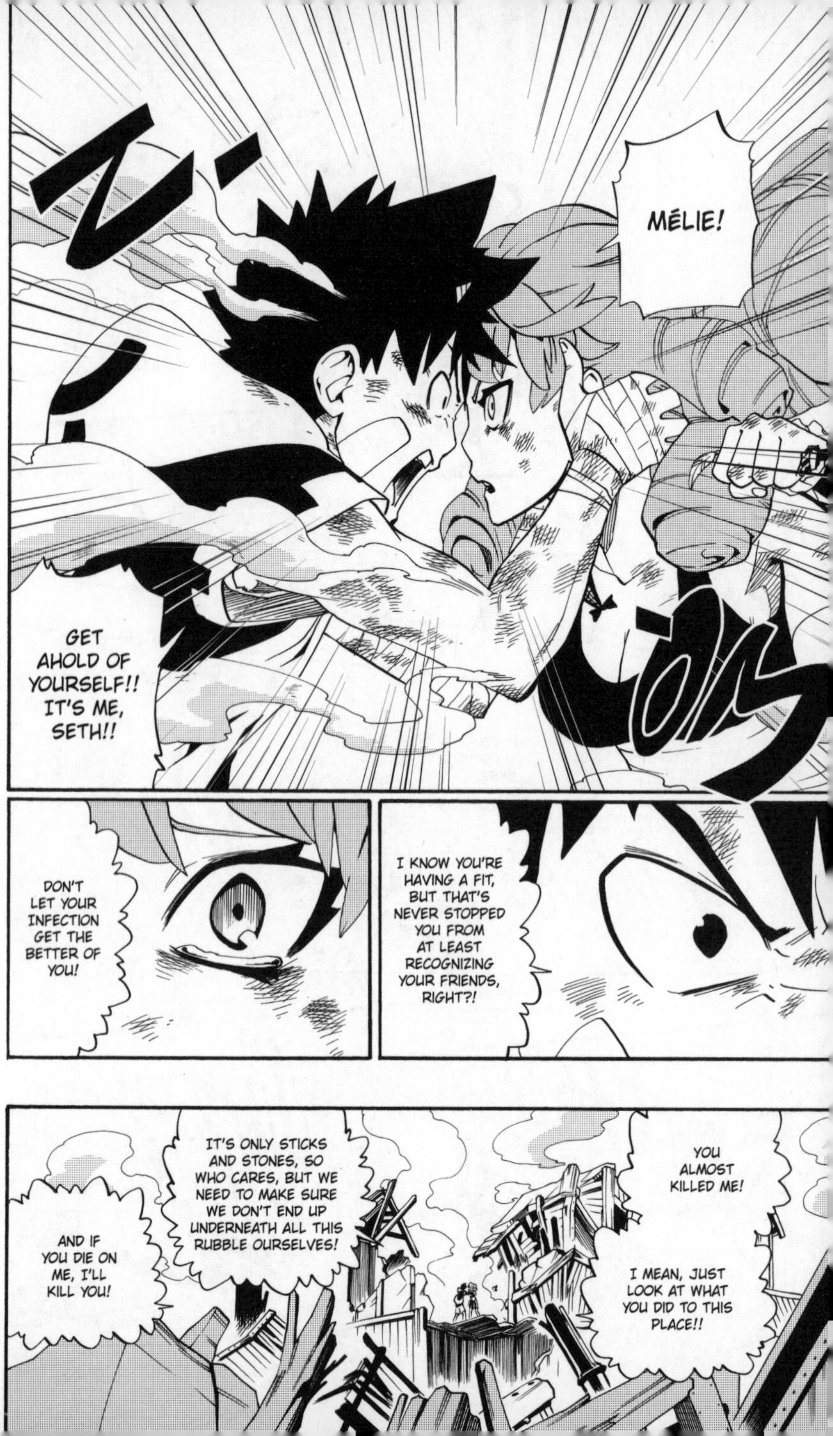
MÉLIE!
GET AHOLD OF YOURSELF!! IT'S ME, SETH!!
I KNOW YOU'RE HAVING A FIT, BUT THAT'S NEVER STOPPED YOU FROM AT LEAST RECOGNIZING YOUR FRIENDS, RIGHT?!
DON'T LET YOUR INFECTION GET THE BETTER OF YOU!
YOU ALMOST KILLED ME!
I MEAN, JUST LOOK AT WHAT YOU DID TO THIS PLACE!!
IT'S ONLY STICKS AND STONES, SO WHO CARES, BUT WE NEED TO MAKE SURE WE DON'T END UP UNDERNEATH ALL THIS RUBBLE OURSELVES!
AND IF YOU DIE ON ME, I'LL KILL YOU!

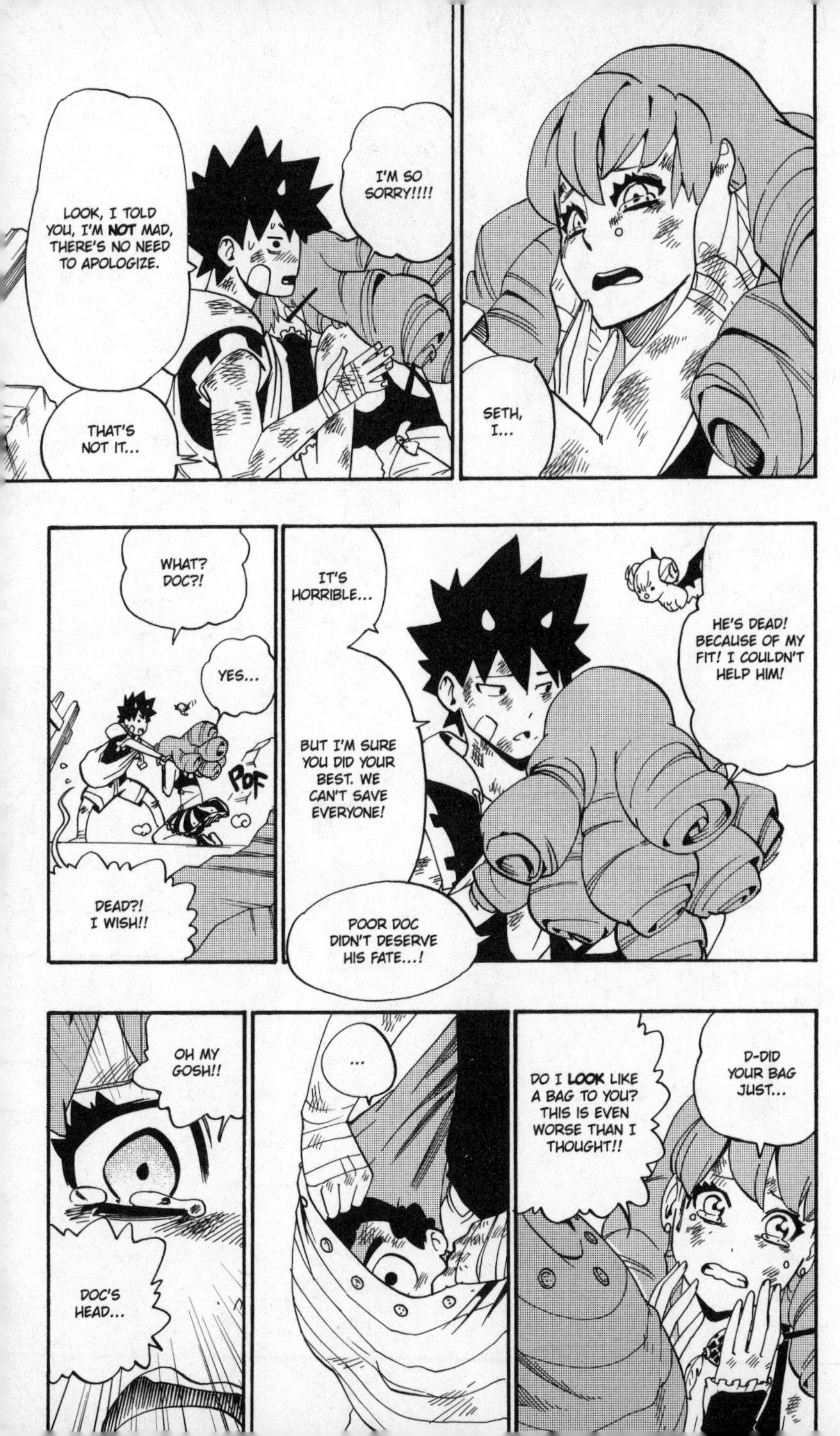
SETH, I...
I'M SO SORRY!!!!
LOOK, I TOLD YOU, I'M **NOT** MAD, THERE'S NO NEED TO APOLOGIZE.
THAT'S NOT IT...
HE'S DEAD! BECAUSE OF MY FIT! I COULDN'T HELP HIM!
IT'S HORRIBLE...
BUT I'M SURE YOU DID YOUR BEST. WE CAN'T SAVE EVERYONE!
POOR DOC DIDN'T DESERVE HIS FATE...!
WHAT? DOC?!
YES...
POF
DEAD?! I WISH!!
D-DID YOUR BAG JUST...
DO I **LOOK** LIKE A BAG TO YOU? THIS IS EVEN WORSE THAN I THOUGHT!!
...
OH MY GOSH!!
DOC'S HEAD...

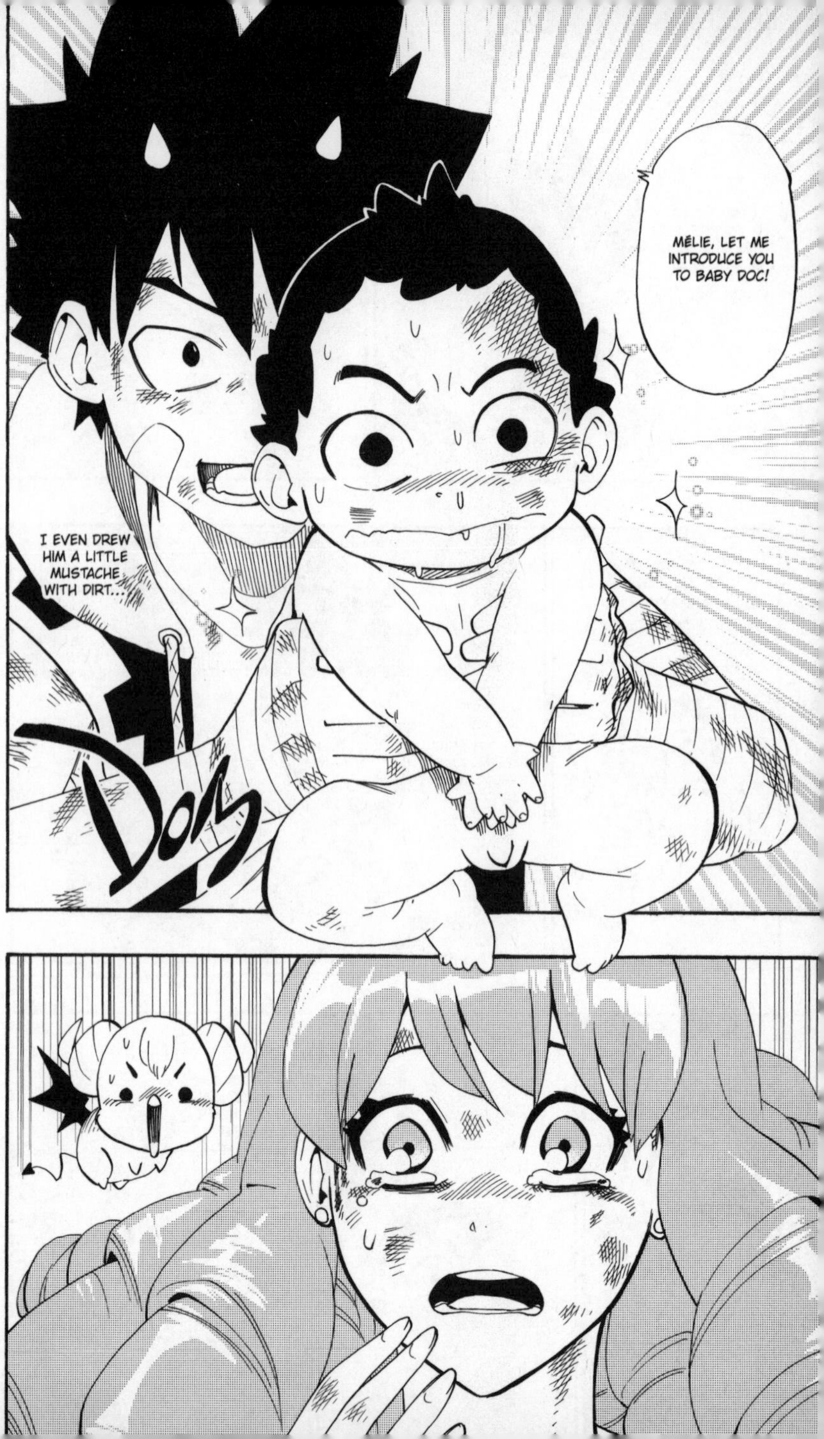
MÉLIE, LET ME INTRODUCE YOU TO BABY DOC!
I EVEN DREW HIM A LITTLE MUSTACHE WITH DIRT...

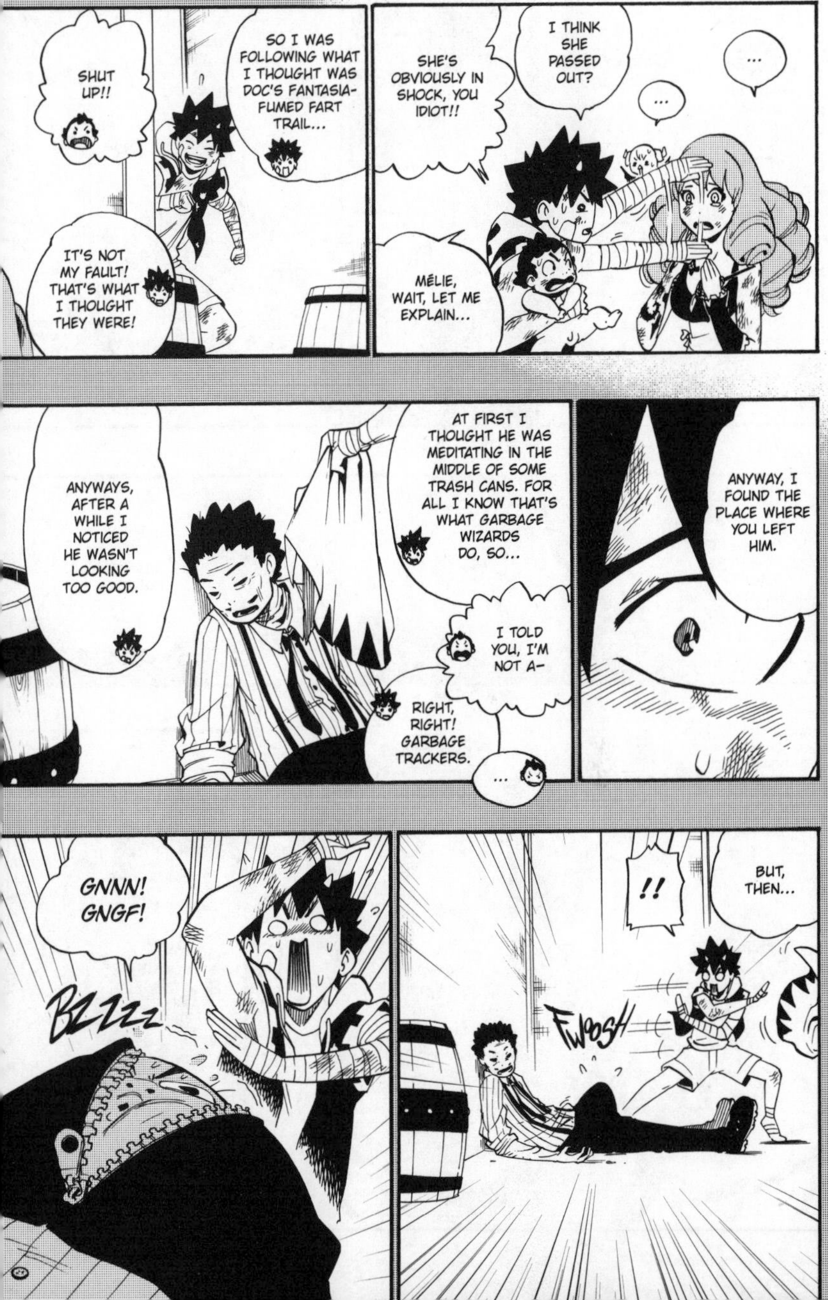
...
...
I THINK SHE PASSED OUT?
SHE'S OBVIOUSLY IN SHOCK, YOU IDIOT!!
MÉLIE, WAIT, LET ME EXPLAIN...
SO I WAS FOLLOWING WHAT I THOUGHT WAS DOC'S FANTASIA-FUMED FART TRAIL...
SHUT UP!!
IT'S NOT MY FAULT! THAT'S WHAT I THOUGHT THEY WERE!
ANYWAY, I FOUND THE PLACE WHERE YOU LEFT HIM.
AT FIRST I THOUGHT HE WAS MEDITATING IN THE MIDDLE OF SOME TRASH CANS. FOR ALL I KNOW THAT'S WHAT GARBAGE WIZARDS DO, SO...
I TOLD YOU, I'M NOT A-
RIGHT, RIGHT! GARBAGE TRACKERS.
...
ANYWAYS, AFTER A WHILE I NOTICED HE WASN'T LOOKING TOO GOOD.
BUT, THEN...
!!
FWOOSH
GNNN! GNGF!
BZZZZ

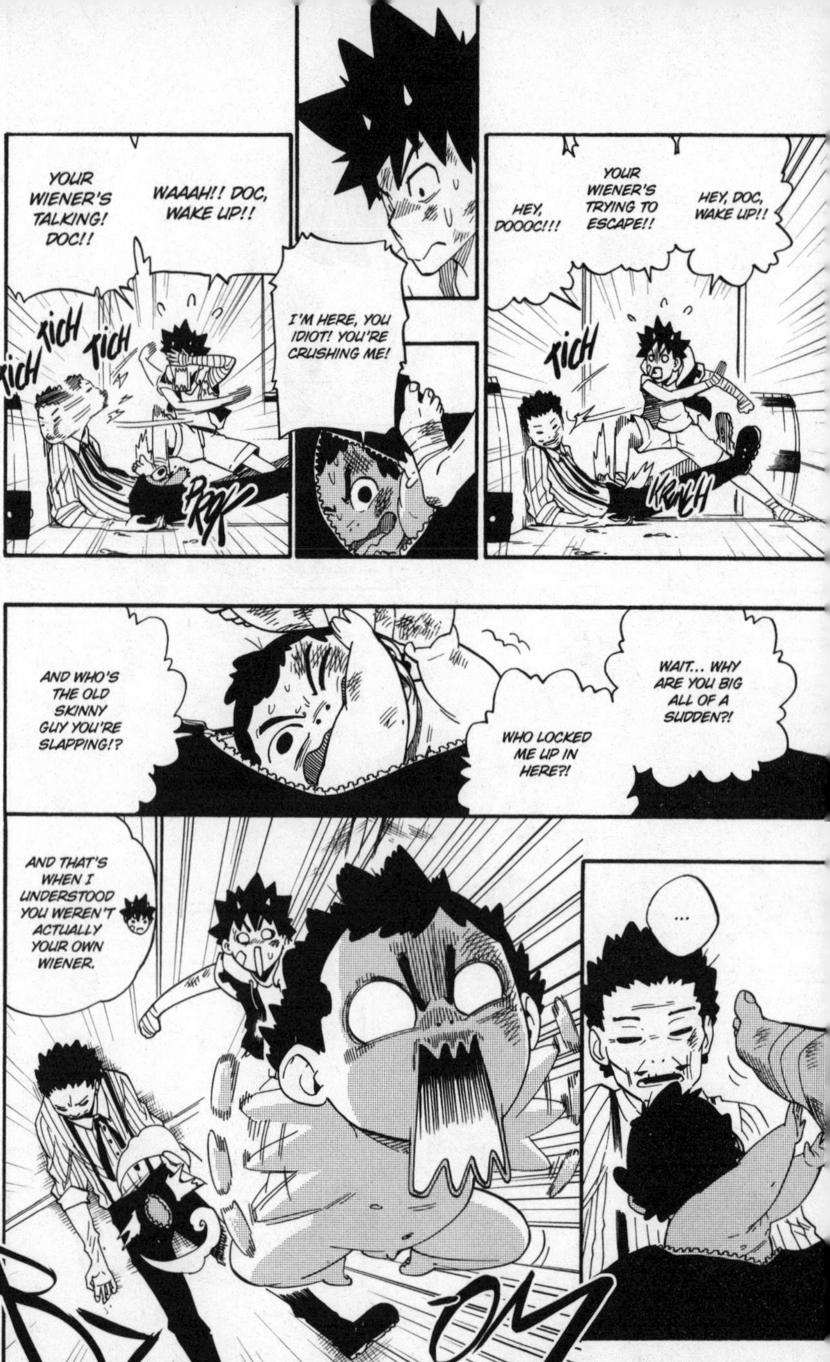
HEY, DOC, WAKE UP!!
YOUR WIENER'S TRYING TO ESCAPE!!
HEY, DOOOC!!!
TICH
KRUNCH
I'M HERE, YOU IDIOT! YOU'RE CRUSHING ME!
WAAAH!! DOC, WAKE UP!!
YOUR WIENER'S TALKING! DOC!!
TICH
TICH
TICH
WAIT... WHY ARE YOU BIG ALL OF A SUDDEN?!
WHO LOCKED ME UP IN HERE?!
AND WHO'S THE OLD SKINNY GUY YOU'RE SLAPPING!?
...
AND THAT'S WHEN I UNDERSTOOD YOU WEREN'T ACTUALLY YOUR OWN WIENER.

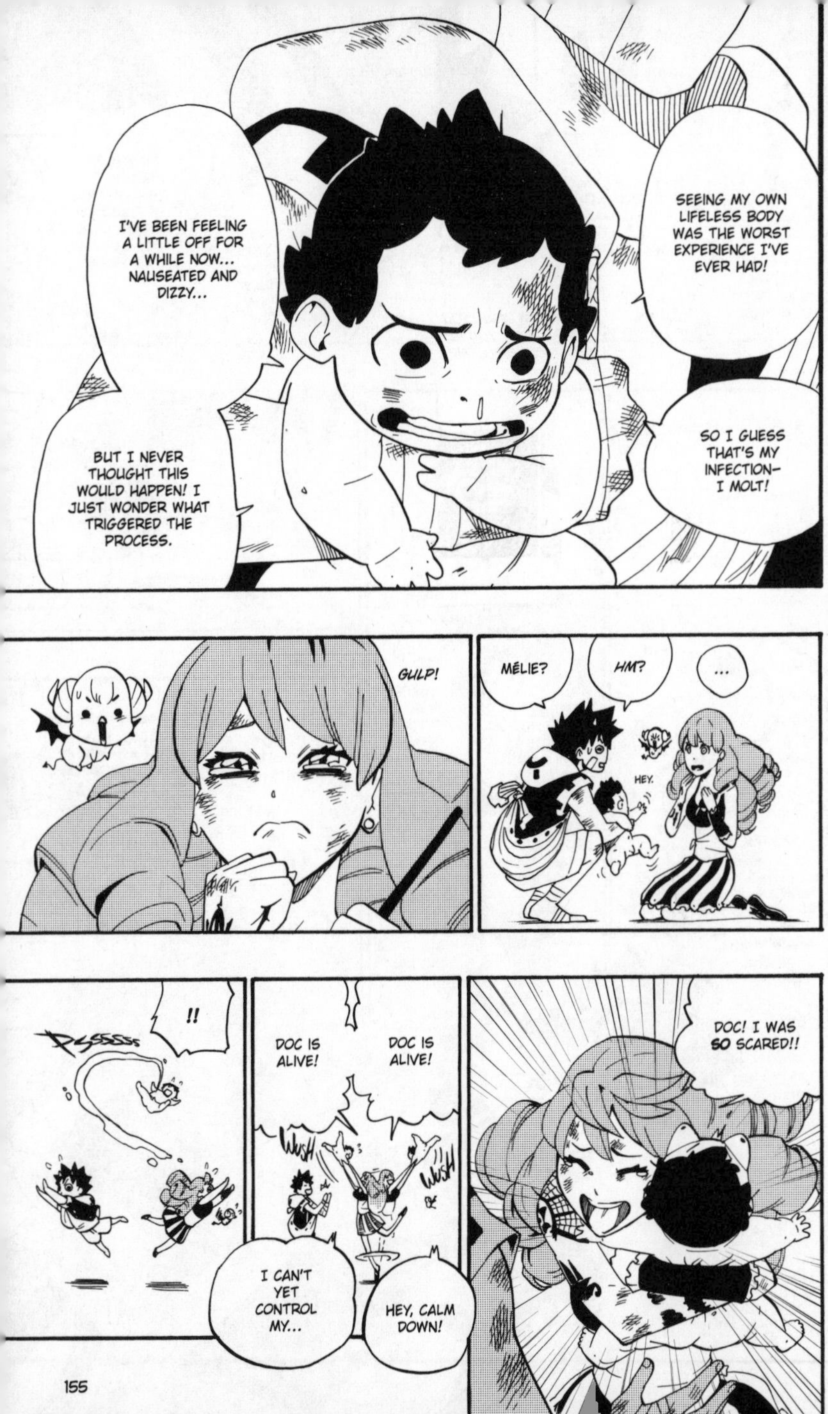
I'VE BEEN FEELING A LITTLE OFF FOR A WHILE NOW... NAUSEATED AND DIZZY...
BUT I NEVER THOUGHT THIS WOULD HAPPEN! I JUST WONDER WHAT TRIGGERED THE PROCESS.
SEEING MY OWN LIFELESS BODY WAS THE WORST EXPERIENCE I'VE EVER HAD!
SO I GUESS THAT'S MY INFECTION— I MOLT!
GULP!
MÉLIE?
HM?
...
HEY.
!!
PSSSSS
DOC IS ALIVE!
DOC IS ALIVE!
WUSH
WUSH
I CAN'T YET CONTROL MY...
HEY, CALM DOWN!
DOC! I WAS SO SCARED!!

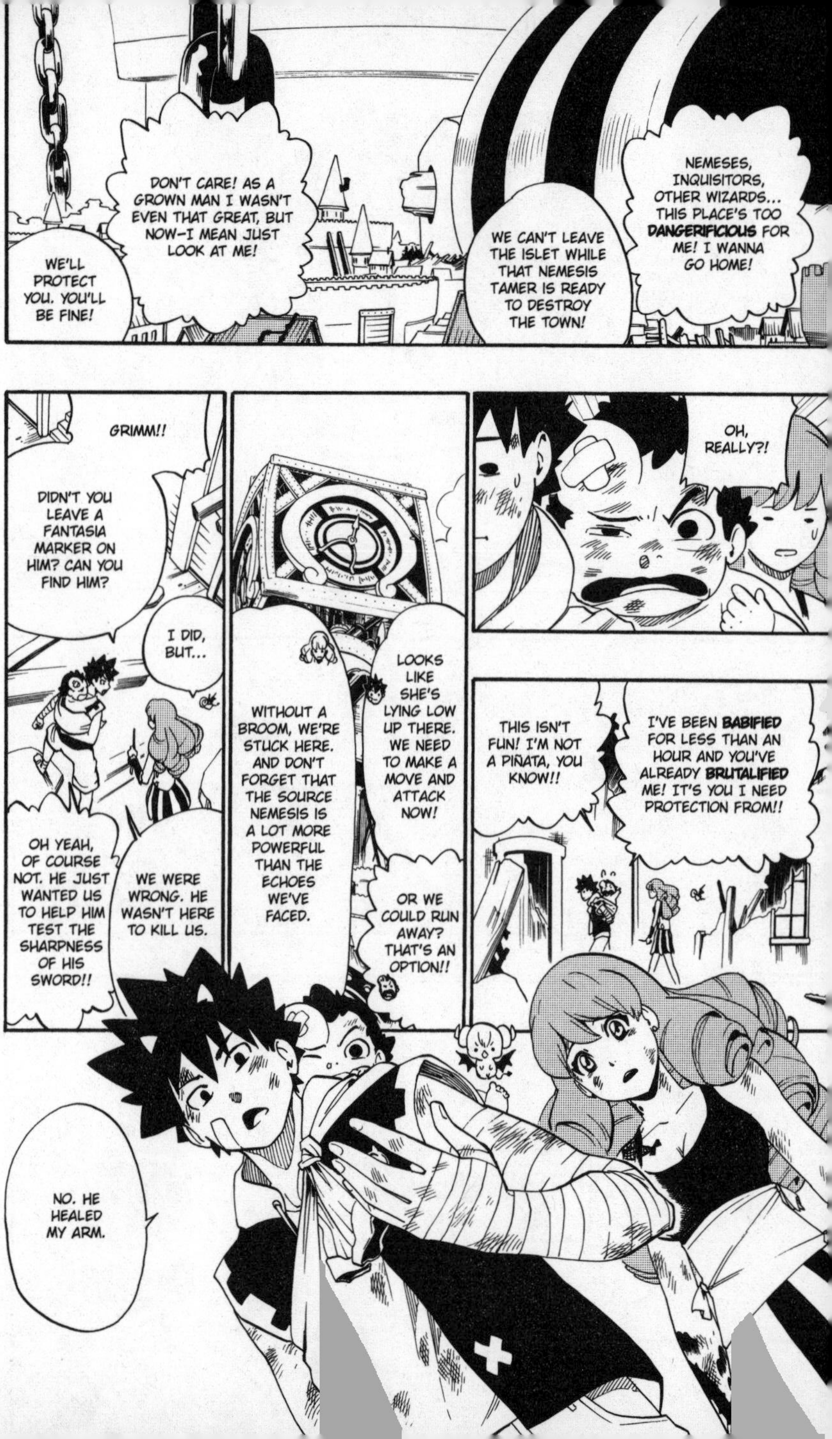
NEMESES, INQUISITORS, OTHER WIZARDS... THIS PLACE'S TOO **DANGERIFICIOUS** FOR ME! I WANNA GO HOME!
WE CAN'T LEAVE THE ISLET WHILE THAT NEMESIS TAMER IS READY TO DESTROY THE TOWN!
WE'LL PROTECT YOU. YOU'LL BE FINE!
DON'T CARE! AS A GROWN MAN I WASN'T EVEN THAT GREAT, BUT NOW—I MEAN JUST LOOK AT ME!
OH, REALLY?!
I'VE BEEN **BABIFIED** FOR LESS THAN AN HOUR AND YOU'VE ALREADY **BRUTALIFIED** ME! IT'S YOU I NEED PROTECTION FROM!!
THIS ISN'T FUN! I'M NOT A PIÑATA, YOU KNOW!!
LOOKS LIKE SHE'S LYING LOW UP THERE. WE NEED TO MAKE A MOVE AND ATTACK NOW!
WITHOUT A BROOM, WE'RE STUCK HERE. AND DON'T FORGET THAT THE SOURCE NEMESIS IS A LOT MORE POWERFUL THAN THE ECHOES WE'VE FACED.
OR WE COULD RUN AWAY? THAT'S AN OPTION!!
GRIMM!!
DIDN'T YOU LEAVE A FANTASIA MARKER ON HIM? CAN YOU FIND HIM?
I DID, BUT...
WE WERE WRONG. HE WASN'T HERE TO KILL US.
OH YEAH, OF COURSE NOT. HE JUST WANTED US TO HELP HIM TEST THE SHARPNESS OF HIS SWORD!!
NO. HE HEALED MY ARM.

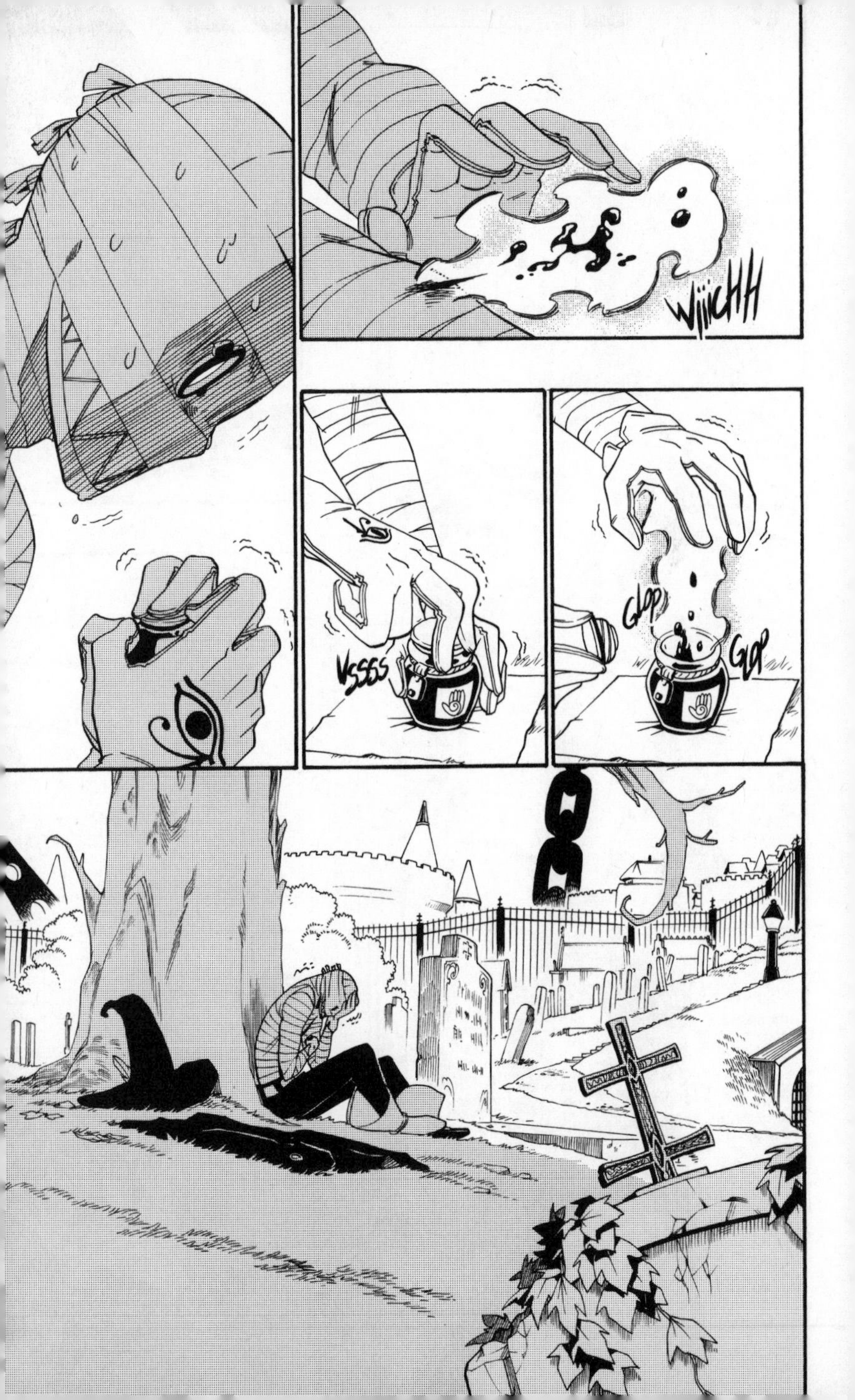

WIIICHH
VSSSS
GLOP
GLOP

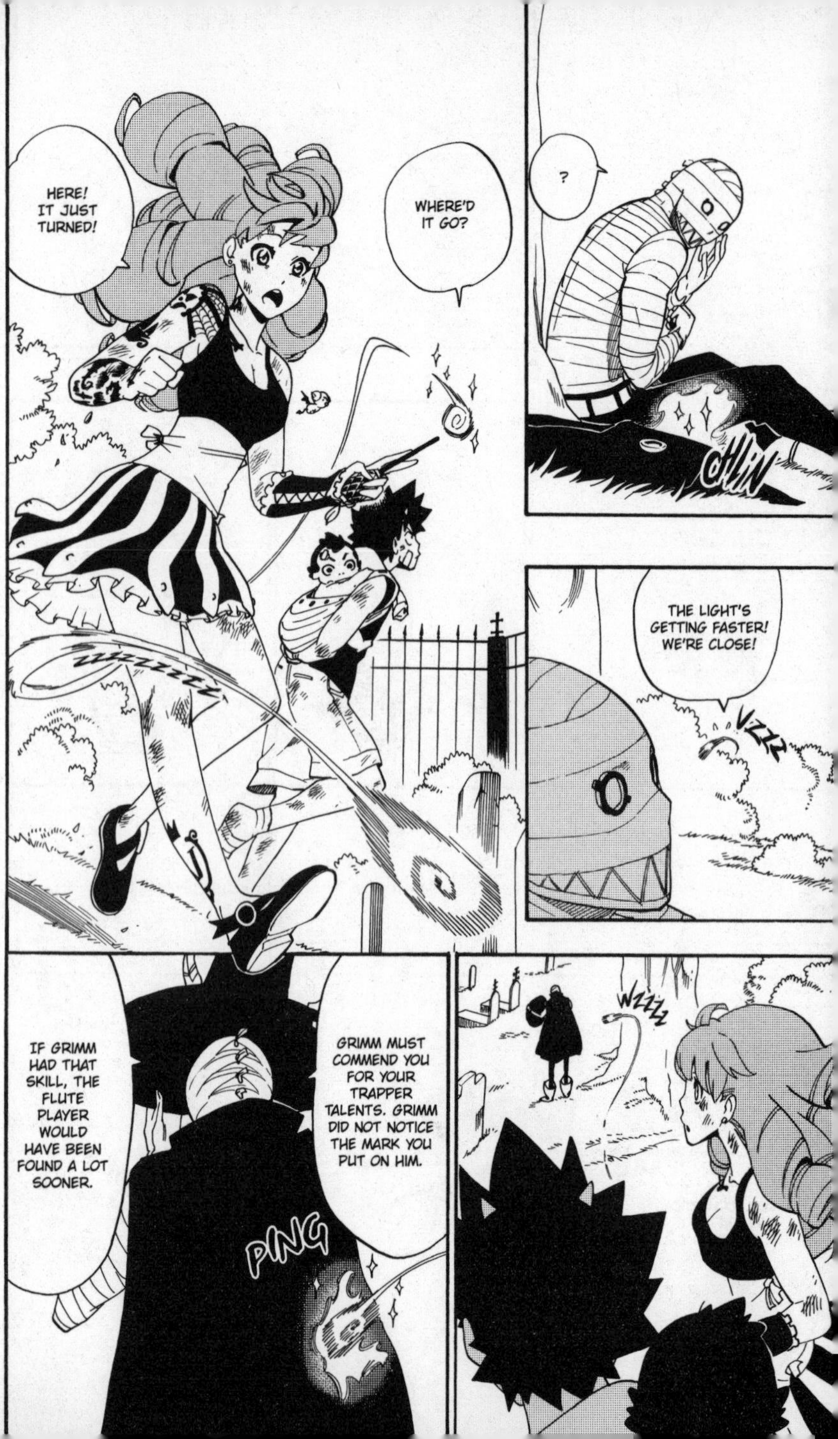
?
CHIN
THE LIGHT'S GETTING FASTER! WE'RE CLOSE!
VZZZZ
WHERE'D IT GO?
HERE! IT JUST TURNED!
ZZZZZZZZZ
WZZZZ
GRIMM MUST COMMEND YOU FOR YOUR TRAPPER TALENTS. GRIMM DID NOT NOTICE THE MARK YOU PUT ON HIM.
PING
IF GRIMM HAD THAT SKILL, THE FLUTE PLAYER WOULD HAVE BEEN FOUND A LOT SOONER.

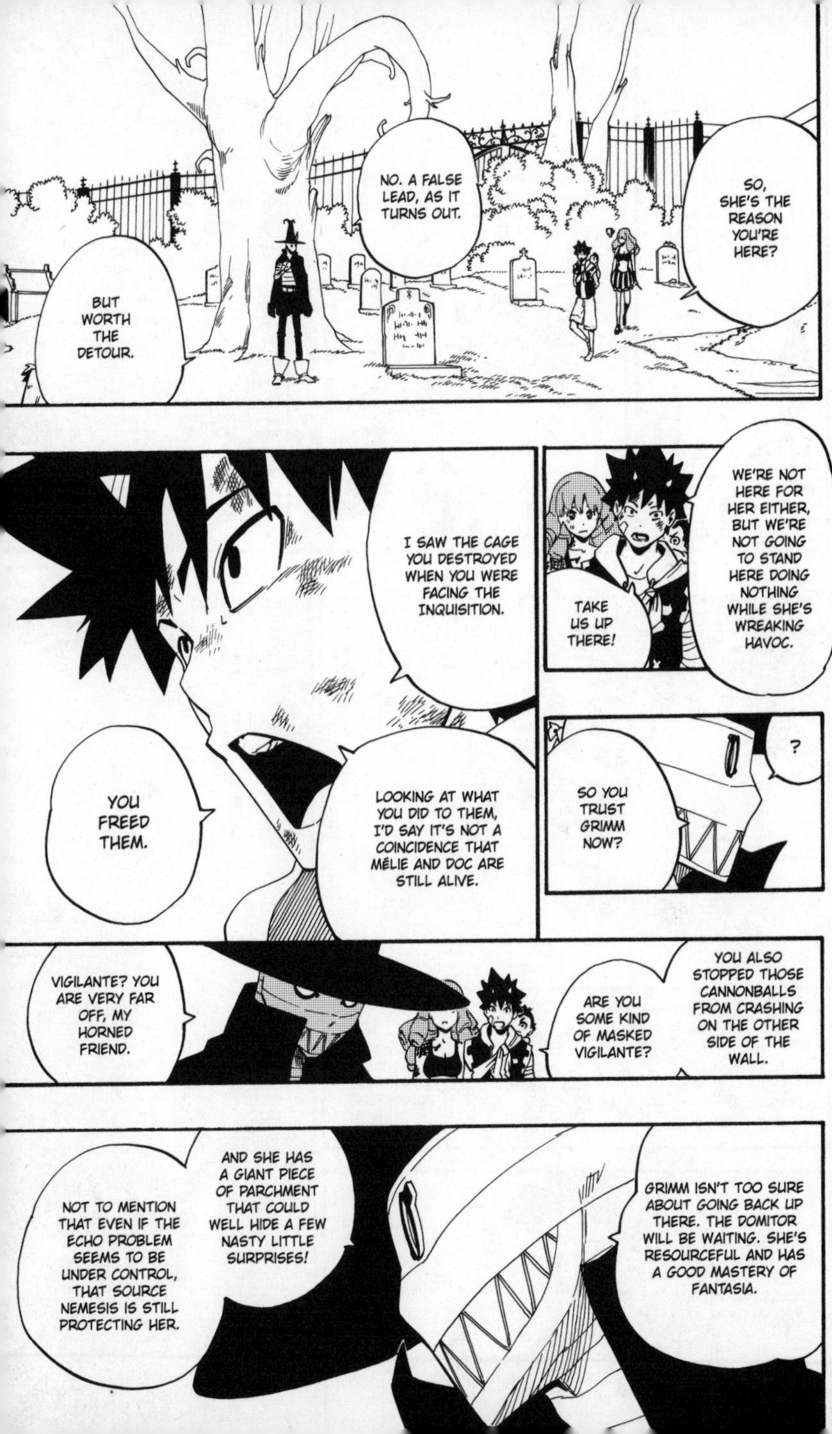
SO, SHE'S THE REASON YOU'RE HERE?
NO. A FALSE LEAD, AS IT TURNS OUT.
BUT WORTH THE DETOUR.
WE'RE NOT HERE FOR HER EITHER, BUT WE'RE NOT GOING TO STAND HERE DOING NOTHING WHILE SHE'S WREAKING HAVOC.
TAKE US UP THERE!
?
SO YOU TRUST GRIMM NOW?
I SAW THE CAGE YOU DESTROYED WHEN YOU WERE FACING THE INQUISITION.
LOOKING AT WHAT YOU DID TO THEM, I'D SAY IT'S NOT A COINCIDENCE THAT MÉLIE AND DOC ARE STILL ALIVE.
YOU FREED THEM.
YOU ALSO STOPPED THOSE CANNONBALLS FROM CRASHING ON THE OTHER SIDE OF THE WALL.
ARE YOU SOME KIND OF MASKED VIGILANTE?
VIGILANTE? YOU ARE VERY FAR OFF, MY HORNED FRIEND.
GRIMM ISN'T TOO SURE ABOUT GOING BACK UP THERE. THE DOMITOR WILL BE WAITING. SHE'S RESOURCEFUL AND HAS A GOOD MASTERY OF FANTASIA.
AND SHE HAS A GIANT PIECE OF PARCHMENT THAT COULD WELL HIDE A FEW NASTY LITTLE SURPRISES!
NOT TO MENTION THAT EVEN IF THE ECHO PROBLEM SEEMS TO BE UNDER CONTROL, THAT SOURCE NEMESIS IS STILL PROTECTING HER.

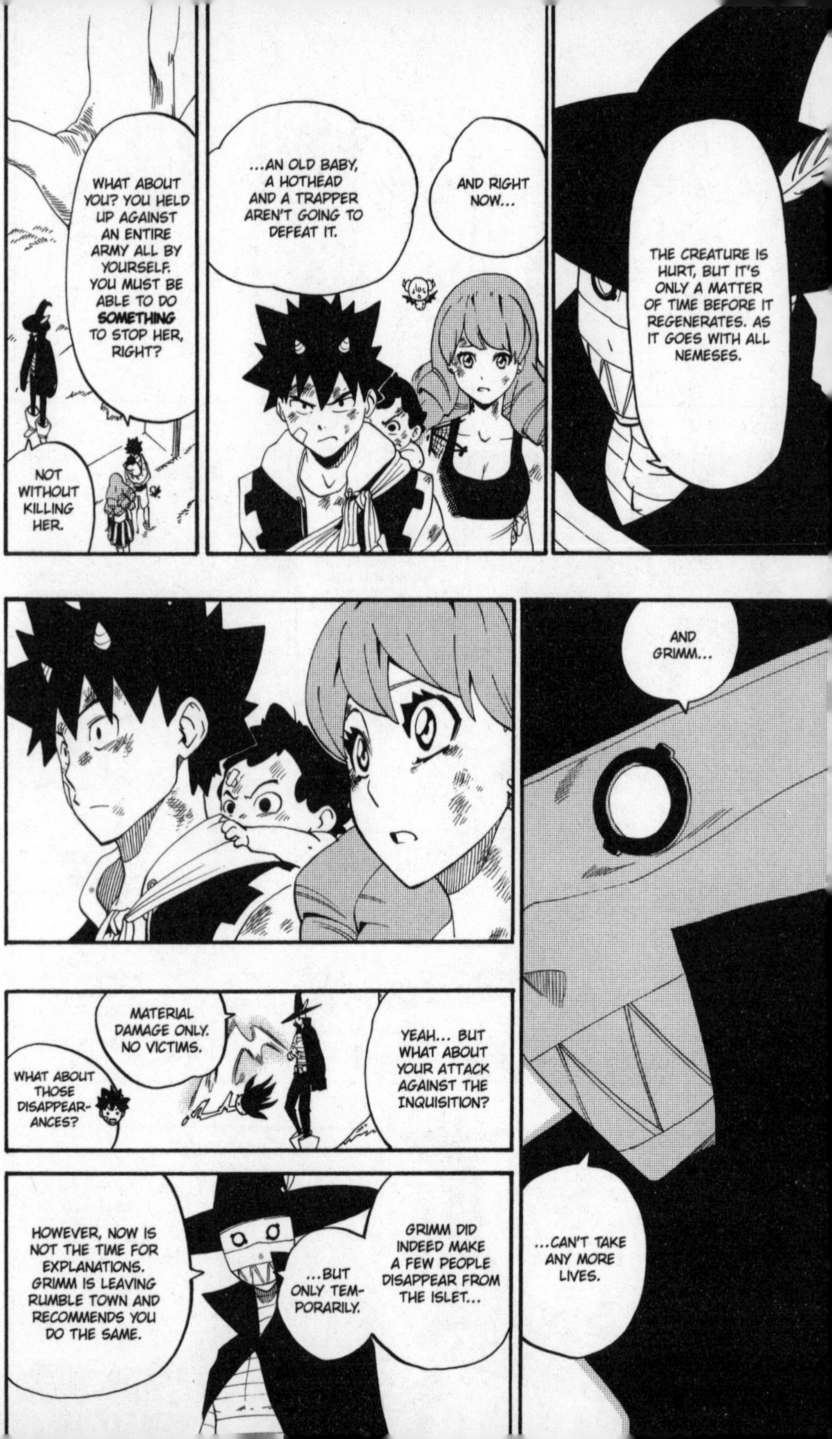
WHAT ABOUT YOU? YOU HELD UP AGAINST AN ENTIRE ARMY ALL BY YOURSELF. YOU MUST BE ABLE TO DO **SOMETHING** TO STOP HER, RIGHT?
NOT WITHOUT KILLING HER.
...AN OLD BABY, A HOTHEAD AND A TRAPPER AREN'T GOING TO DEFEAT IT.
AND RIGHT NOW...
THE CREATURE IS HURT, BUT IT'S ONLY A MATTER OF TIME BEFORE IT REGENERATES. AS IT GOES WITH ALL NEMESES.
AND GRIMM...
...CAN'T TAKE ANY MORE LIVES.
WHAT ABOUT THOSE DISAPPEAR-ANCES?
MATERIAL DAMAGE ONLY. NO VICTIMS.
YEAH... BUT WHAT ABOUT YOUR ATTACK AGAINST THE INQUISITION?
GRIMM DID INDEED MAKE A FEW PEOPLE DISAPPEAR FROM THE ISLET...
...BUT ONLY TEM-PORARILY.
HOWEVER, NOW IS NOT THE TIME FOR EXPLANATIONS. GRIMM IS LEAVING RUMBLE TOWN AND RECOMMENDS YOU DO THE SAME.

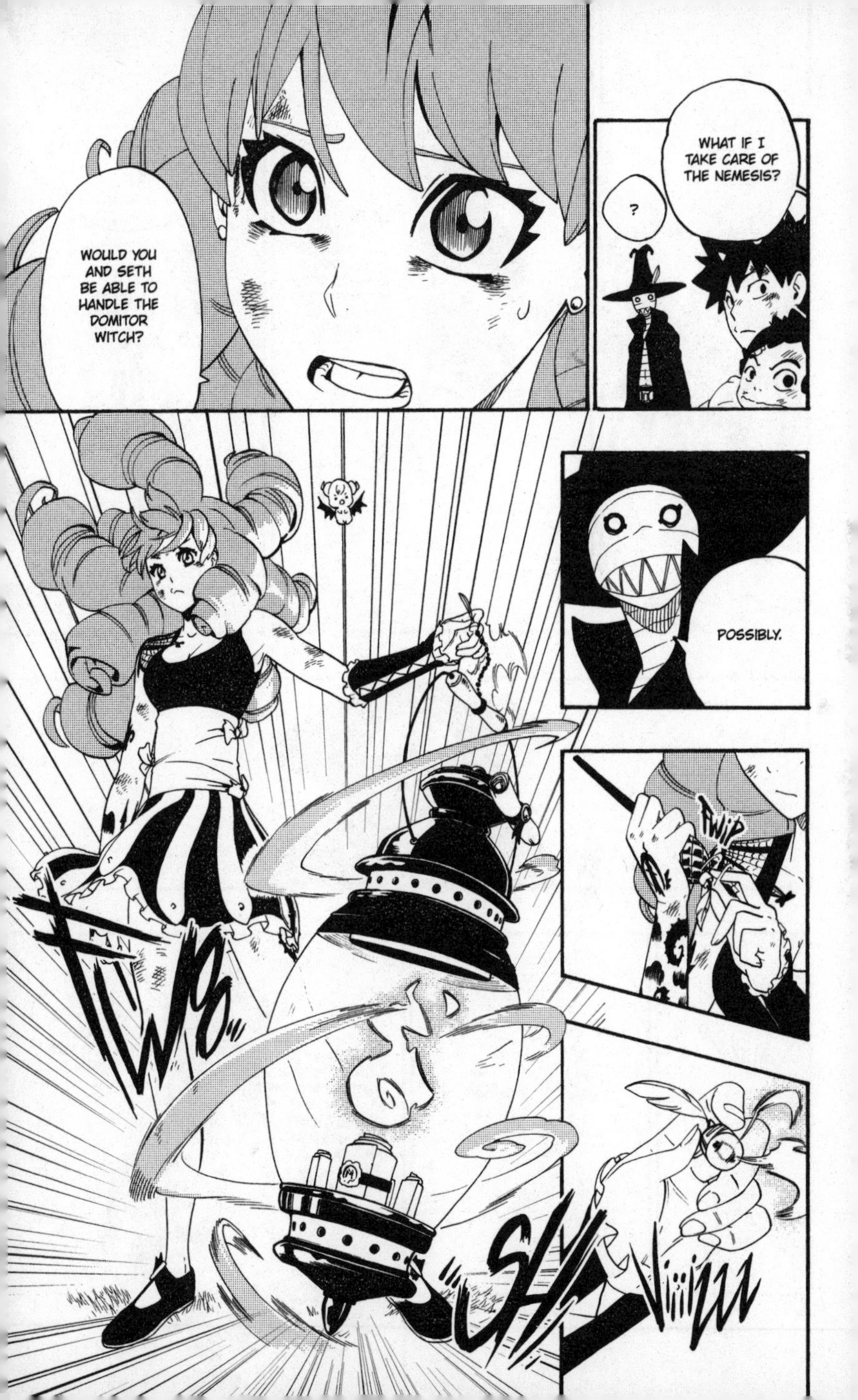
WHAT IF I TAKE CARE OF THE NEMESIS?
?
WOULD YOU AND SETH BE ABLE TO HANDLE THE DOMITOR WITCH?
POSSIBLY.
FWIP

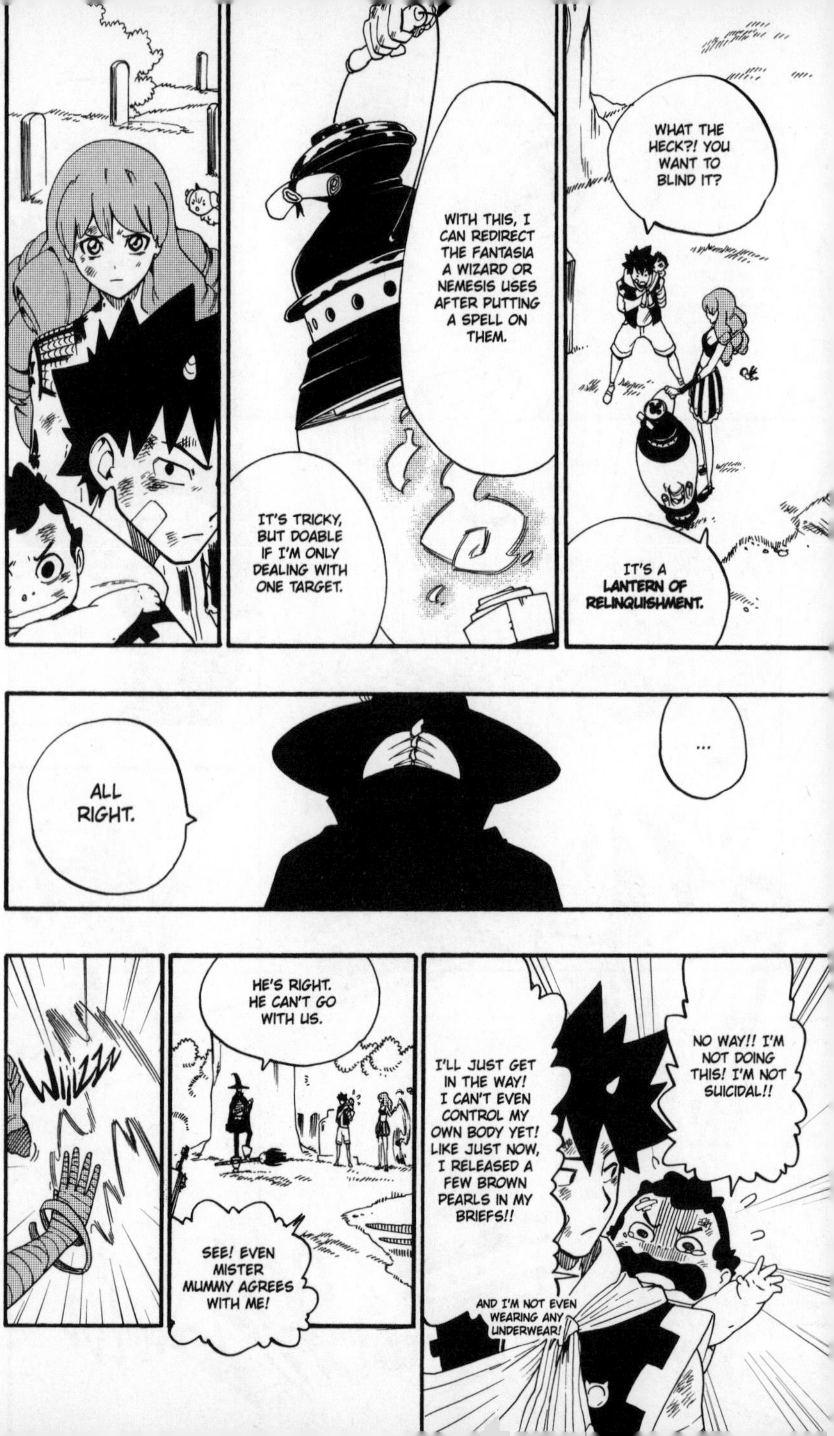
WHAT THE HECK?! YOU WANT TO BLIND IT?
IT'S A LANTERN OF RELINQUISHMENT.
WITH THIS, I CAN REDIRECT THE FANTASIA A WIZARD OR NEMESIS USES AFTER PUTTING A SPELL ON THEM.
IT'S TRICKY, BUT DOABLE IF I'M ONLY DEALING WITH ONE TARGET.
...
ALL RIGHT.
NO WAY!! I'M NOT DOING THIS! I'M NOT SUICIDAL!!
I'LL JUST GET IN THE WAY! I CAN'T EVEN CONTROL MY OWN BODY YET! LIKE JUST NOW, I RELEASED A FEW BROWN PEARLS IN MY BRIEFS!!
AND I'M NOT EVEN WEARING ANY UNDERWEAR!
HE'S RIGHT. HE CAN'T GO WITH US.
SEE! EVEN MISTER MUMMY AGREES WITH ME!
WIIIZZZ

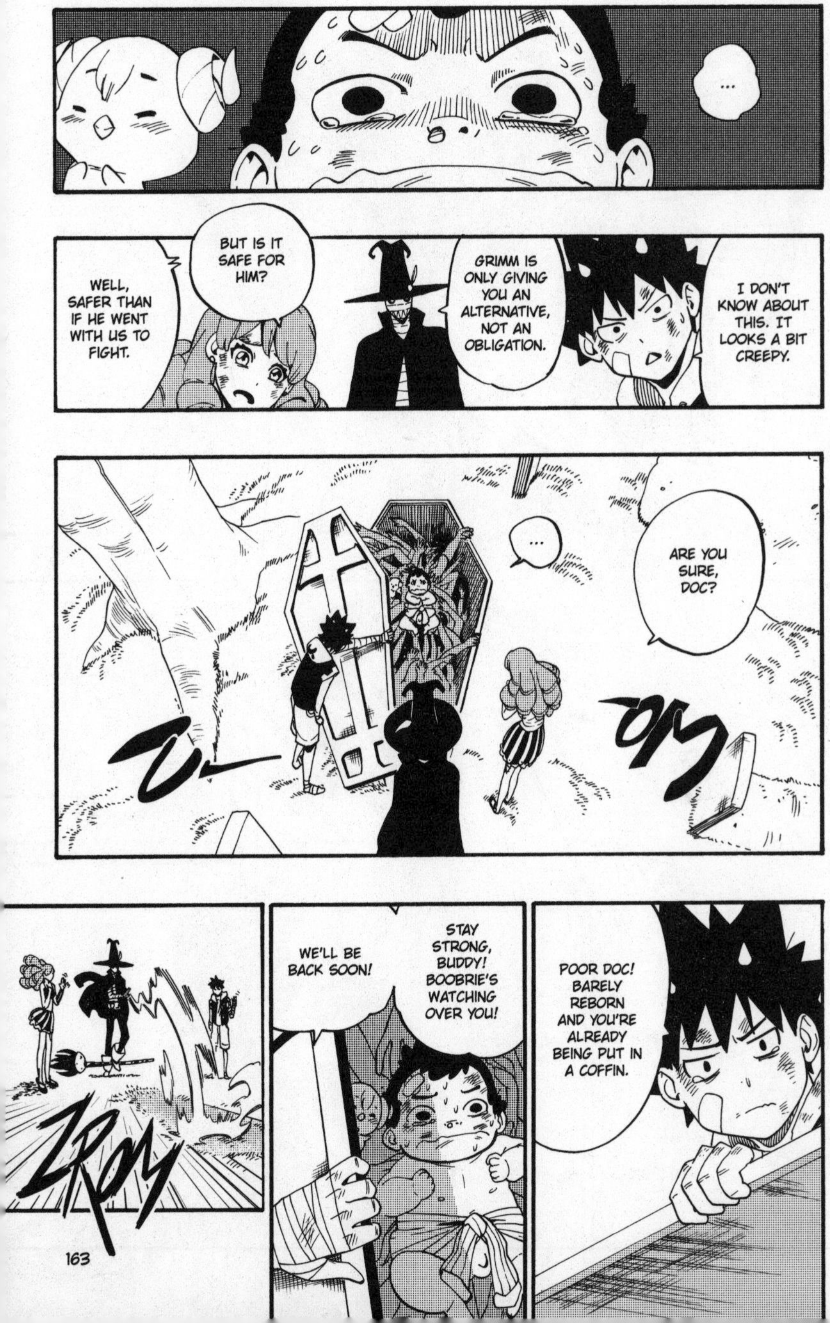
...
I DON'T KNOW ABOUT THIS. IT LOOKS A BIT CREEPY.
GRIMM IS ONLY GIVING YOU AN ALTERNATIVE, NOT AN OBLIGATION.
BUT IS IT SAFE FOR HIM?
WELL, SAFER THAN IF HE WENT WITH US TO FIGHT.
ARE YOU SURE, DOC?
...
POOR DOC! BARELY REBORN AND YOU'RE ALREADY BEING PUT IN A COFFIN.
STAY STRONG, BUDDY! BOOBRIE'S WATCHING OVER YOU!
WE'LL BE BACK SOON!

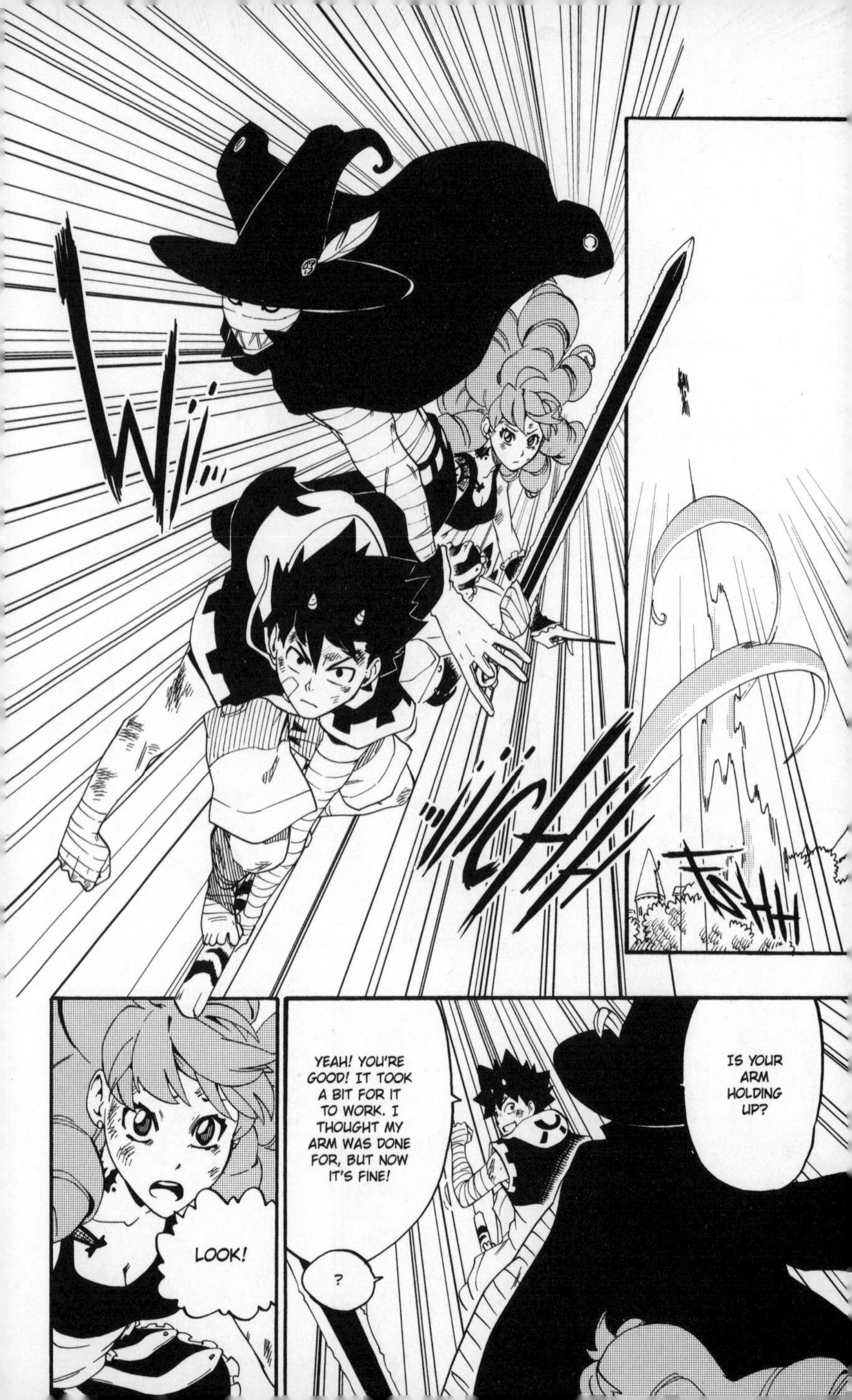
FSHH
WI...
...ICHH
IS YOUR ARM HOLDING UP?
YEAH! YOU'RE GOOD! IT TOOK A BIT FOR IT TO WORK. I THOUGHT MY ARM WAS DONE FOR, BUT NOW IT'S FINE!
?
LOOK!

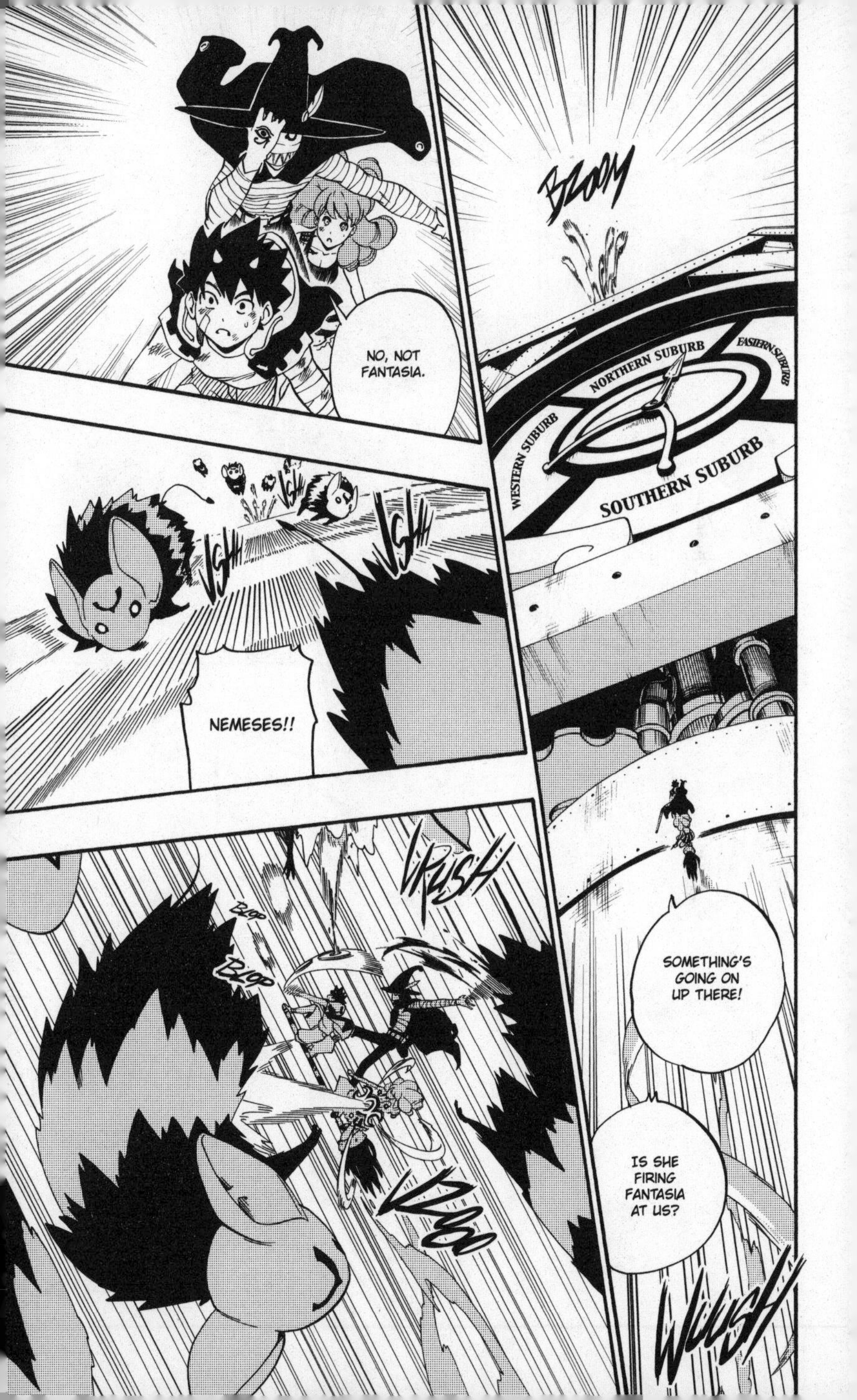
BROOM
NORTHERN SUBURB
EASTERN SUBURB
WESTERN SUBURB
SOUTHERN SUBURB
SOUTHERN SUBURB
SOMETHING'S GOING ON UP THERE!
IS SHE FIRING FANTASIA AT US?
WUSH
NO, NOT FANTASIA.
VSHH
VSHH
NEMESES!!
VRUSH

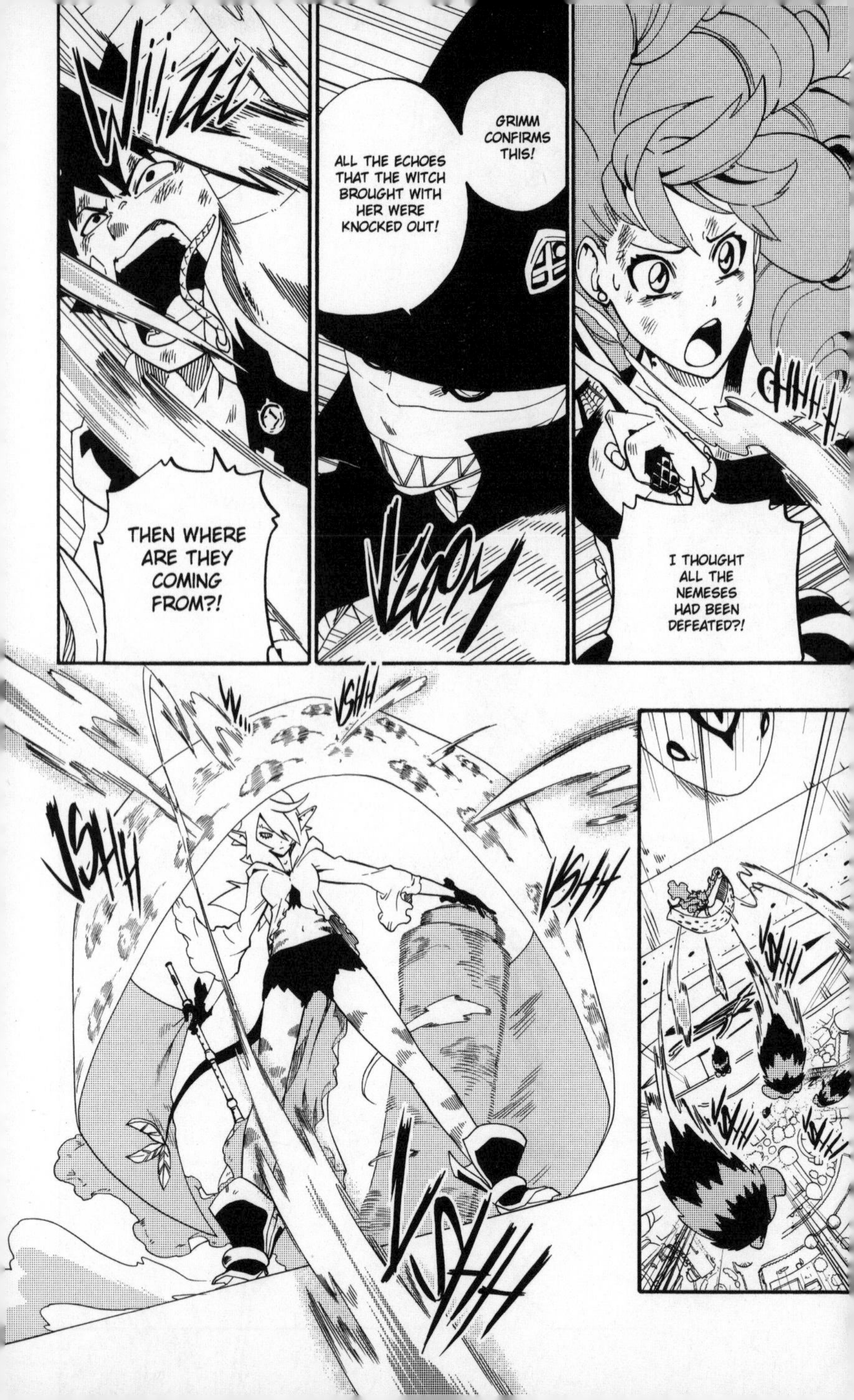
CHHHH
I THOUGHT ALL THE NEMESES HAD BEEN DEFEATED?!
GRIMM CONFIRMS THIS!
ALL THE ECHOES THAT THE WITCH BROUGHT WITH HER WERE KNOCKED OUT!
VROOM
WHIZZZ
THEN WHERE ARE THEY COMING FROM?!
VSHH
VSHH
VSHH
VSHH
VSHH
VSHH
VSHH

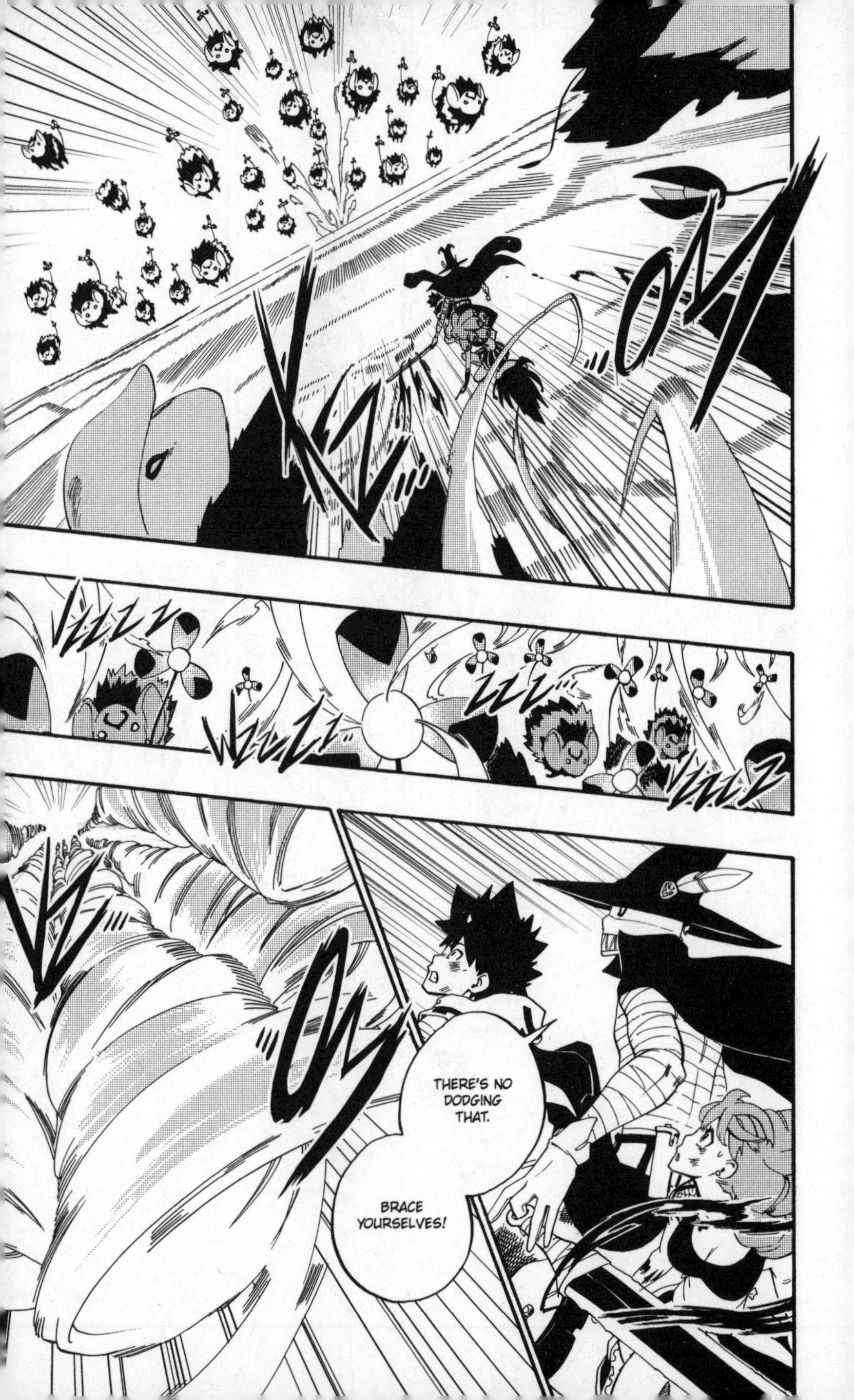
THERE'S NO DODGING THAT.
BRACE YOURSELVES!

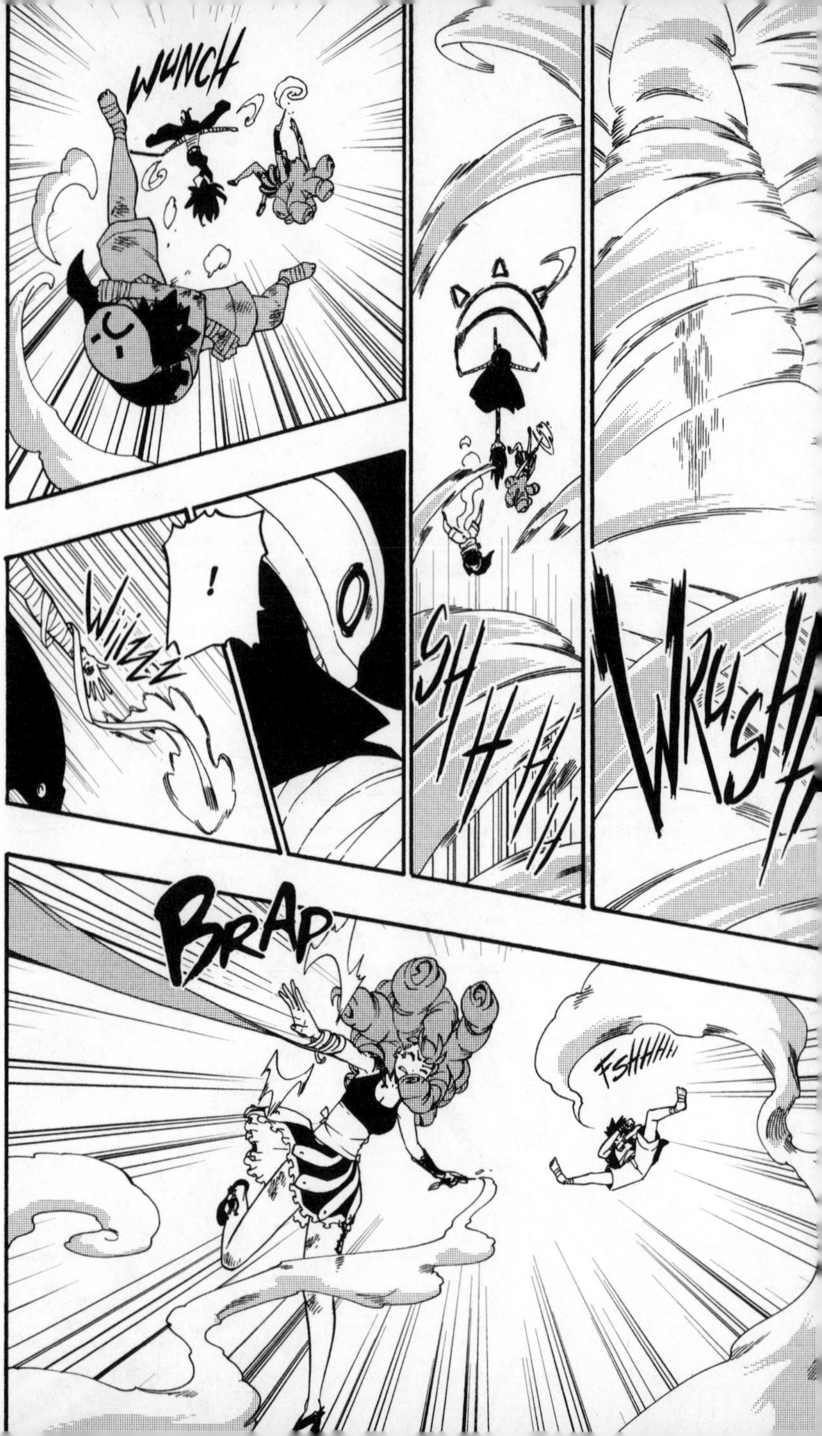
WRUSH
SHHHH
WUNCH
!
WIIIZZZ
BRAP
FSHHHH

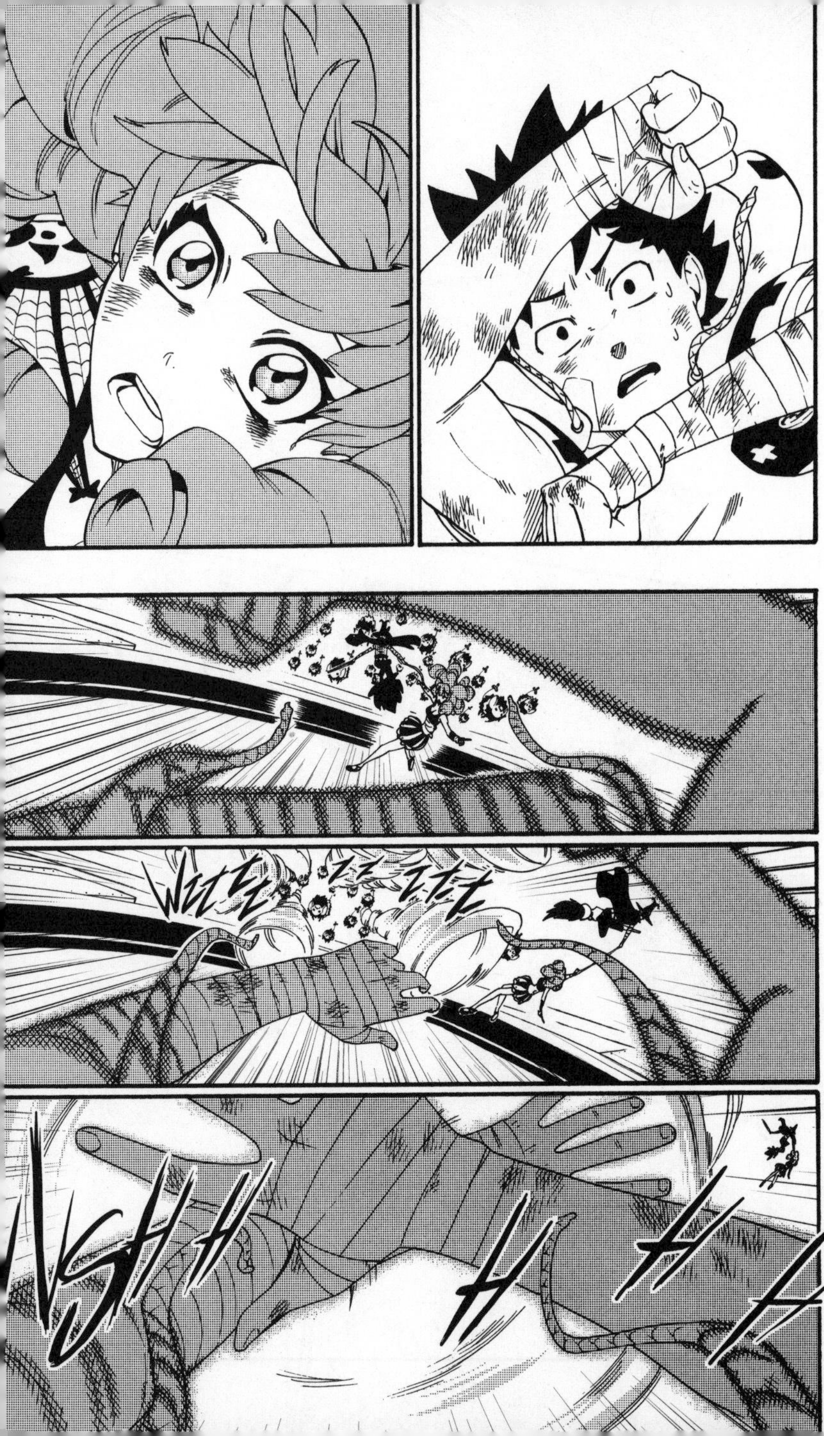

WZZZZZZZZZZZ
VSHHHHHHH

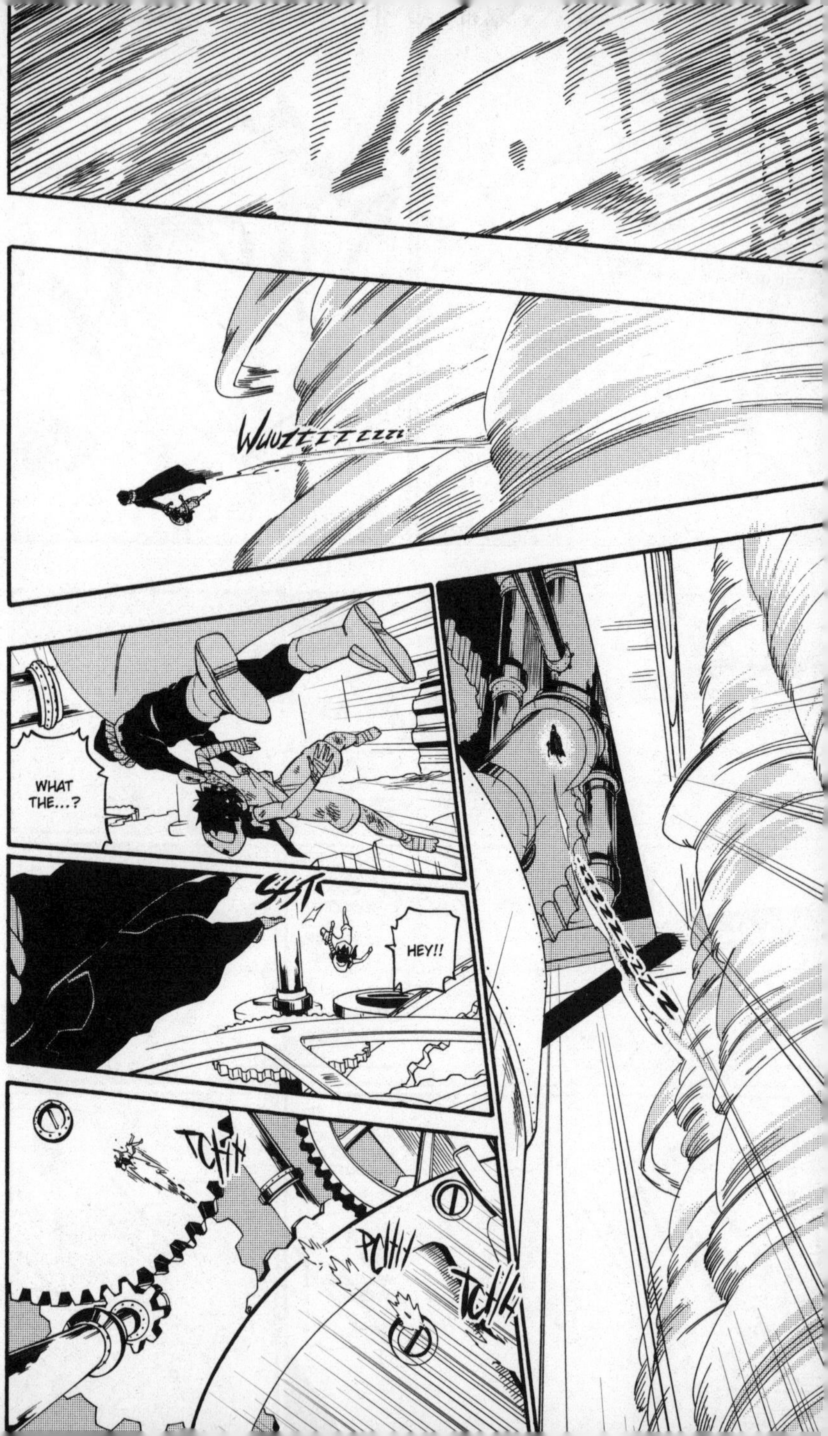
WHAT THE...?
HEY!!

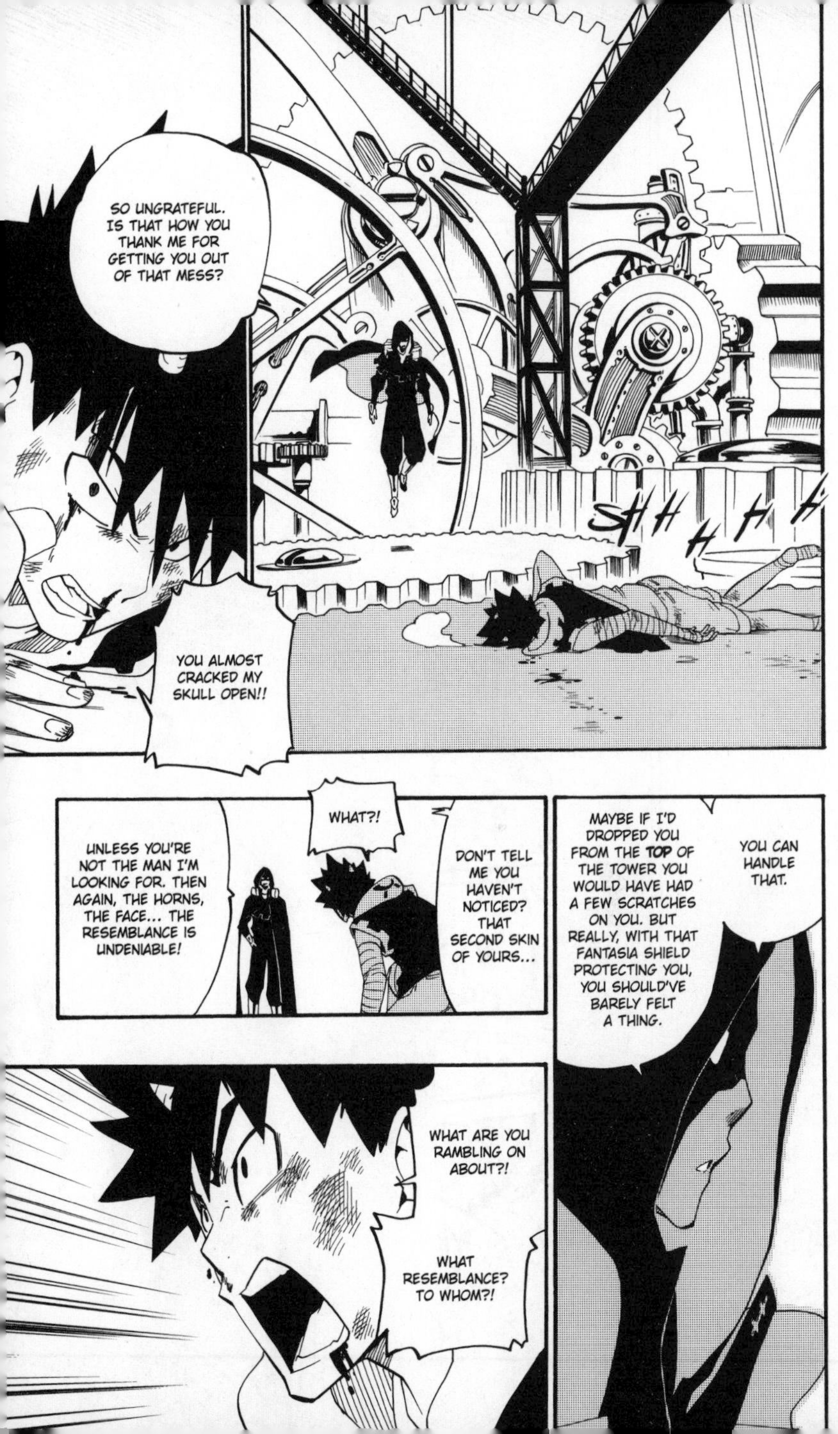
SHHHHHH
YOU ALMOST CRACKED MY SKULL OPEN!!
SO UNGRATEFUL. IS THAT HOW YOU THANK ME FOR GETTING YOU OUT OF THAT MESS?
YOU CAN HANDLE THAT.
MAYBE IF I'D DROPPED YOU FROM THE **TOP** OF THE TOWER YOU WOULD HAVE HAD A FEW SCRATCHES ON YOU. BUT REALLY, WITH THAT FANTASIA SHIELD PROTECTING YOU, YOU SHOULD'VE BARELY FELT A THING.
DON'T TELL ME YOU HAVEN'T NOTICED? THAT SECOND SKIN OF YOURS...
WHAT?!
UNLESS YOU'RE NOT THE MAN I'M LOOKING FOR. THEN AGAIN, THE HORNS, THE FACE... THE RESEMBLANCE IS UNDENIABLE!
WHAT ARE YOU RAMBLING ON ABOUT?!
WHAT RESEMBLANCE? TO WHOM?!

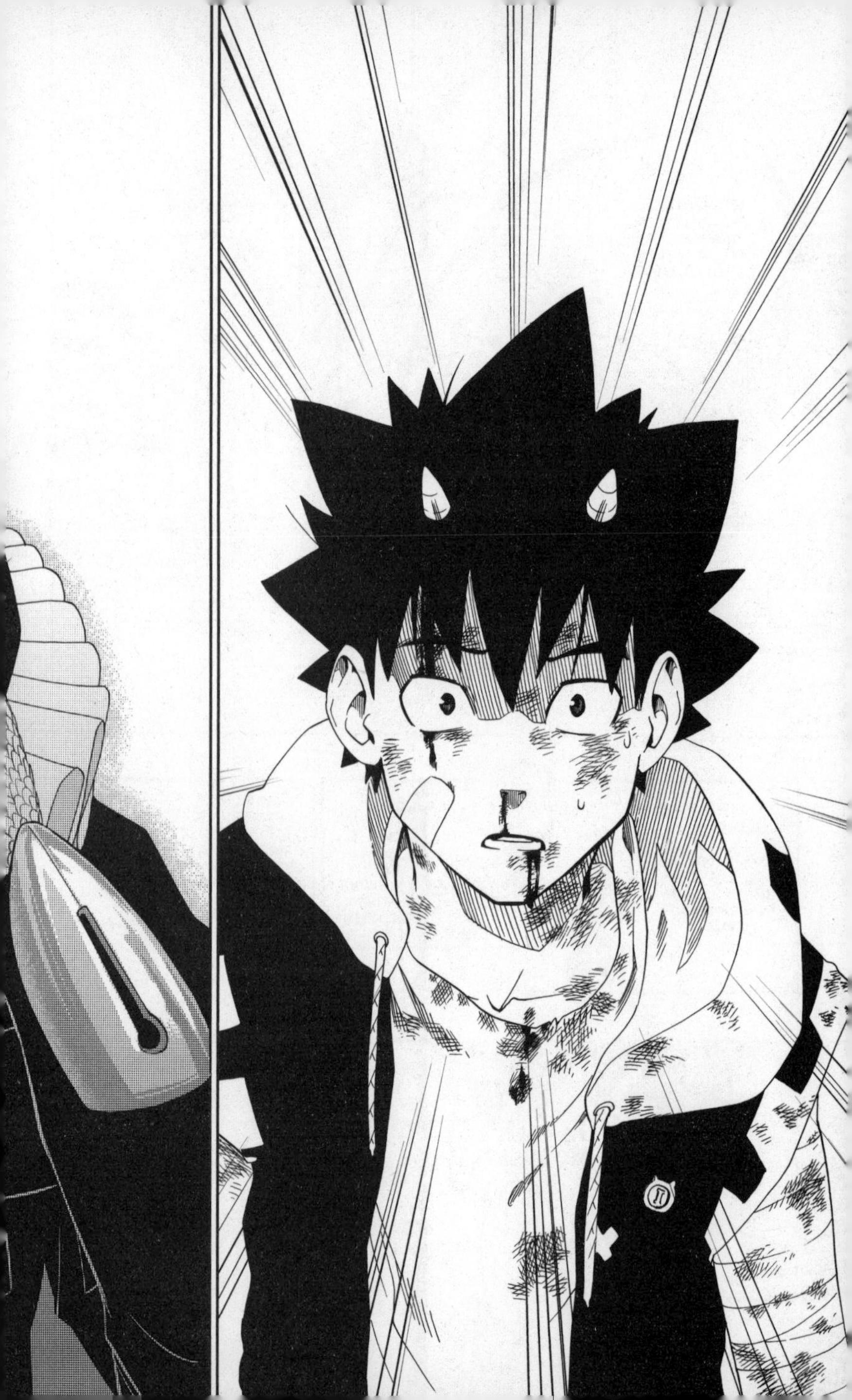

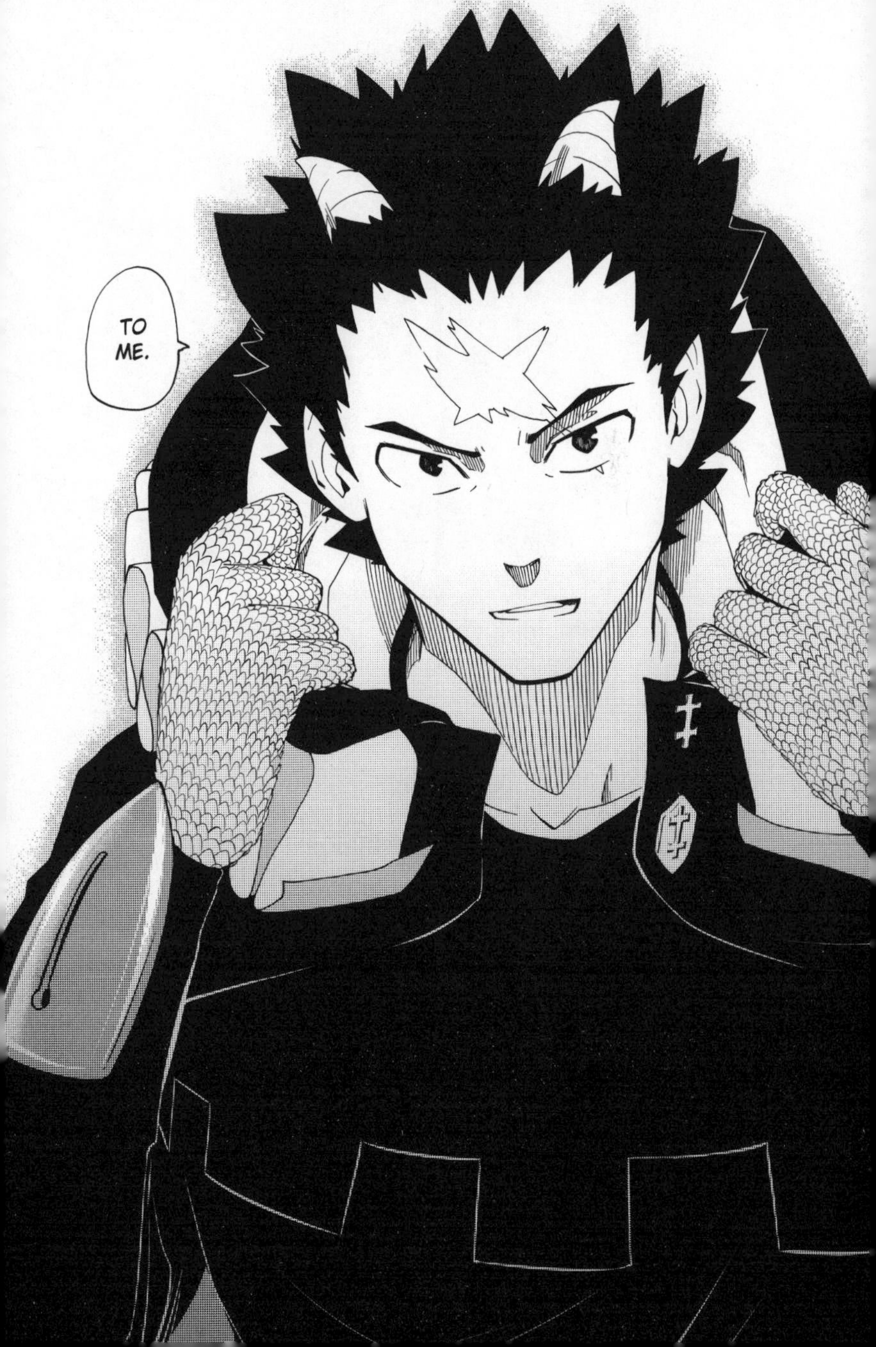
TO ME.

TO BE CONTINUED...

BONUS - CONTEST

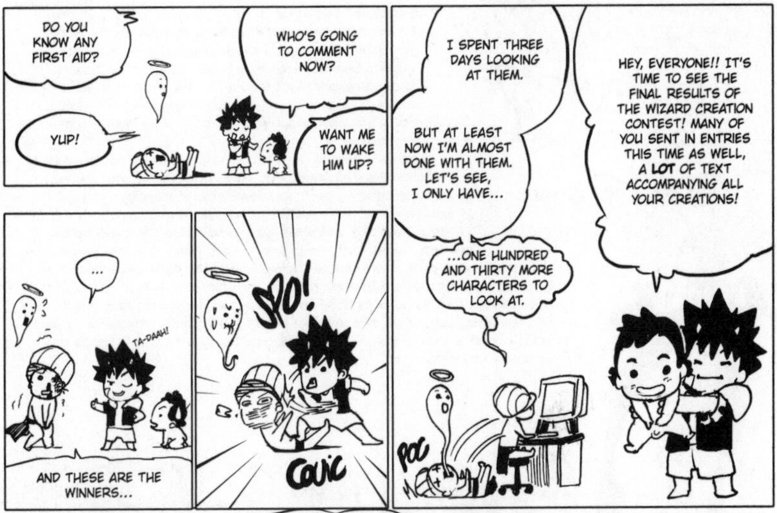

HEY, EVERYONE!! IT'S TIME TO SEE THE FINAL RESULTS OF THE WIZARD CREATION CONTEST! MANY OF YOU SENT IN ENTRIES THIS TIME AS WELL, A LOT OF TEXT ACCOMPANYING ALL YOUR CREATIONS!
I SPENT THREE DAYS LOOKING AT THEM.
BUT AT LEAST NOW I'M ALMOST DONE WITH THEM. LET'S SEE, I ONLY HAVE...
...ONE HUNDRED AND THIRTY MORE CHARACTERS TO LOOK AT.
POC
DO YOU KNOW ANY FIRST AID?
YUP!
WHO'S GOING TO COMMENT NOW?
WANT ME TO WAKE HIM UP?
SPO!
COUIC
...
TA-DAAH!
AND THESE ARE THE WINNERS...

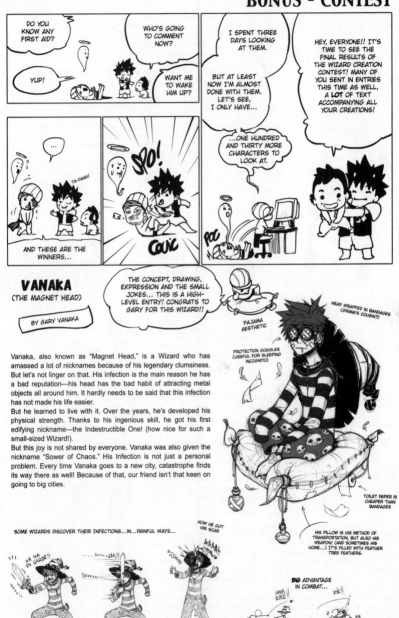

VANAKA

(THE MAGNET HEAD)

BY GARY VANAKA

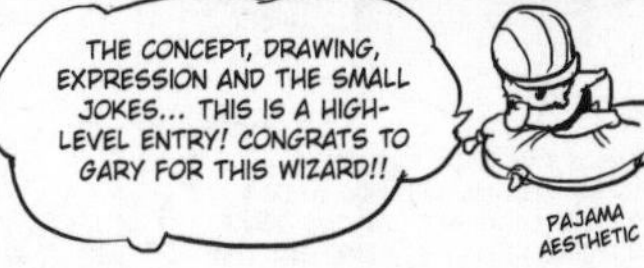

THE CONCEPT, DRAWING, EXPRESSION AND THE SMALL JOKES... THIS IS A HIGH-LEVEL ENTRY! CONGRATS TO GARY FOR THIS WIZARD!!

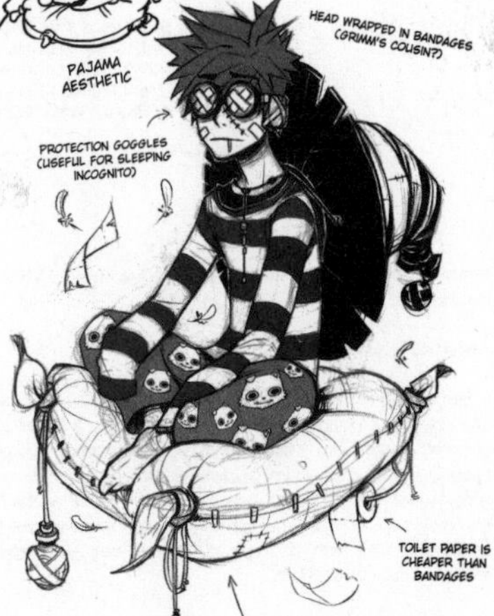

HEAD WRAPPED IN BANDAGES (GRIMM'S COUSIN?)
PAJAMA AESTHETIC
PROTECTION GOGGLES (USEFUL FOR SLEEPING INCOGNITO)
TOILET PAPER IS CHEAPER THAN BANDAGES
HIS PILLOW IS HIS METHOD OF TRANSPORTATION, BUT ALSO HIS WEAPON! (AND SOMETIMES HIS HOME...) IT'S FILLED WITH FEATHER TREE FEATHERS.

Vanaka, also known as "Magnet Head," is a Wizard who has amassed a lot of nicknames because of his legendary clumsiness. But let's not linger on that. His infection is the main reason he has a bad reputation—his head has the bad habit of attracting metal objects all around him. It hardly needs to be said that this infection has not made his life easier.

But he learned to live with it. Over the years, he's developed his physical strength. Thanks to his ingenious skill, he got his first edifying nickname—the Indestructible One! (how nice for such a small-sized Wizard!).

But this joy is not shared by everyone. Vanaka was also given the nickname "Sower of Chaos." His Infection is not just a personal problem. Every time Vanaka goes to a new city, catastrophe finds its way there as well! Because of that, our friend isn't that keen on going to big cities.

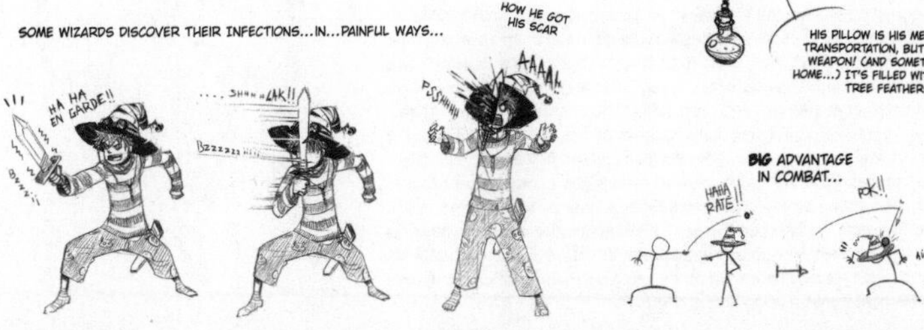

SOME WIZARDS DISCOVER THEIR INFECTIONS...IN...PAINFUL WAYS...
HOW HE GOT HIS SCAR
HA HA EN GARDE!!
....SHHH...LAK!!
AAAAH!!
BIG ADVANTAGE IN COMBAT...
HAHA RATÉ!!
POK!!
AIE

BASS BOOST
Pesnya

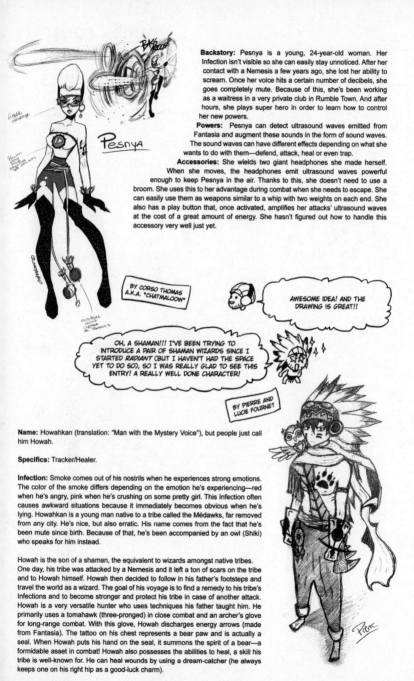

Backstory: Pesnya is a young, 24-year-old woman. Her Infection isn't visible so she can easily stay unnoticed. After her contact with a Nemesis a few years ago, she lost her ability to scream. Once her voice hits a certain number of decibels, she goes completely mute. Because of this, she's been working as a waitress in a very private club in Rumble Town. And after hours, she plays super hero in order to learn how to control her new powers.

Powers: Pesnya can detect ultrasound waves emitted from Fantasia and augment these sounds in the form of sound waves. The sound waves can have different effects depending on what she wants to do with them—defend, attack, heal or even trap.

Accessories: She wields two giant headphones she made herself. When she moves, the headphones emit ultrasound waves powerful enough to keep Pesnya in the air. Thanks to this, she doesn't need to use a broom. She uses this to her advantage during combat when she needs to escape. She can easily use them as weapons similar to a whip with two weights on each end. She also has a play button that, once activated, amplifies her attacks' ultrasound waves at the cost of a great amount of energy. She hasn't figured out how to handle this accessory very well just yet.

BY CORSO THOMAS A.K.A. "CHATMALOOW"

AWESOME IDEA! AND THE DRAWING IS GREAT!!

OH, A SHAMAN!!! I'VE BEEN TRYING TO INTRODUCE A PAIR OF SHAMAN WIZARDS SINCE I STARTED *RADIANT* (BUT I HAVEN'T HAD THE SPACE YET TO DO SO), SO I WAS REALLY GLAD TO SEE THIS ENTRY! A REALLY WELL DONE CHARACTER!

BY PIERRE AND LUCIE FOURNET

Pierre

Name: Howahkan (translation: "Man with the Mystery Voice"), but people just call him Howah.

Specifics: Tracker/Healer.

Infection: Smoke comes out of his nostrils when he experiences strong emotions. The color of the smoke differs depending on the emotion he's experiencing—red when he's angry, pink when he's crushing on some pretty girl. This Infection often causes awkward situations because it immediately becomes obvious when he's lying. Howahkan is a young man native to a tribe called the Médawks, far removed from any city. He's nice, but also erratic. His name comes from the fact that he's been mute since birth. Because of that, he's been accompanied by an owl (Shiki) who speaks for him instead.

Howah is the son of a shaman, the equivalent to wizards amongst native tribes. One day, his tribe was attacked by a Nemesis and it left a ton of scars on the tribe and to Howah himself. Howah then decided to follow in his father's footsteps and travel the world as a wizard. The goal of his voyage is to find a remedy to his tribe's Infections and to become stronger and protect his tribe in case of another attack. Howah is a very versatile hunter who uses techniques his father taught him. He primarily uses a tomahawk (three-pronged) in close combat and an archer's glove for long-range combat. With this glove, Howah discharges energy arrows (made from Fantasia). The tattoo on his chest represents a bear paw and is actually a seal. When Howah puts his hand on the seal, it summons the spirit of a bear—a formidable asset in combat! Howah also possesses the abilities to heal, a skill his tribe is well-known for. He can heal wounds by using a dream-catcher (he always keeps one on his right hip as a good-luck charm).

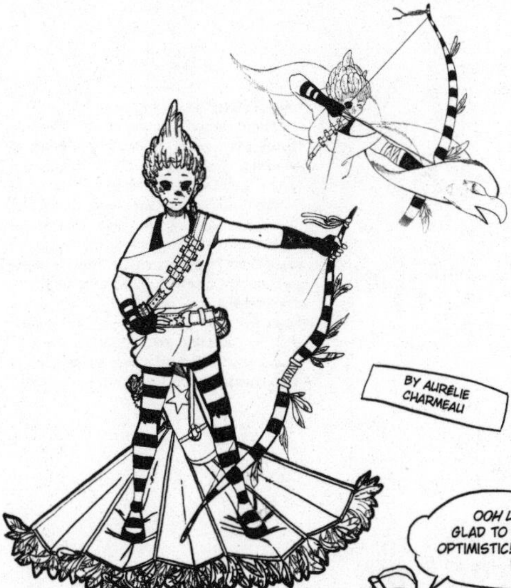
BY AURÉLIE CHARMEAU

Meet Ikäa, an optimistic witch, bubbly and filled with curiosity. Fond of being free, she likes to travel, hike and go to big open spaces.
Ikäa is brave, but not fearless, and specializes in long-distance attacks. Her feather bow allows her to fire off arrows from a very long distances and more or less control their trajectory. Each arrow is equipped with a little space that allows her to fill them with concentrated amounts of Fantasia, thus inflicting damage to a Nemesis over a period of time once attached to its body. Ikäa possesses a plethora of different arrows with different types of effects. She flies on a fan for increased stability. Her Infection is very diverse. Her hair is transformed into feathers, and her eyes have oversized pupils similar to those of a falcon, allowing her to see very far, while being sensitive to over-illuminated areas. The embarrassing part is that instead of poop, she lays eggs... Which really hurts!

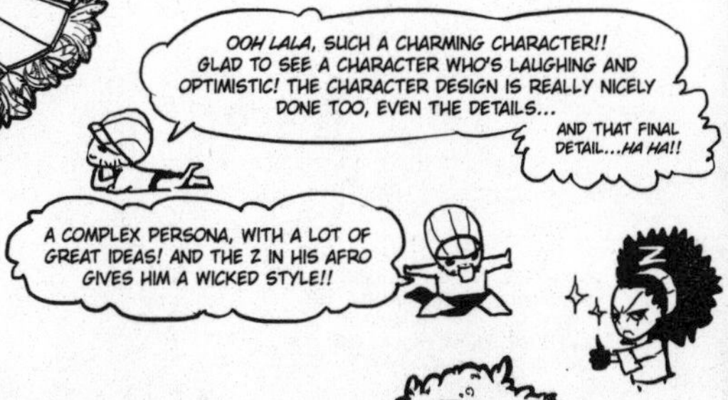
OOH LALA, SUCH A CHARMING CHARACTER!! GLAD TO SEE A CHARACTER WHO'S LAUGHING AND OPTIMISTIC! THE CHARACTER DESIGN IS REALLY NICELY DONE TOO, EVEN THE DETAILS...
AND THAT FINAL DETAIL...HA HA!!
A COMPLEX PERSONA, WITH A LOT OF GREAT IDEAS! AND THE Z IN HIS AFRO GIVES HIM A WICKED STYLE!!

Name: Saül
Infection: He has a problem keeping track of time (everything seems to go in slow-motion), so he needs to be in constant contact with an object from the "real" time flow or he'll lose his grip on reality. The good part is that his Infection sort of handicaps him, but since one second feels like a minute to him, he can observe an opponent's movements, studying their trajectory to better retaliate.
Equipment:
1) Stick of Power: Stays connected to the real time flow (he can replace it with another temporal marker). It also creates bubbles allowing him to recuperate Fantasia.
2) Pillow of Sleep: Allows him to sleep to recharge. Being completely exposed while he sleeps, his companion then takes care of his protection.
Spells: He's specialized in levitation and can also send out a powerful sleeping spell thanks to the "Z" in his hair.
Specialty: Potion making. He's globally well known for his dandelion liquor.
Saül used to be just your average pharmacist. Crazy about science related to Nemeses, he decided to study them more up-close. Too close. He quickly paid the price for this. After a few days of recovery, he discovered his Infection was lethargy of time. Since then, he's teamed up with an ancient mage whose Infection is hyperactivity. Saül is the only one able to understand the rushed ramblings of his companion due to his sickness allowing him to perceive every second as if it were a minute.

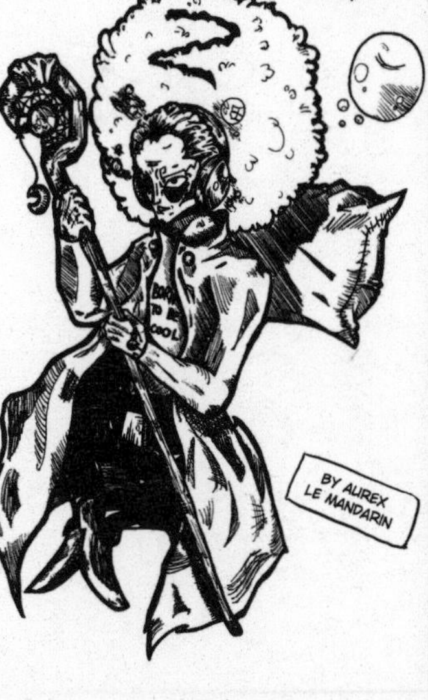
BY AUREX LE MANDARIN

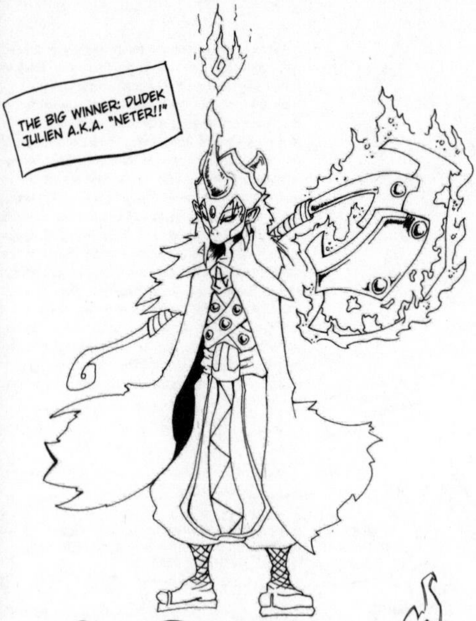
THE BIG WINNER: DUDEK JULIEN A.K.A. "NETER!!"

Neter, Witch Killer

Infection: Neter discovered his house in flames after it was attacked by a horde of Nemeses. Ever since, his Infection sets him on fire at all times. When he's calm, his Infection manifests itself only around his helmet and weapon, but during combat, the Fantasia amplifies his Infection's range and causes him horrendous pain. He only rarely gets hurt by others, with his biggest enemy being himself.

Neter fights with gloves, even if his potions allow him to somewhat contain his Infection. He's also a Wizard Killer, working for good 'ol gold. His allegiances flip regularly.

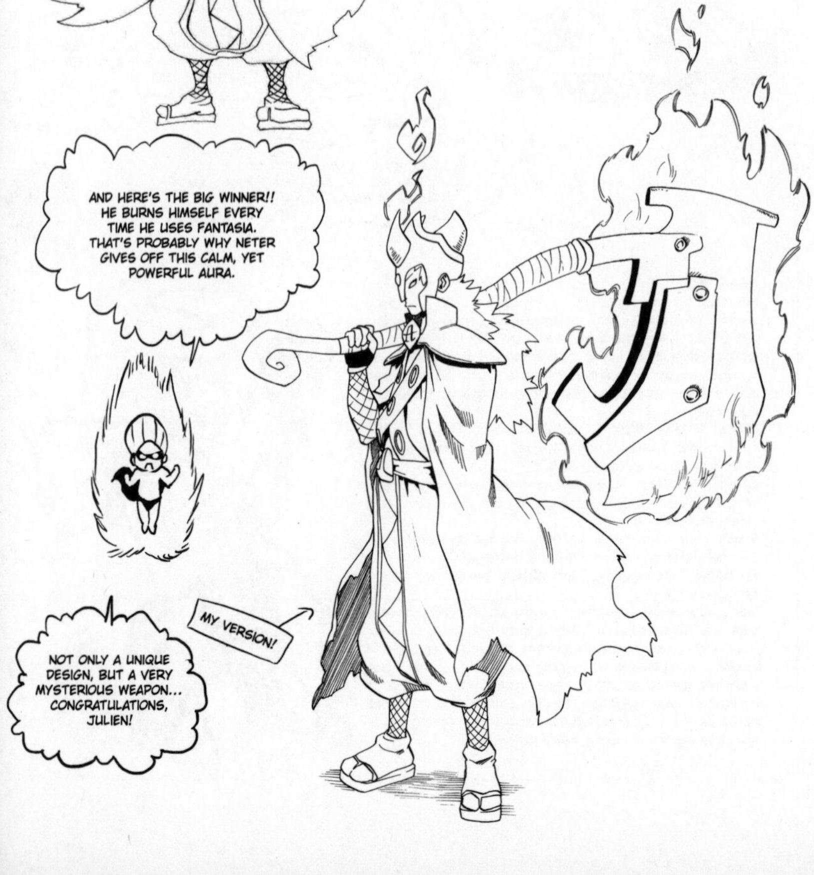
AND HERE'S THE BIG WINNER!! HE BURNS HIMSELF EVERY TIME HE USES FANTASIA. THAT'S PROBABLY WHY NETER GIVES OFF THIS CALM, YET POWERFUL AURA.
NOT ONLY A UNIQUE DESIGN, BUT A VERY MYSTERIOUS WEAPON... CONGRATULATIONS, JULIEN!
MY VERSION!

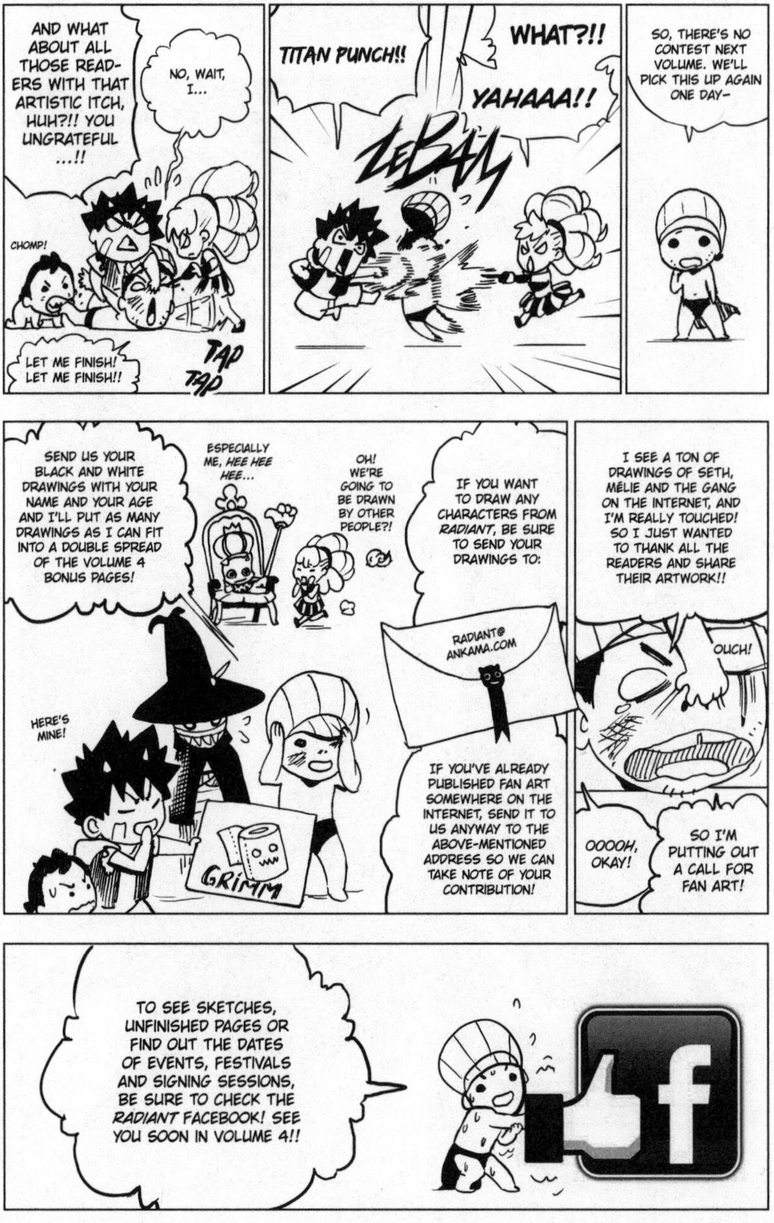
AND WHAT ABOUT ALL THOSE READERS WITH THAT ARTISTIC ITCH, HUH?!! YOU UNGRATEFUL ...!!
NO, WAIT, I...
CHOMP!
LET ME FINISH! LET ME FINISH!!
TAP TAP
TITAN PUNCH!!
WHAT?!!
YAHAAA!!
ZEBAM
SO, THERE'S NO CONTEST NEXT VOLUME. WE'LL PICK THIS UP AGAIN ONE DAY-
SEND US YOUR BLACK AND WHITE DRAWINGS WITH YOUR NAME AND YOUR AGE AND I'LL PUT AS MANY DRAWINGS AS I CAN FIT INTO A DOUBLE SPREAD OF THE VOLUME 4 BONUS PAGES!
ESPECIALLY ME, HEE HEE HEE...
OH! WE'RE GOING TO BE DRAWN BY OTHER PEOPLE?!
IF YOU WANT TO DRAW ANY CHARACTERS FROM RADIANT, BE SURE TO SEND YOUR DRAWINGS TO:
RADIANT@ ANKAMA.COM
HERE'S MINE!
GRIMM
IF YOU'VE ALREADY PUBLISHED FAN ART SOMEWHERE ON THE INTERNET, SEND IT TO US ANYWAY TO THE ABOVE-MENTIONED ADDRESS SO WE CAN TAKE NOTE OF YOUR CONTRIBUTION!
I SEE A TON OF DRAWINGS OF SETH, MÉLIE AND THE GANG ON THE INTERNET, AND I'M REALLY TOUCHED! SO I JUST WANTED TO THANK ALL THE READERS AND SHARE THEIR ARTWORK!!
OUCH!
OOOOH, OKAY!
SO I'M PUTTING OUT A CALL FOR FAN ART!
TO SEE SKETCHES, UNFINISHED PAGES OR FIND OUT THE DATES OF EVENTS, FESTIVALS AND SIGNING SESSIONS, BE SURE TO CHECK THE RADIANT FACEBOOK! SEE YOU SOON IN VOLUME 4!!

GUEST ARTISTS

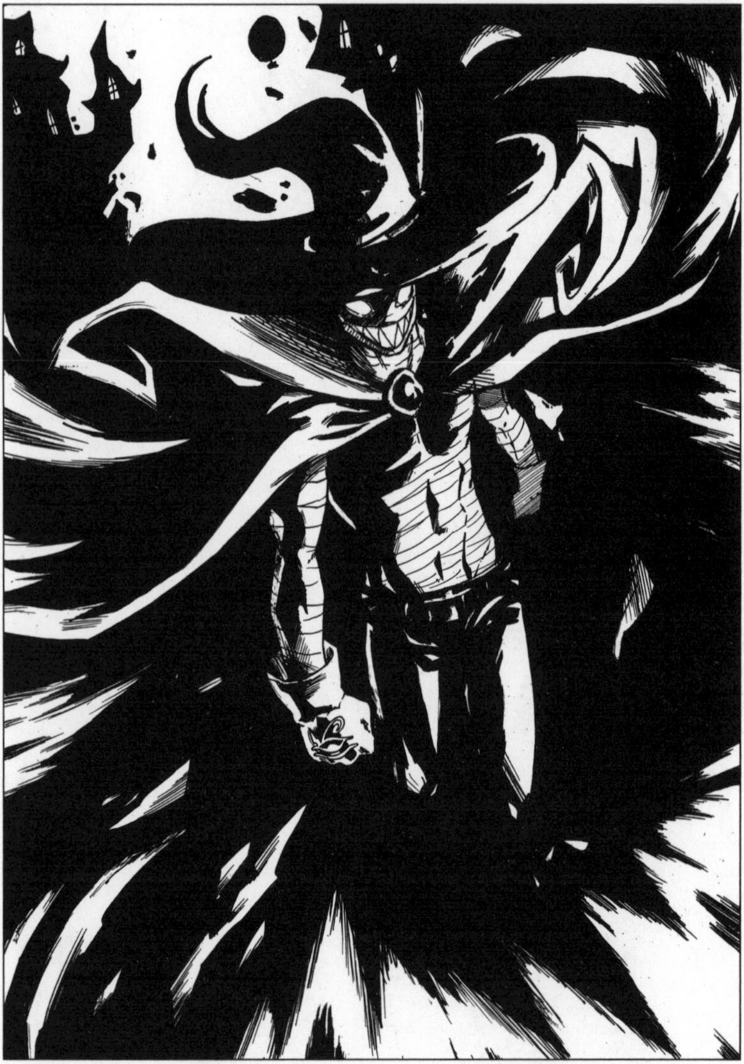

- YO-ONE -

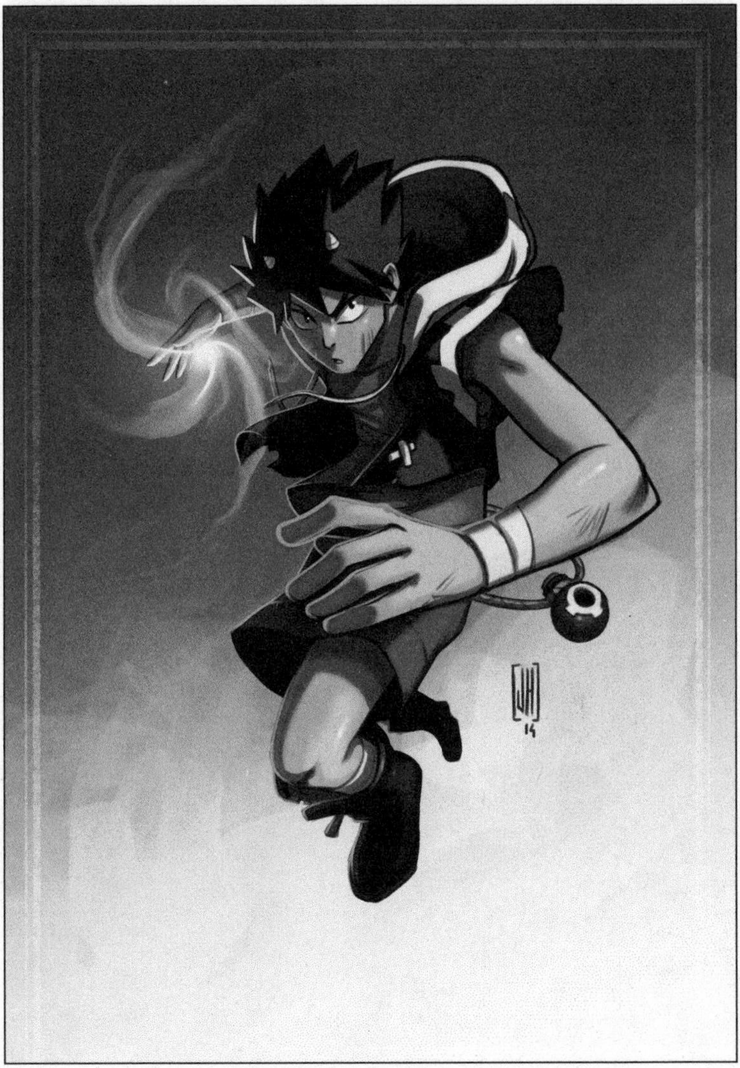

- JONATHAN "CIAN" HARTERT -

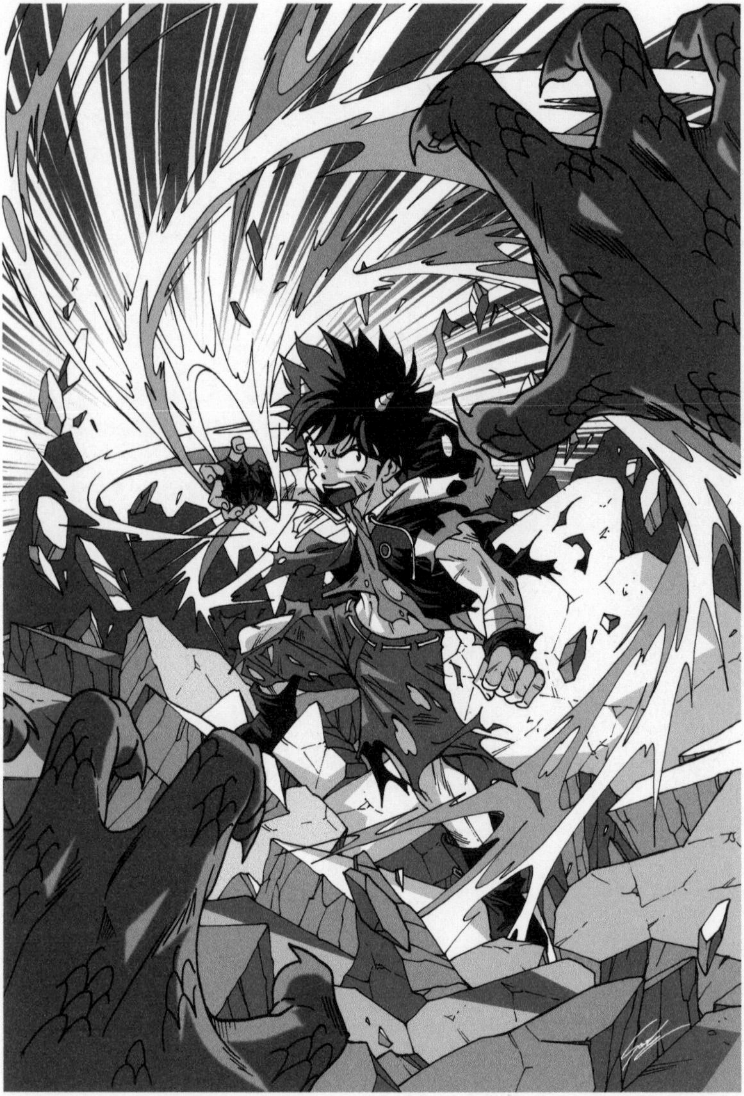

- PATRICK SOBRAL -

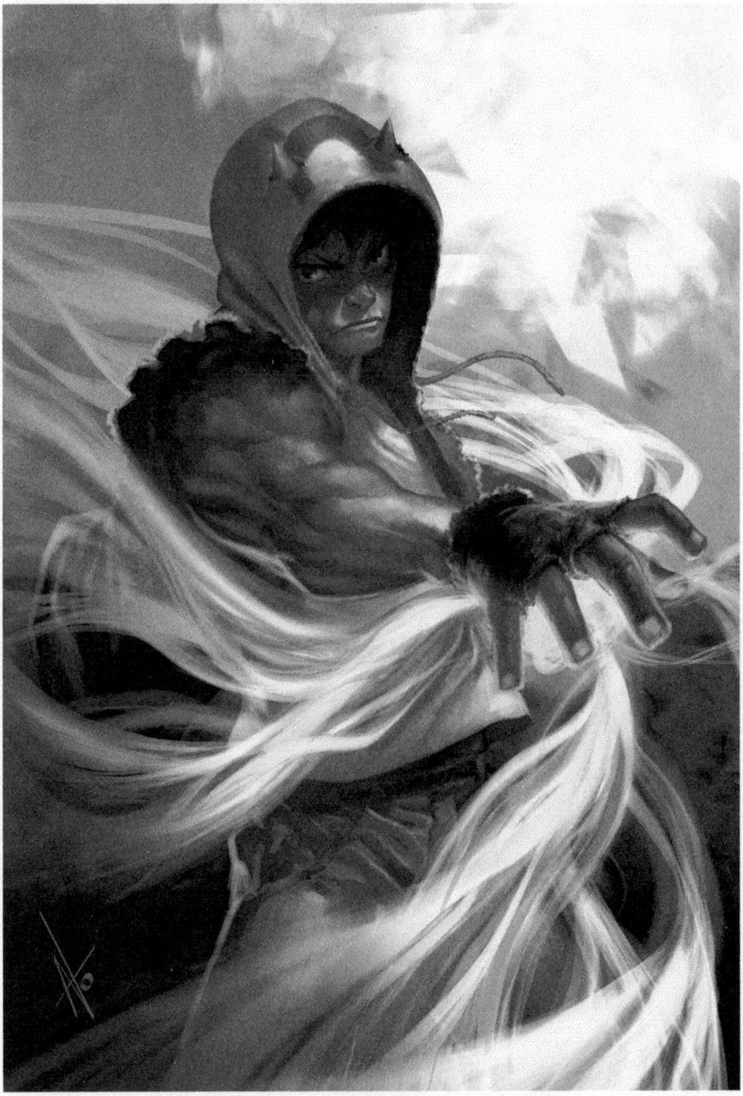

- NTOCHA -

RADIANT

RADIANT VOL. 3
VIZ MEDIA Manga Edition

STORY AND ART BY **TONY VALENTE**

Translation/**(´・∀・`)ｻｧ?**
Touch-Up Art & Lettering/**Erika Terriquez**
Design/**Julian [JR] Robinson**
Editor/**Marlene First**

Published by arrangement with MEDIATOON LICENSING/Ankama.
RADIANT T03

Printed in the U.S.A.

Published by VIZ Media, LLC
P.O. Box 77010
San Francisco, CA 94107

10 9 8 7 6 5 4 3 2 1
First printing, January 2019

VIZ MEDIA
viz.com

ratings.viz.com
RATED T TEEN

PARENTAL ADVISORY
RADIANT is rated T for Teen and is recommended for ages 13 and up. This volume contains fantasy violence.

ME

RYUHEI TAMURA
SENSEI

SHONEN JUMP
EDITOR

RADIANT

A while ago, I had the honor of meeting the author of *Beelzebub*, one of my favorite series!! It was so awesome! I was looking forward to asking him a ton of questions, but he caught me off guard! He'd read *Radiant* a few days before, and he was complimenting me on my work. I didn't know how to react!

(°_°;

I ended up leaving without a single answer to any of my questions, but with a bag full of compliments and with big chunks of undigested praise instead. Thank you so much, Tamura Sensei!!
—Tony Valente

Tony Valente began working as a comic artist with the series *The Four Princes of Ganahan*, written by Raphael Drommelschlager. He then launched a new three-volume project, *Hana Attori*, after which he produced *S.P.E.E.D. Angels*, a series written by Didier Tarquin and colored by Pop.

In preparation for *Radiant*, he relocated to Canada. Through confronting caribou and grizzlies, he gained the wherewithal to train in obscure manga techniques. Since then, his eating habits have changed, his lifestyle became completely different and even his singing voice has changed a bit!

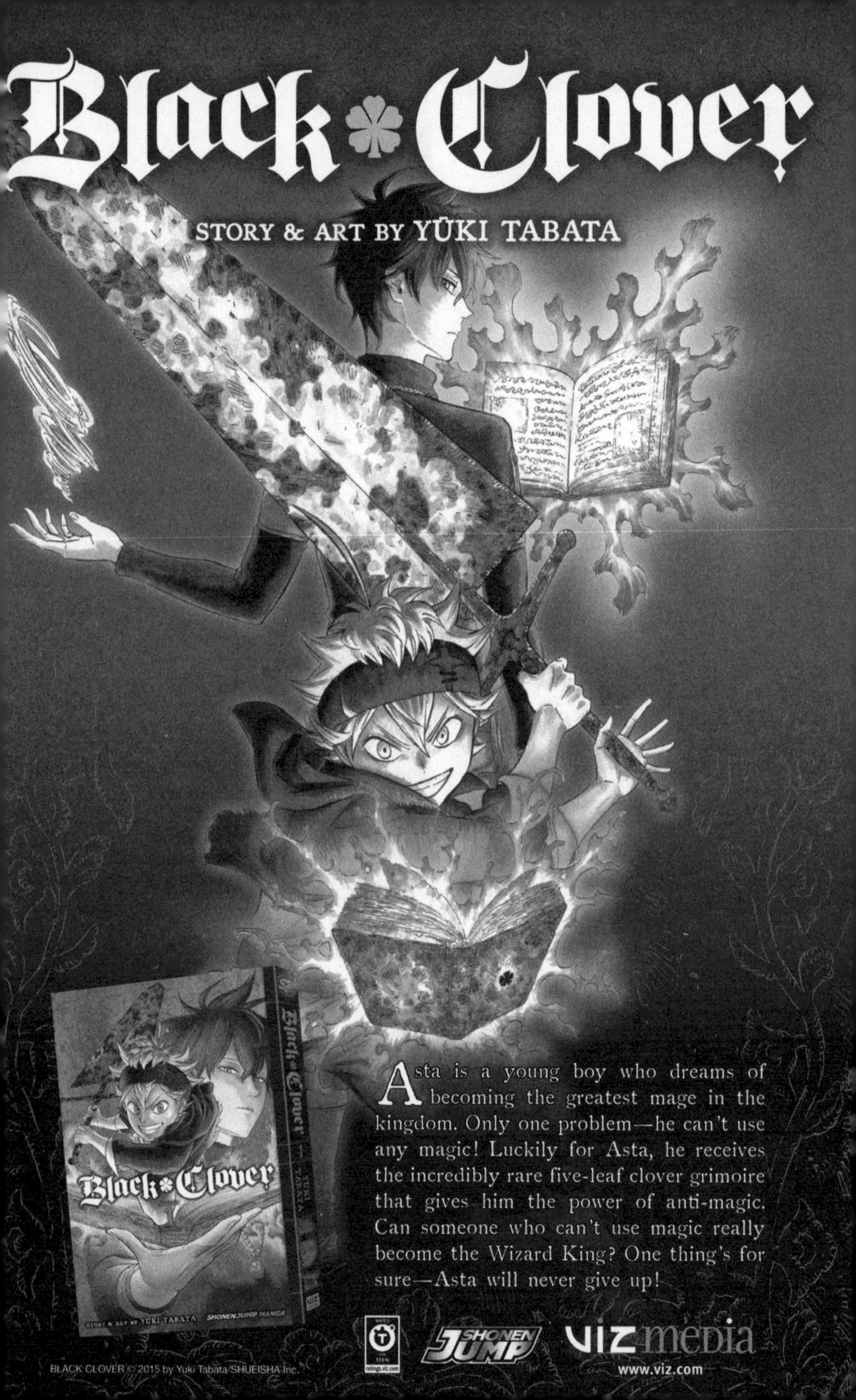
Black Clover
STORY & ART BY YŪKI TABATA
Black Clover
STORY & ART BY YŪKI TABATA
SHONEN JUMP MANGA
Asta is a young boy who dreams of becoming the greatest mage in the kingdom. Only one problem—he can't use any magic! Luckily for Asta, he receives the incredibly rare five-leaf clover grimoire that gives him the power of anti-magic. Can someone who can't use magic really become the Wizard King? One thing's for sure—Asta will never give up!
ratings.viz.com
SHONEN JUMP
VIZ media
www.viz.com
BLACK CLOVER © 2015 by Yuki Tabata/SHUEISHA Inc.

Story and Art by

KOYOHARU GOTOUGE

In Taisho-era Japan, kindhearted Tanjiro Kamado makes a living selling charcoal. But his peaceful life is shattered when a demon slaughters his entire family. His little sister Nezuko is the only survivor, but she has been transformed into a demon herself! Tanjiro sets out on a dangerous journey to find a way to return his sister to normal and destroy the demon who ruined his life.

ASTRA
LOST IN SPACE

CAN EIGHT TEENAGERS FIND THEIR WAY HOME FROM 5,000 LIGHT-YEARS AWAY?

It's the year 2063, and interstellar space travel has become the norm. Eight students from Caird High School and one child set out on a routine planet camp excursion. While there, the students are mysteriously transported 5,000 light-years away to the middle of nowhere! Will they ever make it back home?!

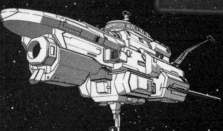

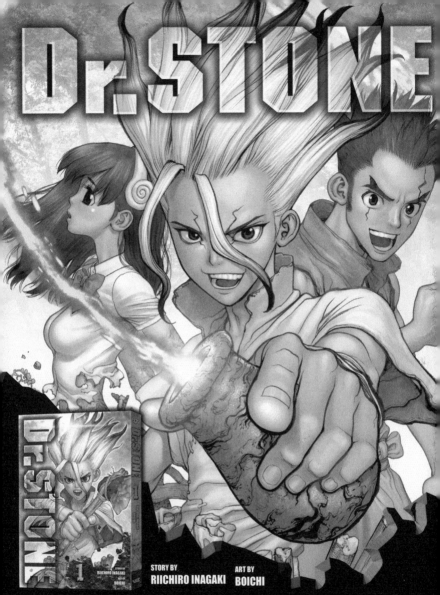

Dr. STONE

STORY BY
RIICHIRO INAGAKI

ART BY
BOICHI

One fateful day, all of humanity turned to stone. Many millennia later, Taiju frees himself from petrification and finds himself surrounded by statues. The situation looks grim—until he runs into his science-loving friend Senku! Together they plan to restart civilization with the power of science!

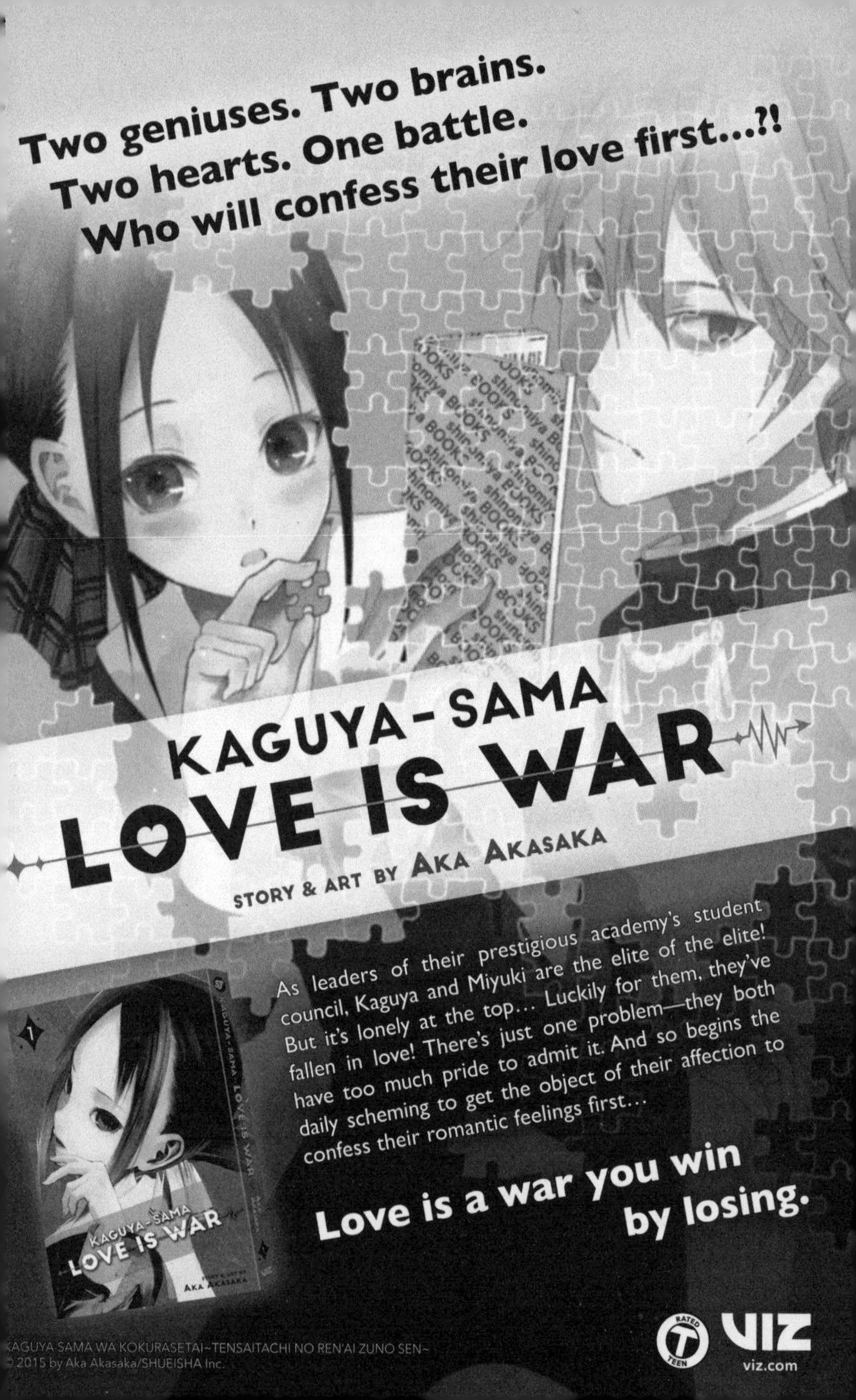
Two geniuses. Two brains.
Two hearts. One battle.
Who will confess their love first…?!
KAGUYA-SAMA
LOVE IS WAR
STORY & ART BY AKA AKASAKA
As leaders of their prestigious academy's student council, Kaguya and Miyuki are the elite of the elite! But it's lonely at the top… Luckily for them, they've fallen in love! There's just one problem—they both have too much pride to admit it. And so begins the daily scheming to get the object of their affection to confess their romantic feelings first…
Love is a war you win by losing.
KAGUYA-SAMA WA KOKURASETAI~TENSAITACHI NO REN'AI ZUNO SEN~
© 2015 by Aka Akasaka/SHUEISHA Inc.
RATED T TEEN
VIZ
viz.com

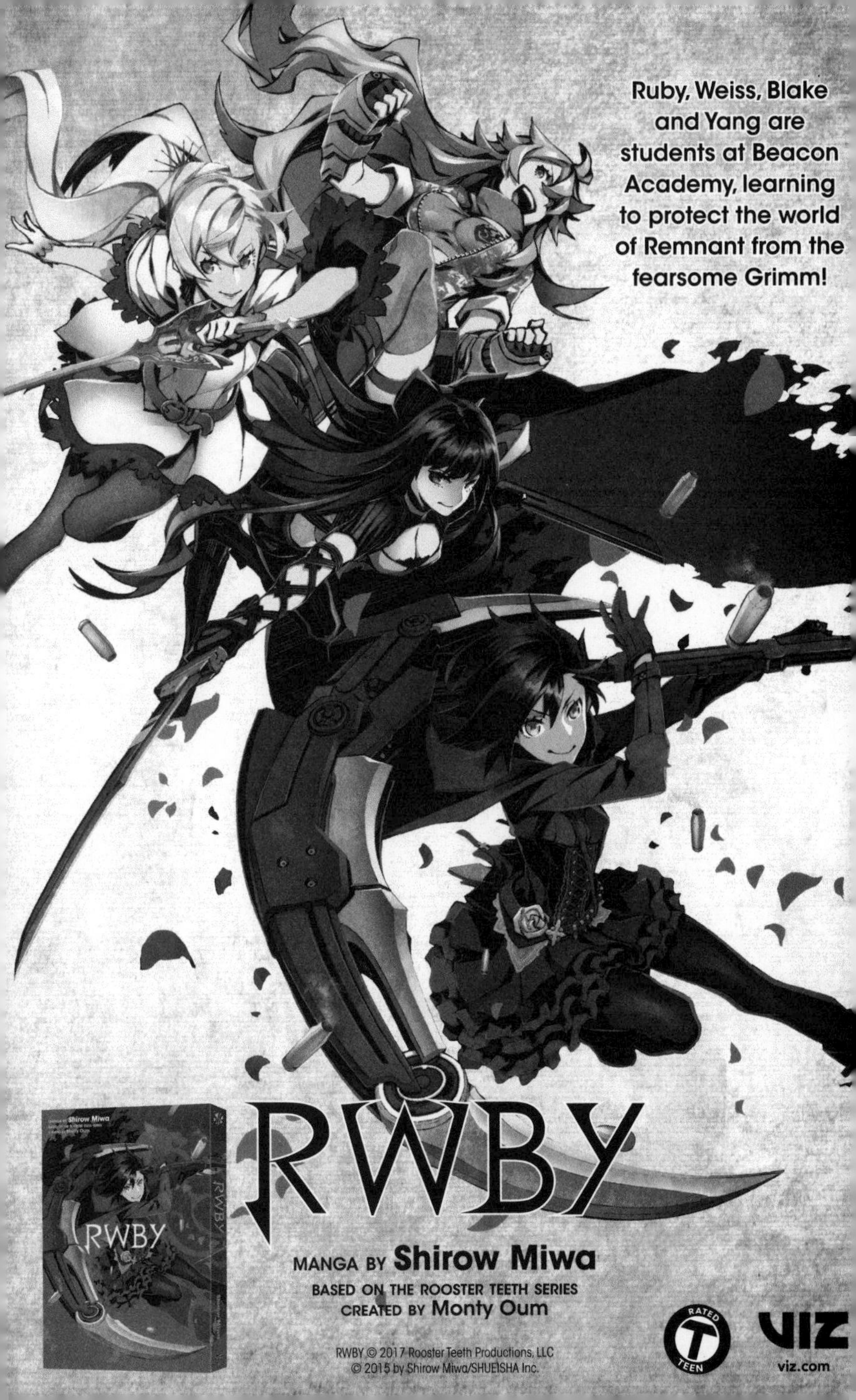
Ruby, Weiss, Blake and Yang are students at Beacon Academy, learning to protect the world of Remnant from the fearsome Grimm!
RWBY
MANGA BY Shirow Miwa
BASED ON THE ROOSTER TEETH SERIES
CREATED BY Monty Oum
RATED T TEEN
VIZ
viz.com
RWBY © 2017 Rooster Teeth Productions, LLC
© 2015 by Shirow Miwa/SHUEISHA Inc.

YOU'RE READING THE WRONG WAY

RADIANT reads from right to left, starting in the upper-right corner, meaning that action, sound effects, and word-balloon order are completely reversed from English order.

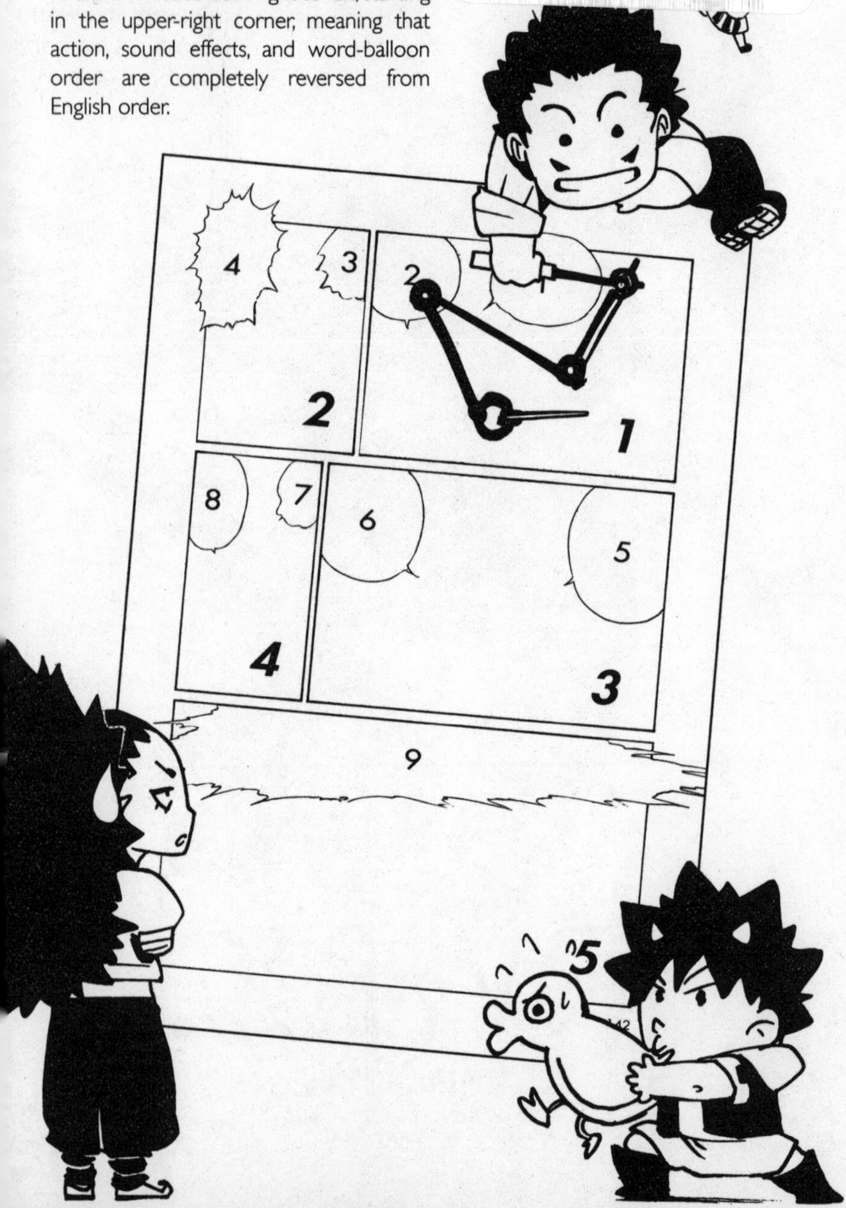
1
2
3
4
1
2
3
4
5
6
7
8
9
5